Global counter-terrorism

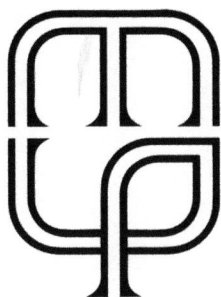

Manchester University Press

Global counter-terrorism

A decolonial approach

Edited by

Sagnik Dutta, Tahir Abbas,
and Sylvia I. Bergh

MANCHESTER UNIVERSITY PRESS

Published by Manchester University Press
Oxford Road, Manchester, M13 9PL

www.manchesteruniversitypress.co.uk

British Library Cataloguing-in-Publication Data
A catalogue record for this book is available from the British Library

ISBN 978 1 5261 7861 9 hardback

First published 2025

Cover image: 'Beautiful context', by Frédérique Bruijnen

EU authorised representative for GPSR:
Easy Access System Europe, Mustamäe tee 50, 10621 Tallinn, Estonia.
gpsr.requests@easproject.com

Typeset by Newgen Publishing UK

Contents

Part I: Colonialism and counter-terrorism

Part II: Global, national, and everyday counter-terrorism practices

Part III: Counter-terrorism, radicalisation, and right-wing extremism

Figures

Tables

Contributors

Tahir Abbas (PhD, FAcSS) is a Professor of Radicalisation Studies at the Institute of Security and Global Affairs at Leiden University in The Hague. He is the Scientific Coordinator of the H2020 RIA DRIVE project (determining multilevel-led causes and testing intervention designs to reduce radicalisation, extremism, and political violence in Northwestern Europe through social inclusion). His recent books are: *Countering Violent Extremism* (Bloomsbury, 2021), *Islamophobia and Radicalisation* (Oxford University Press, 2019), and *Contemporary Turkey in Conflict* (Edinburgh University Press, 2017). His recent edited books are *Political Muslims* (co-ed. with S. Hamid, Syracuse University Press, 2019) and *Muslim Diasporas in the West: Critical Readings in Sociology* (4 vols., Routledge Major Works Series, 2016). Recent peer-reviewed journal articles have appeared in *Journal of Contemporary European Studies, Terrorism and Political Violence, Ethnic and Racial Studies, World Futures, Critical Studies on Terrorism, Ethnicities, Philosophy and Social Criticism, Critical Social Policy, British Journal of Sociology of Education, Turkish Studies, and Journal of Muslim Minority Affairs.*

Naved Bakali (PhD) is an Assistant Professor of Anti-Racism Education at the University of Windsor, as well as a Senior Research Fellow at the Yaqeen Institute for Islamic Research. He is the author of *Islamophobia: Understanding anti-Muslim Racism through the Lived Experiences of Muslim Youth* and co-editor of *The Rise of Global Islamophobia in the War on Terror: Coloniality, Race, and Islam.* He completed his PhD from McGill University, Montreal, in Cultural and International Studies in Education. Drawing from critical race theory, cultural and media studies, and post-colonial theory, Dr. Bakali's research provides a fresh and innovative perspective on Islamophobia within institutional settings, thus demonstrating the institutionalisation of anti-Muslim racism across the Global North and South. He is a dynamic scholar who believes in socially oriented action-research that challenges prejudice and inequality by combining his research with grassroots activism.

Sylvia I. Bergh is an Associate Professor in Development Management and Governance at the International Institute of Social Studies (ISS), Erasmus University Rotterdam, and Senior Researcher at the Research Group Multilevel Regulation, Centre of Expertise on Global and Inclusive Learning at The Hague University of Applied Sciences. She completed both her MPhil in Modern Middle Eastern Studies and her DPhil in Development Studies at the University of Oxford, having previously obtained an MA in Arabic and International Relations from the University of St Andrews. At St Andrews, she took courses on (counter-)terrorism with the late Prof. Paul Wilkinson, Prof. Bruce Hoffman, and Dr. Magnus Ranstorp. Dr. Bergh has published widely on local state–society relations in the Middle East and North Africa, including *The Politics of Development in Morocco: Local Governance and Participation in North Africa* (I.B. Tauris, 2017). She has co-authored the book chapter 'Morocco's governance of cities and borders: AI-enhanced surveillance, facial recognition, and human rights' in *The Cambridge Handbook on Facial Recognition in the Modern State* (2024), and is currently involved in the Artificial Intelligence for Multi-Agency Public Safety (AI-MAPS) research project.

Inés Bolaños-Somoano is Postdoctoral Fellow in International Security at the Institut Barcelona d'Estudis Internacionals (IBEI). She holds a PhD in Political and Social Sciences from the European University Institute (EUI, Leiden University), and is a visiting researcher at the Institute for Security and Global Affairs, where she has also worked as postdoctoral researcher on the DRIVE project: 'Understanding social exclusion, exploring perspectives on polarisation'. Inés Bolaños-Somoano has emerged as a leading voice on (1) the role of Preventing and Countering of Violent Extremism (P/CVE) policies in the European Union's counter-terrorism strategy; and (2) European Islamophobia and the rise of European right-wing extremist groups online. Notable publications on the latter include 'The right-leaning be memeing: Extremist uses of Internet memes and insights for CVE design' in *First Monday*, 2022, which tracks the different usages of Internet memes by extreme online milieus in Europe, and 'Lessons from the Buffalo shooting: Responses to violent white supremacy' (with R. McNeil-Willson), which examines the overlap between online extreme milieus and offline violence in light of the 2022 white supremacist attack in Buffalo, USA. Her work delves into P/CVE as a counter-terrorism policy, illuminating issues of agency in policy creation and implementation, and offering fresh perspectives on knowledge creation and diffusion mechanisms in the European Union security domain. Through rigorous qualitative research and policy analysis, Inés Bolaños-Somoano continues to contribute significantly to the discourses in EU and Terrorism Studies.

Ewan Bottomley is a teaching fellow at the School of Psychology, Aberdeen University. They completed their PhD from the University of St Andrews. Their notable publications include 'Gender and the social cure in undergraduate physics students' and 'The relationship between gender and academic performance in undergraduate physics students' which look at applying social identity approaches in educational contexts. Their work delves into multiple aspects of social psychology, focusing primarily on the role of identity and offering fresh perspectives on how identity functions in particular contexts. Through rigorous research and thoughtful analysis, Ewan Bottomley continues to contribute significantly to the discourse in social psychology.

Sagnik Dutta is a researcher at the Department of Cultural Studies, Tilburg University, and Associate Professor at Jindal Global Law School, OP Jindal Global University. They obtained a PhD in Politics and International Studies from the University of Cambridge supported by the prestigious Gates Cambridge scholarship. Dutta's research focuses on decolonial, postcolonial, and feminist approaches to political theory and IR, as well as minority rights, everyday life of the law, data justice, and algorithmic surveillance. Their doctoral research explored how working-class Muslim women draw upon transnational Islamic feminist ethics as well as local legal cultures in gendered negotiations with the legal framework of minority rights in India and the everyday relationship between Muslim minorities and the right-wing state. Their monograph drawing upon this work is forthcoming with Cambridge University Press. In their work, Dutta aims to decolonise debates on minority rights and gender in political theory and IR. Dutta's work has appeared or is forthcoming in several prestigious journals such as *Journal of Political Ideologies, Critical Studies on Terrorism, Feminist Theory, Law and Social Inquiry, Legal Pluralism and Critical Social Analysis*, and *Ethnicities*. Dutta's other significant strand of research explores right-wing extremism, counter-terrorism, and algorithmic surveillance in India. Their research has been supported by the Gates Cambridge Trust, the Smuts Commonwealth Fund, the American Political Science Association, and a seed grant of Leiden University and The Hague University of Applied Social Sciences.

Alice Finden is an Assistant Professor in International Politics at Durham University. She holds a PhD from SOAS, University of London. Finden is an emerging scholar in Critical Security Studies and Critical Terrorism Studies. Notable publications include 'Pre-criminal: genealogies of suspicion from twentieth century British-occupied Egypt' (*Australian Feminist Law Journal*), which links contemporary pre-criminal practices to colonial understandings of morality, hygiene, vagrancy and extremism. Her work explores the coloniality of counter-terrorism, illuminating how racialised, gendered and classed forms of violence underpin the global War on Terror. She has peer-reviewed publications with *Feminist Review* journal and the *Australian Feminist Law Journal* and was the co-editor of a special journal issue entitled 'Hygiene, coloniality, law' also with the *Australian Feminist Law Journal*. She is a co-convenor for the British International Studies Association's Critical Studies on Terrorism working group.

Marine Guéguin is a Lecturer in International Relations and Security Studies at Leeds Beckett University. She is a Visiting Research Fellow at the Centre for Global Security Challenges at the University of Leeds. She holds a PhD in counter-terrorism (CT) and security studies, and has emerged as a leading voice in critical terrorism studies. A notable forthcoming publication includes 'French normalisation of exceptional powers as a response to terrorism post-Paris attacks' in *Critical Studies on Terrorism*. This article explores the crystallization of CT powers in the French terrorism context post-2015 Paris attacks, exposing the persistent challenge of desecuritization by confronting the paradigm of urgency. Her forthcoming manuscript with Routledge, Critical Studies on Terrorism book series will be forthcoming in 2025 and investigates French counter-terrorism and the colonialities of such counter-terrorism strategy within the French context. Beyond this, her work delves into CT practices, with a particular emphasis on French domestic CT and War on Terror strategies in the Sahel, Syria, and Iraq, where CT interventions take on a colonial dimension. Her work uncovers an inherent colonial continuum shaping French CT approaches. Guéguin scrutinizes constructed and securitized space(s) and body(ies), along with the discourses legitimizing practices, following a decolonial terrorism studies approach.

Sissel H. Jore is a Professor in Risk Management and Societal Safety at the University of Stavanger. With a PhD from the University of Stavanger, Jore has emerged as a leading voice in terrorism and security studies. Key publications are *Countering radicalisation in Norwegian terrorism policy. A welfare state approach to societal security* (Routledge, 2020) and 'Is resilience a good concept in terrorism research? A conceptual adequacy analysis of terrorism resilience' (*Studies in Conflict & Terrorism*). The first publication documents shifts in Norwegian counter-terrorism policy towards a focus on radicalisation. This approach normalises terrorism policy, shifts it to local governance levels, links solutions closely with the apparent benefits of the Norwegian welfare state, and enables practices once seen as violations of civil liberties. The second publication demonstrates that in its current state, resilience serves more as a cultural metaphor than as a well-developed scientific concept. Consequently, the resilience concept can end up more as a utopian goal than an actual means for countering terrorism. Jore's work delves into societal risk perception of terrorism and associated counter-terrorism measures and security management approaches.

Amna Kaleem is a Leverhulme Early Career Fellow at the University of Sheffield. Her research is situated within Critical Terrorism Studies and focuses on the impact of counter-terrorism policies at the grassroots level. She holds a PhD in Security Studies from the University of Sheffield. Her doctoral project studied how the British government's Prevent Strategy is securitising citizenship and turning counter-terrorism work into a component of civic duty. In her current project, Amna is exploring how the British state is co-opting charities and community-based organisations into Countering Violent Extremism (CVE) work and how this impacts third sector organisations and their relationships with the communities they serve. Amna is also a co-convenor of the British International Studies Association's Critical Studies on Terrorism working group. Her publications have appeared in prominent peer-reviewed journals such as *Critical Studies on Terrorism* and *Critical Social Policy*.

Graig R. Klein is an Assistant Professor at the Institute of Security and Global Affairs, Leiden University. Klein holds a PhD in Political Science from Binghamton University (SUNY). Klein's research focuses on the strategic use of political violence by non-state actors (NSAs) and governments, primarily terrorism and protests. It builds from the underlying assumption that government-dissident interactions occur within a bargaining framework to analyse how their choices and behaviours influence tactical and strategic decision-making, conflict evolution, and impact security. Klein considers how political incentives influence both governments' and NSAs' strategic behaviour. In doing so, Klein demonstrates that NSAs have a diverse set of violent and non-violent political tools, such as protests, voting, and terrorism, that are substitutes and compliments depending on government acquiescence or repression. On the government side, his research shows that governments' political goals motivate strategic use of repression and counter-terrorism.

Eviane Leidig (PhD) was recently a Marie Skłodowska-Curie Postdoctoral Fellow at Tilburg University. Her key publications include *The Women of the Far-Right: Social Media Influencers and Online Radicalization* published by Columbia University Press, and 'Not your grandma's fascism: Fame, femininity and race in far-right postcolonial India and Brazil' in the journal *Social Politics*. Leidig's work focuses on the nexus between the global far-right, gender, digital cultures, and platform governance. Her research traces transnational flows between the Global South and Global North using an interdisciplinary approach that draws on media studies, gender studies, sociology, and postcolonial studies. Leidig's analysis contributes to knowledge production that explores gender and global perspectives of the far-right, connected to broader effects of media and digital technologies on users, platform affordances, and socio-political structures, as well as policy frameworks.

Kenneth Mavor is a senior lecturer at the School of Psychology and Neuroscience at the University of St Andrews. Mavor holds a PhD in social psychology from the University of Queensland. He is a social psychologist with particular interests in social identity and self-categorisation theory approaches to self-perception, religion, political ideology, collective action, higher education. Notable publications include two articles with Thomas and McGarty in *Personality and Social Psychology Review* on collective action (with over 350 citations each), and a series of three significant papers on right-wing authoritarianism and fundamentalism with over 100 citations each. He also has fourteen articles and an edited book on social identity in higher education. Ken continues to contribute theoretical and empirical work in all these areas.

Barbara Perry (PhD) is a Professor at Ontario Tech University and the Director of the Centre on Hate, Bias and Extremism housed out of the Faculty of Social Science and Humanities. She has written extensively in the area of hate crime and right-wing extremism. Her books include *In the Name of Hate: Understanding Hate Crimes, Hate and Bias Crime: A Reader*, and *The Silent Victims: Hate Crimes Against Native Americans*. She is also General Editor of a five-volume set on hate crime, and editor of volume 3: *The Victims of Hate Crime*, which is part of that set (published by Praeger). Dr. Perry has also written on policing diverse communities, including work on social control in Native American communities. She has made substantial contributions to the limited scholarship on hate crime in Canada. Most recently, she has contributed to a scholarly understanding of anti-Muslim violence, hate crime against LGBTQ communities, the community impacts of hate crime, and right-wing extremism.

Lumbini Sharma is an independent researcher. She holds a PhD in Indian History from Assam University, Silchar. Sharma has been researching the forbidden propaganda literature of colonial India in the twentieth century. Her interest is aligned with the recent historiographical inquiry to unearth the underexplored phenomenon of the Indian freedom struggle, prioritising the contribution of the revolutionaries in the Indian Independence Movement. Her work to uncover the untold histories of the revolutionaries by analysing propaganda literature is an important contribution to this historiographical trend. Her recent works delve into the role of Bengali police machinery in countering *bhadralok* revolutionaries, illuminating aspects of the counter-terrorism mechanism adopted by the British police and providing a fresh perspective on how the Bengali revolutionaries used to evade those tactics.

Dean J. Smith is a PhD Candidate at the University of St Andrews. Smith works on the psychology of terrorism. Their work delves into social identity models of terrorist radicalisation, illuminating the relationship between conspiracy theory endorsement and perceived legitimacy of violent extremism, and offering fresh perspectives on the radicalisation of lone actor terrorists. Through rigorous research and thoughtful analysis, Dean J. Smith continues to contribute significantly to the discourse relating to the psychology of terrorism.

Farooq Yousaf holds a PhD in Politics from the University of Newcastle (Australia) and is the author of *Pakistan, Regional Security and Conflict Resolution: The Pashtun Tribal Areas* (Routledge, 2020). He has previously worked with Swisspeace (Switzerland). In his research, Yousaf focuses on centre–periphery politics, post-colonialism, as well as gender, peace, and security, more specifically in the Afghanistan-Pakistan region. His research has been published in peer-reviewed journals such as *Interventions, Third World Quarterly, Small Wars and Insurgencies, South Asia Research, Global Policy, Journal of Men's Studies, Social Identities,* and *Journal of Policing, Intelligence and Counterterrorism,* among others.

Preface

The global War on Terror following the 11 September 2001 terror attacks led to a proliferation of counter-terrorism laws and state policies across the world. Counter-terrorism policies are manifested in regimes of investigation, interrogation, detention, and surveillance on a global scale and in everyday public life. Yet there is little scholarship that draws out the conceptual links between the practice of counter-terrorism in the Global North and the Global South. Counter-terrorism has become a global, national, and local phenomenon. With the upsurge of right-wing populist ideologies in the Global South, counter-terrorism policies have become all-pervasive in public life. While existing scholarship has focused on counter-terrorism policies in everyday life across the world, there is little exploration of counter-terrorism from a comparative perspective. This book aims to bring together scholars studying counter-terrorism in the Global North and South to explore convergence and divergence in how counter-terrorism policies function across national and local contexts.

Acknowledgements

We are grateful to the former Centre of Expertise on Global Governance at The Hague University of Applied Sciences and the Institute of Security and Global Affairs at Leiden University for the seed grant that made it possible to host a workshop on 'Counter-terrorism in a global perspective'. We also acknowledge the support of the Research Group Multilevel Regulation and the Centre of Expertise on Global and Inclusive Learning at The Hague University of Applied Sciences for the research time spent on this book project, as well as funding for open access and indexing costs. In addition, we are grateful to Robert Byron, Humairaa Dudhwala, and Deborah Smith at Manchester University Press for their support and patience. Finally, our thanks are due to Mridini Kulkarni, an undergraduate student at Jindal Global Law School, OP Jindal Global University, for research assistance, and to Michelle Luijben for producing the index.

Introduction: A decolonial approach to counter-terrorism in a global context

Sagnik Dutta, Tahir Abbas, and Sylvia I. Bergh

Since the events of 9/11 and the onset of the War on Terror in 2001, scholars have paid considerable attention to issues of terrorism, radicalisation, and political violence across the world. Governments, academia, and civil society continue to invest significantly in investigating and preventing terrorism and 'radicalisation'. Post 9/11, counter-terrorism policies have expanded to many parts of the world, including the Global South, such as India, Egypt, Turkey, and Malaysia. Counter-terrorism legislation mostly takes the form of pre-emptive security legislation and is premised on the assumption that potential terrorists can be identified, detected, and terror acts prevented through adequate measures of surveillance. Counter-terrorism policies in various shapes have become pervasive in both the Global North and the Global South over the last two decades (Amoore 2009; de Goede 2014; Sian 2017). Many of these counter-terrorism policies have not only enhanced securitisation of religious and racial minorities but also massively expanded the surveillance capacities of the state. With the upsurge of authoritarian states and populist governments, counter-terrorism legislation has become yet another tool that augments state power and places curbs on the civil liberties of vulnerable minority populations (Suresh 2019).

Much of the policy-related and academic scholarship on counter-terrorism has been preoccupied with the causes of violent extremism and its supposed solutions. Counter-terrorism policies have thus habitually focused on short-term national and international security priorities and paid little attention to the material or cultural needs of local communities and structural inequalities. Practices of Countering Violent Extremism (CVE) have only worsened systemic discrimination and marginalisation of minority communities in Europe and other parts of the world. The fixation of policy discourses on radicalisation, deradicalisation, and the implementation of CVE has taken attention away from deeper historical and structural factors that mediate the discourse and practice of counter-terrorism (Abbas 2021). CVE, especially as it principally operationalised in most parts of

Europe, is premised upon the assumption that radicalisation is a function of primordial religious beliefs rather than of socio-economic inequalities. This conception of radicalisation as linked to religion has had the unfortunate impact of augmenting Islamophobia and racism in counter-terrorism practice. Predominant frameworks for understanding CVE policies have reified religious identities and ignored historical processes that produce the categories of terrorism and counter-terrorism.

Though counter-terrorism policies have significantly augmented state power and criminalised 'suspect communities' post 9/11, it would be myopic to construe them merely as an outcome of the War on Terror. Counter-terrorism policies often feed off historically embedded orientalist tropes about the Muslim other (Sian 2017). They draw upon racist and gendered assumptions about Muslim minorities. The intersection of counter-terrorism and coloniality animates counter-terrorism policies both in the Global North and the Global South. We cannot understand counter-terrorism and its proliferation across the Global North and the Global South without paying attention to global historical processes such as colonialism that connect them. There are enduring legacies of colonialism and colonialism's racist and gendered construction of the civilisational other that feed into counter-terrorism practice. Scholarly discussions, as well as policy conversations on counter-terrorism and security, have been fixated upon the causes and consequences of counter-terrorism policies to the neglect of enduring legacies of racialisation, colonialism, and quandaries of global and nationalist discourses that produce counter-terrorism policies. To this end, this volume proposes a decolonial approach to the study of counter-terrorism by bringing together scholarship from across the Global North and the Global South that engages coloniality and the legacies of colonialism. This volume, therefore, broadens both the theoretical and empirical focus of counter-terrorism studies through a deeper engagement with postcolonial approaches.

When 9/11 or the global War on Terror are taken as the starting point for exploring the practice of counter-terrorism, iterations of counter-terrorism policies in other parts of the world merely appear as effects of an event in the Global North. This framework has ignored more complex tangles between global, nationalist, and everyday processes that produce counter-terrorism policies. Consequently, one sees a Eurocentric bias inherent in most approaches to the study of counter-terrorism. Counter-terrorism appears to be a phenomenon that started in the West and spread to other parts of the world. This approach to the study of counter-terrorism elides more complex relations between global, transnational, national, and everyday discourses about race, gender, and religion that constitute counter-terrorism policies and practices. Challenging these existing frameworks for studying counter-terrorism is in itself a decolonial contribution to the study of counter-terrorism. In decentring existing ways of studying counter-terrorism that privilege the experiences of the Global North, we acknowledge and recognise how colonial hierarchies and neo-colonial modes of knowledge production have informed scholarship in politics and international relations broadly (Acharya 2022; Getachew 2019; Iqtidar 2021).

Existing approaches in counter-terrorism studies demonstrate this preoccupation with the Global North as well. In this collection, we challenge the coloniality of counter-terrorism studies in multiple ways. This collection uses a range of case studies from India, Egypt, and Pakistan as well as locations in the Global North, to show how counter-terrorism policy and practice are closely tethered to particular negotiations with imperial legacies and colonial modes of knowledge about the law, politics, and terror. We also challenge colonial epistemologies of studying counter-terrorism by delineating transnational connections as well as the various scales, spaces, and levels at which counter-terrorism policies work. This collection of chapters proposes a novel contribution to counter-terrorism studies by challenging Eurocentrism and methodological nationalism in existing approaches. It does so by opening up three new areas of enquiry: (1) colonialism, coloniality, and the role that colonial epistemes play in shaping counter-terrorism policies; (2) the role of the global, transnational, and national in everyday discourses of (in)security in shaping counter-terrorism policies; (3) practices of everyday securitisation and counter-terrorism and their knots with other ideologies such as right-wing extremism and right-wing radicalisation.

In exploring these myriad aspects of counter-terrorism policies, we unsettle a Eurocentric and 9/11-centric narrative of counter-terrorism. These three major themes of the book all contribute to our overall project of decolonising counter-terrorism studies. The first section of this collection focuses on colonialism and its legacies to unsettle an epochal and Eurocentric approach to counter-terrorism. Such an approach conceptualises events such as 9/11 and the consequent War on Terror as marking some sort of break in a normative, liberal democratic order. In contrast, this collection throws light on the colonial genealogy of terrorism and how colonial legacies inform postcolonial engagements with counter-terrorism. Hence, this collection produces new knowledge on counter-terrorism that foregrounds its intimate connections with colonialism both historically and in the postcolonial present. The second section of this collection, which highlights the connections between global, transnational, and national discourses that shape counter-terrorism policies, also contributes to a decolonial approach to counter-terrorism. This section traces the various scales – the global, transnational, national, and everyday – at which counter-terrorism policies and laws function and draws out both the entanglement as well as the overlap between security logics at these various scales.

Chapters 5–8 help us untangle the myriad ways in which the everyday, the international, and the transnational intersect to produce counter-terrorism policies across the Global North and the Global South. Hence, we move beyond an approach to counter-terrorism based on particular events that privileges the Global North. We thereby unsettle colonial modes of knowledge production that traditionally privilege the Global North as the site of knowledge and theory. Relatedly, the third section of this collection of essays, which focuses on the interaction between counter-terrorism and other ideologies such as right-wing extremism, explores the life of counter-terrorism policies and laws in relation to a range of political ideologies in both the Global North and the Global South such as Hindu right-wing nationalism and the Q-Anon movement. This section sheds light on a range of ideologies that animate the practice of counter-terrorism across the Global North and the Global South and traces the connections between them. The essays in this section show how historical conceptions of race, gender, and ethnicity are mobilised by counter-terrorism rhetoric and strategies in multiple contexts. These moments of negotiation are ultimately negotiations with colonial epistemes of race and gender in both the Global North and the Global South. Hence, this section also traces the enduring influence of and negotiations with colonial forms of knowledge in counter-terrorism practice in both the Global North and the Global South. This section speaks to the overall aim of the collection: to present a decolonial approach to counter-terrorism studies. Together, the sections demonstrate the multiple and ongoing negotiations with coloniality that produce counter-terrorism policies across the world.

This is an important contribution to the project of decolonising counter-terrorism studies. The chapters in this volume adopt a range of methodologies and use an array of empirical materials to speak to the broad theme of counter-terrorism and coloniality. While some chapters take a squarely historical approach, others are more invested in exploring contemporary negotiations with coloniality. The collection consciously brings together a range of approaches and methods to encourage a methodological and epistemological diversity in exploring the question of counter-terrorism and coloniality. Our aim is to consider rich discussions of the colonial genealogy of counter-terrorism as well as engage scholarship that explores the contemporary usage of a range of sources, such as social media data, etc. This methodological and disciplinary pluralism is essential for understanding a complex phenomenon like counter-terrorism and the lived experience of colonialism. The range of case studies as well as the connected categories and scales of exploration of counter-terrorism also help us expand our horizons of knowledge on counter-terrorism and coloniality. The contributors to this volume come from various disciplines including political science, international relations, sociology, media studies, and history. They bring to bear multiple disciplinary perspectives to their explorations of counter-terrorism.

Scholars from a range of disciplinary backgrounds shed light on the politics of counter-terrorism. The multiple disciplinary perspectives enrich our understanding of the various aspects of the colonial legacies of counter-terrorism and the shapes and forms they take in a range of national contexts. The chapters in this collection provide a sense of both the richness of the history and genealogy of counter-terrorism practice as well as an understanding of the everyday lived experience of counter-terrorism mediated by digital media practices and negotiations between multiple state and non-state actors. A transdisciplinary approach is useful for understanding a multi-faceted phenomenon such as counter-terrorism. The book itself draws upon a principle of methodological pluralism that enhances our understanding of counter-terrorism in a global context and contributes to decolonising existing debates on counter-terrorism. The compartmentalisation of knowledge production in social sciences into specific disciplines is a marker of a Eurocentric and neo-colonial approach towards knowledge. We challenge disciplinary and methodological silos by adopting a more plural approach that draws upon the strengths of various disciplines and methodologies. Another collection of essays (Silke 2018) explores major approaches to counter-terrorism in several national contexts such as Argentina, Canada, China, France, Great Britain, India, Iraq, Israel, Italy, Spain, and Russia. This volume traces the multiple responses to counter-terrorism but stops short of analysing the links with colonialism and coloniality.

In the past decade, several scholars have explored how counter-terrorism policies permeate everyday life in myriad ways in the Global North (Amoore 2009; Kundnani 2015; Sian 2017). This scholarship dwells on various modes of securitisation following the War on Terror in the Global North. Securitisation in the Global North has taken the form of pre-emptive security legislation based on the assumption that objects and individuals can be identified and detained through mechanisms of surveillance (Wojczewski 2020).[1] Scholars have explored various iterations of counter-terrorism policies, pre-emptive security legislation, and CVE policies such as PREVENT in the UK. It has been argued that CVE has only led to the profiling of minority groups as potential terror suspects (Kundnani 2015; Sian 2017). The pervasiveness of CVE is borne out by the gradual involvement of a vigilant public (Amoore 2009) as well as a range of non-state actors such as school and university administrators in the implementation of CVE policies (Quraishi 2017; Taylor and Soni 2017). Countering violent extremism also shapes how minority populations and those deemed suspicious by the state perform their own identity through negotiations with CVE policies (Elshimi 2015). Recent scholarship has explored counter-terrorism practices in a range of non-Western contexts (Boyle 2019) but this scholarship does not engage the legacies of colonialism and coloniality in a sustained manner. For example, Boyle (2019), while providing a comprehensive and rich account of counter-terrorism practices in non-Western contexts, takes 9/11 and US foreign policy responses to the same as a starting point for the analysis of global trends in counter-terrorism practice. This collection departs significantly from this epochal approach to present a more historically situated and contextual approach to counter-terrorism. Our authors engage themes such as race, gender, and colonial genealogies. Our collection demonstrates a deeper awareness of the specific contexts that enable counter-terrorism practices across the Global North and the Global South as well as the connected histories and epistemologies of colonialism that shape counter-terrorism practice. We are sceptical of the use of frames such as 'non-Western' and focus instead on the connected histories and genealogies of counter-terrorism that are shaped by the shared experiences of colonialism and globalisation.

This important body of scholarship, however, is predominantly focused on counter-terrorism policies such as CVE in the Global North and does not explore counter-terrorism from a comparative perspective. This body of scholarship also shows little engagement with questions of coloniality and colonial epistemes of terrorism. Scholarship on CVE, in centring the experiences of the Global North, thus suffers from the Eurocentrism and privileging of the experiences of the Global North that plagues much of the discipline of Politics and IR. Moreover, the presentism of some of this scholarship is evinced by a lack of sufficient attention to connected historical processes that mediate the practice of counter-terrorism policies across the Global North and the Global South. CVE policies are often more than just a form of extraordinary emergency legislation, and build upon racialised hierarchies and colonial forms of knowledge. Exploring CVE merely as a form of extraordinary security legislation and a form of surveillance ignores deeper and more enduring links between counter-terrorism practice and transnational historical processes.

Seeing CVE merely as a form of surveillance has restricted scholarly understanding of how counter-terrorism and securitisation work through connected ideas and shared pasts across the world. Ideas that shape the practice and discourse of CVE circulate across the Global North and the Global South in various iterations and are often tethered to a range of nationalist and local discourses on terrorism as well as historically linked notions of gender, religion, and ethnicity. In expanding the field of counter-terrorism studies, it is therefore imperative to adopt a more holistic approach towards counter-terrorism that moves beyond the preoccupation with CVE linked to 9/11 and the experiences of the Global North.

This will be an important scholarly contribution as it will enhance our understanding of the gradual and rapid increase of securitisation of the state and society in many parts of the world today, as well as the enabling role that counter-terrorism has played in this process. We cannot understand the global spread of counter-terrorism without adopting a global approach that moves beyond the experiences of the West with counter-terrorism. At the same time, it is imperative to understand the complex ways in which counter-terrorism is negotiated in non-Western contexts as well as to examine the larger postcolonial conundrums that animate the practice of counter-terrorism. Comparative approaches thereby help in challenging the hegemony of a Eurocentric way of exploring counter-terrorism as well as provide a lens for understanding the connections, convergences, and divergences in counter-terrorism practices across the world.

With the global upsurge of authoritarianism and populism, securitisation is increasingly becoming part of the everyday lives of democracies. Scholars need to explore what factors enable and mediate the rapid expansion of securitisation in many states today, including states in the Global South. As CVE practices and modes of securitisation spread to many parts of the world, it would be myopic to merely understand CVE from a Eurocentric or Global North perspective. This phenomenon calls for a global approach and framework for studying counter-terrorism that moves beyond a particular event. Merely focusing on 9/11 and the War on Terror does not enable a comprehensive understanding of securitisation.

A comparative approach, as proposed in this collection, by bringing together chapters on counter-terrorism practice in a range of cases across the Global North and the Global South, will successfully expand and deparochialise existing interventions in the scholarship on counter-terrorism that remains fixated upon recent developments in the Global North as a point of entry into studying counter-terrorism. Such a fixation on the Global North and the epochal events of 9/11 and the global War on Terror betrays a parochial, Eurocentric understanding of the phenomenon of counter-terrorism. Like much else in the study of politics and international relations, approaches to counter-terrorism draw upon events and theorising that centres the Global North. Such approaches severely limit a holistic understanding of historical processes as well as larger questions about negotiating coloniality and postcolonial agency that are inextricably linked to the practice and discourse of counter-terrorism.

This methodology sheds light on the connected processes, shared practices, and repertoires that produce counter-terrorism policies. In offering a comparative approach, we seek to understand counter-terrorism as part of a larger set of negotiations with coloniality and the technologies of colonialism in the postcolonial present and thereby expand the horizons of studying counter-terrorism. We also aim to unsettle binaries between the Global North and the Global South through our comparative exploration of counter-terrorism. Tracing connections and convergences as well as shared epistemes of counter-terrorism across the Global North and the Global South enables us to challenge these binaries as well as approaches to counter-terrorism that privilege the events and experiences of the Global North.

This collection builds upon some recent efforts by scholars to study counter-terrorism policies in the Global North and the Global South from a comparative perspective (Bastani and Gazotti 2021; Chan 2018). Building upon a rich comparative ethnographic study of counter-terrorism practices by non-state actors in the UK and Morocco, Bastani and Gazotti (2021) outline how counter-terrorism practices for preventing 'radicalisation' carried out by non-state actors such as school and university administrators across the Global North and the Global South draw upon similar notions of care and duty. Similarly, Chan argues that counter-narratives in counter-terrorism policies serve to secure a sense of ontological security for the Malaysian state, a Muslim majority state, in the face of the upsurge of transnational jihadist terrorism (2018). Our contribution also builds upon recent calls for a more comprehensive, historical, and interdisciplinary approach to counter-terrorism studies (Crelinsten 2014; Silke 2018; Youngman 2020). These recent approaches to counter-terrorism alert us to the need to critique and move beyond the centrality of 9/11 in counter-terrorism studies and the need for a more historical approach to counter-terrorism (Youngman 2020).

Recent comprehensive surveys of counter-terrorism touch upon multiple aspects of counter-terrorism practices, such as various models of counter-terrorism policy, including the criminal justice model and the military model, the role of intelligence in counter-terrorism, an approach towards creating sensitisation or a 'hearts and minds' approach (Silke 2018), as well as case studies of the workings of counter-terrorism in various parts of the world (Boyle 2019; Spalek and Weeks 2020). Yet these comprehensive, recently edited collections on counter-terrorism do not engage postcolonial scholarship. They do not adequately explore the extensive engagements with coloniality as well as the various scales and levels at which counter-terrorism laws and policies work. Some recent work has highlighted the need to take seriously the particularities of non-Western cases in terrorism studies to avoid uncritically importing theoretical and epistemic frameworks of thinking about non-Western contexts (Barnard-Wills and Moore 2010).

This collection of chapters significantly expands these recent efforts by focusing on questions of coloniality and decoloniality, transnational connections, interactions between transnational and nationalist discourses, as well as overlaps between everyday securitisation and right-wing extremist ideologies.

Primary contribution to the collection

Colonialism and its enduring legacies: A comparative approach and a decolonial lens

This book makes an original contribution by bringing together a range of studies on counter-terrorism policies from both the Global North and the Global South that show how the legacies of colonialism and coloniality reproduce practices of counter-terrorism. The comparative perspective is especially useful in enhancing our understanding of counter-terrorism and its iterations as constituted by the connected histories and legacies of colonialism. The contributions in this collection demonstrate how states across the world continue to draw upon colonial ideologies of racial hierarchies and the civilisational other as they implement counter-terrorism policies. To that extent, it expands our theoretical understanding of counter-terrorism. Research on counter-terrorism can be a productive site for exploring how colonial ideas persist and how they are engaged and appropriated in the postcolonial present. All chapters advance research in this direction as they shed light on how counter-terrorism and coloniality are negotiated in a range of spaces and contexts.

In doing so, this collection proposes a decolonial lens for the study of counter-terrorism. Recent approaches to decolonise political theory and IR can be a useful tool for enhancing our understanding of the tangles between colonialism and counter-terrorism (Iqtidar 2021). Decolonial approaches have highlighted how racism and imperialism constitute the very edifice of the liberal international order (Acharya 2022; Getachew 2019). Colonial hierarchies and colonial modes of knowledge creation have played a central role in producing particular ways of theorising in politics and international relations. The project of decolonising knowledge, however, does not merely entail critiquing coloniality and the project of colonialism but also being alive to the legacies and afterlives of colonialism and how they animate our postcolonial present (Iqtidar 2021). The project of decolonisation, therefore, needs to do more than merely include voices from the Global South in the study of politics and international relations. A decolonial approach can stem from a sustained engagement with coloniality and its various iterations to delineate the myriad negotiations with the same in multiple contexts.

This collection speaks particularly to decolonial and postcolonial approaches to the study of security, terrorism, and emergency politics. In the disciplines of political science and IR as well as critical legal studies, counter-terrorism policies have been conceptualised as an expression of sovereign state power that comes into play particularly through the suspension of the rule of law (Kundnani and Hayes 2018; Walker and Cawley 2022). But these conceptualisations of counter-terrorism envisage a normative vision of a liberal state based on the rule of law. In doing so, they privilege a Western European normative vision of a liberal state that overlooks the historical entanglements of liberalism with imperialism and colonialism (Alice Finden's essay in this volume). Hence, some critical legal and postcolonial scholars have cautioned against working with binaries of normal, liberal democratic, and emergency politics (Nucleolus 2006; Hussain 2007). The proliferation of counter-terrorism laws and policies has been read by scholars of colonialism as not merely an exception to liberal democratic norms but part of a historical process enabled by imperialism and colonialism of the use of fragmented forms of law as well as dual systems of law for colonised subjects based on hierarchies of race, gender, and multiple conceptualisations of communities (Eckert 2008; Hillyard 1993; Hussain 2007; Johns 2005; also see Finden's chapter 1 in this volume).

The pervasive use of counter-terrorism laws mirrors the use of martial law and emergency laws for colonial subjects. In postcolonial contexts, multiple processes of normalisation have rendered such temporary and emergency legislation more permanent and pervasive (Hussain 1999; Neocleolus 2007; Reynolds 2017, also see Finden in this volume). To that extent, most postcolonial and feminist scholars have conceptualised the law itself as a form of violence (Cohn 2013; Hamzić 2018; Heathcote 2012; Sjoberg and Gentry 2007). Scholars of colonialism have conceptualised emergency laws and methods of governance as a 'patchwork' of laws and policies that are deployed throughout the metropole and the colonies and are tethered to hierarchies based upon class, gender, race, and categorisation of particular communities as threats (Likhovski 2006; Zichi 2021, also see Chapter 1 by Finden in this volume). Critical terrorism scholars have also shown how counter-terrorist responses often instrumentalise and maintain gendered and racialised hierarchies within society and overlook the violence of patriarchal white, supremacist political structures (Gentry 2020; see also Eviane Leidig's essay in this volume). Building upon these postcolonial approaches to emergency laws and counter-terrorism, this volume further explores the myriad engagements with coloniality and colonial forms of knowledge in relation to the historical and contemporary use of counter-terrorism.

Inspired by recent moves to decolonise political theory and IR, our approach in this collection is to decolonise the study of counter-terrorism through a productive critique and engagement with the legacies of colonialism and coloniality. The case studies in this collection dwell upon a wide range of cases including France, Pakistan, India, Egypt, and Canada. These cases provide insights into a wide range of ways in which colonial legacies and colonial conceptions of race and civilisational hierarchies are appropriated in diverse contexts in both the Global North and the Global South. Be it the colonial forms of pre-emptive security logics in Egypt, orientalist representation of Pashtuns by the Pakistani security state, representation of the cultural 'other' in French counter-terrorism discourses, or the global spread of counter-insurgency networks from colonial Bengal, the chapters show a wide array of ways in which colonial logics intersect with the discourse and practice of counter-terrorism. This collection thereby challenges a Eurocentric and Global-North-oriented approach to the study of counter-terrorism.

Predicaments of the global, the nationalist, and the everyday

The second part of this collection of chapters challenges the methodological nationalism in counter-terrorism studies and pays closer attention to the connections between the Global North and the Global South in the conception and practice of counter-terrorism.[2] This second theme of the collection also speaks to the broad, overall theme of coloniality and decolonisation in counter-terrorism studies. As the chapters draw out the complex relations between global, transnational, and nationalist discourses of counter-terrorism in multiple contexts, we challenge a Eurocentric and Global-North-oriented approach to the study of counter-terrorism. In drawing out these multiple relations, we unsettle approaches to counter-terrorism that often presume 9/11 or the global War on Terror as the point of genesis of counter-terrorism policies, which then spread to the rest of the world. This approach shows an inherent Eurocentrism in conceptualising counter-terrorism. In drawing out the connections between the global, the transnational, and the everyday in the conception and practice of counter-terrorism, we present an epistemic challenge to contemporary ways of studying counter-terrorism that privilege events in the Global North as the starting point for knowledge production on counter-terrorism. Further, drawing out these embroglios shows how historical conceptions of race, gender, religion, and ethnicity work at multiple scales to produce practices of counter-terrorism.

Our empirical case studies move beyond this approach as we focus on the various scales at which counter-terrorism policies work. For example, in Chapter 8, Amna Kaleem focuses on how the international and domestic security logics produced by race, religion, gender, and class converge in the everyday life of the individual under PREVENT, a policy of countering violent extremism practised in the UK. Kaleem traces a 'symbiotic exchange of technologies' between domestic and international security logics that play out in the life of the individual.

Our aim in bringing together these chapters is to show how a range of discourses, agents, and practices, both transnational and national, intersect with the practice of counter-terrorism. In doing so, we unsettle a narrative of the unidirectional flow of counter-terrorism policies in response to 9/11 from the Global North to the Global South.

Counter-terrorism, radicalisation, and right-wing extremism

The third section of this collection enriches counter-terrorism studies through sophisticated analyses of the interactions between counter-terrorism and ideologies such as right-wing extremism and Islamophobia in many parts of the world. The chapters in this section tie up with the overall aim of decolonising and deparochialising the study of counter-terrorism through an exploration of how counter-terrorism works at various scales and intersects with a range of ideologies. In doing so, this section also unsettles a Eurocentric and North American focus on counter-terrorism. This section demonstrates how colonial conceptions of race, gender, and religion feed into counter-terrorism discourse and are then mobilised by a range of ideologies. To that extent, this section contributes to the overall aims of the volume to engage the myriad iterations of coloniality as well as understand the multiple negotiations with the same. The chapters in this section show how discourses of counter-terrorism are creatively appropriated and reshaped by right-wing extremists using a range of resources, especially in non-Western contexts. Therefore, we aim to challenge a unidirectional narrative of counter-terrorism and consequent securitisation as a practice originating in the Global North and circulating to other parts of the world. We also expand on the predominant ways of studying counter-terrorism and securitisation in the Global North, paying careful attention to their overlap with other ideologies. The chapters in this section show a rich interplay of discourses and ideas that produce everyday practices of counter-terrorism and everyday securitisation enabled by right-wing extremists and the security apparatus. This is an important contribution to the scholarship on counter-terrorism.

For example, Leidig's contribution shows how far-right discourses on gender representations, nationalist far-right anxieties about demographic change, and global far-right discourses of Islamophobia influence counter-terrorism discourse and practice in India and the UK. Bakkali and Perry show how the securitisation of Muslims in Canada has drawn attention away from the rapid growth of far-right extremist activism. The latter has largely been ignored in the discourse of security. The chapters in this section of the book show how far-right invocations of security threats at a national, local, and everyday level interact with discourses of counter-terrorism.

Summary of the chapters

The first part of the book, comprising four chapters, dwells upon colonialism and its legacies. The individual chapters focus on how colonial hierarchies and colonial forms of knowledge persist in the practice of counter-terrorism. The contributions in this section show how these are negotiated in the everyday.

Part I: Colonialism and counter-terrorism

In Chapter 1 titled 'Colonial law and normal violence: The racialised, gendered, and classed development of counter-terrorism', Alice Finden traces the history of pre-criminal technologies to show how coloniality persists in contemporary counter-terrorism practices in Egypt. Whereas pre-criminal tools – instruments that purport to detect 'potential' extremists before they are radicalised – are primarily construed as post-9/11 developments that erode liberal democratic values, Finden shows how pre-criminal thinking was inextricably linked with colonial law-making in British-occupied Egypt. This chapter uses archival research to show how the development of pre-emptive governance relies on colonial erasure and the rewriting of marginalised modes of thinking and being. Finden analyses legal moments in the British occupation of Egypt where pre-criminal thinking was enacted and institutionalised through the law. Additionally, Finden also presents interviews with Egyptians that demonstrate the persistent effects of colonial forms of pre-emption. This chapter thereby shows the continuities between contemporary Egyptian law-making and colonial notions of pre-emption. Through an exploration of everyday forms of violence in law-making, Finden shows how contemporary counter-terrorism is dependent upon the production of categories of difference and classifications of suspicion.

In Chapter 2, Farooq Yousaf shows how the colonial and postcolonial representations of the Pashtun community in Pakistan are weaponised in Pakistan's war on terror and enable the consolidation of power by the country's military establishment. Yousaf shows how Pashtuns, especially those based in the former FATA (Federally Administered Tribal Areas) region of the Afghanistan–Pakistan border, have been portrayed as 'violent' and 'warrior-like' by colonial writers during the British military expeditions against Pashtun insurgencies. Even after the independence of Pakistan, these perceptions about Pashtuns have persisted and are today weaponised by the Pakistani state. Consequently, Pashtun nationalist non-violent movements demanding equal rights have been branded as being against Pakistan's interests. The Pashtun Tahafuz (Protection) Movement (PTM), a non-violent Indigenous peace and human rights movement in the former FATA region, has been blacklisted by Pakistan's military. This shows how Pashtun's demanding peace, justice, and accountability from the state are only termed a 'security threat' by the military.

In Chapter 3, Lumbini Sharma explores the growth of counter-terrorism machinery in early twentieth-century colonial Bengal as a response to growing 'terrorist' activities in the province. The chapter shows how British counter-terrorism practice relied on extensive intelligence apparatus to locate propagandists, agents, and secret presses associated with 'terrorist' activities in the dark, dingy lanes of central Calcutta. Sharma shows how Bengal emerged as an important centre for counter-insurgency networks, from which the British government traced the network of terrorists spreading across the globe. In Bengal, activities of colonial intelligence agencies such as the Special Branch of the Calcutta Police and the Intelligence Branch of the Bengal Police proliferated. The chapter also takes note of the novel counter-terrorist propaganda adopted by the imperial government to influence public opinion that was aimed at countering 'terrorist' propaganda. The extensive surveillance technologies and counter-terrorism policing strategies of the empire continue to shape the practice of counter-terrorism in contemporary India.

In Chapter 4, Marine Guéguin proposes a decolonial approach to understanding French counter-terrorism. The chapter aims to delineate how coloniality and colonial structures of counter-terrorism animate the practice of counter-terrorism in contemporary France. Using a discourse analysis of the French response to terrorism in the aftermath of the Charlie Hebdo and the Paris attacks in 2015, Guéguin shows how the use of emergency legislation following terror attacks in France has colonial roots. This legislation is embedded in the practice of French colonialism during the Algerian War. Guéguin shows how French counter-terrorism practices depart from the predominant post-9/11 discourses on counter-terrorism with their depiction of the 'enemy within' as an internal threat to national security.

Part II: Global, national, and everyday counter-terrorism practices

The second part of the book, comprising four chapters, traces the relations between global, transnational, and national discourses of counter-terrorism to challenge a Eurocentric and Global North oriented approach to the study of counter-terrorism.

In Chapter 5, Graig Klein argues that the traditional Western-centric focus on counter-terrorism impedes our ability to systematically study and access counter-terrorism in the Global South. Klein's Comparative Counterterrorism Project (CCTP) uses a cross-national database from 2016 to 2019 to explore the counter-terrorism legislative, investigative, and detention practices of national governments around the world. CCTP allows for the ability to develop non-Eurocentric or non-Global-North perspectives, models, and implementations of counter-terrorism that provide a roadmap for how to approach, organise, and coordinate counter-terrorism responses among highly heterogeneous countries. As a result, CCTP provides the foundation to conduct cross-national and country-specific analyses and comparisons of the practices, connections, divergences, trends, and effectiveness of counter-terrorism in the Global North and Global South. This helps overcome the limitations of primarily Western, Global North, or Eurocentric studies of local, regional, and transnational counter-terrorism cooperation, practices, and policies.

In Chapter 6, Sissel Haugdal Jore examines the evolution of counter-terrorism policies in Norway from the 1990s to 2020 through the lens of the attack on the Norwegian government complex. It shows how the 22 July 2011 attack impacted the legitimacy of security measures in the public realm. Jore shows how terrorism and counter-terrorism measures become highly visible in the public discourse on the rebuilding of the government quarter and in the urban landscape. The chapter shows how conceptions of terrorism change as well as how counter-terrorism measures are legitimised through an exploration of the changing contours of the urban landscape in Norway.

In Chapter 7, Inés Bolaños-Somoano shows how Member States of the European Union and EU institutions participate in a collective securitisation process for the prevention of terrorism. The chapter outlines the composite nature of agency in the EU as it implements counter-terrorism measures. It examines the securitising move and audience response dynamics between EU institutions and Member States. This chapter combines secondary literature, policy analysis, and novel interview materials to outline the roles and phases in the collective securitisation process of prevention, a relatively new model of counter-terrorism in the European Union. This chapter takes into consideration both the priorities of the Member States as well as external discursive conditions that facilitate a process of securitisation. Bolaños-Somoano chapter, therefore, delineates the various scales – transnational, national, and institutional – at which counter-terrorism functions and brings out the various agents involved in the operationalisation of counter-terrorism.

In Chapter 8, Amna Kaleem challenges the predominant paradigms of understanding Preventing and Countering Violent Extremism (P/CVE) policies, which often focus on the migration of policies from the international to the domestic sphere. Kaleem, instead, urges attention to how international and domestic security logics converge at the grassroots level. Drawing on the experiences of ordinary citizens conducting counter-terrorism surveillance under the Prevent Duty in England, her chapter explores how the body of the individual becomes the terrain where international and domestic logics of counter-terrorism converge. As a result, ordinary interactions turn into (in)security-making opportunities and spaces that turn into domestic outposts of the global War on Terror. Domestic counter-extremism technologies feed into the international by constructing the securitisation of civic life as a preventative rationality that can be replicated elsewhere. These technologies are also reflected in the categories of race, gender, religion, and class. Kaleem contends that there is a symbiotic exchange of technologies between the domestic and the international, instantiated in the micro-level interactions of individuals.

Part III: Counter-terrorism, radicalisation, and right-wing extremism

The third part of the book draws attention to the discourse and practice of counter-terrorism and a range of ideologies such as far-right extremism and Islamophobia.

Chapter 9 by Naved Bakali and Barbara Perry argue that the securitisation of Muslims in Canada is part of broader historic practices associated with the racialised logic of coloniality. They also show how the securitisation of Muslims draws attention away from serious threats to Canadian society, such as the rapid growth of white supremacist and far-right extremist groups, which have targeted many racialised and minority communities, including Muslims. Their chapter explores how racialised logic undergirding the securitisation of Muslims is also manifested in the neglect of far-right extremist activism in security discourses. This contribution shows how racialised logic is central to the practice of counter-terrorism and how this logic exacerbates white nationalist and right-wing extremist ideologies. These prejudiced logics of counter-terrorism have had fatal consequences for Muslims as they both criminalise and dehumanise Muslims and gloss over the rise of right-wing forces that attack Muslim minorities.

In Chapter 10, Eviane Leidig explores the convergence between anti-Muslim political activism and counter-terrorism policies. She shows how international counter-terrorism policies have responded to, and been shaped by, far-right metapolitics concerning gendered narratives of Muslim male sexuality. This chapter presents a comparative analysis of two case studies: 'love jihad' in India and the Great Replacement theory in Europe and America. Building upon these narratives, this chapter analyses social media content related to love jihad and the Great Replacement produced by far-right activists and traces how local ideological narratives of Muslim sexuality are embedded into global Islamophobic tropes. Leidig then explores the connections between the far-right metapolitical discourse on gendered representations and its impact on counter-terrorism policies in India. In India, state-led legislation prohibiting interfaith marriage and religious conversion has been propelled by Hindu nationalist activists campaigning against love jihad. Similarly, in Europe, the passage of anti-immigrant and anti-refugee legislation spearheaded by populist radical right parties can be construed as a function of far-right metapolitical activism on the issue expressed through the Great Replacement theory. Leidig uses counter-terrorism as an analysis for understanding these policies.

Dean J. Smith, Ewan Bottomley, and Ken Mavor in Chapter 11 explore the relationship between the right-wing Q-Anon movement, conspiracy theories, and perceptions of a threat from particular communities or groups. Through a content analysis of material associated with the Q-Anon movement, the authors suggest that believers hold an extreme perception of danger from a malevolent, secret organisation. This contribution discusses the relationship between right-wing extremism and conspiracy theories using a social identity model of collective violence, with an emphasis on the roles of threat perception and defensive violence. The authors also provide a social psychological account of conspiracy theories, in particular the relationship between conspiratorial thinking and threat perception.

Counter-terrorism beyond binaries: Interrogating prevailing frameworks

This collection represents a pivotal intervention in critical terrorism studies by outlining new directions for scholarship on counter-terrorism. The contributors compellingly make the case for moving beyond dominant binaries and prevailing assumptions that have constrained the field. Central prevailing tendencies that are constructively critiqued include:

- binaries between liberal democracy and emergency politics that neglect colonial histories;
- Eurocentrism and methodological nationalism that reduce counter-terrorism to 9/11 and the West;
- presentism and epochal thinking that overlook enduring legacies and continuities;
- binaries between domestic and international spheres that ignore convergences and connections.

The contributors highlight the need to transcend such binaries through deeper historical, postcolonial, and transnational analyses that reveal the complexity of counter-terrorism practices worldwide. One crucial binary interrogated is between normal and emergency politics, with counter-terrorism seen as an exception or departure from liberal democratic norms. The chapters reveal the colonial continuities and genealogies underlying contemporary counter-terrorism tools, from pre-emptive logics to ethnic profiling. Far from an anomaly, today's counter-terrorism practices mirror colonial strategies of emergency legislation, fragmentation, and racialised governance. Another pernicious binary is between the West and the non-West, whereby Eurocentric approaches reduce counter-terrorism to post-9/11 policies spreading from the Global North. The contributors highlight connected histories and multifarious flows shaping counter-terrorism through diverse cases spanning the Global North and

South. Examining cases beyond the West throws into sharp relief the need to analyse counter-terrorism as a global, interconnected phenomenon. The collection also challenges binaries between the past and present by emphasising colonial afterlives and enduring imperial legacies that constitute the present. Contemporary counter-terrorism practices worldwide are situated within deeper histories of colonial violence, racist surveillance, and discourses of dangerous cultures that endure today. Epochal thinking that separates the past from the present is profoundly interrogated. Finally, binaries between international and domestic counter-terrorism are questioned. The chapters reveal complex cross-scalar connections, whereby global and local discourses interact in spaces like the surveilled themselves. International security logics fuse with domestic policies; discourses circulate transnationally; and diverse actors and interests shape policies at multiple levels.

This collection represents the best of critical scholarship, challenging prevailing binaries, questioning worn assumptions, and expanding theoretical horizons. It models new ways of studying counter-terrorism beyond trappings like Eurocentrism, epochal thinking, and conceptual silos. The potency lies in revealing counter-terrorism as a profoundly complex global phenomenon shaped by interconnected histories, identities, spaces, and ideas. In focusing on multiplicity, these scholars compellingly gesture towards decolonising and deparochialising critical terrorism studies. Their bold, imaginative analyses provide a guidepost for the field to move forward. In sum, this collection demonstrates the urgency and potential of new postcolonial, transnational, and multi-scalar approaches that avoid the binaries undergirding traditional scholarship. The authors model generative new ways of studying counter-terrorism in all its complexity, contingency, and connectedness across time and space. Their critical analyses point persuasively towards decolonising counter-terrorism studies in theory and practice.

Notes

1　Securitisation as a concept builds upon post-structuralist conceptions of security. Security can be considered as a speech act through which a target audience is convinced that a specific issue poses an 'existential threat to a designated referent object' that has a 'legitimate claim to survival' and thereby adopts extraordinary measures to deal with it.
2　Methodological nationalism is the preoccupation of lot of social science scholarship with the unit of the nation-state construed as the 'natural social and political form of the modern world' (Wimmer and Schiller 2002, 217).

References

Abbas, T. (2021). *Countering Violent Extremism: The International Deradicalization Agenda*. London: Bloomsbury Academic.

Acharya, A. (2022). 'Race and racism in the founding of the modern world order', *International Affairs*, 98(1), 23–43.

Amoore, L. (2009). 'Algorithmic war: Everyday geographies of the War on Terror', *Antipode*, 41(1), 49–69.

Barnard-Wills, D. and Moore, C. (2010). 'The terrorism of the other: Towards a contrapuntal reading of terrorism in India', *Critical Studies on Terrorism*, 3(3), 383–402.

Bastani, N. and Gazzotti, L. (2021). ' "Still a bit uncomfortable, to be an arm of the state": Making sense and subjects of counter-extremism in the UK and Morocco', *Environment and Planning C: Politics and Space*, 40(2), 520–40, 23996544211031914.

Boyle, M. J. (2019). *Non-Western Responses to Terrorism*. Manchester: Manchester University Press.

Chan, N. (2018). 'The Malaysian "Islamic" state versus the Islamic State (IS): Evolving definitions of "terror" in an "Islamising" nation-state', *Critical Studies on Terrorism*, 11(3), 415–37.

Cohn, C. (2013). *Women and Wars: Contested Histories, Uncertain Futures*. Cambridge and Malden: Polity Press.

Crelinsten, R. (2014). 'Perspectives on counterterrorism: From stovepipes to a comprehensive approach', *Perspectives on Terrorism*, 8(1), 2–15.

De Goede, M., Simon, S., and Hoijtink, M. (2014). 'Performing preemption', *Security Dialogue*, 45(5), 411–22.

Eckert, J. (2008). 'Laws for enemies', in Eckert, J. (ed.) *The Social Life of Anti-Terrorism Laws: The War on Terror and the Classifications of the Dangerous 'Other'*. Bielefeld: transcript, pp. 7–32.

Elshimi, M. (2015). 'De-radicalisation interventions as technologies of the self: A Foucauldian analysis', *Critical Studies on Terrorism*, 8(1), 110–29.

Genty, C. (2020). *Disordered Violence: How Gender, Race and Heteronormativity Structure Terrorism*. Edinburgh: Edinburgh University Press.

Getachew, A. (2019). 'The limits of sovereignty as responsibility', *Constellations*, 26(2), 225–40.

Hamzić, V. (2018). 'International law as violence: Competing absences of the other', in Otto, D. (ed.) *Queering International Law: Possibilities, Alliances, Complicities, Risks*. New York: Routledge.

Heathcote, G. (2012). *The Law on the Use of Force: A Feminist Analysis*. Oxon and New York: Routledge.

Hillyard, P. (1993). *Suspect Community: People's Experience of the Prevention of Terrorism Acts in Britain*. London: Pluto Press.

Hussain, N. (1999). 'Towards a jurisprudence of emergency: Colonialism and the rule of law', *Law and Critique*, 10(2), 93–115.

Hussain, N. (2007). 'Hyperlegality', *New Criminal Law Review*, 10(4), 514–31.

Iqtidar, H. (2021). 'Jizya against nationalism: Abul A'la Maududi's attempt at decolonizing political theory', *The Journal of Politics*, 83(3), 1145–57.

Kundnani, A. (2015) *The Muslims Are Coming! Islamophobia, Extremism, and the Domestic War on Terror*. London: Verso.

Kundnani, A. and Hayes, B. (2018). *The Globalisation of Countering Violent Extremism Policies: Undermining Human Rights, Instrumentalising Civil Society*. Amsterdam: Transnational Institute.

Likhovski, A. (2006). *Law and Identity in Mandate Palestine*. Chapel Hill, NC: University of North Carolina Press.

Neocleous, M. (2006). 'The problem with normality: Taking exception to "permanent emergency"', *Alternatives: Global, Local, Political*, 31(2), 191–213.

Neocleous, M. (2007). 'From martial law to the War on Terror', *New Criminal Law Review: An International and Interdisciplinary Journal*, 10(4), 489–513.

Qurashi, F. (2017). 'Just get on with it: Implementing the Prevent duty in higher education and the role of academic expertise', *Education, Citizenship and Social Justice*, 12(3), 197–212.

Reynolds, J. (2017). *Empire, Emergency, and International Law*. Cambridge: Cambridge University Press.

Sian, K. (2017). 'Born radicals? Prevent, positivism, and "race-thinking"', *Palgrave Communications*, 3(1), 1–8.

Silke, A. (2018). 'The study of terrorism and counterterrorism', in Silke, A. (ed.) *Routledge Handbook of Terrorism and Counterterrorism*. London: Routledge, pp. 1–10.

Sjoberg, L. and Gentry, C. E. (2007). *Mothers, Monsters, Whores: Women's Violence in Global Politics*. London: Zed Books.

Spalek, B. and Weeks, D. (2020). 'The role of communities in counterterrorism: Analyzing policy and exploring psychotherapeutic approaches within community settings', in Spalek, B. and Weeks, D. (eds) *Communities and Counterterrorism*. Abingdon, NY: Routledge, pp. 5–7.

Suresh, M. (2019). 'The social life of technicalities: "Terrorist" lives in Delhi's courts', *Contributions to Indian Sociology*, 53(1), 72–96.

Taylor, L. and Soni, A. (2017). 'Preventing radicalisation: A systematic review of literature considering the lived experiences of the UK's Prevent strategy in educational settings', *Pastoral Care in Education*, 35(4), 241–52.

Walker, C. and Cawley, O. (2022). 'The juridification of the UK's counter terrorism Prevent policy', *Studies in Conflict & Terrorism*, 45(11), 1004–29.

Wimmer, A. and Glick-Schiller, N. (2002). 'Methodological nationalism and beyond: Nation–state building, migration and the social sciences', *Global Networks*, 2(4), 301–34.

Wojczewski, T. (2020). ' "Enemies of the people": Populism and the politics of (In) security', *European Journal of International Security*, 5(1), 5–24.

Youngman, M. (2020). 'Building "terrorism studies" as an interdisciplinary space: Addressing recurring issues in the study of terrorism', *Terrorism and Political Violence*, 32(5), 1091–105.

Zichi, P. (2021). 'Prostitution and moral and sexual hygiene in Palestine: The criminal code for Palestine (1921–1936)', *Australian Feminist Law Journal*, 47(1), 47–65.

Part I

Colonialism and counter-terrorism

1

Colonial law and normal violence: The racialised, gendered and classed development of counter-terrorism

Alice Finden

Twenty years after the declaration of the global War on Terror and the creation of Guantánamo Bay, states around the globe continue to adopt increasingly restrictive, permanent, and pre-emptive laws and policies to counter-terrorism. Over the past two decades, liberal democracies in the Global North – in particular the UK, Germany, Denmark, Sweden, and the Netherlands – have led on the development of countering extremism tools such as deradicalisation programmes (Ministry of Refugee, Immigration and Integration Affairs 2010). Such programmes have particularly expanded since the 2014 UN Security Council Resolution 2178 encouraged member states to 'engage relevant local communities and non-governmental actors in developing strategies to counter the violent extremist narrative that can incite terrorist acts'.[1] These counter-extremism programmes have alarmed scholars and practitioners alike because they extend the temporality of a crime to actions taken before a crime has occurred. These 'pre-criminal' tools (McCulloch and Wilson 2016; see also Heath-Kelly 2013) increasingly work from a discriminatory and identarian basis and destabilise the rule of law (Ní Aoláin 2020). In the UK, the Terrorism Act 2000 was the first of several terrorism laws that increasingly squeeze freedoms, broaden definitions of terrorism, and afford more powers to the police and the Secretary of State (Bradley 2018).

Global South states have developed their anti-terror laws and policies on a similar trajectory. Egypt has been effective in leading the way in the Middle East and North Africa. Since 2013, under the military regime of Abdel Fattah el-Sisi, the passing of anti-terror decrees and laws has accelerated at a high rate, many of which mirror Global North laws in their pre-emptive style (Welchman 2005). Many such laws are used by el-Sisi's government to detain people en masse for 'infringing on public peace' or 'disturbing public order' (International Commission of Jurists 2016). Under former President Mubarak, Egypt's promulgation of its anti-terror law no. 97 in 1992 was already influential to the shaping of the Arab Convention for the Suppression of Terrorism (Welchman 2005). Egypt has also been developing

counter-extremism approaches since 1997, through prison-based deradicalisation programmes focusing on re-education, religious discourse, psychological counselling, and family and financial support (Kruse 2016).

While both states of the Global North and Global South use similar tools
for countering terrorism, scholars risk making generalisations as to the
development of such policies, according to whether the state in question is
considered to be a liberal democracy or authoritarian. The use of authoritarian tools within liberal democracies such as the UK is often framed as
exceptional to the values of a liberal democracy. Such tools are understood
to stand outside of the rule of law and threaten to erode it. In authoritarian states like Egypt, however, such tools are framed as part of the normal
procedure of what are often generalising and naturalising terms, 'reflecting
long-standing orientalist tropes about non-European countries' (Pratt and
Rezk 2019: 243).

Formerly colonised states, like Egypt, however, carry through colonial structures of law and government that were imposed upon them, and
indeed make use of such colonial security tools to counter terrorism today
(Abdelrahman 2017; Abozaid 2022; Berda 2020; Brankamp and Glück
2022; Chukwuma 2022; McQuade 2020; Oando and Achieng 2021;
Parashar and Schultz 2021; Whittaker 2015). Further than this, colonialism underpins the entire epistemic creation of 'modernity' and along with
it, the norms of the international community (Parashar and Schultz 2021;
Quijano 2007). Here, modern systems of government and law depend upon
the reproduction of colonial categories of humanity based on racialised,
gendered and classed frames (Quijano 2007). However, the postcolonial
experience cannot be solely reduced to European colonialism if we are to
take decolonial and Indigenous forms of knowledge seriously and aim to
move away from a Eurocentric blueprint of statehood (Parashar and Schultz
2021; Ismail 2006; Rao 2020; Salem 2020). Such a move would reduce
non-Western political interventions in international relations to the colonial
story (Agathangelou and Lin 2004). It is instead necessary to pay attention
to the nuanced and differentiated forms of power involved in the creation
of authoritarian tools today, for instance through Agathangelou and Lin's
(2004) framework of 'worldism' that acknowledges the existence of multiple and changeable worlds.

As an alternative to the traditional comparative approach, therefore,
this chapter presents a postcolonial feminist methodology for assessing the
development of anti-terror laws and policies which is sensitive to both the
colonial imposition of modern legal systems and the role of the postcolonial
state in refashioning authoritarian tools. I argue that these laws and policies
should be understood as *fragmented authoritarian tools* that have developed

through power struggles between colonial and postcolonial states, manifesting through the securitisation of racialised, gendered, and classed communities. Theoretically, this approach hinges upon viewing authoritarianism not as exceptional in liberal democracies, nor as a corrosion of liberal values such as the rule of law, but instead upon viewing violence and the law as co-constitutive. In this way, this chapter illustrates a key argument of this edited collection: that counter-terrorism is mediated through the messy entanglement of historical and transnational processes.

Looking at the historical period of British-occupied Egypt (1882–1956), this chapter combines critical legal studies with feminist and postcolonial theories as a means to trace the development of some countering terrorism tools and their historical interaction with law.[2] In particular, I use and expand Hussain's (2007a) theory of 'hyperlegality' to develop a lens that can account for the production and deployment of categories of suspicion and dangerousness through everyday administrative encounters with law. This approach situates violence within the law and argues that the development of colonial authoritarian tools – many of which are still in use today – were formed upon the suppression of marginalised communities in response to political anxieties over sovereignty. Through developing hierarchical and fragmented systems of law (Eckert 2008; Hillyard 1993; Johns 2005) that provided alternative arrangements for 'not yet civilised' subjects, colonial administrative systems paved the way for present day countering terrorism legislation which allows for the above-described differential treatment of marginalised subjects.

It should be noted that I am not trying to relativise the Egyptian and British application of terrorism laws, nor the experiences of them which are markedly more widespread and violent in Egypt. Rather I argue that by looking to the uneven history of the development of violent securitising practices and their social dynamics, we gain a more empirically rich and grounded view of contemporary terrorism laws that contextualise the state in everyday and global dynamics. Such an approach tells us around which bodies and communities, and at what moments, states continue to develop authoritarian technologies, and further interrogates potential cultural essentialisations within scholarship. In what follows, I first present an overview of how framing countering terrorism as 'exceptionalism' prevents us from viewing the law as violent and risks culturally essentialist arguments that frame Global South states as 'naturally' authoritarian. Next, I provide my alternative methodological approach which combines critical legal studies with postcolonial and feminist theories. The following two sections then use my case study of British-occupied Egypt to illustrate this approach.

Countering terrorism as exceptionalism

A major theoretical framing of the actions of Global North states within the War on Terror is the lens of exceptionalism that posits countering terrorism as threatening the integrity of liberal democracies and undermining judicial procedures (Kundnani and Hayes 2018). Through this lens, mechanisms of the global War on Terror such as arbitrary arrest, torture, detention without trial, and pre-criminal methods, are cast as effects of a state of exception (Johns 2005). In a state of exception, the state is ruled by sovereign power and law is suspended by the executive branch. It is often cast as a 'return' to the past or a 'regression' from democratic and liberal values (Gökariksel and Türem 2019). For Nazi jurist Schmitt (2005), the state of exception entailed the suspension of law which was ultimately at the whim of the sovereign who held legitimate power. Here, sovereign power and thus the state of exception is constitutive of juridical order, or as Van Munster (2004: 143) puts it: 'the sovereign declaration of the state of exception simultaneously creates the state of nature and the rule of law'.

The philosopher Agamben (2005: 50) reframed Schmitt's theory and effectively rescued the rule of law through holding the exception as 'law's "other": as a zone where law is suspended, a space devoid of law, a zone of anomie'. Guantánamo Bay is often given as an example where the exception reigns free, ungoverned by the 'lawful' order in the United States (Humphreys 2006). A geographical and jurisdictional difference is therefore drawn between a 'lawful' USA and a 'lawless' Guantánamo Bay. For Agamben, the military order issued by President George W. Bush on 13 November 2001 that authorised indefinite detention, of which Guantánamo Bay was part, 'radically erases any legal status of the individual, thus producing a legally unnameable and unclassifiable being' (Agamben 2005: 3). Being a Guantánamo detainee – a place where indefinite detention, lack of legal representation and constant interrogation and torture is the norm – is thus understood as the pinnacle of dehumanisation.

Butler rethinks exceptionalism through the lenses of governmentality and performativity, framing the state of exception as discursive and tactical. By relocating exceptionalism within practices of governmentality, Butler interrogates Schmittian and Agambenian framings that invest all power in the sovereign to suspend law and renders the exception a product of multiple actors (Butler 2004: 54). As Neal (2008) explains, Butler rethinks exceptionalism as performative, as the repetitive discursive production of a justification for a political course of action. For Butler, the suspension of law is a political practice or a 'tactic' of governmentality. In this way, 'the suspension of law is not the exception in itself, but rather part of the performative constitution of "exceptionalism" as a normalised and legitimate mode of government' (Neal 2008: 51).

However, for Butler, it appears that the suspension of law still ultimately gives way to executive decision-making that sits outside of the 'true' rule of law. Speaking about decisions taken about detainees at Guantánamo Bay, Butler (2004: 54) explains:

> Neither the decision to detain nor the decision to activate the military tribunal are grounded in law. They are determined by discretionary judgements that function within a manufactured law or that manufacture a law as they are performed. In this sense, both of these judgements are already outside of the sphere of law, since the determination of when and where, for instance, a trial might be waived and detention deemed indefinite does not take place within a legal process.

What is curious is Butler's differentiation between executive actions that manufacture the language of law, and the rule of law as a space in which real legal processes take place. While Butler's interrogation of the state of exception as tactical and performative is useful for conceptualising how discursive framings of countering terrorism as a necessary exception help to justify excessively violent state actions, they continue to situate the rule of law as a separate sphere in which proper legal processes take place.

In the disciplines of political science and critical legal studies, the increasingly restrictive practices of liberal democracies under the guise of counter-terrorism are often understood through this same framing: as an unveiling of sovereign power, whereby the executive rules and corrodes the rule of law. For instance, Kundnani and Hayes (2018) note pre-criminal approaches to be primarily enacted through policy reform, executive decree, or the allocation of funds, rather than through primary legislation. They consider deradicalisation programmes to be the cause of problems of democratic accountability and compliance with human rights standards. Using this framing, scholars have ended up commending the juridification of the pre-criminal space. Walker and Cawley (2020) give the example of the UK's Prevent agenda which was made a legal duty in 2015, and argue that the juridification of countering extremism policies brings about legal constraints through accountability, transparency, and fairness. Others like Hawley (2008) frame the conceptualisation of the 'citizen-terrorist' as causing the fundamental structures of liberalism to shift from a situation where citizens are afforded the protection of the social contract to one in which the liberal state wages war against its own citizens.

However, some critical legal scholars warn of the dangers of separating legal and political spaces in such a way. For Neocleous (2006: 207), the imagining of a 'normal' and an 'emergency' rule as two oppositional forms of governance assumes that the emergency is an aberration that happens in a space separate to the normal constitutional order 'thereby preserving the Constitution in its pristine form while providing the executive with the power to act in an emergency'. This framing is problematic because it is based upon an assumption and the 'serious misjudgement' that legality is the ultimate space of protection for human rights from state violence (Neocleous 2006: 207). Furthermore, the state of exception as a philosophical portrayal of the contemporary post-9/11 moment relies upon teleological understandings of a universal linear time that can end up reaffirming dichotomies drawn between states of the Global North as progressive and states of the Global South as backward. Here, the exception is deemed an aberrational rift in time where we can see echoes of the violent past. As Hutchings (2008: 129–30) explains, the operation of time within grand theories of world politics is 'necessarily exclusionary' in that what is counted as significant change or progress is always 'bound up with specific normative stances, and it always relies on treating the time of world politics in unifying and universalising terms'.

Because of this, the use of authoritarian tools to counter terrorism in Global North states can be framed as exceptional whereas in Global South states such use is framed as the norm or a different kind of law. For instance, Cooley (2016) considers the post-9/11 turn towards counter-terrorism to be one of the more powerful sources of 'counternorms' that has led towards the erosion of the liberal democracy worldwide. While I do not dispute that governments around the globe have been harnessing counter-terrorism discourse to further their own agendas, it is Cooley's framing that I take issue with. Cooley argues that the post-9/11 backlash against democratic norms have developed among predominantly Global South states that take issue with the universalising effects of liberal democracy and are pushing instead for the recognition of 'civilisational diversity' and the defense of 'traditional values'. Such framings are limited in that they frame the liberal democracy as devoid of authoritarian leanings, thus erasing the epistemic and totalising violence upon which the liberal self-determination principle was built (Mitchell 2002) and further characterise authoritarianism as a cultural phenomenon.

While I do not deny the real forms of safety that can be accessed through democratic processes and the law, it is crucial to look to how law and politics overlap in the creation of authoritarian tools in order to understand how violence is normalised and legitimised. By looking to a historical context, the persistence of colonial forms of governance is unveiled, challenging the Eurocentrism of many contemporary accounts of countering terrorism.

Looking to the violence of colonial law: An alternative approach

In contrast to the state-of-exception approach, the increasing proliferation of counter-terror laws and practices is understood by Hussain (2007a) and others not as an encroachment of exceptional executive measures onto the liberal democracy, but as the contemporary face of a longer history of the use of fragmented and hierarchical forms of law for colonised subjects (Hillyard 1993; Johns 2005). Colonial law and in particular the use of martial law and emergency laws for colonial subjects are widely understood to be the roots of contemporary counter-terrorism law in that various processes of liberalisation and normalisation have, over time, made them palatable to democratic societies all the while turning such temporary measures into more permanent and pervasive frameworks (Hussain 1999; Neocleous 2007; Reynolds 2017). Such approaches are based on conceptualising the law as bound up in violence through the creation of hegemonic legal truths and the denial of the speech of colonised subjects (Quijano 2007). Indeed, centring the experiences of colonial and queer communities, many postcolonial and feminist scholars understand the law itself as violence (Cohn 2013; Hamzić, 2018; Heathcote 2012; Sjoberg and Gentry 2007).

Hussain provides a theoretical approach that does not consider the use of emergency laws to be a different kind of law to the normal, ordinary law, but instead shifts our focus to the interaction of law and politics in administrative sites. Routed through critical historical and legal approaches, he shows how situations that are at first considered to be the most 'lawless' and exceptional, are in fact similarly based upon 'a range of regular law and daily disciplinary state practices... the difference being one more of degree than kind' (Hussain 2007b: 735). Hussain explains this as a 'typically colonial' set up, noting that colonial states cast the permanent use of emergency law as providing 'rules and rights' in the colonies. In this sense, colonial powers held that permanent emergency law could create norms and rules in the same way that the 'ordinary law' could. The difference was the more immediate violence and less checks that emergency law provided.

Reynolds (2010) argues the imagined distinction between a metropole where the ordinary law ruled and the colonies where emergency law ruled was not possible or always desirable to maintain. Indeed, scholars like Likhovski (2006), Reynolds (2010), and Zichi (2021: 56) instead understand the development of methods of governance as a changeable 'patchwork' of laws and policies throughout the metropole and the colonies, attaching to classed, gendered and racialised bodies and communities cast as threatening at different moments. The constant movement of colonial officers and administrators, of soldiers and tourists, of missionaries and of colonial subjects themselves throughout the British Empire facilitated the movement of narratives about Britishness and belonging and helped shape and share methods of governance. From this perspective, whereas the colonies are often framed as 'lawless' spaces where colonial subjects were subject to the violent whim of a colonial authority unrestrained by the metropole, such violence was often mediated by an overlapping of different emergency codes and legal orders.

Hussain (2007b: 102) describes a 'colonial rule of law' to be one that claims legitimacy through law but one that is also 'full of law, full of rules that hierarchize, bureaucratize, mediate and channel power'. He terms this administrative process 'hyperlegality'. Hyperlegality is characterised by the increasing and overwhelming administrative classification of persons within the law, aided by the use of special tribunals and commissions. New classifications within the law go further than simply developing new subcategories or types of criminality. Instead, 'the process has a strong predictive quality, combining who people supposedly are with what they are likely to do, and, as with much predictive activity, invariably involves racial and cultural presumptions' (Hussain 2007b: 102). In this sense, we begin to see a law that is fragmented, changeable, and able to adapt to new contexts, adding in 'special measures' for those deemed 'not yet ready' for full civilisation.

From this perspective, the colonial development of differentiated practices in the colonies was part of a hierarchical system of law rather than a system of exceptionalism in which no law existed. By understanding the development of colonial law as the precursor to contemporary terrorism laws, we start to see how contemporary variations of legal proceedings, including the increasing uses of pre-criminal law for 'terrorist' crimes, allow for different standards of evidence to be met for different subjects. To illustrate this with the example of Guantánamo Bay, this approach would suggest that many of the so-called 'exceptional' practices of liberal democracies – detention without trial, torture, and pre-criminal methods – are actually provided for through law. Countering the framing of Guantánamo Bay as a lawless 'black hole', Hussain (2007b: 735) details an overlapping 'excess' of laws and administrative orders, showing that 'many of the mechanisms and justifications we find there [Guantánamo Bay] are continuous and consonant with a range of regular law and daily disciplinary state practices'. For Hussain (2007b: 740), the rendering of Guantánamo Bay as a space that produces unnameable subjects is inconsistent with 'the profusion of names and classifications–enemy alien, unlawful belligerent, enemy combatant'.

In this way, law can be understood as part of the larger architecture of colonial truth-making whereby the continuous publishing of security documents aims at foreclosing the freedoms of colonised communities (Stoler 2010). Quijano (2007) understands colonialism as the 'systematic repression' of the knowledge systems of the colonised alongside the expropriation of their products and work, and the imposition of colonial truth. After the formal decolonisation of many parts of the world, structures of governance shifted in postcolonial states to a combination of imperialism, as the external governance by former colonial states, and local administration. Through this shift, Quijano (2007: 169) understands that what persisted in new forms was a 'coloniality of power' through modern knowledge systems that continued to produce hierarchical categories of humanity based on race, class and gender. Underpinning such forms of power is the 'colonisation of the imagination of the dominated' and thus the continual erasure of alternative truths.

When looking to the origins of authoritarian tools, it is therefore not sufficient to trace the material development of laws and policies alone, as we stand to lose the discursive power behind them. Instead, we must look not only to the reappropriation of policies today, but to how such laws and policies feature as examples of a broader 'truth regime'[3] of imperialism and modernity. We must ask how the classifications of race, ethnicity, gender, class, and sexuality, and the erasure of non-hegemonic modes of being made such truth regimes possible and continue to underscore the development of authoritarian tools today. Rather than solely looking at the material legal structures present and the classifications that are developing, postcolonial and feminist scholars look to the way in which the creation of norms can alter the constitution of subjects on affective and psychic levels. This means looking to the creation and disciplining of 'acceptable' and 'suspect' subjects in similar colonising ways that rescripts ways of thinking, feeling and being (Lugones 2007; Quijano 2007; Takla 2021).

This level of analysis not only provides a more holistic and subaltern view of the effects of security laws and policies, but also offers methods to expose the development of classifications of 'suspicion' and 'dangerousness' as multiple and attached to changeable markers of gender, race, and class. For instance, the production of the 'vulnerable' subject comes hand in hand with the production of the 'terrorist' subject, and has a history situated in the adoption of 'softer' methods to pacify, discipline, and educate colonial communities out of immoral attitudes. The 'danger' posed by Egyptian working-class subjects, at a time when anti-colonial resistance was growing, was not solely cast as a fanatical or extremist political influence, but also as a contagion that could infect whole communities with bad morals through illicit sexuality (Finden 2021; Takla 2021). Combining a critical legal studies approach with a postcolonial feminist theoretical lens then provides a methodology to assess the development of authoritarian counter-terror tools today as formed from fragmenting and hierarchical colonial law that develops on the level of official politics as it does through the everyday creation of norms.

It is further necessary to delineate the paths taken by the colonising power and the colonised state after struggles for independence and decolonisation. As I demonstrate in the case of British-occupied Egypt, security tools were indeed imposed upon Egypt throughout the late nineteenth and early twentieth century, many of which continue to structure Egyptian counter-terrorism today. However, postcolonial work risks reifying Eurocentric frameworks and disregarding Indigenous and local agency if it only recognises the power of the coloniser (Agathangelou and Ling 2004; Ismail 2006; Parashar and Schultz 2021). Indeed, scholars demonstrate how Egyptian elites working with the British administration perpetuated and reframed narratives of morality, moderacy, and extremism around the working classes, women, and particular forms of Islam (Ahmed 1992; Omar 2017; Takla 2021). Furthermore, British security laws provided the newly independent Egyptian regime with its own toolbox to suppress the same communities framed as 'threatening' (Abozaid 2022; Alzubairi 2019). When considering the colonial logics of present-day authoritarian tools, therefore, it is crucial to pay attention to shifting power dynamics, 'including those that enable formerly colonised states to become colonial in their own right' (Rao 2020: 9).

The next two sections will illustrate this approach through my case study, exposing the colonial logics that underpin aspects of contemporary countering terrorism thinking, including the development of new systems that came to 'know' and administer Egyptian communities through martial law, and an early shift to pre-emptive methods justified around curtailing the movement of racialised, classed, and gendered subjects.

Justifying a hierarchical legal set-up in British-occupied Egypt

The British entered and occupied Egypt in 1882 following the 'Urabi revolt in which Arab nationalists revolted against European influence in the region and control over the Egyptian economy. The British remained in Egypt in some form until 1956. From 1882 to 1914, the British held a Veiled Protectorate over Egypt, in which they had restricted access to the country. This period under the first and most notorious Consul-General to govern Egypt, Lord Cromer, saw the British carry out what were termed 'exceptional' measures against Egyptians which he cast as justifiable and necessary for a country accustomed 'to lawless and despotic government' (Brown 1995: 111). From 1914, the British promulgated martial law and defended it as a relatively 'civilised' set up, and closer to the rule of law, when compared to the 'exceptional' measures that had been carried out by Cromer. As I demonstrate, the particular framing of martial law in Egypt as 'humanising' and 'civilising' at a point in time when the British Empire was crumbling illustrates the legitimisation of fragmented and hierarchical forms of law for different racialised, classed and gendered subjects. This framing allowed for the strategic normalisation of forms of violence and the development of authoritarian tools through law.

When Britain invaded and began occupying Egypt in 1882, there was already a complex legal system in place. This was formed of a mixture of Shari'a-based personal status codes and the Ottoman treaties of Capitulations which granted extraterritorial status to citizens of European states (Brown 1995: 107). In this system, the 'Native Courts' would try Egyptian nationals, and separate consular courts would try the cases of foreign nationals until the Mixed Courts were set up in 1876. Gradually, a legal code was developed which borrowed from the French, as well as a separate judiciary and eventually a system of National Courts in 1884 (Brown 1995: 109). The systems of Capitulations and Mixed Courts represented a constant source of frustration for both the British and the Egyptian authorities in that they restricted the ability to enforce civil and criminal law against foreigners. This lack of power frustrated Lord Cromer to no end. Cromer referred to the breakdown of authority in 1882 as requiring a system 'tantamount to the introduction of martial law' (Brown 1995: 271). In this way, both the British and Egyptian governments had reasons to desire a set up like martial law, or a state of emergency, that would overrule the Capitulations.

Martial law was promulgated in Egypt by the British in 1914 as World War One broke out. At this point martial law was already determined to be a draconian framework in many parts of the Empire and had begun to be replaced by statute-based emergency laws deemed to be more 'humane' and therefore more appropriate for a liberal state (Reynolds 2017). The early twentieth century saw pressures from the international community and the metropole to acknowledge the self-determination of colonies, and pressures from anticolonial resistors themselves. European civilisation missions were greatly impacted by the acceleration of independence movements and the Wilsonian principle of self-determination which came to shape the proceedings of international law and the formation of the League of Nations. At the same time, back in Westminster, members of the Labour party called for decolonisation and demanded to know 'has there ever dawned on the Government the advisability of leaving Egypt to the Egyptians?' (Parliamentary Question 1923).

On this backdrop, the British had to devise a narrative for implementing martial law that would be acceptable to changing Western and international political tastes. The conceptualisation of Egypt as a 'different sort' of colony – one that was not 'fully' colonised – provided the scope for the British

administration to adapt and 'stretch' (Reynolds 2017) martial law in new
'humanising' forms through increased access to administrative and public
services such as transportation, the police, and border controls. Martial
law was promulgated on 2 November 1914 in the official journal of the
Egyptian government by the Commander of the British forces Lieutenant-
General J. G. Maxwell (Proclamation by the General Officer Commanding
His Britannic Majesty's Forces in Egypt). In doing so, the British announced
Egypt to be a Protectorate, thus terminating Ottoman Suzerainty.

Despite ostensibly being promulgated throughout Egypt in reaction to
World War One to regulate the behaviour of British and allied troops, martial law also gave the British the much-desired access to administrative and
judicial spaces throughout the country, including the ability to regulate
working class and rural districts against the spread of disease and disor-
der. With relief at a system that would allow them to bypass the difficult
Egyptian legal structure, the British administration promulgated martial
law, describing it as 'the only system under which everyone can be held'
(Murray 1916). Considered threatening to the morality and hygiene of the
troops, sex workers were deemed enough of a risk to justify their trial by
military court as recorded in the following passage written by an army colonel lamenting the retraction of martial law in 1924 (Letter from Colonel):

> The situation [regarding the transmission of venereal diseases] has become
> worse since the abolition of martial law, and after full consideration, I formed
> the opinion that the increase in disease is mainly due to the lack of efficiency
> in the measures adopted by the civil authorities for the control of prostitutes,
> both registered and unregistered... During the operation of martial law such
> persons [sex workers] were arrested and tried before military courts and on
> conviction, were awarded punishments ranging from 14 days to 6 months
> imprisonment with hard labour, and/or fines of from 10/- to £10 – this action
> proved an efficient deterrent. At the present time, although they are constantly
> arrested by the civil police, the punishments awarded vary, I believe, from only
> PT5 – PT100.

As scholars demonstrate, the colonial spatial regulation of certain districts
was constructed upon racialised, gendered and classed perceptions of moral
and social 'hygiene' (Bashford 2004; Biancani 2013) At the time, 'vice' and
venereal disease were framed as markers of degeneracy and bad morals and
so, martial law provided increased access to such spaces and justification for
their regulation.

Looking into archival records, we witness a shift in the location of martial
law from the military space into civil and administrative spaces and such a
development as indicative of the framework as being 'humanising'. Sir M. S.
Amos (1925: 8) described martial law as setting an 'unfamiliar standard of
care and deliberation' in Egypt, noting that 'in one instance the trial of seventeen persons charged with criminal conspiracy lasted without intermission

for nine weeks', as exemplary of this. Martial law was therefore increasingly framed as less of a draconian emergency structure, and closer to the rule of law. Commander in Chief of the Egyptian Expeditionary Force, General A. J. Murray (1916), observed that, 'as an instrument of Government, as distinct from an instrument of repression, it [martial law] has... been used almost exclusively by the Civil Authorities'. Murray pressed that it was necessary for the application of martial law to affect 'to a greater or lesser extent, every department of the Civil Administration', before going onto list how every public service, including the state railways, the department of public works, the postal and telegraph services, the ports and lights administration, the administration of civil law, and the control of police, should be manipulated. In fact, it was framed so much in this way that it was considered by Murray as 'probably wholly unnecessary as a military measure...' (1916). While there had been a push towards agricultural reform in the period preceding 1914, the promulgation of martial law provided for direct British control over the economy such as the systematic requisition of land, the ban on sugar imports, and the manipulation of house rents.

In this way, British access to everyday and inner workings of Egyptian society was expanded through martial law which also set up new administrative sites for dealing with 'suspicious' and 'dangerous' characters. At the same time, martial law was rendered a normal and humanising type of law, closer to the rule of law than it was to an emergency code. Going back to Hussain, the grafting of different forms of law for colonial subjects was a normal occurrence and helped create a fragmented and hierarchal system of law whereby different avenues were created for colonial subjects seen as 'not quite ready' for total civilised law.

Power struggles and the normalisation of authoritarian tools

As this section demonstrates, the development of authoritarian tools took place on a backdrop of intense episodes of power struggle between the British and Egyptian governments. The desire to maintain control led to authorities developing increasingly oppressive tools formed around the regulation of the Egyptian public (see Abozaid 2022; Alzubairi 2019). As I detail in this section, the development of the 1909 Police Supervision Act in Egypt was one such pre-emptive, future-focused tool developed throughout a major power struggle between the British and Egyptian authorities. Furthermore, the development of this tool demonstrates the influence of security tools developed prior to the British arrival. Such messy and non-linear interactions point to the complexities of postcolonial states' relationship with oppressive tools (see Ismail 2006 for a discussion of temporality and coloniality within Egypt).

The development of the 1909 Police Supervision Act was part of the systematic and institutional creation of the criminal category 'banditry' that was a direct product of the power struggle between the Egyptian government and the British occupiers (Brown 1990). The law provided the ability to curtail and monitor the movement of 'suspicious' characters. However, this law found some of its origins in Ottoman regulations that had already been enacted in Muhammad Ali's early nineteenth century rule. As Fahmy (2012) explains, in the early nineteenth century, the modern Egyptian state was tightening its control over rural areas of the country and measures were imposed to monitor the movement of the fellaheen (rural communities) in particular. The Ottoman authorities felt anxiety most 'in the case of people who had no domicile and who roamed around the city with no clear residence and/or profession' (Fahmy 2012: 350), and in 1830, the 'Government Department of Catching Absconders' (ma'mūriyyat dhabt al-missahhabīn) decreed that every villager should carry a passport with them when they left their village.

On this backdrop, the 1883 Egyptian 'Commissions of Brigandage' was introduced by Prime Minister of Egypt Nubar Pasha quickly following the British arrival in 1882. The Commissions was a system that provided quick access to a criminal sentence; by bypassing the formal legal system, they did not have to wait for the notification of crimes – they worked in a pre-emptive manner, and forcibly took confessions. The Commissions were used to curtail and detect bandits throughout the countryside, working on a classed basis to mark the working classes and fellaheen as suspicious. Brown (1990: 271) explains that the Commissions of Brigandage constituted 'an attempt by the Egyptian government to retain a measure of control over state building, to ensure that Egyptians would still control law enforcement and local administration even as the British occupied the country'. He continues that while forms of banditry had occurred for decades before, the Prime Minister strategically chose to treat it as an emergency to be dealt with through the Commissions, thereby effectively 'inventing' the crime of banditry through institutionalisation.

As the power struggle intensified between the British and the Egyptian governments, the monopoly over the control of state security became the desire of the British occupiers. The British relied on the colonial ideology of representing Egyptian institutions as 'backwards' and 'lawless' in order to frame their own systems as 'civilised'. While the Egyptian Commissions of Brigandage were certainly not a fair institution – they became notorious for torture including hanging people from iron collars (Brown, 1990: 271) – the British used this a means to institute their own version that relied upon the law to give it legitimacy.

In 1909, the British promulgated the Police Supervision Act which similarly sought to limit the movement of 'suspicious' characters. Nineteenth century British legal conceptions of dangerousness were associated with individuals or groups who were seen to 'threaten the domestic order as well as the very existence of the state' which included classed, gendered, and racialised notions of vagrancy, sex work, and diseases (Finnane and Donkin 2013: 10). Referring to concerns over 'dangerous characters', Consul-General (1907–1911) Sir Eldon Gorst, explained that 'the idea is to create a special settlement for them, rather on the lines of what has been proposed for the unemployed in England, where they would be kept under special supervision and prevented from doing further harm' (Letter to Sir Edward Grey 1909). He noted that 'nothing will be done outside the law', and in July, the Police Supervision Act was introduced which expanded the capacity to arrest, trial, and detain those deemed potential criminals (Esmeir 2012: 277). As Esmeir describes in detail, in practice, a committee of local omdas (mayors) had the job of collating lists of 'suspicious' individuals from villages around Egypt. The first list came to a total of around 12,000 names. After checks made by provincial governors and British inspectors, this list was reduced to 283 men, out of whom 263 had no previous convictions. These 283 were then tried before a commission and consequently were sentenced to a period not exceeding five years living under police supervision in their village and the security payment of LE100–1000. If the defendant could not pay the security fee, they would be exiled to the settlement Gorst referred to. One hundred and sixty-seven men, without previous convictions, were exiled here. As Brown (1990: 279) states, 'the only qualification to deserve this punishment was a bad reputation'.

The 1909 law therefore provided for pre-emptive suspicion-based detentions without trial. However, by framing themselves in contrast to the Egyptian Commissions and as part of a 'lawful' and 'civilised' manner of achieving security, class-based British systems found a more permanent home in Egypt. Indeed, years later such powers were coveted by the Egyptian government. Despite nationwide protests for years that culminated in the 1919 revolution, the British proved difficult to get rid of as they negotiated several legal and administrative agreements with the Egyptian government that would provide for their ongoing influence in the region. The Egyptian government itself was invested in an outcome that would end the Protectorate but would grant them some of the same powers of national security that the British had developed. Prime Minister of Egypt (1921–2 and 1926–7) Adly Yakan Pasha agreed to ask for the suspension of martial law 'as soon as an Egyptian law is promulgated giving the Government adequate powers to deal with demonstrations and to effect preventive arrests' (Letter to Foreign Office 1923). Egyptian officials painted anticolonial protests and demonstrations as a justification for the continuation of martial law, despite claims that they desired to repeal it. Adly Yakan Pasha's concern over maintaining tools to enact preventive arrest suggests that British martial law and the various statutory laws enacted throughout the occupation were central in providing the government and military with such powers, and further, that the period of British occupation had facilitated the development of some pre-emptive practices within the law.

The British occupiers relied on the colonial ideology of representing Egyptian institutions as 'backwards' and 'lawless' in order to frame their own as civilising. The development of such tools to pre-emptively curtail and control the movement of racialised, classed and gendered subjects suggests Hussain's hyperlegal set up of a fragmentation of legal standards whereby the working classes were naturalised as dangerous, denied testimony and that this standard was normalised into statute-based laws. Some such laws were carried through by the newly independent Egyptian state in 1952, and indeed Egypt continues to rely upon an almost permanent emergency rule set up today which forms the basis of its counter-terrorism agenda along with other colonial laws (Abozaid 2022; Alzubairi 2019). The development of authoritarian tools in both Global North and Global South states today therefore retain colonial hierarchies and with them the badge of legitimacy that the rule of law affords.

Conclusion: Interrogating contemporary applications of 'authoritarianism'

These early twentieth century developments provide a more holistic picture of authoritarianism, liberalism, and the law today. From what the archives tell us, the deployment of martial law in Egypt as a 'humanising' tool at a time when it was increasingly considered to be a draconian framework internationally is proof that legal narratives can be used effectively to normalise and legitimise increased control and securitisation of a population. Linking to the work of Hussain, Reynolds, and others, the deployment of martial law in this period was part of a wider development of fragmented systems of law that differentiated between the 'civilised' and the 'not yet civilised'. Colonial law was formed upon the theory of racialised, gendered, and classed 'difference' which legitimised the creation of 'special' identarian methods of treatment for colonial subjects, and thus the normalisation of such hierarchies within legal spaces. Such framings are a crucial part of the history of contemporary counter-terror tools that appear at first to be too draconian and thus 'exceptional' within a liberal democracy. In fact, contemporary authoritarian tools like identitarian and pre-emptive offences used today have developed from liberal states' attempts to deal with their 'uncivilised' colonial subjects by creating separate avenues of 'justice'. The liberal framing of the law is precisely what is used to both erase and justify continued violence.

But such tools were not only developed by liberal nations. As shown above, archival records of British-occupied Egypt suggest that such authoritarian tools were developed as forms of governance sometimes through power struggles between the two powers to quell the Egyptian population. In both instances, racialised, classed, and gendered sections of the Egyptian population were constructed as particularly dangerous or vulnerable and new legal and administrative tools were created to suppress them. This suggests that not only did some of the tools we see being used today develop from the suppression of colonial populations, but that we must also pay attention to the ways in which postcolonial states draw on pre-colonial structures, identities, and versions of morality in the formation of security structures (Abozaid 2022; Ismail 2006; Rao 2020; Takla 2021). This demands that the researcher does not simply apply a Western theoretical blueprint to a Global South state, but that we attend to the ways in which the Egyptian state refashions colonial hierarchies of subjects in response to the changeable local and global political context.

Tracing some of the origins of contemporary securitising legal developments, the myth of a liberal democracy immune from authoritarianism is shattered. Furthermore, states like Egypt which has continued to use emergency law as an almost permanent method of governance since the British finally left in 1956, can be thought of not as a qualitatively different 'type' of state to a liberal democracy like the UK, but that it is more a question of degree of authoritarianism (Hussain 2007b: 735). Through situating violence as central to law, focusing on the increasing administration of law and law's effects such as the hierarchising of humanity, the naturalisation of dangerousness, and the law's ability to normalise and legitimise such processes, we access different stories about violence and authoritarianism. Rather than comparing between types of law or states, this type of analysis asks questions about the norms produced by the administrative processes attached to law and finds that sometimes the violent effects are in fact similar.

Notes

1 UN Security Council Resolution 2178 (24 September 2014) UN Doc S/RES/ 2178, 16.
2 This chapter uses a genealogical method by critically engaging with archival sources. This chapter is limited to an assessment of primary British colonial records because of restrictions throughout the research process. However, it uses the work by critical middle east studies scholars as a means to interrogate this bias.
3 Michel Foucault (1977) considered 'truth' to be a made up of 'types of discourse it [society] harbours and causes to function as true'.

References

Abdelrahman, M. (2017). 'Policing neoliberalism in Egypt: The continuing rise of the "securocratic" state', *Third World Quarterly*, 38(1), 185–202. https://doi.org/10.1080/01436597.2015.1133246

Abozaid, A. M. (2022). *Counterterrorism Strategies in Egypt: Permanent Exceptions in the War on Terror*. London and New York: Routledge.

Ahmed, L. (1992). *Women and Gender in Islam: Historical Roots of a Modern Debate*. New Haven, CT: Yale University Press.

Agamben, G. (2005). *State of Exception*. Chicago, IL: University of Chicago Press.

Agathangelou, A. M. and Ling, L. H. M. (2004). 'The house of IR: From family power to the poisies of worldism', *International Studies Review*, 6(4), 21–49. www.jstor.org/stable/3699724

Alzubairi, F. (2019). *Colonialism, Neo-Colonialism, and Anti-Terrorism Law in the Arab World*. Cambridge: Cambridge University Press.

Amos, M. S. (1925) *Martial Law in Egypt, 1914–23*. London: The National Archives. FO 141/671/4337.

Bashford, A. (2004). *Imperial Hygiene: A Critical History of Colonialism, Nationalism and Public Health*. London: Palgrave Macmillan.

Berda, Y. (2020). 'Managing "dangerous population": How colonial emergency laws shape citizenship', *Security Dialogue*, 51(6), 557–78.

Biancani, F. (2013). *Sex Work in Colonial Egypt: Women, Modernity and The Global Economy* London: I.B. Tauris.

Bradley, G. (2018). 'Some of the worst excesses of the counter-terror bill are gone, but without further changes it is still a threat to our civil liberties', *Liberty*, 20 November. www.libertyhumanrights.org.uk/issue/some-of-the-worst-excesses-of-the-counter-terror-bill-are-gone-but-without-further-changes-it-is-still-a-threat-to-our-civil-liberties/

Brankamp, H. and Z. Glück (2022). 'Camps and counterterrorism: Security and the remaking of refuge in Kenya', *Environment and Planning D: Society and Space*, 40(3), 528–48. https://doi.org/10.1177/02637758221093070

Brown, N. (1990). 'Brigands and state building: The invention of banditry in modern Egypt', *Comparative Studies in Society and History*, 32(2), 258–81. https://doi.org/10.1017/S0010417500016480

Brown, N. (1995). 'Retrospective: law and imperialism: Egypt in comparative perspective', *Law & Society Review*, 29(1), 103–26. https://doi.org/10.2307/3054055

Butler, J. (2004). *Precarious Life: The Powers of Mourning and Violence*. London and New York: Verso.

Chukwuma, K. H. (2022). 'Critical terrorism studies and postcolonialism: Constructing ungoverned spaces in counter-terrorism discourse in Nigeria', *Critical Studies on Terrorism*, 15(2), 399–416. https://doi.org/10.1080/17539153.2022.2048990

Cohn, C. (2013). *Women and Wars: Contested Histories, Uncertain Futures*. Cambridge and Malden: Polity Press.

Cooley, A. (2016). 'Countering Democratic Norms', in Plattner, M. F., Diamond, L., and Walker, C. (eds) *Authoritarianism Goes Global: The Challenge to Democracy*. Baltimore, MD: Johns Hopkins University Press, pp. 117–34.

Eckert, J. (2008). *The Social life of Anti-Terrorism Laws: The War on Terror and the Classifications of the 'Dangerous Other'*. Bielefeld: transcript.

Esmeir, S. (2012). *Juridical Humanity: A Colonial History*. Stanford: Stanford University Press.

Fahmy, K. (2012). 'The birth of the "secular" individual: Medical and legal methods of identification in nineteenth-century Egypt', in Breckenridge, K. and Szeter, S. (eds) *Registration and Recognition: Documenting the Person in World History*. Oxford: Oxford University Press and The British Academy, pp. 335–56.

Finden, A. (2021). 'Hygiene, morality and the pre-criminal: Genealogies of suspicion from twentieth century British-occupied Egypt', *Australian Feminist Law Journal*, 47(1), 27–45. https://doi.org/10.1080/13200968.2021.1923189

Finnane, M. and Donkin, S. (2013). 'Fighting terror with law? Some other genealogies of pre-emption', *International Journal for Crime and Justice*, 2(1), 3–7. https://doi.org/10.5204/ijcjsd.v2i1.85

Foucault, M. (1977). 'The political function of the intellectual', *Radical Philosophy*, 17, 12–4. www.radicalphilosophyarchive.com/issue-files/rp17_article2_politicalfunctionofintellectual_foucault.pdf

Gökariksel, S. and T. Z. Umut. (2019). 'The banality of exception? Law and politics in "Post-Coup" Turkey', *South Atlantic Quarterly*, 118(1), 175–87. https://doi.org/10.1215/00382876-7281684

Hamzić, V. (2018). 'International law as violence: Competing absences of the other', in Otto, D. (ed.) *Queering International law: Possibilities, Alliances, Complicities, Risks*. New York: Routledge, pp. 77–90.

Hawley, T. M. (2008). 'Liberalism versus terrorism: Welfare, crime control, and the United States after 11 September', in Eckert, J. (ed.) *The Social life of Anti-Terrorism Laws: The War on Terror and the Classifications of the "Dangerous Other"*. Bielefeld: transcript, pp. 33–54.

Heath-Kelly, C. (2013). 'Counter-terrorism and the counterfactual: Producing the "radicalisation" discourse and the UK PREVENT strategy', *The British Journal of Politics & International Relations*, 15(3), 394–415. https://doi.org/10.1111/j.1467–856X.2011.00489.x

Heathcote, G. (2012). *The Law on the Use of Force: A Feminist Analysis*. Oxon and New York: Routledge.

Hillyard, P. (1993). *Suspect Community: People's Experience of the Prevention of Terrorism Acts in Britain*, London: Pluto Press.

Humphreys, S. (2006). 'Legalizing lawlessness: On Giorgio Agamben's *State of Exception*', *European Journal of International Law*, 17(3), 677–87. https://doi.org/10.1093/ejil/chl020

Hussain, N. (1999). 'Towards a jurisprudence of emergency: colonialism and the rule of law', *Law and Critique*, 10(2), 93–115. 10.1023/A:1008993501958.

Hussain, N. (2007a). 'Hyperlegality', *New Criminal Law Review*, 10(4), 514–31. https://doi.org/10.1525/nclr.2007.10.4.514

Hussain, N. (2007b). 'Beyond norm and exception: Guantánamo', *Critical Inquiry*, 33(4), 734–53. https://doi.org/10.1086/521567

Hutchings, K. (2008). *Time and World Politics: Thinking the Present*. Manchester: Manchester University Press.

International Commission of Jurists. 2016. *Egypt's Judiciary: A Tool of Repression. Lack of Effective Guarantees of Independence and Accountability*.

Geneva: International Commission of Jurists. www.icj.org/wp-content/uplo ads/2016/10/Egypt-Tool-of-repression-Publications-Reports-Thematic-repo rts-2016-ENG-1.pdf

Ismail, S. (2006). *Political Life in Cairo's New Quarters: Encountering the Everyday State*. Minneapolis: University of Minnesota Press.

Johns, F. (2005). 'Guantanamo Bay and the Annihilation of the Exception', *The European Journal of International Law*, 16(4), 613–35. https://doi.org/10.1093/ ejil/chi135

Kruse, M. (2016). 'Countering Violence Extremism Strategies in the Muslim World', *The ANNALS of the American Academy of Political and Social Science*, 668(1), 198–201. https://doi.org/10.1177/0002716216671706

Kundnani, A. and Hayes, B. (2018). *The Globalisation of Countering Violent Extremism Policies: Undermining Human Rights, Instrumentalising Civil Society*. Amsterdam: Transnational Institute https://www.tni.org/files/publication-downlo ads/cve_web.pdf

Letter from Colonel on the Staff i/c Administration British Troops in Egypt to the First Secretary, the Residency, Alexandria, 28 June 1924, Prostitution and vene-real diseases. Part 1, FO 141/466/2, The National Archives, Kew Gardens, UK.

Letter from Sir Eldon Gorst to Sir Edward Grey, 31 January 1909, Egypt, FO 800/ 47/36, The National Archives, Kew Gardens, UK.

Letter to Foreign Office 28 February 1923, Administration of Martial Law in Egypt (The National Archives, Kew Gardens), FO 141/671/4337/60.

Letter to the Secretary, War Office in London from A. J. Murray, General, Commander in Chief, Egyptian Expeditionary Force, 26 November 1916, Administration of Martial Law in Egypt, FO 141/671/4337/1, The National Archives, Kew Gardens, UK.

Likhovski, A. (2006). *Law and Identity in Mandate Palestine*. Chapel Hill, NC: University of North Carolina Press.

Lugones, M. (2007). 'Heterosexualism and the colonial/modern gender system', *Hypatia*, 22(1), 186–209. https://doi.org/10.1111/j.1527–2001.2007.tb01156.x

Martial Law in Egypt, 1914–23. Pamphlet written by Sir M.S. Amos, August 1925, Administration of Martial Law in Egypt, FO 141/671/4337/95, The National Archives, Kew.

McCulloch, J. and Wilson, D. (2016). *Pre-crime: Pre-emption, Precaution and the Future*. Oxon: Routledge.

McQuade, J. (2020). *A Genealogy of Terrorism: Colonial Law and the Origins of an Idea*. Cambridge: Cambridge University Press.

Ministry of Refugee, Immigration and Integration Affairs. 2010. *The Challenge of Extremism: Examples of Deradicalisation and Disengagement Programmes in the EU*. Denmark: Ministry of Refugee, Immigration and Integration Affairs www. youthpolicy.org/library/wp-content/uploads/library/2010_Challenge_Extremi sme_Deradicalisation_EU_Eng.pdf

Mitchell, T. (2002). *Rule of Experts: Egypt, Technopolitics, Modernity*. Berkeley, LA: University of California Press.

Neal, A. W. (2008). 'Goodbye War on Terror: Foucault and Butler on discourses of law, war and exceptionalism', in Dillon, M. and Neal, A. W. (eds) *Foucault on Politics, Security and War*. London: Palgrave Macmillan, pp. 43–64.

Neocleous, M. (2006). 'The problem with normality: Taking exception to "permanent emergency"', *Alternatives: Global, Local, Political*, 31(2), 191–213. https:// doi.org/10.1177/030437540603100204

Neocleous, M. (2007). 'From martial law to the War on Terror', *New Criminal Law Review: An International and Interdisciplinary Journal*, 10(4), 489–513. https://doi.org/10.1525/nclr.2007.10.4.489

Ní Aoláin, F. (2020). 'Report of the special rapporteur on the promotion and protection of human rights and fundamental freedoms while countering terrorism', *United Nations General Assembly*, Human Rights Council 43rd Session Supp No 3 UN Doc A/HRC/43/46.

Oando, S. and Achieng, S. (2021). 'An indigenous African framework for counterterrorism: Decolonising Kenya's approach to countering "Al-Shabaab-ism"', *Critical Studies on Terrorism*, 14(3), 354–77. https://doi.org/10.1080/17539153.2021.1958182

Omar, H. (2017). 'Arabic thought in the liberal cage', in Devji, F. and Kazmi, Z. (eds) *Islam After Liberalism*. Oxford: Oxford University Press.

Parashar, S. and Schulz, M. (2021). 'Colonial legacies, postcolonial "selfhood" and the (un)doing of Africa', *Third World Quarterly*, 42(5), 867–81. https://doi.org/10.1080/01436597.2021.1903313

Parliamentary Question, 28 February 1923, Administration of Martial Law in Egypt FO 141/671/4337, The National Archives, Kew Gardens, UK.

Pratt, N. and Rezk, D. (2019). 'Securitizing the Muslim Brotherhood: State violence and authoritarianism in Egypt after the Arab Spring', *Security Dialogue*, 50(3), 239–56. https://doi.org/10.1177/0967010619830043

Quijano A. (2007). 'Coloniality And Modernity/Rationality', *Cultural Studies*, 21(2–3), 168–78. https://doi.org/10.1080/09502380601164353

Rao, R. (2020). *Out of time: The Queer Politics of Postcoloniality*. Oxford: Oxford University Press.

Reynolds, J. (2017). *Empire, Emergency, and International Law*. Cambridge: Cambridge University Press.

Reynolds, J. (2010). 'The long shadow of colonialism: The origins of the doctrine of emergency in international human rights law', *Comparative Research in Law & Political Economy*, 6(5), 1–50. https://papers.ssrn.com/sol3/papers.cfm?abstract_id=1625395

Salem, S. (2020). *Anticolonial Afterlives in Egypt: The Politics of Hegemony*. Cambridge: Cambridge University Press.

Schmitt, C. (2005). *Political Theology: Four Chapters on the Concept of Sovereignty*, Translated by G. Schwab. Chicago: University of Chicago Press.

Sjoberg, L. and Gentry, C. E. (2007). *Mothers, Monsters, Whores: Women's Violence in Global Politics*. London: Zed Books.

Takla, N. (2021). 'Barbaric women: Race and the colonization of gender in interwar Egypt', *International Journal of Middle East Studies*, 53(3), 387–405. https://doi:10.1017/S0020743821000349

Van Munster, R. (2004). 'The war on terrorism: When the exception becomes the rule', *International Journal for Semiotics of Law*, 17, 141–53. https://doi.org/10.1023/B%3ASELA.0000033618.13410.02

Walker, C. and Cawley, O. (2020). 'The juridification of the UK's counter-terrorism prevent policy', *Studies in Conflict & Terrorism*, 45(11), 1004–29. https://doi.org/10.1080/1057610X.2020.1727098

Welchman, L. (2005). 'Rocks, hard places and human rights: Anti-terrorism law and policy in Arab states', in Ramraj, V. V., Hor, M., and Roach, K. (eds) *Global Anti-Terrorism Law and Policy*. Cambridge: Cambridge University Press.

Whittaker, H. (2015). 'Legacies of empire: State violence and collective punishment in Kenya's north eastern province, c. 1963–present', *The Journal of Imperial and Commonwealth History*, 43(4), 641–57. https://doi.org/10.1080/03086 534.2015.1083232

Zichi, P. (2021). 'Prostitution and moral and sexual hygiene in mandatory Palestine: The criminal code for Palestine (1921–1936)', *Australian Feminist Law Journal*, 47(1), 47–65. https://doi.org/10.1080/13200968.2021.1933806

2

Pashtun stereotyping and the marginalisation of non-violent movements in post-9/11 Pakistan

Farooq Yousaf

The Pashtuns,[1] especially in the Federally Administered Tribal Areas (FATA) on Pakistan's border with Afghanistan,[2] have historically been portrayed as 'violent' and 'warrior-like' in both colonial and modern literature. This representation is largely based on generalisations propagated by colonial writers during the British military expeditions against Pashtun insurgencies. Non-violent Pashtun movements, such as Ghaffar Khan's Khudai Khidmatgar (Servants of God), have challenged these stereotypes even before Pakistan's independence from the British Raj. However, these generalisations and perceptions have persisted since Pakistan's independence, where Pashtun nationalist non-violent movements calling for equal rights have been viewed with suspicion and branded as against Pakistan's interests. These representations have also been reinforced by the rise of the Taliban, a predominantly Pashtun group that has been associated with terrorism. In Pakistan, the national discourse on terrorism mainly focuses on Pashtuns, even though militants and terrorists from other ethnic groups also participate in terrorist activities (Yousaf 2017). As a result, the Pashtun Tahafuz Movement (PTM), a non-violent Indigenous peace and human rights movement from the former FATA region, has been blacklisted by the state and military, indicating that even non-violent Pashtuns demanding peace, justice, and accountability from the military establishment are seen as a security threat. Against this backdrop, this chapter explores the postcolonial representations of Pashtuns and how these stereotypes continue to be weaponised in Pakistan's war on terror.

The chapter uses an interpretive approach, which means it focuses on understanding the perspectives of participants involved in the situation (Frechette et al. 2020). The chapter also uses a case study method, which allows for a more comprehensive and in-depth exploration of the issue, while remaining focused on the Pashtuns based in the former FATA region. In terms of data, both primary and secondary sources are used, such as literature, interviews, and media analysis. In terms of its analytical lens, the chapter employs a postcolonial framework, which helps to understand the historical and cultural factors that influence the treatment of Pashtuns in Pakistan. This framework considers the country's colonial past and the inheritance of colonial legacies, which continue to impact its politics and society. The use of this framework provides a broader perspective on the issue of Pashtun marginalisation and representation, and it helps to explain the complexity of the situation.

Pashtuns, orientalism, and violence

In recent decades, scholars interested in critical research in the Global South have emphasised the need to deconstruct colonial narratives based on 'racialisation' and generalisation of native and Indigenous groups in Western (colonial) ethnographic accounts. Among these groups are the Pashtuns in Afghanistan and Pakistan who have historically been subjected to similar racialised colonial narratives and representations. Pashtuns, who make up a major ethnic group in Afghanistan and the largest ethnic minority in Pakistan, are mostly situated in the country's north-western (Khyber Pakhtunkhwa) and southern (Balochistan and Sindh) parts. During the time of the British Raj in the Indian subcontinent, colonial archives and literature often portrayed Pashtuns in a negative light, using terms such as 'uncivilised', 'primitive', 'semi-savages', 'treacherous', and 'violence-condoning', particularly to describe those based in rural and remote parts on both sides of the Durand Line (Borthakur 2021; Yousaf 2019b). These representations were a result of the British invasions of Afghanistan and the Pashtun 'tribal' areas, which led to Indigenous resistance and insurgencies against the Raj.

Despite the mainstream academic and media discourses often associating Pashtuns, particularly those based in rural and remote areas, with militant, war-like, and violent tendencies, these portrayals are often misleading. The predominant Pashtun composition of the Taliban and its splinters, albeit a minority of the overall Pashtun population, has contributed to negative representations of Pashtuns. However, the antithesis of the 'violent Pashtun' in the form of Abdul Ghaffar Khan's (commonly known as Bacha Khan) non-violent Khudai Khidmatgar (Servants of God) struggle against the British Raj, and the current non-violent Pashtun Tahafuz (Protection) Movement against the Pakistani state and military get little attention (Yousaf 2019a; Daud 2019).

The lack of counter-narratives on Pashtuns in the literature is exacerbated by the 'systematic destruction of crucial archival material during the colonial era, as well as by the Pakistani authorities following independence' (Bala 2013: 132). According to Shah Mahmoud Hanifi (2016), the works of Mountstuart Elphinstone and Louis Dupree have normalised and propagated the persistence of an orientalist picture of the Pashtuns. In reviewing colonial archives on Pashtuns and British expeditions in the Pashtun borderlands, one finds recurring themes and terms used to describe and identify Pashtuns. Some of these terms include 'noble savages', 'primitive', 'thievish', 'untrustworthy', and 'violent' (see, e.g., Elphinstone 1839; Enriquez 1921; Warburton and Warburton 1900). Colonial writings on Pashtuns also demonstrate a clear sense of 'superiority' in terms of civilisation, which British writers and officers assumed they had in comparison with the 'primitive' Pashtuns (Yousaf 2020: 30). Such representations of Pashtuns were based on 'political expediencies demanded of colonialism' and were constructed on 'simplifications and limited, sometimes inconsistent and contradictory data' (Hanifi 2016: 395; Manchanda 2017). Despite critiques and flaws in this overall representation, historical colonial stereotyping of Pashtuns has persisted and is 'weaponised' by governments and media to portray the ethnic group in a negative light

Following the US invasion of Afghanistan in 2001, scholars in Pakistan and abroad continued to promote representations of Pashtuns as 'lawless' in literature on the 'tribal region' situated on the Afghanistan–Pakistan border (see, e.g., Bergen and Tiedemann 2013; Nawaz 2009). Similarly, some Western writers have interpreted contemporary actions of Pashtun tribes, in the wake of the US-led War on Terror, in terms of dominant colonial narratives. David J. Kilcullen's *The Accidental Guerrilla* (2011: 229) draws directly on Winston Churchill's narrative on Pashtuns to ascribe similar 'warlike' characteristics to contemporary Pashtuns. Pakistani policymakers and security experts, primarily based in the centre (Punjab province), also perpetuated these representations and failed to acknowledge the consequential role of the colonial legacies of the Durand Line (Afghanistan–Pakistan border) and the Frontier Crimes Regulations (FCR) 1901, which made the 'tribal' Pashtun region an 'area of legal exception', keeping it out of the scope of the Pakistani constitution. As a result, even today, Pashtuns are perceived as suspicious, terrorist sympathisers, and traitors (Afzal 2020; Khattak 2017; Pashteen 2019; Yousaf 2019c).

Until the 'tribal' region's merger with the Khyber Pakhtunkhwa province and mainstreaming in May 2018, 'tribal' Pashtuns were treated as second-class citizens. This treatment not only caused issues within Pakistan, but their negative representation in the national and international media also meant that students from the region aspiring to study at international universities had to wait months, and sometimes years, to obtain necessary background checks for their study-abroad visas. Raza Wazir, a young student and writer from Waziristan, highlights that the Pashtun identity of 'tribal' Pashtun turned the ethnic group into a target for domestic racial profiling. The local police in other provinces, particularly in Punjab, often raided university dorms and isolated Pashtun students for anti-terror investigations (Wazir 2018: para. 14).

Pashtuns and 9/11: From Mujahideen to terror suspects

Between 1947 and the 1970s, Pakistan's erstwhile FATA region experienced relative calm. However, in the late 1970s, Pakistan, with support from Saudi Arabia and the United States, began funding and training the so-called Mujahedeen groups to engage in an insurgency against Soviet forces in Afghanistan. It was during this time that a systematic policy of Islamisation was implemented in the region, coinciding with the arrival of Osama bin Laden. Bin Laden played a significant role in establishing training camps and financial networks in Afghanistan and Pakistan's erstwhile FATA for the Afghan Jihad, with the support of Abdullah Yusuf Azzam, a Palestinian Sunni Islamic scholar teaching at the Islamic International University in Islamabad, who used his networks and sermons in different countries to spread his message of Jihad against the Soviets (Rana 2010; Yousaf 2020: 63–4). Their mission was also supported by Jalaluddin Haqqani, an influential Afghan cleric and father of the current Taliban interior minister and Haqqani Network leader Sirajuddin Haqqani. Islamic (missionary) charities also had a significant presence in the former-FATA region after 1979, some of which had connections to the Jihadi operations directed at the Soviets in Afghanistan (Yousaf 2020: 63–4). Consequently, a combination of geopolitical, economic, and social factors led to a monumental change in the cultural fabric of the region, where less conservative elders were being replaced by hard-line clerics (Feyyaz 2019).

After the US invasion of Afghanistan in 2001, militants not only found support in erstwhile FATA but their influx into the region also laid the foundation for the creation of local militant and terrorist groups due to the region's historical exploitation for the Afghan Jihad. Pakistan, under military dictator General Pervez Musharraf, became a frontline ally of the US-led coalition, which contradicted with the previous state policy of supporting militants and Jihadists in the 1980s. Consequently, Pashtuns in erstwhile FATA became the primary victims of the War on Terror. They faced indiscriminate shelling during military operations, lost lives as collateral damage in US drone strikes, and were punished by terrorist groups for siding with the state. As a result, Pashtun elders, who were once a source of cohesion and maintenance of order in their respective areas, were systematically targeted and killed by terrorist groups. Furthermore, the majority of civilian casualties between 2003 and 2016 were Pashtuns or religious minorities, while among the 6,000 security forces' casualties, the majority were police or Pashtun paramilitary personnel deputed in erstwhile FATA (Sahill 2018: 328).

In response to the spike in terrorist attacks, the Pakistani military launched major and minor operations resulting in the internal displacement of Pashtuns from erstwhile FATA. However, Pashtun IDPs (internally displaced persons) and Afghan refugees were subjected to profiling in other provinces of the country (Yousaf 2017). In the wake of a major military operation in Wana in 2004, the provincial governments of Punjab and Sindh placed an informal embargo on the entry of Pashtun IDPs from erstwhile FATA (Khan 2017b). Similarly, in 2017, after a series of terrorist attacks in Lahore, the provincial capital of Pakistan's largest Punjab province, there was a widespread crackdown against 'Pashtun-looking' and 'Afghan-looking' people. Official and unofficial circulars and notices implied that Pashtuns and Afghans were 'suspected terrorists'. For example, a traders' association of Lahore sent a notice to all business owners in the area, asking Pashtun traders to submit their national identity card copies, photos, and business details to the nearest police station, or face legal action from the government (Cheema 2017).

> **Translation:** The market informs our respected Pathan (Pashtun) brothers that the Government of Punjab's security agencies' officers visited the traders association office and met traders. After the meeting, they instructed the Pathan brothers, who are directly or indirectly related to the association, to submit their identity documents within 48 hours so that those documents could be submitted at the local police station. If they (Pathan traders) fail to do so, the association would not be responsible for any further legal action taken by the government. The following documents are required: 1 – two photos, 2 – two copies of the National Identity Card, 3 – a visiting card of the business you own or work at. (Cheema 2017)

In another Urdu language circular – issued by a local police station in District Mandi Bahauddin of the Punjab province – people were asked to inform the police immediately if they saw a street vendor in 'Pashtun attire, and having Pashtun looks' (Yousaf 2017). The notification implied that anyone who 'looked Pashtun' might be a potential terrorist. The full notification stated the following:

> **Translation:**

> In light of the current incidents of terrorism (in the country), people are requested that if they see anyone **who looks Afghan or Pathan** and sells Peshawari green tea, dried fruits, toys, or items of domestic consumption and **can conduct terrorist attacks** (due to their ill intentions) in any part of the

country, if you see someone who looks like that or looks suspicious, please inform your nearest police station or call 15.

Your cooperation is the guarantee for your protection.
Spokesperson Police
District Mandi Bahauddin (Yousaf 2017)

Initially, there were concerns that the circular and the notice regarding Pashtun profiling may be part of fake news. However, a journalist working with Pakistan Today confirmed on a talk show with Dawn News that the circular was indeed issued by the District Police Office, which was directed by the Punjab Police (Khan 2017a). This was not the first incident where Pashtuns were being profiled. In 2014, both the Sindh and Punjab governments implicitly barred any Internally Displaced People (IDP) belonging to erstwhile FATA from entering either of these provinces, fearing they might engage in terrorist activities (Saeed 2014). The profiling of Pashtuns has extended to Pakistan's entertainment industry as well. In 2020, ARY news network's entertainment channel aired an Urdu language comedy show in which Pashtuns were generalised as either 'naswar (dipping tobacco) consuming people' or 'terrorists' (Tahir 2020). The actor who made the insensitive joke later apologised on his social media handles, but the incident reflected the realities of Pashtun profiling throughout the country. In response to this controversy, Alamzaib Mahsud, a prominent member of the Pashtun Tahafuz Movement from erstwhile FATA, tweeted a screenshot of his profile on the ARY channel after his arrest, saying that the channel had profiled him as a suspected terrorist when he was out fighting for justice, humanity, and the rule of law (Mahsud 2020).

Translation: Breaking News: Karachi: Arrested Suspect shifted to an unknown location for further interrogation. (Mahsud 2020)

Mehsud's imprisonment for ten months under false charges for campaigning against military-planted landmines in erstwhile FATA is noteworthy. He was picked up in broad daylight by men allegedly belonging to security agencies in plain clothes who put guns to his head during the arrest after Mehsud criticised the military for its lack of action on removing landmines from the region and actively campaigning for the PTM on social media. The manner of his arrest indicated that anti-terrorism activists like Mehsud, critical of the military, were perceived as a significant threat. However, negative portrayal of Pashtuns did not end here. The Punjab Government released a public service anti-sectarian and anti-terrorism multimedia message in September 2018, which featured a short video of a muted speech from PTM leader Manzoor Pashteen, coinciding with the voiceover alluding to 'hate and sectarian speech'.

The association of Pashtun nationalism with terrorism in Pakistan has become all too common. Rubina Saigol (2012: 198) criticises the association of Pashtun nationalism with the Taliban and fundamentalism, particularly since 2001, by arguing that it overlooks the ethnic dimension of the religious conflict in Pakistan's border regions, fusing simplistic notions of ethnicity with older orientalist notions of Pashtun clannishness and ideas of resistance to foreign intervention. Proponents of this view conclude that the military fight against the Taliban is unwinnable due to its ethnicity. Therefore, to understand the association and treatment of Pashtun nationalists in Pakistan, particularly those critical of the state and demanding rights, it is imperative to have a cursory look at the history of Pashtun nationalism both in the Indian subcontinent and modern-day Pakistan.

Pashtun nationalism and the 'perceived threat' to the Pakistani Federation

Pashtuns, on both sides of the Durand Line, are considered by Amin Saikal (2010: 5) to constitute an ethnic-based nation, which Anthony Smith defines as 'a named population sharing a collective proper name, a presumed common ancestry, shared historical memories, one or more differentiating elements of a common culture, an association with a specific "homeland" and a sense of solidarity for significant sectors of the population' (Smith 2000: 65). Due to this shared history and identity, the Durand Line (the Afghanistan–Pakistan border) remains a major unresolved colonial legacy between Pakistan and Afghanistan. The Durand Line Agreement was signed in 1893 between the British colonial diplomat Henry Mortimer Durand and the then Emir of Afghanistan, Abdul Rehman, to negotiate a final border between Afghanistan and British India. The agreement divided Pashtuns based in the northwest due to the colonial demarcation. Even after the British left the Indian subcontinent in 1947, the colonial legacy of the Durand Line remained the biggest issue between Afghanistan and Pakistan, with the Pakistani state using it as an excuse to justify its interventions in Afghanistan. Nationalist leaders, on the other hand, made efforts to unite the Pashtuns on both sides for years to come.

Historically, the earliest political efforts to unite the Pashtuns in Afghanistan were made by Khushal Khan Khattak, a renowned Pashtun poet and leader of the Khattak tribe, during his time working for the Mughal Empire and Mughal King Aurangzeb. Although Khattak failed in uniting the Pashtuns, his efforts did create a sense of nationalism among the Pashtuns (Saikal 2010: 7). However, when discussing the history of modern-day Pashtun nationalism, one cannot overlook the role of Abdul Ghaffar Khan in reviving the consciousness of nationalism among Pashtuns in the Indian subcontinent. Born in 1890 in the Utmanzai district of Peshawar, Khan was educated in both religious and modern schools and later established the educational institutions of Dar ul Ulum in Utmanzai and Gaddar (Mardan) in 1910, which taught children both religious education and concepts of patriotism. After a series of setbacks, arrests, and a brief period of migration to Afghanistan, Khan established the Anjuman-i-Islah-ul-Afghana (the Society for the Reformation of Afghans) in April 1921, with himself as its President and Mian Ahmad Shah as Secretary (Shah 2007: 91). In September 1929, the formation of a 'revolutionary' forum for young Pashtuns was proposed by Mian Akbar Shah, an active member of the Anjuman who had been to the Soviet Union via Afghanistan. Ghaffar Khan liked the idea, which led to the formation of the Zalmo (youth) Jirga (council). The Jirga led to the formation of the Khudai Khidmatgar (Servants of God) movement in November 1929, which sought to accommodate Pashtuns from all age groups and backgrounds (Bala 2013). The movement resonated with Pashtuns, especially in rural areas, who had been previously ignored by mainstream political parties in the Indian subcontinent. Although the recruits were organised and trained in a military fashion, there was a major focus on discipline and tolerance, with all volunteers pledging to adhere to non-violence before joining the movement (see Easwaran 1999).

Abdul Ghaffar Khan's non-violent philosophy of struggle was successful in convincing Pashtuns that it was the only solution to their marginalisation, factional feuds, and miseries. The Khudai Khidmatgar movement, based on these principles, attracted not only Muslims but also many non-Muslims. Though Khan was an ally of the Indian National Congress and a close friend of Mahatma Gandhi, he was unhappy with the Congress' acceptance of the Indian partition plan and the proposed referendum in NWFP, to decide whether the province should join India or Pakistan. After the partition, Khan pledged allegiance to Pakistan but demanded Pashtun autonomy. However, the Pakistani government arrested him several times, between 1948 and 1956, due to his demands for Pashtun autonomy and opposition to the One Unit policy (Haqqani and Ahmad 2018). In the 1960s and 1970s, he spent much of his life either in prison or in self-exile in Afghanistan. Upon his death, in accordance with his will, on 20 January 1988, Khan was buried in Jalalabad, Afghanistan.

Khan's political stance on Afghanistan and Pashtuns was always viewed with suspicion by the Pakistani state. This perception, combined with Afghanistan's active support for Pashtun nationalism, influenced Islamabad's strategic direction, which resembled the British colonial forward policy and involved interventions in Afghanistan, primarily in the form of the anti-Soviet Jihad. Reflecting on the Pakistani government's view of Pashtun nationalism as a threat, Tarzi and Lamb (2011: 4) argue that Pashtun societies in both the Khyber Pakhtunkhwa province of Pakistan and the FATA continue to undergo major changes. The introduction of an alien Islamist ideology in the 1980s and the subsequent three decades of war waged mostly from their territories have affected Pashtuns' worldview and systematically deprived them of their traditional leadership in both secular and religious realms.

Following the death of Abdul Ghaffar Khan, his son Abdul Wali Khan continued his father's Pashtun nationalist politics. He first led the National Awami Party (Wali Group) and later founded the Awami National Party (ANP), which remains one of the major political parties in the Khyber Pakhtunkhwa province today. Despite facing several challenges and accusations of having a hidden agenda for establishing greater Pashtunistan, the ANP has recently become a symbol of the status quo for many Pashtun nationalists. The party has been accused of appeasing the military establishment. For instance, the ANP suspended the memberships of Afrasiyab Khattak, Bushra Gohar and Mohsin Dawar in 2018 due to their active support for the Pashtun Tahafuz Movement (Mir 2018). The vacuum for Pashtun nationalist politics in Khyber Pakhtunkhwa has contributed to the rise and prominence of the Pashtun Tahafuz (Protection) Movement in recent years.

Pashtun Tahafuz Movement and the Pakistani state

The rural and 'tribal' Pashtuns in Pakistan experienced a significant turning point with the formation and rise of the Pashtun Tahafuz (Protection) Movement (PTM) in 2018. Initially launched as the Mehsud Tahafuz Movement in 2015 by fifteen young men from Waziristan, the PTM evolved into its current form after a protest was sparked by the extrajudicial killing of Naseemullah Mehsud, also known as Naqeebullah Mehsud, by local police in Karachi (Yousaf 2019). Mehsud was a former resident of erstwhile FATA who fled his home in 2008 due to a military operation that resulted in a mass exodus of Pashtuns from North and South Waziristan. Mehsud was allegedly murdered by Rao Anwar, a police officer notorious for his fake police encounters, and his dead body was later dumped with a gun to make him appear as a suspected terrorist (Yousaf 2019). Pashtuns from erstwhile FATA, led by Manzoor Pashteen, held a ten-day sit-in in Islamabad, Pakistan's capital, in February 2018 to protest his murder and demand equal rights, security, and peace. The sit-in transformed into a nationwide movement of Pashtuns, known as the PTM, calling on the state to respect basic human rights, release illegally detained individuals, and remove landmines, among other demands (Zahoor 2020).

The peaceful nature of the PTM has helped to bring the grievances of Pashtuns, particularly forced disappearances, to the global stage. The movement has also called for better treatment of locals at military checkpoints, more stringent measures against the Pakistani Taliban, and an end to curfews in erstwhile FATA (Zahoor 2020). Unlike mainstream political parties in the region, the PTM has supported women's participation in politics and challenged religious and cultural conservatism. According to Farhat Taj (2021: 75), the PTM is a movement of 'children of war' who grew up during the War on Terror in erstwhile FATA.

The PTM has demanded the establishment of a Truth and Reconciliation Commission to investigate alleged state crimes and rights violations in erstwhile FATA (Taj 2021). Despite the legitimacy of its demands, the PTM has been viewed with suspicion by the Pakistani state, which has retaliated against its leaders by blacklisting them from the media, restricting their movement, targeting their families, and imprisoning them (Khan et al. 2021). Although the military initially received the PTM positively and instructed against using force against it, the association of Pashtuns in Afghanistan with the PTM and its advocacy on anti-Pakistan Army online platforms became problematic for the military establishment. The slogans and manifesto of the PTM highlight the social and historical awareness of young Pashtuns. The PTM's leaders and members are blacklisted from appearing on any late-night shows of mainstream news media channels, and the military, through its spokespersons, has often insinuated that the PTM is working on a 'foreign agenda' against the state (Shah 2020). Furthermore, the movement's leaders are often prohibited from speaking at events and rallies in other provinces. For example, in December 2021, the government of Pakistan-administered Kashmir banned PTM leader Manzoor Pashtun from entering the region to speak at the convention of the National Students Federation, a pro-independence organisation (Naqash 2021). In November 2021, the provincial government of Balochistan province, where significant support for PTM exists, placed a two-month ban on all major PTM leaders, including Mohsin Dawar, Ali Wazir, Sana Ejaz, Said Alam, and Abdullah Nangyal (Dawn 2021). In June 2018, a Political Agent of North Waziristan banned Mohsin Dawar from entering his village, citing that he was 'acting in a manner prejudicial to public peace and tranquillity... and he was instigating the people through provocative speeches against the state' (Daily-Times 2018), which indicates the tacit state policy against the PTM.

The treatment of the PTM by the Pakistani state stands in contrast to that of violent and religious extremist groups in the Punjab province such as Tehrik e Labaik Pakistan (TLP) (Al Jazeera 2021). While the TLP often engages in violent protests that have resulted in the deaths of police personnel, its arrested supporters and leader were released after tacit deals were signed between the government and the TLP (Al Jazeera 2021). In contrast, since its formation, the PTM and many of its prominent leaders have been arrested or faced some form of state retribution, including black-listing from media, limitations on their movement, targeting of their family members, and incarceration (Khan et al. 2021).

For example, Manzoor Pashteen, the face of the Pashtun awakening in erstwhile FATA, has been barred from entering other provinces and has been arrested multiple times on various charges, including treason (Sirajuddin 2021). Similarly, Ali Wazir, a current member of the National Assembly, has suffered the most among all PTM leaders and members. He remained in police custody until February 2023, despite being granted bail by the apex court in November 2021, and his lawyer's house was allegedly raided by the Rangers force in Sindh province on 7 January 2022 in his absence (Yousaf 2016). It was only on 14 February 2023, and a few months after the retirement of the former military chief General Bajwa, that Wazir was finally released from prison. Sana Ejaz, a prominent woman leader of the PTM, was arbitrarily terminated from her job as a news anchor and talk show host at Pakistan Television due to her association with the PTM (Malik 2018). Other PTM members, such as Mohsin Dawar and Gulalai Ismail (currently in exile), have also faced harassment and been arrested multiple times by state authorities (Hashim 2021). These policies and actions show that despite being a non-violent movement, the PTM has been looked upon with suspicion by the Pakistani state, with its leaders often accused of working on a foreign agenda against the state (Shah 2020).

These examples of the state's action against PTM and its leaders also highlight the red line that exists in Pakistan for political activism, which concerns the military and the consequences of criticising the country's most powerful institution. Thus, non-violent groups like the PTM are not only met with a heavy-handed response but are also subject to allegations of anti-state activities and foreign influence. This situation has been further complicated by the Taliban takeover of Afghanistan (in August 2021) and the escalation of terrorist activities in the erstwhile FATA region. Despite the state's efforts, the PTM will continue to play a vital role in the region's future. However, the movement's survival is being tested by reports of internal conflicts, with Mohsin Dawar, who still considers himself a member of the PTM, forming a new political party called the National Democratic Movement (NDM).

Concluding remarks

The Pashtun community in Pakistan, particularly those residing in the former FATA region on the Afghanistan–Pakistan border, has long been stereotyped as 'violent' and 'warrior-like', a perception that can be traced back to the British government's policies towards Afghanistan in the Indian subcontinent, as well as Pakistan's anxiety about Pashtun nationalism undermining its federation. Despite the passage of time, these colonial narratives about Pashtuns have persisted, particularly after the United States' War on Terror began in Afghanistan. Furthermore, the chapter argues that non-violent Pashtun nationalist movements, particularly those that criticise the Pakistani military establishment, are perceived as a significant threat. Considering these issues, the emergence of the Pashtun Tahafuz Movement (PTM) marks a critical moment in post-9/11 Pashtun nationalist politics, prompting the military to consider it a significant challenge. As a result, the Pakistani state has dealt with the PTM with an iron hand, imposing embargoes and arresting its leaders. The state's opposition to the Pashtun Tahafuz Movement is a clear indication of how the post-9/11 era has allowed the Pakistani military to perpetuate colonial-era prejudices against rural Pashtuns. These stereotypes have been used to suppress any local movements that challenge the military's authority in state and security affairs and endanger the status quo. Furthermore, the state's actions against the PTM suggest that it is more concerned with maintaining its power and control over people than addressing their concerns and grievances. In conclusion, the state's policy towards the PTM reflects the wider issue of how colonial era prejudices continue to shape the Pakistani state's approach to governance.

Notes

1 Pashtuns are also known by exonyms such as Pashtoon, Pushtoon, Afghan, Pathan, Pakhtoon, Pakhtun, and Pukhtoon. The chapter, for consistency, will use the term *Pashtuns*.

2 In colonial and contemporary literature, Pashtuns living on the Afghanistan-Pakistan border region (formerly known as the Federally Administered Tribal Areas, FATA) in Pakistan, have been commonly referred to as 'tribal' Pashtuns, due to their segmentary nature and inter- and intra-group divisions. However, the term 'tribal' often carries negative, and sometimes oriental, connotations. This chapter will refer to Pashtuns, based in former FATA, as 'rural' Pashtuns, whereas the term 'tribal', wherever rarely used, will only either signify the original usage in the quoted texts or the location of Pashtuns, instead of applying the term's (colonial) anthropological usage.

References

Afzal, M. (2020). 'Why is Pakistan's military repressing a huge, nonviolent Pashtun protest movement?', 7 February, *Brookings*. www.brookings.edu/blog/order-from-chaos/2020/02/07/why-is-pakistans-military-repressing-a-huge-nonviolent-pashtun-protest-movement/ (accessed 12 December 2021).

Al Jazeera (2021). 'Four Pakistani police killed in violence at far-right TLP protest', 27 October, *Al Jazeera*. www.aljazeera.com/news/2021/10/27/pakistani-police-killed-at-tlp-protest (accessed 16 January 2022).

Bala, S. (2013). 'Waging nonviolence: Reflections on the history writing of the Pashtun nonviolent movement Khudai Khidmatgar', *Peace & Change*, 38(2), 131–54.

Bergen, P. and Tiedemann, K. (2013). *Talibanistan: Negotiating the Borders Between Terror, Politics, and Religion.* Oxford: Oxford University Press.

Borthakur, A. (2021). 'The Pashtun trajectory: From the colonially constructed notion on "violent" Pashtun tribe to "non violent" Pashtun Tahafuz Movement', *Asian Journal of Middle Eastern and Islamic Studies*, 15(3), 360–78.

Cheema, U. (2017). 'How stupid. Is Trump ruling Punjab?', *Twitter*. https://twitter.com/UmarCheema1/status/835526294880288768?s=20 (accessed 29 December 2021).

Daily Times (2018). 'Ban on PTM leader's entry in hometown set aside', *Daily Times*. https://dailytimes.com.pk/253709/ban-on-ptm-leaders-entry-in-hometown-set-aside/ (accessed 9 January 2022).

Daud, B. (2019). 'Peacemaker from the past: Bacha Khan's challenge to radical islamic narrative', *IIC Quarterly*, 46(1), 26–37.

Dawn (2021). 'Ban imposed on PTM leaders' entry to Balochistan', 23 November, *Dawn News*. www.dawn.com/news/1659715 (accessed 9 January 2022).

Easwaran, E. (1999). *Nonviolent Soldier of Islam: Badshah Khan, a Man to Match His Mountains.* Tomales, CA: Nilgiri Press.

Elphinstone, M. (1839). *An Account of the Kingdom of Caubul, and Its Dependencies, in Persia, Tartary, and India: A View of the Afghaun Nation, and a History of the Dooraunee Monarchy.* Vol. 2. London: R. Bentley.

Enriquez, C. M. (1921). *The Pathan Borderland: A Consecutive Account of the Country and People on and Beyond the Indian Frontier from Chitral to Dera Ismail Khan.* Calcutta: Thacker, Spink & Company.

Feyyaz, M. (2019). 'Countering terrorism in Pakistan: Challenges, conundrum and resolution', in Boyle, M. J. (ed.) *Non-Western Responses to Terrorism.* Manchester: Manchester University Press, pp. 184–218.

Frechette, J., Bitzas, V., Aubry, M., Kilpatrick K., and Lavoie-Tremblay, M. (2020). 'Capturing lived experience: Methodological considerations for interpretive phenomenological inquiry', *International Journal of Qualitative Methods*, 19. 1609406920907254.

Hanifi, S. M. (2016). 'The Pashtun counter-narrative', *Middle East Critique*, 25(4), 385–400.

Haqqani, H. and Ahmad, T. (2018). 'Reimagining Pakistan', in *Transforming A Dysfunctional Nuclear State.* Noida: Harper Collins Publishers India, pp. 97–8.

Hashim, A. (2021). 'Father of Pakistani rights activist arrested on "terror" charges', *Al Jazeera*. www.aljazeera.com/news/2021/2/3/father-of-pakistani-rights-activist-arrested-on-terror-charges (accessed 4 January 2022).

Khan, U. A. (2017a). 'Do Raye', in Khan, A. R. (ed.) *Do Raye (Talk Show).* Pakistan: Dawn News.

Khan, U., Cheng, Y., Shah, Z. A., Ullah, S., and Jianfu, M. (2021). 'Reclaiming Pashtun identity: The role of informal spaces in developing an alternative narrative', *Interventions*, 23(8), 1166–86.

Khan, Y. H. (2017b). 'The discriminated Pashtun', 5 March, *The News on Sunday*. www.thenews.com.pk/tns/detail/562817-discriminated-pashtun (accessed 7 January 2022).

Khattak, S. G. (2017). *Why Pakistan Associates Terrorism with Pashtuns and Afghans*. Edited by S. Shams. Germany: Deutsche Welle.

Kilcullen, D. (2011). *The Accidental Guerrilla: Fighting Small Wars in the Midst of a Big One*. Oxford: Oxford University Press.

Mahsud, A. Z. (2020). 'When I was picked up by the ISI &.........', 23 July, *Twitter*. https://twitter.com/AlamzaibMahsud/status/1286241689544396801 (accessed 2 January 2022).

Malik, A. (2018). 'PTV terminates anchor Sana Ejaz "on association with PTM"', 10 May *Daily Times*.. https://dailytimes.com.pk/238116/ptv-terminates-anchor-sana-ejaz-on-association-with-ptm/ (accessed 9 January 2022).

Manchanda, N. (2017). 'The Imperial Sociology of the "Tribe" in Afghanistan', *Millennium: Journal of International Studies*, 46(2), 165–89.

Mir, N. A. (2018). 'Pashtun nationalism in search of political space and the state in Pakistan', *Strategic Analysis*, 42(4), 443–50.

Naqash, T. (2021). 'Entry of PTM chief banned in AJK', *Dawn News*. www.dawn.com/news/1665257 (accessed 9 January 2022).

Nawaz, S. (2009). 'FATA—A most dangerous place', *Center for Strategic and International Studies*, 15, 1–44.

Pashteen, M. A. (2019). 'The military says Pashtuns are traitors. We just want our rights', *The New York Times*. www.nytimes3xbfgragh.onion/2019/02/11/opinion/pashtun-protests-pakistan.html (accessed 9 December 2021).

Rana, M. A. (2010). 'Role of Arab militants and charities during and after Soviet-Afghan War', in Rana, M. A., Sial, S., and Basit, A. (eds) *Dynamics of Taliban Insurgency in FATA*. Islamabad: Pak Institute for Peace Studies, pp. 13–39.

Saeed, S. (2014). 'Barred from Sindh and Punjab, displaced Pashtuns see discrimination', *The Express Tribune*. https://tribune.com.pk/story/745842/barred-from-sindh-and-punjab-displaced-pashtuns-see-discrimination/ (accessed 10 January 2022).

Sahill, P. H. (2018). 'The terror speaks: Inside Pakistan's terrorism discourse and national action plan', *Studies in Conflict & Terrorism*, 41(4), 319–37.

Saigol, R. (2012). 'The multiple self: Interfaces between Pashtun nationalism and religious conflict on the frontier', *South Asian History and Culture*, 3(2), 197–214.

Saikal, A. (2010). 'Afghanistan and Pakistan: The question of Pashtun nationalism?', *Journal of Muslim Minority Affairs*, 30(1), 5–17.

Shah, A. R. (2020). 'The rise of the Pashtun Protection Movement (PTM): Polemics and conspiracy theories', *Asian Affairs*, 51(2), 265–85.

Shah, S. W. A.(2007). 'Abdul Ghaffar Khan, the Khudai Khidmatgars, Congress and the Partition of India', *Pakistan Vision*, 8(2), 86–115.

Sirajuddin (2021). 'PTM's Manzoor Pashteen released nearly 8 hours after being detained in Kohat', 4 June, *Dawn News*. www.dawn.com/news/1627498/ptms-manzoor-pashteen-released-nearly-8-hours-after-being-detained-in-kohat (accessed 10 January 2022).

Smith, A. D. (2000). *The Nation in History: Historiographical Debates about Ethnicity and Nationalism*. Hanover, NE: University Press of New England.

Tahir, J. (2020). 'Pashtuns are asking to boycott ARY after "Bulbulay" made insensitive jokes about them', 23 July, *MangoBaaz*. www.mangobaaz.com/pashtuns-are-asking-to-boycott-ary-after-bulbulay-made-insensitive-jokes-about-them (accessed 4 January 2022).

Taj, F. (2021). 'Stable regime, historiography and truth commissions: A case study of Pashtun Tahafuz Movement of Pakistan', *Review of Human Rights*, 7(1), 67–88.

Tarzi, A. and Lamb, R. D. (2011). *Measuring Perceptions about the Pashtun People.* Washington, DC: Center for Strategic and International Studies.

Warburton, R. and Lady Warburton, M. C. (1900). *Eighteen Years in the Khyber, 1879–1898*: London: J. Murray.

Wazir, R. (2018). 'To be young and Pashtun in Pakistan', 9 March, *The New York Times*. www.nytimes.com/2018/03/09/opinion/pashtun-pakistan-young-killing. html (accessed 29 October 2021).

Yousaf, F. (2016). '"Collective Punishment" in Pakistan's tribal areas', 13 December, *The Diplomat*.https://thediplomat.com/2016/12/collective-punishment-in-pakist ans-tribal-areas/ (accessed 11 December 2021).

Yousaf, F. (2017). 'Pakistan's Pashtun Profiling', 1 March, *The Diplomat*. https://thed iplomat.com/2017/03/pakistans-pashtun-profiling/ (accessed 11 December 2021).

Yousaf, F. (2019a). 'Pakistan's "tribal" Pashtuns, their "violent" representation, and the Pashtun Tahafuz movement', *Sage Open*, 9(1), 1–10. DOI: 10.1177/ 2158244019829546.

Yousaf, F. (2019b). 'Pakistan's colonial legacy: FCR and postcolonial governance in the Pashtun tribal frontier', *Interventions*, 21(2), 172–87.

Yousaf, F. (2020). *Pakistan, Regional Security and Conflict Resolution: The Pashtun 'Tribal' Areas*. Abingdon and Oxon: Routledge.

Zahoor, M. A. (2020). 'Social movements in hybrid regimes: The case of Pashtun Tahafuz (protection) movement of Pakistan (PTM)', Central European University.

3

Policing 'terrorist' propaganda: A study of counter-terrorism strategies in colonial Bengal 1908–18

Lumbini Sharma

India has been dealing with terrorist outrages and insurgencies ever since it became independent. Waves of outrages in India's North and North-East have been causing instability for the last five decades. India faces a complex amalgam of Indigenous, proxy, and transnational threats, which mark its experience with terrorism as highly unusual in scale, scope, and complexity (Boyle 2019). To combat terrorism, colonial laws and policies were adopted (Kalhan et al. 2006).

While it is debatable to what extent the independent government of India succeeded in combatting the threats posed by the insurgents and terrorists, it could be said that they were successful in adopting the blueprint of British counter-terrorism mechanisms both at the state and central levels, from police structure to gathering intelligence via agents. In this chapter, I will discuss the precursor of the modern Indian counter-terrorism mechanism by focusing on the historical narrative of the development of British India's counter-terrorism laws and strategies in the context of propaganda, published and disseminated by the 'Bengali terrorists'. It is beyond the scope of this chapter to discuss the implementation of their strategies, or to compare modern Indian and British Indian counter-terrorism practices.

Now, the question arises: who were the Bengali terrorists, and why were they called 'terrorists'? During early twentieth century, there was a group of young Bengalis who used political violence to spread terror among the ranks of British officials. While some scholars have recently contested the use of the term 'terrorism' to describe revolutionaries, we have chosen it here due to its widespread usage by the British to characterise members of underground political groups who advocated militant anti-colonialism (Ghosh 2017). Interestingly, these people belonged to an upper-caste, mostly Hindu, educated class, who were called 'bhadralok' (gentlemen) in the Bengali vernacular. For the British officers, they were 'anarchists' or 'terrorists' as they were posing threats to the security of the empire. Though the common knowledge defined 'terrorism' as an uncivil and irrational form of seditious behaviour, Bengali 'terrorists' took this path to demand complete independence.

The 'terrorist' movement started gathering force in Bengal as early as 1902 with the establishment of 'akhras' (a Bengali term for physical exercise clubs). The resistance organised by the people of Bengal after the declaration of Partition by Curzon provided an impetus to this movement. By the end of 1917, more than two thousand youths from Bengal had participated in this resistance. Their initial aim was to destabilise the British administration by spreading 'terror' among the ranks of British officials, attacking colonial officials, institutions, and buildings with armed robberies, bombs, and assassinations.

These gentleman 'terrorists' were able to spread their ideas, influence public opinion, and shake the British officials to such extent that the latter responded by bringing about novel repressive legislation, one after another, to stop their 'outrages'. The Sedition Committee reported that '[t]he connection between this leaflet literature and the outrages has over and over again been accepted and dwelt upon by the courts. These leaflets embody a propaganda of bloodthirsty fanaticism directed against the Europeans and all who assist them' (Sedition Committee Report 1973: 17–18). This was the extent to which this propaganda evoked terror among the British.

Richard J. Popplewell is the first historian to study British intelligence and counter-insurgency methods carried out both in India and London, in the broader rubric of the revolutionary movement in India. By analysing the role of the Home Department and the India Office in the making of imperial intelligence in India during the first two decades of the twentieth century, he focuses on the developments of counter-insurgency strategies as a response to the 'insurgency' ('terrorist') movement in India. He, further, deals with the British intelligence operations on a global scale; these played an important role in defending the British Empire during the First World War (Popplewell 2015).

Scholar Erin M. Giuliani (2013) deals with the features of policing strategies as well as infrastructural growth in nineteenth and early twentieth century Bengal. Giuliani's unpublished thesis centres around the organisation and evolution of police systems in the context of the development of surveillance strategy in Bengal during the period between 1861 and 1913 (Giuliani 2013: 25). Her work provides a thorough understanding of how surveillance systems work in preventative policing while validating that the Indian police system relies heavily on the collection and analysis of information.

Michael Silvestri conducts a thorough analysis of the organisation and strategies of counter-insurgency used to police 'Bengali terrorism' (Silvestri 2019). He discusses how colonial anxieties about the 'Bengali terrorism' lead to the development of an extensive intelligence apparatus in Bengal. Intelligence expertise acquired in Bengal was in turn applied globally, both to the policing of Bengali revolutionaries and to other anti-colonial movements which threatened the Empire.

Following Silvestri's direction, I particularly focus on counter-terrorism practices adopted for controlling 'seditious' propaganda which was 'very serious, for it gets youth thinking on terrorist lines and this widens the field for terrorist recruitment to huge dimensions' (Mclean 2014).

Emergence of early 'terrorist' groups

As a centre of trade and commerce, Calcutta became the hub of Western education in India. Consequently, the growth of English education in Bengal was rapid, and by the twentieth century there existed a considerable number of people who regularly read newspapers in both the vernacular and English. Therefore, since the early twentieth century, common people of Bengal became increasingly aware of the oppression of the British government, and many participated in nationalist politics. The popularity of print journalism and mass participation in nationalist politics made the public receptive to propaganda published by the revolutionaries. Bengal revolutionaries used to compose, publish, and disseminate political propaganda in the early twentieth century, following in the footsteps of the revolutionaries of Maharashtra.

As the Swadeshi movement and the anti-partition movement gathered its strength, the division between the moderates and the extremists became clear. People who believed in a violent overthrow of the British rule were disappointed by the 'prayer-petition' methods of the Congress. From the early twentieth century on, they were organising into secret samitis,[1] and by 1906, they started to publish newspapers and weeklies. Their main objectives were twofold: one was to pursue the mass to follow their path of violence towards complete independence, and another was to prepare the public for a nationwide revolution to overthrow the oppressive government. However, for the British government, it was a medium to manipulate public opinion with 'deception and lies'. The colonial government castigated revolutionary pamphlet propaganda as 'seditious' literature that aimed at spreading disaffection and defiance against the rulers (Sanyal 2014: 4).

British police tried to repress the revolutionaries' use of print media to rouse the people into open rebellion. Initially, stringent repression and prosecutions forced the revolutionaries to stop their publications, followed by the introduction of the Newspapers Act of India, 1908. *Jugantar* (New Era) was stopped from publishing after suffering three consecutive prosecutions by Mr. Kingsford; *Bande Mataram (Hail! Mother)* ceased to be published on 30 April 1908;[2] and another seditious newspaper, *Sandhya (Twilight),* in 1907.[3] James Campbell Ker (ICS officer who was responsible for compiling report of revolutionary activities between 1907 and 1917) reported that '[t]he Newspapers Act provided for the forfeiture of presses in which newspapers containing incitements to murder, or to any offence under the Explosives Substances Act, 1908, or to any act of violence, were printed. This brought the "*Yugantar*"[4] as a newspaper to an end' (Ker 1960: 65).

Bengali revolutionaries envisaged a new method to reach the public. Previously, in the case of the publication of newspapers or weeklies like *Jugantar, Bande Mataram,* or *Sandhya,* they mentioned the name and location of the press in the paper, rendering the tracing by the police easy and simple. Now, they began to publish materials that were ephemeral and short-lived in character, namely the leaflets and pamphlets. They discovered the Newspapers Act (1908) was only applied to the newspapers and did not incorporate other forms of propaganda. Therefore, they started to issue their revolutionary appeals in the form of leaflets. 'British reports frequently pointed out that the appearance and widespread dissemination of pamphlet propaganda in a particular area was an indication of the increasing vitality of the "anarchists" movement in this region' (Sanyal 2014: 30).

For composition and printing purposes they made use of secret presses and circulated their word through elusive figures, either sending it by post or pasting it up on the walls of populous areas. The first pamphlet that blazed a trail of violent vituperation against the government was *Raja K?*[5] (Who is the King?). It can be considered as the first pamphlet issued in Bengal. It was published in August 1905 in Dacca in the wake of the anti-partition movement. *Sonar Bangla,* another anti-colonial pamphlet, appeared at the same time in Calcutta. The leaflet was issued by the revolutionaries during the anti-partition meeting at the Town Hall in Calcutta on 7 August 1905 (Ray 2008: 199). However, pamphlet propaganda had not flourished during that time – it was about 1910 when pamphlets appeared in flurries in almost all districts of Bengal. Despite the government's repressive measures, a series of proscriptions and house raids, pamphlet propaganda went on increasing in vigour and strength. All throughout the colonial period the British police tried to stamp out the underground pamphlet press, but, except for slowing down its flow from time to time, it did not prove to be effective enough to put a permanent stop to it.

In February 1910, a new pamphlet started to appear, titled *Swadhin Bharat* (Free India), in different parts of Bengal. These pamphlets targeted the students at Bengal schools and colleges who received them in large numbers. In most cases, they were pasted on the walls of the institution, and some were posted to the addresses of students. These pamphlets were also sent to students who had been residing in hostels or messes. They were also received by pleaders, bar libraries, teachers, headmasters, and doctors.

In connection with the investigation of the Moulvi Bajar and Raja Bajar bomb cases,[6] the Inspector General of Bengal Police asserted that '[t]hroughout the long period during which the Police of Bengal and Eastern Bengal have been dealing with political criminal organization, they have always held that one of the most dangerous weapons which has been systematically employed against the government has been the Swadhin Bharat and similar publications' (Letter from IG of Police, Bengal, 6 January 1914). This remark reflects on how the revolutionary propaganda became an object of anxiety in the ranks of the British administration. While tracing the perpetrator responsible for the production of the Swadhin Bharat leaflet, the police made an unprecedented discovery: a propaganda network existing across Bengal, ranging from Dinajpur in the north to Chittagong in the south. This network was effectively used by the revolutionaries, to encourage the readers to join their force.

Police measures to cope with revolutionary literature

For most of the nineteenth century, the Bengal Police remained a class of government officials who were regarded as 'far less important than the executive officers' (Robb 1991: 150). They were poorly paid, and their social status was exceptionally low. Besides doing the regular policing work they were also associated with revenue collection responsibilities. The detection of crime was left to the regular police who had to carve out time from an already busy schedule cramped with an array of various police work (watch and ward, daily patrol, court duty) to identify and pursue the perpetrators when a crime was reported (Sengupta and Das 2021: 20).

By the end of the nineteenth century, it became apparent that the Bengal Police was understaffed and in dire need of reformation. In 1905 Lord Curzon set up a Police Commission to reform the Indian police system. Accordingly, in 1905, he introduced a Central Intelligence Department (Department of Criminal Intelligence) at Delhi, and CIDs in every province of India, thereby giving it a much-needed disciplined structure. Accordingly, a CID was attached to the Bengal Police. In Bengal, colonial intelligence organisations were housed within the police: the Special Branch of Calcutta Police and the Intelligence Branch of Bengal Police. The latter was part of the Criminal Investigation Department of Bengal Police established in 1904.

The accumulated number of insurgency cases from 1907 to 1911 was 69, which alarmed the colonial government about the seriousness of the situation (Sedition Committee Report 1973). They retaliated by enforcing counter-insurgency methods to control these violent outrages and strengthening the town and rural police forces. Eastern Bengal districts were very notorious for revolutionary outrages and, to cope with this problem, the police were armed. In March 1913, the Bengal Government supplied arms in selected police stations and outposts in the province for the prevention of 'political dacoities' (violent robbery). Previously, the rural police were scarcely armed to confront the armed dacoit (bandit) groups. Accordingly, sanction was given to 1215 muskets with ball and buckshot ammunition in some of the district police stations. Nevertheless, by August 1916, in view of the increase of 'anarchist crimes', all the inspectors, sub-inspectors, and sergeants of the Calcutta Police were armed with revolvers and two muskets (Gupta 1979: 309). Despite all these revolutionary outrages, propaganda continued to stir the public opinion until 1947. Therefore, it remained a step ahead of government intelligence.

As the publication and spread of revolutionary propaganda formed one of the basic features of the revolutionary movement, the Intelligence Branch of Calcutta Police, with the help of District Intelligence Branches, attempted to control its dissemination. The investigation of revolutionary movements was closely linked with the investigation of tracing the propagators of 'seditious' pamphlets. While police raided houses or messes of the suspected terrorists in accordance with information provided by numerous 'agents' or spies, they got hold of a bunch of pamphlets stacked in those residences, intended for circulation. Though police could not convict the residents for possessing those materials, they opened a conspiracy case under 124A of the IPC Act. During this time, the Delhi bomb case and the Lahore bomb case were two of the most important conspiracy cases started against the revolutionaries.[7] Nevertheless, from 1913 on, police and IB officers urged the Home Department to introduce a legislation by which they could punish the person who possessed this kind of 'objectionable' publication.

Bengal IB and Calcutta Police had little success in arresting the culprits who were involved in drafting and circulating those inflammatory tracts and pieces. After examining these contents, IB officers reported that they were either written by Anushilan samiti members or by revolutionaries in West Bengal. However, they could hardly catch any perpetrator involved in the circulation of these pamphlets.

Discoveries of pamphlets in connection with the Raja Bajar bomb case unfolded a network of propaganda across Bengal. But no definite clue was found with which they could convict anyone. During 1913 Denham arrested and prosecuted two Telegu students of the National Medical College who were involved in circulating *Liberty* leaflets from Calcutta to Bombay and Madras. But the real culprits, Nalini and Hedgawar, could not be convicted. The Calcutta Police had knowledge that two MA students at Calcutta

University were associated with the composition of the February 1916 edition of *Swadhin Bharat*. However, without obtaining any concrete evidence against them, the IB could not convict them. Meanwhile, in 1917, one Jogesh Agarwala of Old Malda was arrested on the night of 6 March, 'having been detected in the act of pasting up seditious leaflets' (police report regarding West Bengal affairs, 1917). Enquiries followed to discover his party affiliation and family background.

However, in most cases, the pasting work was performed by people who did not know anyone from the inner ring of the secret samiti. They might have been newly admitted members of the samiti, friends of some samiti members, or had been sympathetic to the revolutionary cause. In 1913, regarding the investigation of the second edition of Swadhin Bharat leaflets, SP Hill Tippera remarked: 'The youths who circulated these papers did not even know who the printer and composer were. The composition was made in Calcutta but printed at a house in Dacca. Two or three youths posted it from there' (from a confidential letter by S.P. Hill Tippera to Calcutta IB, 1913).

Adopting secret enquiry system

One of the salient aspects of counter-terrorism practices of British intelligence was their secret enquiry system to get inside the 'conspiracy'. For this they recruited agents and informers who operated secretly to watch over the 'terrorist'. In 1932, Intelligence Bureau Director, Horace Williamson, remarked that 'the main method of fighting terrorism in Bengal for the last quarter of a century had been that of "getting inside" the conspiracy' (Silvestri 2019: 96).

In the case of controlling the spread of revolutionary propaganda, the Bengal Police (Intelligence Branch) employed adopted the same strategy. They recruited informants, agents, and watchers to know the movements of those who participated in the spreading of 'terrorist' voices and causing outrages. In many instances, they deployed agents who were ex-samiti members. This source of 'human intelligence' was used to provide the bulk of the information about the movement. In cases where the police had been suspicions about some students at schools where some 'seditious' propaganda had been found to be pasted on the blackboard or noticeboard, they employed another student to watch the movements of suspected individuals.

Sometimes ex-samiti members thus became police agents or spies. It was typical that if they were caught by any of their fellow comrades, they would eventually have killed them. Abdur Rahman, probably the most hated informer in the Midnapore bomb case,[8] was attempted to be killed several times. On 13 December 1912, there had been a dangerous attempt to murder him with a powerful picric acid bomb believed to be manufactured in Chandernagore (Sedition Committee Report 1973: 58). It was thrown in the room where he usually slept; however, he did not sleep there that night, and no life was lost. Exactly one year after that, in December 1913, another attempt was carried out to bomb Abdur Rahman while he was walking in a religious procession (Sedition Committee Report 1973: 58). The bomb failed to explode and he escaped again.

Police officers, constables, agents, and sub-inspectors who were engaged in various investigations, on searching for the revolutionary groups and samitis who were operating secretly and spreading their propaganda among the people, were killed by the revolutionaries. In March 1913, one Constable of CID, Haripada Deb, found four copies of 'Om Bande Mataram Swadhin Bharat' leaflets pasted in different parts of College Square and saw approximately twenty-five young people reading them earnestly at the time (police report regarding Om Bande Mataram Swadhin Bharat, 1913). Sub-Inspector S.C. Mukherjee found the same edition of the leaflet pasted on a palm tree in Beadon Square and some copies in Cornwallis Square. Five months after this incident Haripada Deb was shot dead by three young Bengalis at the banks of a lake in College Square – the same spot where he had found those leaflets. It was reported by the Sedition Committee that the 'murdered officer had succeeded in getting into touch with a revolutionary section and it is clear they had seen through him and decided to put him out of the way' (Sedition Committee Report 1973: 58). The police could not catch his assailants as he was assassinated in the middle of the throng and the culprits disappeared in the crowd. Later in March 1914, S.C. Mukherjee was killed while on duty to supervise arrangements in connection with a ceremony at Calcutta University.

Moreover, in 1913 Inspector Bankim Chandra Chaudhuri who had been investigating the Dacca Conspiracy Case,[9] was killed by a bomb attack in his house. The most important of all these murders was the assassination of Deputy Superintendent Basanta Chatterji in 1916. Moreover, Charles Tegart was the most notorious among the revolutionaries; they intended to kill him three times but failed miserably.

Countering global network of 'terrorists' propaganda

Bengal revolutionaries started to spread their influence outside India from early twentieth century. They made contacts with students studying in American universities and started importing propaganda from America to India as early as 1903. Since then, *Gaelic American,* an Irish anti-British newspaper, began to import to India. Eventually two important centres of revolutionaries came into prominence: one was in New York, USA, and the other was in Paris and London. Revolutionaries who escaped from India to fight anti-British war joined hands with either of these two groups. After Baraktullah, an important figure who had fought anti-British campaign, moved from New York to Japan, the centre of activity was shifted to California, USA. During this time several Indians immigrated to the west coast of Vancouver, Canada in search for jobs or higher studies.

In Europe, Krishnaverma, Madam Cama, and Raoji Rana all started their anti-British campaign through publishing and spreading propaganda around the same time (Mukherjee 1981: 72). They observed that even Indians enjoyed considerable free speech and freedom of movement in England. Eventually, a network of Indian revolutionaries was established in both sides of the Atlantic as well as in the Far East. They spread their words by publishing and disseminating 'terrorist' propaganda and sent it to different addresses in Calcutta. IB soon discovered this propaganda network and spent no time to prevent its dissemination.

Interception of letters and envelopes by postal censors in GPOs and notorious post offices in Calcutta was a regular method of preventing the circulation of revolutionary leaflets. Calcutta General Post Office and Bowbazar Post Office were two among many places where revolutionaries used to post envelopes containing 'seditious' leaflets. These leaflets were detained before proscription. In 1927 there was an amendment to the Indian Post Office Act that empowered any postal official duly authorised in this behalf to detain any document in transmission through the post that he may suspect to contain seditious matter without reference to the fact that such a document had been proscribed or prohibited by an order of the government.

A pamphlet titled *Ca Ira* was popular among the Bengal revolutionaries. This pamphlet came from Paris and was written by E. H. James. Bengal Police intercepted this in 1913 and, by the Sea Customs Act it, was prohibited from entering India. Another pamphlet, *Free Hindustan*, published by the New York group of Bengal revolutionaries, headed by Taraknath Das, was also banned from entering India. Interception directed under Section 26 of the Post Office Act on 23 October 1908, and importation prohibited several weeklies, journals, and pamphlets like *Gaelic American, Yugantar Circular-The Delhi Bomb* (published by the Ghadr Party), *Indian Sociologist, Kumar Singh-May 1910 in Memoriam*, or *Methods of the Indian Police in Twentieth Century*.

Indian Sociologists began to publish in 1905 in London and they were continuously imported to India until 1914. Though their importation was prohibited on 19 September 1907, copies continued to be sent to India in covers that were changed from time to time so as to escape detection in the Post Office.

However, the most notorious and widespread was the reach of *Ghadr*. Bengal CID felt threatened at the instance of the importation of *Ghadr* pamphlets on 30 January 1914, among all the imported propaganda from several revolutionary parties of abroad. Initially, *Ghadr* leaflets were intercepted in large numbers at Bombay, Hosiarpur, Lahore, Amritsar, Ferozpore, Gurudaspur, Ambala, Gujranwala, Delhi, Lyallpur, Montogomery, Multan, Hissar, Jullunder, Hosiarpur, Mysore, Kapurthala, Patiala State, Faridkot State, Burma, and so on.

Around this time, *Ghadr* started to appear in Calcutta. DCI Simla alerted all the superintendents of Bengal Police to be vigilant for the appearance of this pamphlet. After scrutinising the addressee list, police inquired about the recipients of those leaflets and found that the propagandists 'intended to appeal to the martial races of India' (Ker 1960: 112), residing in different parts of Bengal, to spread their words. Most of these pamphlets were posted from New Orleans, Vancouver, New Westminster, Portland, and Strawberry Hill, USA.

The first *Ghadr* pamphlet, imported to Calcutta, was addressed to one Jamadar Basanta Singh, Budge Budge (Confidential letter to L. N. Bird from Calcutta IB, 1914). The writer was Bishen Singh, a watchman in Panama. He suggested that Basant Singh would join him in California and advised him to write to an agency in Calcutta for further particulars. This was also sent to the editor of the *Al-Hilal* newspaper in Calcutta, Haji Gul Muhammad Khan. In May 1914, *Ghadr* started to appear in another language, this time it was Gujarati. One copy of this edition was intercepted by the censor in Karachi (Bombay Police report of 9 January, 1915).

Tracing underground presses

'Terrorists' were extremely cautious in publishing 'seditious' pamphlets; they were aware that to maintain anonymity, they need to keep the location of the press hidden. Tracing those hidden presses became a nightmare for the police. In this section we will see how the 'terrorists' made use of them and how the intelligence traced them.

When the first *Swadhin Bharat* leaflets began to appear in Bengal, the police had no clue about its authors or where they were printed. They were found to be pasted in conspicuous areas of the town and sent by post to Eastern Bengal districts. They were addressed to a large number of students and teachers at schools and colleges in Bengal. IB, in collaboration with DIBs, started to search for the writers and printers of those seditious documents. Finally, in 1914, in connection with the investigation of the *Liberty* pamphlet, they were informed that some Lokenath Yantra Press was engaged to print *Liberty* and *Swadhin Bharat* leaflets.

When the fourth edition of the *Liberty* leaflet was found to be circulated in Calcutta, Faridpur, and Dacca, Bengal police led a thorough investigation to trace the press. They discovered that two Madrasi students at the National Medical College, B. S. Ramaya and Y. J. Shastri, were involved in its circulation. Ramayya confessed that he posted some copies of *Liberty: The Divine Heritage of Man* (third edition) leaflets to various people in Madras and Bombay. He was arrested for the same thing. After enquiring with Ramayya, the police came to know that he had received these envelopes from someone who called themselves 'U. A. or A. U. Ray', who Ramayya says, 'is in point of fact a Madrasi student at the National Medical College of Calcutta named Yerramillay Jaganna Shastri' (Bombay Police report regarding seditious leaflet *Liberty*, 5 September 1914).

Police inquired about all the Madrasi student messes in Calcutta and wasted no time in finding Y. J. Shastri, who had been residing at Andhra Lodge in Harrison Road. Shastri was arrested immediately (police report about the investigation of *Liberty*, 1914). His residence was searched, and he confessed after being arrested by the police. He informed the police that he received these pamphlets from a Maratha student Hedgawar, who was also a student at the National Medical College. Later, Shastri was introduced to Nalini Guha (arrested in the Barisal Conspiracy Case),[10] who got them printed at a press in College Street. Nalini planned to print the leaflet on 20 August 1914 and wanted Shastri to print the same edition on the same day from Madras. Shastri agreed to the proposal. Relying on Shastri's statement, the police discovered and raided the messes where Nalini, Hedgawar, and two Telegu people were residing. They searched their houses and tried to find the press from which they had printed the *Liberty* leaflets. Shastri admitted that he did not know the press from which Hedgawar had brought the leaflets. Regarding the press, the police recognised Nalini as a member of the Dacca Anushilan samiti and had knowledge that one Loknath Yantra Press was used by the samiti. But it seemed difficult for Denham to find the press 'amongst the thousands in Calcutta' (G.C. Denham's confidential letter to Griffiths, 13 November 1914). Police searched 51 Bowbazar Street and found the press was owned by one Surendra Nath Bose of Amherst Street (police report regarding the investigation of 'Liberty', 1914). Later, police suspected that this press might be the Loknath Yantra Press. The inquiry on the circulation of Liberty in 1914 revealed that a nationwide propaganda network existed during this period.

In connection with the investigation of the Benaras Conspiracy case,[11] in December 1916, Bengal police searched some of the houses in Chandernagore. The police got hold of a large quantity of revolutionary literature (mainly *Swadhin Bharat* and *Liberty*) from one of the houses that they had searched on that occasion. After scrutinising them, intelligence officers suspected that they had been printed at 23/2 Mirzaffer Lane, Calcutta, which was used as a printing centre for most of the secret samitis in Western Bengal (IB Reports on Investigation of Chandernagore, Bulletin 2, 1917).

Next, when Kalipada Das, an associate of Amrita Lal Hazra, was arrested in connection with the investigation of the Maulvi Bazar and Raja Bazar bomb cases, ten *Liberty* leaflets were found in his possession, which further revealed the propaganda network that existed between the Calcutta group and the group of North Bengal. Police suspected Lalit Mohun De as the composer of the *Liberty* leaflet, but could not trace him as he was absconding after the Maulvi bazaar bomb outrage. Later, Dacca DIB employed Kalipada as a Police agent (Confidential Letter from Dacca DIB to G. C. Denham, 10 July 1914). But he too could not help them find Lalit Mohun De. Also, a startling discovery in the course of the Raja Bazar Bomb Case showed that bombs used in Delhi and Lahore as well as in Bengal were manufactured in Bengal while at least some editions of the *Liberty* and *Swadhin Bharat* had been composed and printed in Loknath Yantra Press (Letter from the Inspector-General of Police, Bengal to the Chief Secretary of Bengal, 6 January 1914, Letter 229, 1914). Hence, it became apparent from these discoveries that the bomb and the pen went hand in hand towards furthering revolutionary objectives.

Raiding houses to prevent 'terrorism'

The revolutionary leaflets were discovered in great numbers at searches where revolutionaries had been arrested and organisation documents and arms recovered. Besides this, samiti members often referred to them when being arrested. Sometimes revolutionaries were arrested for possession of seditious leaflets. In connection with the Raja Bazar conspiracy case, in November 1913, a raid on a house in the heart of Calcutta brought to light one of the sources. A room was discovered thereafter containing both revolutionary literature and cigarette tins, the latter in the process of being manufactured into bombs. The men found in this room were put on their trial for infringing the Explosives Act and for conspiracy to commit crime.

In 1917, seditious pamphlets were seized during house searches, notably at 12/1 Hara Dhar's Lane, Calcutta, and during the searches in North

Bengal, while among the articles seized during the Kalta Bazar raid in Dacca was a revolutionary document entitled 'Revolution and Constitution' (IB Bulletin regarding Seditious Pamphlets No. 7 to 9, third quarter 1918). In September 1917, in connection with the circulation of copies of a 'short seditious notice' in manuscript in Sirajganj, Dacca Police raided the houses of members of Anushilan samiti. However, the raid was unsuccessful. But after some days of the raid, eighteen copies of the said notice were recovered from the Bar Library. The police were certain that a branch of Anushilan samiti in Sirajganj was responsible for this circulation.

In 1908, police also raided the premises of the Dacca Anushilan samiti at Bhuterbari, Dacca and found some documents through which they came to know about the organisational structure of the samiti. 'The vows', 'The rules for members', 'district organisation scheme', and 'General principles' were all invaluable documents to understand the line upon which the samiti was established and the members would act (Sedition Committee Report 1973: 96).

Emergency litigations to combat the upsurge of 'terrorist' propaganda during the Great War

With the commencement of the First World War, the number of revolutionary outrages grew exponentially in Bengal. Anandaswarup Gupta had pointed out that '[c]rime in 1916 continued to be more than in the pre-war days' (Gupta 1979: 320). The most important among them was the loot of arms from Rodda & Company on 26 August 1914 and the *Komagatamaru* incident of 19 September 1914 in Budge Budge where 351 Sikhs and 21 Punjabi Muslims appeared in the port from North America and a fight broke out with the police. Bengal revolutionaries were engaged in the loot and fifty Mauser pistols and 46,000 rounds of ammunition were stolen.

Early 1914 witnessed an influx of propaganda importing from abroad into India. The Colonial Police in India was anxious to prevent these importations and implemented novel censorship and custom interception rules. To stop the spread of propaganda coming from abroad, they depended on Sea Customs Act. Despite implementing all the regulations and legislations they failed miserably to control the importation of seditious materials into India.

Colonial Police had taken a preventive measure to put a bridle on the face of appearance of revolutionary propaganda in flurries during this time. As in 1915, Bengal Government passed a draconian law through which it was able to supersede the provisions of the criminal law and institute summary trials by special tribunals, each consisting of three commissioners appointed by the local government. Nine conspiracy cases were tried by

Special Tribunals and altogether 174 persons were put on trial for general conspiracies. This Act further authorised the government to detain anyone if they consider the movement of this person is prejudicial to public safety. It also empowered the hands of police as they could raid anyone's residence without warrant and seize anything found there related to any person which they regarded was used in prejudicial purpose.

However, with the increasing appearance of revolutionary propaganda in Bengal, the Chief Secretary of Bengal government proposed to the Legislative Assembly to draft a rule which would enable the possession of revolutionary literature a crime. However, in April 1915, mere possession of revolutionary literature could not be made a criminal offence due to the absence of conscience among the home members and disapproval of the proposed scheme by the Viceroy, Hardinge.

On that occasion Reginald Craddock, while admitting the pressing need to fight against 'Bengal anarchists', drew the attention of the members of the Council to other kind of seditious propaganda which were spread extensively across India (Recommendations of the Bengal Govt. that the possession of seditious Literature inciting to mutiny or crimes of violence should be made punishable; November 1916). He further pointed out that the position of NWFP, United Provinces, Punjab, and Sind was vulnerable as these governments had seen considerable number of influxes of 'seditious' propaganda. Craddock proposed that the government should introduce a rule by which the local governments could put a stop to these kinds of 'seditious' propaganda in their provinces. He wrote that

> '[t]here is no doubt that so far as revolutionary propaganda are concerned, there is need of a permanent law, but that need not prevent us using the Defence of India Act so long as its use is at the time appropriate. I contemplate approaching the Legislative department soon in regard to a permanent law for dealing with the Bengal anarchists, but that is different matter. For the proposed rule is not the peculiar necessity of Bengal. All the local Governments were unanimous in favour of such a rule, and it might be just as handy in the North-West Frontier Province, in the Punjab, the United Provinces or Sind as in Bengal.' (Recommendations of the Bengal Govt. that the possession of seditious literature inciting to mutiny or crimes of violence should be made punishable; November 1916).

While the association of Bengal revolutionaries with the Indo-German conspiracy was revealed,[12] Bengal Government insisted on central government to make a law which would penalise the possession of revolutionary literature. Accordingly, the Defence of India Act was amended, and the Seditious Literature Rule was passed with the result that possession of certain category of documents became illegal by Section 2 of the Defence of India Act.

The pamphleteers responded with fresh issues of pamphlets. The most important among them was a pamphlet entitled 'Antarin Bhikkhya' (the beggary of internment) which was received by the Bengal Civil Rights Committee in 1918 and contained 'many misstatements of facts regarding detenus and the working of the Defence Act' (CID reports regarding seditious leaflets in Bengal, 1917).

Controlling the recruiting ground

After realising that revolutionaries were using schools and colleges as recruiting grounds by disseminating 'seditious' propaganda, the CID of Bengal decided to put all the government and government-aided schools and colleges under vigilance. From 1908, the Bengal Police and Intelligence Branch started to include headmasters and principals of schools and colleges in their network for collecting intelligence. To control the spread of 'seditious' ideas, the Bengal government ordered that any packet or letter addressed generally and not to a student should be delivered to the principal or headmaster 'who, if they contained anything of an objectionable nature, would detain it on his own responsibility' (letter from the Inspector-General of Police, Bengal to the Chief Secretary of Bengal, 6 January 1914, Letter 229,1919). However, the government of India was apprehensive that these kinds of orders would incur criticism from the liberal press, thereby deciding that 'these instructions should be communicated orally to the heads of the institutions by officers of the education department' (letter from the Inspector-General of Police, Bengal to the Chief Secretary of Bengal, 6 January 1914, Letter 229, 1919).

On 4 May 1910, a circular was issued by the Bengal government by which all unregistered postal matter addressed generally or by the names of students at a school or college was to be placed by the postal peon in a locked box to which the headmaster or principal kept the key. In this way headmasters and principals were incorporated into the system of prevention of the circulation of revolutionary literature by 1908.

After the Barisal conspiracy case (1910; see Table 3.1 for an overview of conspiracy cases during the period under review), the Director of Public Instruction, CID, Dacca and Calcutta IB took strong measures to introduce some regulations for the prevention of the exploitation of schools and colleges in East Bengal and Assam by the revolutionaries. In 1912, in an effort to curb the participation of schoolboys, students, and professors in political agitation and the growth of the revolutionary propaganda in schools and colleges, the government issued an order that showed the three-tier surveillance system of the proposed 'preventative mechanism'.

Table 3.1: Overview of conspiracy cases in colonial Bengal

Year	Conspiracy case	Note
1908	Howrah Conspiracy Case	Fifty persons were charged for waging war against the King, and with committing dacoities in districts around Calcutta in order to collect money in pursuit of their scheme.
1910	Alipore Bomb Case	Related to the house raid of secret den of Barindra Ghosh and associates in Maniktola Garden House where many documents and materials used for making bombs were discovered.
1910	Midnapore Conspiracy Case	The discovery of the Maniktola group of revolutionaries (1908) and the eventual house raids and arrests of revolutionaries located in Midnapore. Maniktola group of revolutionaries were convicted for attempted assassination of District Magistrate of Midnapore, Kingsford and the murders of Mrs. and Miss. Kennedy (by mistake for Mr. Kingsford). This conspiracy case cast a heavy blow in the revolutionary movement of Bengal.
1910	Barisal Conspiracy Case	Three cases of gang robbery took place in Dacca, Faridpur and Bakarganj during 1910. A group of students was convicted for this crime. Later it was discovered that these groups of students came from Sonarang National School which became the breeding ground of spreading 'terrorism'. A case was started to punish the convicts of these robberies which is called Barisal Conspiracy Case.
1913	Delhi Bomb Case	Rash Bihari Bose devised a plan to throw a bomb at Viceroy Hardinge in the celebration of capital transfer from Calcutta to Delhi in December, 1912. Initially, police could not trace the culprits, but after thorough investigation they charged the whole group for the Delhi bomb case.

(*continued*)

Table 3.1 (Cont.)

Year	Conspiracy case	Note
1913	Raja Bazar Bomb Case	This was related to the discovery of a room in the Raja Bajar area of Calcutta in connection with the investigation of throwing bombs in various incidents in districts of Eastern Bengal between 1910 and 1913.
1915	Benaras Conspiracy Case	Rash Bihari Bose devised a plan of armed uprising by Bengal, Punjab and UP revolutionaries acting in unison with British Indian army. Bose sent out emissaries to various cantonments in Upper India to procure military aid for the appointed day. Unfortunately, for the last-minute betrayal by Kirpal Sing, police discovered the plot and Rash Bihari Bose's plan was foiled.
1915	Indo-German Conspiracy Case	During the Great War, Bengal revolutionaries, with the help of revolutionaries located in Germany, devised a plan to import arms and money with the help of the German Govt.

Source: author's own work.

When a suspect, whether under police surveillance or not, is found to be a member of any government-aided school or college, that fact should be promptly reported in writing by the Deputy Inspector General, Special Department, to the Chief Secretary (orders about sedition in schools and colleges: Postal Delivery and Undesirable Literature, 1919).

A history sheet was advised to be prepared to accompany the report, showing all that was done by the suspect. This report would then go to the authorities of the institution, and they would be called on to keep the suspect under observation. Next, the Director of Public Instruction would receive the history sheet of the suspect, and he in turn would be directed to correspond with the headmaster or principal of the institution concerned.

The Director of Public Instruction should then address the principal or headmaster confidentially, and point out that, if the suspect is still retained, the governing body of the institution concerned must hold themselves responsible for his future conduct to the extent of furnishing:

1. He will be kept under special observation, and a report on the steps taken to this end will be submitted by the headmaster or principal to the Director of Public Instruction.
2. Reports will be submitted to the DoPI on the general conduct of the suspect, not only at regular intervals of three months, but also whenever they are warranted by general misbehaviour on his part (orders from Director General of Public Education, Bengal, about sedition in schools and colleges: Postal Delivery and Undesirable Literature, 1919).

During 1913, the discovery of an extract of a paper entitled 'District organization scheme', revealed how the revolutionaries had been operating in middle and high schools and colleges in Bengal. The scheme deserves to be quoted here.

> The district organiser shall first make himself acquainted with the number of entrance and middle English schools or colleges in his centre. He shall influence at least one boy in each class of the school or college and through him, he will disseminate the idea to the whole class. He shall have connections with the higher-class students under the teacher or professor of the school or college. This higher-class student will have connections with the monitors and other classes. (Sedition Committee Report 1973: 25)

In the wake of the Barisal Conspiracy Case (1913) and the arrest of a teacher at Sonarang National School, a confession by this teacher revealed the grave and grim situation of the schools and colleges of Bengal. The government had classified all schools into two categories as early as 1908: (a) those that had turned themselves into regular organisations for sedition and (b) those that had kept no proper control over their students.

Students from institutions in class (b) should only be accepted in government service with great caution and those from class (a) were to be debarred altogether from such employment. Between 1911 and 1913 twelve, nine, and seven schools and PM Not sure about tcolleges were blacklisted all over Bengal, respectively. Students of these blacklisted school were barred from entering any government or government-aided institution. In some cases, they would require a verification certificate from the police (orders relating to Postal Delivery and Undesirable Literature, 1919).

Revolutionaries had been using schools and colleges as recruiting grounds, by influencing the minds of the youth through seditious propaganda. These propaganda materials were sent to schools, hostels and messes. Alongside these, many members of secret samitis worked as teachers in different schools all over Bengal. The local government as well as the Government of India retaliated by blacklisting schools and colleges that were used by the insurgents as the breeding grounds for 'terrorism'. Nevertheless, schools and colleges in Bengal enjoyed a stable recruiting ground for the Bhadralok 'terrorist gang' as late as 1947.

Conclusion

In their effort to put an end to the 'terrorist' movement in Bengal, Intelligence Branch officers had perceived that they were close to inflicting a final blow to the movement since 1913. They firmly believed that they understood the machinations of the Bengal revolutionaries better than their counterparts elsewhere in the Empire (Silvestri 2019: 197). However, Rash Bihari Bose's flight from India on 12 May 1915 indicated a rather contradictory perspective. (After the failure of his plan, he had been residing in Chandernagore in disguise of a Brahmin cook and left for Japan from Calcutta port a few days later; CID had no clue about that.) Despite building modern apparatus and taking every precaution to repress the revolutionaries of Bengal, in most cases they outsmarted the police scanner. This was validated by their continued 'outrages' until 1947.

However, after 1947, there was a paradigm shift. The newly independent Indian state, as a successor of the colonial state, continued the basic tenets of the counter-terrorism policies of earlier regimes. The counter-terrorism practices of controlling funding, checking ideological propaganda, and prohibiting the import of arms from external and internal sources remained the same. The sleek entry of 'terrorist' organisations under the cover of various social and political organisations, including broader political entities, also persisted. Prohibition and the smart changing of the names of openly operating outfits still continued. The Indian state also spawned various counter-terrorist organisations in national and international domains, operating secretly, similar to the days of Charles Tegart. These organisations maintain communication with international counter-terrorism agencies from different countries.

Notes

1 An important aspect of the revolutionary movement of Bengal was its secret clubs. The members of these secret clubs operated secretly because of the seditious nature of their activities. Anushilan and Jugantar are the two most prominent secret samitis that had been active during the early twentieth century.

2 Bande Mataram was translated by J. C. Ker in his book *Political Trouble in India: 1907–1917* as 'Hail! Mother'.

3 J. C. Ker mentioned in his book that 'the title of the paper means "Twilight", and the point of it may be found in remark made in the paper in September, 1907, warning the English that after the passing of the *Sandhya* comes nightfall when the squaring of accounts with the Feringhi will begin.'

4 *Yugantar* and *Jugantar* is the same newspaper, J. C. Ker, in his book, uses the former spelling.

5 Brahmabandhab Upadhyaya was allegedly the author of *Raja K.*

6 During the year 1913, there was a series of bomb outrages in Eastern Bengal and Assam, and Western Bengal (including the Moulvi Bazar outrage in Assam). Upon examination of these bombs, police found a similarity in construction and thought those to be the work of the same gang. A series of inquiries led them to a house at Upper Circular Road (local name Raja Bazar), which initiated a raid of the house bringing to light explosive materials and revolutionary propaganda. 'The men found in this room were put on their trial for infringing the Explosives Act and for conspiracy to commit crime and, it was held by the High Court that the tins were intended to be used as bombs and that their purpose was endanger life' (Sedition Committee Report).

7 The Delhi Bomb Case refers to an attempt made in 1912 to assassinate the then Viceroy Lord Hardinge while he was in a procession in Chandni Chawk, Delhi, celebrating the capital transfer from Calcutta to Delhi. In the course of investigation, it was discovered that Rash Bihari Bose, an active member of Bengal revolutionary samiti, was the mastermind behind this outrage. The Lahore Bomb Case refers to the incident where Basanta Biswas and Abad Bihari dropped a bomb in Lawrence Gardens (May 1913), Lahore, where one peon was killed. As the result of enquiries in this case Basanta Kumar Biswas, Abad Bihari, Bhai Balmokand, and Amir Chand were sentenced to death.

8 The Midnapore Bomb Case refers to the discovery of the Maniktola group of revolutionaries (1908) and the eventual house raids and arrests of revolutionaries located in Midnapore. The Maniktola group of revolutionaries was convicted for attempted assassination to District Magistrate of Midnapore, Kingsford and the murders of Mrs. and Miss. Kennedy (by mistake for Mr Kingsford). This conspiracy case cast a heavy blow in the revolutionary movement of Bengal.

9 On 4 November 1908, a charge of kidnapping a minor boy was made against Pulin Bihari Das, head of Anushilan samiti. During the enquiries, the particular member who had enticed the boy into samiti, Sukumar Chakravarti, was arrested at his house, where he made a statement to the police, and bound over to come before the DM on 12 November. The next day, he was murdered by his samiti members. This case led to a thorough search of the premises of the samiti on 15 November, where documents were discovered. In connection with the evidence, the govt. declared Anushilan samiti as an unlawful association under the Indian Criminal Law Amendment Act of 1908.

10 In later half of 1910, three cases of gang robbery took place in Dacca, Faridpur, and Bakarganj. A group of students was convicted for this crime. Later it was discovered that these groups of students come from Sonarang National School which became the breeding ground of spreading 'terrorism'. A case was started to punish the convicts of these robberies which is called Barisal Conspiracy Case.

11 Benaras Conspiracy Case (1915) refers to the affairs where Rash Bihari Bose devised a plan of armed uprising by Bengal, Punjab, and UP revolutionaries acting in unison with the British Indian army. Bose sent out emissaries to

various cantonments in Upper India to procure military aid for the appointed day. Unfortunately, for the last-minute betrayal by Kirpal Sing, police discovered the plot and Rash Bihari Bose's plan was foiled.

12 Bengal revolutionaries, with the help of revolutionaries formed as Berlin-India Committee, devised a plan to import arms and money with the help of German Govt. While the German Govt. intended to destabilise British power base in India, Indian revolutionaries wanted to achieve independence by means of organising a national armed uprising with German money and arms.

References

Boyle, J. M. (2019). *Non-Western Responses to Terrorism*. Manchester: Manchester University Press.

Giuliani, E. M. (2013). 'Policing knowledge: Surveillance in colonial Bengal 1861–1913', PhD diss., Kingston: Queens University.

Gupta, A. (1979). *The Police in British India 1861–1947*. New Delhi: Concept Publishing House.

Ghosh, D. (2017). *Gentlemanly Terrorists: Political Violence and the Colonial State in India, 1919–1947*. Cambridge: Cambridge University Press.

Kalhan A., Conroy G., Kaushal M., and Miller S. (2006). 'Colonial continuities: Human rights, terrorism, and security laws in India', *Columbia Journal of Asian Law*, 20(1), 93–234.

Ker, J. C. (1960). *Political Trouble in India*. Calcutta: Editions India.

Kishor Rakkhit, B. (2015). *Sobar Olokkhe, Banglar Biplob Itihaser Oprakishito Kahini*. Calcutta: Radical Impression.

Majumdar, R. C. (1963). *History of Freedom Movement in India, Vol. III*. Calcutta: Firma K. L. Mukhopadhyay.

Mclean, K. (2015). *A Revolutionary History of Interwar India: Violence, Image, Voice and Text*. London: Hurst and Company.

Mukherjee, U. (1981). *Two Great Indian Revolutionaries: Jatindranath Mukherjee and Rash Bihari Bose*. Calcutta: Firma K. L. Mukhopadhyaya.

NAI, New Delhi, Simla Records, Proceeding No. 302–311 (November 1916). Legislative Department notes, recommendations of the Bengal Govt. that the possession of seditious literature inciting to mutiny or crimes of violence should be made punishable.

Pakrashi, S. (1947). *Agnidiner Kotha*. Calcutta: National Book Agency.

Popplewell, R. (2015). *Intelligence and Imperial Defence: British Intelligence and the Defence of the Indian Empire 1904–1924*. New York: Routledge.

Ray, K. (2008). *Revolutionary Propaganda in Bengal: Extremist and Militant Press (1905–1918)*. Calcutta: Papyrus.

Robb, P. (1991). 'The ordering of rural India: The policing of nineteenth-century Bengal and Bihar', in Anderson, D. M. and Killingray, D. (eds) *Policing the Empire: Government, Authority and Control, 1830–1940*. Manchester: Manchester University Press, pp. 126–50.

Sanyal, S. (2014). *Revolutionary Pamphlets, Propaganda and Political Culture in Colonial Bengal*. New York: Cambridge University Press.

Sedition Committee Report (1973). Calcutta: New Age Publishers.

Silvestri, M. (2019). *Policing 'Bengali Terrorism' in India and the World: Imperial Intelligence and Revolutionary Nationalism, 1905–1939*. Hampshire: Palgrave Macmillan.

Silke, A. (2019). *Routledge Handbook of Terrorism and Counter-Terrorism*. New York: Routledge.

Sarkar, S. (1973). *Swadeshi Movement in Bengal: 1903–1908*. New Delhi: People's Publishing House.

Sengupta, K. and Das, T. (eds) (2021). *Rethinking the Local in Indian History: Perspective from Southern Bengal*. India: Routledge.

Tripathi, A. (1967). *The Extremist Challenge: India between 1890–1910*. Bombay: Orient Longman.

WBSA, Kolkata, 321/17 (Part I), IB Records, 'Seditious leaflets', 1917.

WBSA, Kolkata, 321/17 (Part II), IB Records, IB Reports on investigation of Chandernagore, Bulletin 2, 1917.

WBSA, Kolkata, 71/19, Home Political Records, 'Orders about sedition in schools and colleges: postal delivery and undesirable literature, 1919.

WBSA, Kolkata, 1318/10, IB Records, 'Seditious leaflet wadhin Bharat or Free India, circulation Eastern Bengal and Assam', 1910.

WBSA, Kolkata, 380/13, IB Records, 'Pamphlet Swadhin Bharat: Second edition of seditious leaflet', 1913.

WBSA, Kolkata, IB Records, 9/1914, 'Letter from the Inspector-General of Police, Bengal to the Chief Secretary of Bengal', 6 January 1914, Letter 229, 1914.

WBSA, Kolkata, IB Records, 586/1914, 'Lithographed under paper called "Ghadr" by Jugantar Ashram, San Francisco, USA', 1914.

WBSA, Kolkata, IB Records,1290/14, 'Liberty leaflets and other confidential reports', 1914.

WBSA, Kolkata, IB Records, 1465/16, 'Independent India', 1916.

4

The French domestic counter-terrorism framework: Unravelling the colonial matrix in shaping bodies and the response to terrorism

Marine Guéguin

The portrayal of the 'cultural other' in French counter-terrorism narratives is a focal point of the present analysis and speaks to this volume in examining counter-terrorism in a global context. This chapter further expands recent efforts in literature by focusing on questions of coloniality and decoloniality, particularly looking at the French case and its CT practices. This chapter offers valuable perspective on colonial influences, colonial conceptual of race, and civilisational hierarchies entrenched in the French CT context. The construction of polarised identities in political discourse is integral to and an essential feature of the language of securitisation and security politics (Campbell 1998), which aim at legitimising counter-terrorism policies. Identities of the self and the other are discursively constructed through the language of counter-terrorism (Jackson 2007: 395) as a manifest political consequence of selecting one mode of representations over another (Campbell 1998). The terrorism scholarship argues that the discursive construction of the other is event- and policy-driven. I demonstrate that it is also embedded in a context. While it is essential for political actors to build a binary self–other identity within discourse, my analysis does not focus on the political construction of the French national self. Instead, it centres on the depiction of the terrorist 'other' excavating colonial legacies from political discourse and political constructions, a matrix that unveils coloniality of the French counter-terrorism strategy (i.e., powers, being/non-being, knowledge [Quijano 2000]). Within this analysis, I refer to 'postcolonial enemy within' furthering the dichotomy insider/outsider and representing the status of the second generation of French-born immigrants (Rigouste 2011). Critical to (re)constructing and maintaining a national self-identity as a collective identity, the notion of difference is embedded in political discourse via a series of identity markers: those who belong to a 'shared and imagined community' (Anderson 1991: 6) and those who do not (Rigouste 2011).

The chapter adopts a critical discourse analysis (CDA) approach to explore the political rhetoric, declarations, and media statements of French political elites in 214 texts. The analysis spans from January 2015, post-Charlie Hebdo attacks, up until October 2017 when the SILT Bill was enacted.[1] By employing a CDA method, the study delves into the language, ideologies, and power dynamics embedded in political communication and narratives. This period is particularly significant as it covers a critical juncture in France's response to terrorism and the subsequent implementation of the SILT Bill. The chapter sheds light on the underlying themes and power structures within the French political landscape during this pivotal time, contributing to a deeper comprehension of how terrorists and securitised bodies were framed and how terrorism was addressed following the post-2015 attacks. The chapter provides a comprehensive analysis of how the French counter-terrorism response is embedded in colonialities reproducing and reifying colonial structures.

Terrorism studies have been significantly shaped by the impact of the 9/11 attacks, with a strong emphasis on Anglo-Saxon perspectives, dominated by UK, US, and Australian case studies and research (Boyle 2021). Recently, there has been a shift in critical terrorism studies (CTS) to unveil other examples crucial for a comprehensive understanding of terrorism and various approaches to counter-terrorism. The chapter comfortably sits within this comparative perspective, deepening our comprehension of counter-terrorism, shaped by interconnected histories and the enduring impacts of colonialism, as this volume illustrates. Expanding on these postcolonial frameworks concerning emergency laws and counter-terrorism, this volume delves into the diverse ways in which colonial legacies and colonial knowledge intersect with the historical and present-day implementation of counter-terrorism strategies. The French case study offers the literature an original approach in counter-terrorism by focusing on the constructed categories of bodies. CTS literature actively involves marginalised and silenced perspectives in its research, as evidenced by the incorporation of these voices in analyses (Breen-Smyth 2014; Holland 2016: 209; Khalid 2017; Toros 2012). However, it is essential to recognise that decolonial theory transcends this aspect and should not be confined solely to this inclusion. To comprehensively address the issues of orientalism and the coloniality of power within Western hegemonic security structures, further exploration is warranted. Thus, the objective of this chapter is to broaden the scope and explore the French construction of the terrorist 'other' and its counter-terrorism measures, utilising decolonial and orientalist critical perspectives. The otherness metanarrative is an essential component in understanding the political construction of terrorism, powers, and structures. There is a necessity to widen CTS' research scope and examine 'other-centric' research which focus on the phenomenon of political language depicting terrorism. The chapter provides a critique of the Western hegemonic construction of the terrorist other as a modern taboo and a marker of Western identity. Additionally, it examines the differentiation of the self and the other within the category of the self, that is 'French by birth' and the 'French Muslim' (Rigouste 2011: 60),[2] a body located within the national French body (Rigouste 2011: 56), a product of colonial genesis imprinting contemporary discourse, a 'real' French and a 'postcolonial second generation of immigrant'. The dichotomy of and/or postcolonial hierarchy of who is French citizen, and the second generation of French-born immigrants depicted within political discourse uncovers the colonial episteme of race. Western hegemonic powers fix meaning in discourse inextricably linked to power of representational practises in identity-making (Doty 1996: 8–10). Those hierarchies and forms of exclusion remain invisible in mainstream approaches to security and still constitute an additional layer of power relations (Adamson 2020). Said (2003) demonstrates that the discourse is ever-changing, largely influenced by the context in which it is produced. Therefore, the identity self/West versus other/East is not static, but rather entrenched in historical, social, intellectual, and political processes (Said 2003: 332). The French case study offers the opportunity to observe the racial hierarchies, and imperial and colonial settings embedded in discourse and response to terrorism. The chapter analyses the understanding of the racial othering components which compose the French political discourse adopting a decolonial approach. The understanding of discourse, for the purpose of the analysis, rests upon a system of meaning-production constructing new realities, as a site of construction of meaning (Foucault 1993: 32–3). It structures signification and constructs social realities, defines subjects and establishes relational positions, produces subjects authorised to speak and act, and legitimises knowledge and political practice (Jackson 2007: 396).

First, it finds significance within the French political language game through the construction of the terrorist radical other, underlining an orientalist narrative by decision-makers to construct the 'Islamic radical terrorist'. Not only does the analysis cover the orientalist narrative of 'Islamic terrorism' but it also illustrates the use of the meta-narrative of civilisation and barbarism to dehumanise, depersonalise, and depoliticise the terrorist enemy, ultimately creating a hierarchy of civilisations. This nourishes the orientalist and racial discourse on terrorism and questions the political interest in implementing counter-terrorism measures based on those orientalist and racial assumptions. The first section highlights and demonstrates the colonial continuum of the enemy depiction in the French counter-terrorism strategy and political narratives. Second, the analysis delves into the French response to terrorism domestically by dissecting the state of emergency post-Paris 2015 attacks considered a 'new' counter-terrorism approach, which originates from the French colonial context of the Algerian War. French CT measures further the internal other political construction and the logic of 'suspect community' which ultimately (re)produces a 'postcolonial enemy within' and (re)creates within the 'self category' a self and an other. Those components can be traced back to colonial historical settings and they help to excavate colonialities of power, being/non-being within French contemporary counter-terrorism approaches and discourse.

The depiction of the terrorist enemy other: Coloniality of being/non-being

Understanding the racial othering process – 'Islamic radical terrorism'

To emphasise the negation of the enemy other and promote the superiority of the self-identity, political actors deploy a series of terms to delineate the terrorist enemy other through the narrative of 'Islamic radical terrorism'. As Jackson (2005) underlines in his analysis of post-9/11 discourse, this is a very common discursive strategy employed by Western hegemonic powers. As evidence, the French political discourse delineates terrorism using various labels: 'Islamism', 'extremism', 'obscurantism', 'fanatics', 'jihadi-terrorism', 'radicals', 'extremists', 'dividers', and 'Salafists', to depict the terrorist enemy without providing any definition of these concepts. Yet these labels are culturally loaded, highly deployed, and function therefore to construct the radical 'Islamic terrorists' in opposition to the self (Jackson 2007). After the Charlie Hebdo attacks in 2015,[3] to further mark the binary self–other, the enemy is depicted as coming from an outside. Political actors delineate terrorists' obscure beliefs and wrong ideology, portraying them as external and outsiders and reinforcing the negation of the 'other' and furthering the orientalist construction. The terrorist other is located in an external space and created in direct opposition to the 'self', 'us', or 'we' embodied by values such as freedom, liberties, fraternity, solidarity, unity; feelings such as love and care – everything that the other is not which by political actors is portrayed as a 'divider'. Empirically, post-Charlie Hebdo attacks, terrorists are depicted as 'external' in various forms – culturally, politically, and territorially. Post-Paris attacks, the political framing evolves to depict terrorists as the enemy within, external culturally and politically, but within the territory/inside space. This serves to securitise the body as 'other', demarcating the 'self within' from the 'other within'. However, the political framing goes further than this, as it involves racial and colonial dimensions of political narrative constructions. Through these continuous (re)constructions, French political actors securitised bodies and territorial spaces.

François Hollande, former French president, declared:

> War acts on Friday were decided and planned in Syria; they were organised in Belgium, perpetrated on our soil with French accomplices. (2015a) (translation by the author)

Manuel Valls, the former Prime Minister, claimed:

> This radical Islamism, these jihadists, were born in our suburbs, in our *quartiers populaires*[4]. (2015c) (translation by the author)

Discourse links the terrorists' place of birth with their religion, thereby differentiating them from French citizens, the 'us'. Political actors bear a significant responsibility for the meaning-production concerning Islam and Arabs, their stigmatisation, and the exacerbation of Islamophobia among the population. Through in-depth analysis of political discourse, the discursive construction of terrorism post-Charlie Hebdo emphasised the depiction of terrorists as 'killers', *'individus'* (see below), the 'outsiders', and 'Islamists' which further evolved after the Paris attacks to depict them as 'dividers', 'extremists', 'Salafists', and 'fundamentalists' within.

Hollande, the former French president, argued:

> Salafism… which got inspiration from radical jihadism… represents a real danger, and we need to fight it, hence our wish to dissolve a few groups, close mosques, deport radical imams… . (2015a) (translation by the author)

As Jackson (2007) demonstrates, the discourse of Islamic terrorism, and particularly the terrorism–extremism nexus, works to produce knowledge that terrorism and religion are intrinsically linked. It reinforces discrimination, impacts the Muslim community, and highlights how the orientalist construction of a terrorist other by Western hegemonic powers has deep colonial roots. This discourse not only leads to the closure of places of worship but also results in the disproportionate and discriminatory implementation of emergency powers by decisions-makers. The discourse of Islamic terrorism and its implementation targets Muslims using house arrest and police raids solely based on religious practices and beliefs (Amnesty International 2017). Consequently, it contributes to further polarise French society and securitise bodies. Political narrative illustrates fragmented categories of people, a French subject and a 'Islamic radical other' terrorist subject, by linking Islam to this narrative, further securitising the Muslim body (the other within the self category – see in the following section). Tuastad (2003) demonstrates that such narratives and politics of representations of Arabs and Islam highlight the hallmarks of orientalism by fundamentally dividing the East and the West, the self and the other, and essentially define the knowledge–power nexus of orientalism, embedded in contemporary French political discourse.

Not only do they securitise the terrorist enemy within, but they also (re)produce the 'French by birth and the 'French Muslim' dichotomy. As reported by Attalai and Moussi (2020), Islamophobia is a political phenomenon, shared by the entire political spectrum, which resulted, in the aftermath of the Paris attacks – just to name one example, in the closure of nineteen places of worship. Said (2003) notes that the oriental other reflects deeper socio-cultural fears and stereotypes that can be traced back to the imperial age, based on a long tradition of orientalist scholarship on the Middle East and Arab culture and religion. The French discursive assumptions rest upon a long colonial tradition of cultural stereotypes, representations and depictions of Islam. Not only do they depoliticise Islam by linking terrorism to extremist forms of religion, but they also depoliticise the terrorist enemy delineated as a sub-human, monster, savage, and barbarian to legitimate the War on Terror's counter-violence (Jackson 2005: 75).

'Individus': Dehumanisation and depersonalisation processes

The political discourse participates in dehumanising the terrorist embedded in a civilisation–barbarism meta-narrative. This meta-narrative further distinguishes the self from the other and shapes the public audience's perception of the terrorist threat. Scrimin and Rubaltelli (2021: 2707) argue that blatant and explicit dehumanisation processes impact the perception of terrorist events and of an out-group. Dehumanisation was first observed in a context of conflict and mass violence (Kelman 1979). It encompasses the act of withholding complete humanity from the portrayal of 'others', characterising their deeds as brutal and leading to suffering as a direct consequence (Haslam 2006: 252). Kelman (1979) conceptualises dehumanisation as denying a person 'identity' – defined as the perception of the person as an individual, independent, and distinguishable from others – and 'community' – the perception of seeing the other as part of an interconnected network where individuals care for each other. Dehumanisation is understood as an extreme phenomenon deployed to justify acts of violence (Haslam 2006). In this chapter, I focus on the dehumanisation process embedded in political discourse vis-à-vis a perceived threat of terrorism and the promotion of the securitised out-group/enemy through depersonalisation, depoliticisation, and depictions of bestiality and irrationality.

A specificity of the French case study is the label *individus* embedded in political discourse to refer to terrorists. The French wording *individu* should be understood as a generic way to describe someone. Its use suggests a distinct identity separate from the self, which is systematically employed within the French political discourse after the Charlie Hebdo and Paris attacks.

The French juridical meaning of *individu* refers to someone whose identity is unknown, and/or someone who needs to be kept anonymous because they have been (or might be) convicted for crimes. Such wording suggests a certain type of dehumanisation taking the form of a depersonalisation of the subject/individual. In other words, terrorists are stripped of any identifiable characteristics that would construct the unique individual with individual characteristics, emotions, feelings, and human identity markers. The categorisation of the terrorists as *individus* contributes to the process of depersonalisation. While victims are consistently named and described within the discourse, terrorists are equated with being inhuman, savages, monsters, and *individus*, suggesting a political choice to not identify them with human markers, ultimately uncovering a process of not naming.

Valls, the former Prime Minister, stressed:

> the one – I always struggle to pronounce their names – the one who operated, the one who killed the police officer.... . (2015b) (translation by the author)

Christiane Taubira, the former Minister of Justice, advocated:

> this brutality... this monstrosity... this cowardice because there is unspeakable cowardice... Yes, I'm talking about monstrosity. There is something incomprehensible, for us humans, when you look at this coldness. (2015) (translation by the author)

The narrative of *individus* underlines a strategic discursive process of depersonalising the terrorists and is extensively used by French political actors, to associate them with the lexical field of monstrosity, cowardice, and brutality. In contrast, the French and the victims are detailed as human beings, united, suffering, crying, and shouting; they have feelings and families. The use of specific terminologies in the process of othering and dehumanisation are highlighted aims to depersonalise terrorists, denying their humanness and excluding them from the human species (Haslam 2006). By avoiding direct identification and attributing sub-human behaviours to them, they are distinguished from the citizens. All these characteristics help political actors to (re)construct a dichotomy between good and bad – 'good' encompassing the French citizens and 'bad' encompassing the terrorists. The application and employment of the term *individu* consequently contributes to the othering process entrenched in political discourse. This indicates that dehumanisation is associated with a diverse assortment of individual differences (personality traits, ideologies, attitudes) and contextual factors (emotions, motives, threats, social positions) rather than being solely driven by hate or hatefulness (Halsam and Loughnan 2014).

As delineated in political narratives, terrorists do not express feelings and emotions as 'our civilisation' would do. They are portrayed as acting with cold blood, and, therefore, as lacking personality, identity, and community – they belong to their own community of terrorists but are not deemed worthy of being considered as human. This establishes a hierarchy and superiority of 'our' civilisation in comparison to the external other. Reflecting on Mbembe (2011), in his preface of Fanon's book, the use of the concepts of civilisation and groups, dehumanised and humanised, (re) create racial hierarchies to describe different populations, bodies, or people, along with their distribution within those hierarchies. It refers to the logic of enclosure during colonial regimes, aimed at controlling potential dangers and ensuring general safety in the mind of political actors who construct and (re)adapt those hierarchies as an expression of coloniality. It is particularly significant to reflect on Césaire's development and critique of the constructed superiority of the West, in Europe, where the West constantly (re)produces its 'race superiority' (2000: 33). Ultimately, his critique unveils a political strategy in creating characteristics of barbarism which entail irrationality and bestiality correlated to the terrorist's depiction. Killing defines the very nature of the terrorist (Jackson 2005: 153) and suggests bestial characteristics linked to their identity (see Taubira's quote). Combining the civilisation and barbarism narratives to delineate the two opposite identities underscores a meta-narrative of civilisation–barbarism. Dehumanising the terrorists means emptying their actions of any political content. Their acts are defined by their nature – they kill, torture, and kidnap innocent people because they are considered monsters and 'because this is what evil, demonic terrorists do' (Jackson 2005: 153).

Valls, the former Prime Minister, described:

> They… behaved … like soldiers, like killers. Their modus operandi is that of people trained to kill. (2015a) (translation by the author)

Bernard Cazeneuve, the former Interior Minister, declared:

> What I see is the mark of savagery. Individuals who, in cold, blood murder… individuals who, with such savagery, point blank, in cold blood, are capable of murdering… are extraordinarily dangerous individuals, inhabited by savagery… No matter what has caused them inspiration, what inspires them is savagery, it is crime, it is barbarism. (2015) (translation by the author)

The rhetoric of savagery and barbarism stresses the depersonalisation and dehumanisation of terrorists, depicting them as nothing more than savages, murderers, and barbarians. These narratives play a crucial role in constructing the enemy, and are central to the post-Charlie Hebdo discourse, further exemplified after the Paris attacks. Ultimately, it securitises the body of the terrorist enemy (Guéguin 2022).

Not only is the terrorist depicted as a wrongdoer, inferior in moral and cultural terms but also portrayed as a radical other. As Jackson (2005) argues, the most noticeable feature of the language of counter-terrorism is its appeal to identity produced by political actors to demonise the terrorist as evil, barbarian, and inhuman. He demonstrates that the discursive construction of the terrorist's identity as a radical other is not a natural consequence; rather, it serves several political objectives, especially to make the War on Terror and policies curb human rights that would otherwise not be legitimate under normal circumstances more acceptable to the wider public. Therefore, the discursive construction of the terrorist identity has a political purpose: stripping terrorists of any personality and humanity serves to justify counter-terrorism measures and contributes to the public's perception of the threat. The narratives of radical otherness and the production of the other aid in justifying the War on Terror (Wilhelmsen 2017). This is not only a matter of legitimising measures that justify curtailment and breach of human rights and civil liberties, or the construction of an exceptional threat and enemy, as highlighted by scholars; the political language game also underscores a phenomenon of orientalist construction as a relic of colonisation deeply embedded in French political narratives.

In conclusion, the dehumanisation process is highly evident within political discourse and is correlated with various individual differences in depersonalising terrorists, such as personality traits, ideologies, behaviours, and contextual factors such as threats, objectives and emotions which underpins terrorism and the terrorist threat (Haslam and Loughnan 2014).

Depoliticisation of the terrorist enemy

While seeking the depoliticisation of the terrorist enemy, the depiction of the terrorist enemy in political discourse is highly politicised. Depoliticisation, as defined by Tsoukala (2008), refers to portraying a terrorist attack as devoid of any political objective, turning the act of terrorism into a goal in itself, with the sole aim of inflicting pain and suffering on 'our' civilisation according to decision-makers. Reflecting on poststructuralism, language is not a neutral medium serving to communicate information. Instead, language fixes meaning in discourse. Political language possesses the power to construct meaning, and hegemonic rhetoric is linked to representational practices that establish binaries, where one element is privileged over the other element (Doty 1996: 8–10). The superiority–inferiority identity-making nexus, reflected through the meta-narrative civilisation–barbarism, represents a regime of truth for political actors and therefore is also used as a mean to depoliticise the terrorist. Terrorist acts are for political actors not political actions, but products of irrational hatred and fanatical ideologies aimed at destroying our civilisation (Tsoukala 2008: 64), labelling terrorists as 'dividers' (Hollande 2015b).

Depoliticisation must also be understood as racial (Haslam and Loughnan 2014), and the analysis of French political discourse sheds light on an orientalist construction of the terrorist other through the constructed nexus of inferiority–superiority within identities. Orientalism is defined as positioning the West at a superior point in civilisation, and the orientalist scholarship was originally developed in the service of imperialism and colonialism (Said 2003). It is a way to establish boundaries between the West and the East. Said describes orientalism as the construction of an 'other Orient' inferior in comparison to the West, based on an ontological and epistemological distinction between East and West (Khalid 2017). By depoliticising the terrorist enemy, the other is in an inferior position in terms of civilisation, seen as an 'outsider' or a 'divider', reduced and voided of political content, and instead driven solely by irrational hatred and violence. Combined with the civilisation–barbarism narratives, this leads to a hierarchy of civilisation. This hierarchy classifies civilisations by what Mbembe (2011) called the fragmented logic of enclosure, with the self positioned at the top and the terrorists excluded from this civilisational hierarchy further distinguishing the self from the uncivilised other. It establishes a hierarchy of values where the West is considered as superior and civilised compared to the terrorists (Zulaika and Douglas 1996). The dehumanisation processes demonstrate the exclusion from this hierarchy, not as a position at the bottom of a hierarchy, but rather as a value of non-belonging.

Ultimately, the existing political discursive hierarchy and construction of the self versus an other, the distinction between who can be represented in the hierarchy of civilisation and those who do not belong to it, illustrates continuous colonial and imperialist legacies in Western societies (Toros 2016; Zulaika and Douglas 1996). Depoliticising the terrorists' aims and goals not only facilitates the legitimation of counter-terrorism policies (Jackson 2005) but indicates a colonial continuum in French security policies. I have used Said's critique of orientalism and Khalid's (2017) work as a model to demonstrate how to analyse political discourses and the political language game on 'Islamic terrorism', claiming to understand the East by discursively constructing it, and using persistent racialised assumptions along an East–West binary, and self–other nexus. Political discourse and political language game securitise the bodies of the enemy as a political manoeuvre, while depoliticising the terrorists, removing any political goals and objectives from their acts, and portraying them as the abnormality.

Hence, depoliticisation, depersonalisation, and dehumanisation narratives are co-constitutive – one concept reinforces the other within the discourse. Nonetheless, coloniality is not reduced to 'terrorist other' identity-making in the French approach. The French contemporary CT is entrenched in colonial legacies duplicating powers originating from the Algerian War to respond to terrorism in the present day.

The coloniality of powers of the French counter-terrorism framework

The West (re)produces and shapes representations by (re)creating binaries that purposely imply its superiority through discourse by depoliticising, dehumanising, and depersonalising the terrorist enemy other, as covered in the previous section. Indeed, the narrative of 'Islamic terrorism' is deeply ingrained in the discursive constructions of Western society (Jackson 2007) and serves as an illustration of contemporary forms of imperialism. The use of representational politics has devastating consequences for and impacts on the Muslim community, perpetuating islamophobia and racial and orientalist assumptions by the Western hegemonic powers (Majozi 2018). Moreover, within the French counter-terrorism approach, the orientalist construction of the terrorist enemy and coloniality of counter-terrorism powers (re)produce an 'internal racial other' (Rigouste 2011: 182): a postcolonial enemy within.[5] In this section, I demonstrate this coloniality in language and power to provide a comprehensive understanding of French counter-terrorism legacies.

Déchéance de nationalité: A French nationality ladder?

Discourse excludes and silences some modes of representation over others, revealing contemporary forms of imperialism and colonial structures, present within the French discourse on terrorism. Adopting a decolonial perspective and an orientalist critical lens, this section explores the framing of terrorism by French political actors to shed light on the dynamics of inclusion/exclusion and the politics of representation in global counter-terrorism research. Decolonial approaches enable scholars to investigate how and why the field of security studies legitimises certain voices while silencing others (Adamson 2020). Through this decolonial lens, we can investigate the historical exclusions and their ties to colonial, racial, and imperial legacies. In practice, and with reference to the French case study, there exists a legacy of racial politics that needs to be examined to deconstruct the orientalist construction of the 'other' identity, manifesting as a continuum embedded and perpetuated in contemporary terrorism discourse: the postcolonial enemy within. Significantly, not only does the political discourse perpetuate colonial structures; CT measures also expose and reinforce these colonial structures and legacies, as this section reveals. As a preliminary step towards analysing the French orientalist construction, we must contextualise the concept of *déchéance de nationalité*.[6] Its origins date back to 1848, with the abolition of slavery in France, when it allowed for the exclusion of those involved in slavery from French nationality. During wars of independence and decolonisation, inhabitants of former colonies had their French nationality revoked. In the contemporary times, fourteen nationalities have been revoked between 1989 and 1998, seven between 1998 and 2007, and five in 2015, due to terrorism-related reasons. The aftermath of the Charlie Hebdo attacks reignited the debate on and conceptualisation of *déchéance de nationalité*. This concept illustrates the moral, cultural, and identity inferiority attributed to the 'other', extending beyond the narratives following the Charlie Hebdo attacks. It not only reinforces the self–other dichotomy, but also serves to enhance the creation of meaning of Western identity as superior – culturally, morally, politically – in comparison to the terrorist other (Khalid 2017). The orientalist construction of identities escalated, and after the Paris attacks, the debate centred around the possibility of depriving someone suspected and/or convicted of terrorism of their French nationality, regardless of whether they hold a dual or single nationality.[7] The speech made by former French president Hollande on 16 November 2015 raises questions about the colonial continuum of counter-terrorism powers and the racialisation of the terrorist other.

Hollande declared:

> The deprivation of nationality must not result in making someone stateless, but we must be able to deprive of their French nationality an individual sentenced for an attack on the fundamental interests of the Nation or an act of terrorism, even if he was born French. I say 'even if he was born French' when he has another nationality. (2015a) (translation by the author)

The way political language is structured after the Paris attacks implies racial considerations, establishing divides between individuals perceived as worthy of French nationality and those who are not (Lambert 2021: 257). These narratives on *déchéance de nationalité* illustrate the colonial aspects of such measure, structures, and the state of being within the French counter-terrorism framework – colonialities. The explanation lies in the means implemented to control French nationality and territory, involving surveillance of both the physical space and the bodies of individuals within the space. Ultimately, the *déchéance de nationalité* highlights the superiority–inferiority nexus and recreates a hierarchy of the French nationality, producing an 'enemy within' by revoking their French nationality to reinforce the superior identity of the French national self. The national self is represented by the French national body, within which the other body would be located (Rigouste 2011: 56). Thus, it establishes a division between the 'self' (to be protected) and the 'other' (the enemy). However, within the 'self' category, it constructs the other as a securitised body to be suspected. The Defender of Rights argues against the *déchéance de nationalité* for French who only have one nationality, as it would create a distinction: those with a contested French nationality (the body other) and those with an uncontested one (the

French national body), further stigmatising French citizens with immigrant origins and distinguishing 'the French born with immigrant background' and the 'French by birth' (Geissier 2015). The debate around the *déchéance de nationalité* was discussed to be applied to French nationals who only had one nationality (i.e., the French one) and were suspected of and/or convicted for terrorism. Hollande and political decision-makers justified this possibility based on the presumption of an immigrant background that could be attributed to these terrorists, or the nationality of the country they were allegedly 'originally from', even though they had never lived there or had any connection to that country. Remarkably, it is similar to what was done during the Algerian War when the French authority sent Algerians to 'where they are from' or their 'country of origin', assuming they were never French (Lambert 2021: 79). Hence, coloniality is expressed through constructing this 'postcolonial enemy within' (Rigouste 2011). The political narratives distinguish between 'French by birth' and 'French with immigrants backgrounds', and question the assumption that the 'French by birth' cannot be suspected or convicted of terrorism. Allowing this *déchéance de nationalité* would create a hierarchy of Frenchness called the 'scale of Frenchness or purity of identity'[8] (Geissier 2015: 11), and this analysis demonstrates how it is juridically, morally, and culturally wrong. However, Hollande's attempt to include the *déchéance de nationalité* within the constitution was declared unconstitutional.

This political debate echoes historical discussions during the War in Algeria, revealing the distinction between nationality and citizenship deeply embedded in a colonial matrix and rule. The political orientalist discourse functions to construct and maintain national identity, defining the self through negation (Jackson 2007: 420). Importantly, Quijano (2000; 2007) notes that race is significant when discussing the coloniality of power and structures. The *déchéance de nationalité* only (re)inforces and intensifies Islamophobia and stigmatisation, creating a 'postcolonial internal other' that became more pronounced in the aftermath of the Paris attacks. This suggests that race is a criterion for activating the *déchéance de nationalité* as a measure of French national CT strategy.

State of emergency as a colonial legacy

On the night of the 2015 Paris attacks, Hollande declared a state of emergency in France and raised the *Vigipirate* level to its maximum.[9] The state of emergency, known as *état d'urgence* in France, has its origins in the context of the Algerian War, representing a manifestation of 'modern war' at that time. It grants military-political powers without declaring war across the whole territory, and activates war powers during peace time (Rigouste

2011; Guéguin 2022). The Law of 1955 was created during the Algerian War, following a series of terrorist attacks by the *Front de Libération Nationale Algérien* in November 1954 (Joffé 2021: 278), and it established what is now known the state of emergency regime. Empirically, and reflecting upon historical settings of those emergency powers, French decision-makers implemented the state of emergency eight times since 1955. That is, during the Algerian War and its creation (1955–62), during the revolt against colonial powers in France's Outre Mer territory, that is Kanaky (1985), Wallis, Futuna (1986), and the Polynesian archipelago îles du Vent a Ma'oji Nui (1987), during the riots in the *quartiers populaires* (2005–6), and then for the cases of Islamic terrorism after the Paris attacks (2015–17).

The purpose is not to delve into the details of the application of emergency measures, but to illustrate the continuum of the colonial matrix, the coloniality of the power and structure of the regime of emergency, and its impact on targeting such policies as the 'racialised internal other' or 'racialisation of the bodies' (Lambert 2021: 136). These policies not only securitised the space but also securitised the internal other and the terrorist enemy,[10] still demarcating the difference as a 'post-colonial enemy from within' (Rigouste 2011: 182).[11] The state of emergency is based on racial assumptions and builds upon a colonial continuum in its application. Both are intertwined, as the racialisation of bodies is genealogically rooted in the colonial history; the state-of-emergency measure was previously applied in historical colonial contexts and is today entrenched in ordinary law (see SILT bill 2017). Therefore, it illustrates the coloniality of a legal measure (SILT bill 2017: 136) incorporated in the present. Empirically, the emergency powers targeted securitised Algerians fighting against colonial power, then securitised Kanak seeking independence, reproduced against the securitised youth from the *quartiers populaires* the majority of whom came from families who experienced French colonisation (second generation of immigrants), French with immigrant's background, and then the securitised Muslims assimilated by the Government to terrorism since 2015 (Mechaï and Zine 2018; Lambert 2021). In 2005, a shift occurred as the enemy was depicted by political actors to be inside French metropolitan borders with the youth in *quartiers populaires*, necessitating the securitisation of the body and the territorial space (see also Bakkali and Perry in this volume). Then, in 2015, the securitised terrorist enemy is located in the inside. Terrorists that are born in France and perpetrate acts of terrorism inside the French borders are identified as a postcolonial enemy within (Rigouste 2011). Emergency powers were implemented and normalised, securitising the everyday as an expression of colonialities. From 2015 to 2017, France was under the regime of exceptional powers, where the exception became normalised (Guéguin 2022), specifically targeting the French Muslim community. Anti-terrorist measures were implemented in the everyday life, expressing colonial continuities. A recent example of this was the deployment of anti-terrorist police during the 2023 French revolts, which further highlights the impact of these policies on the community in the everyday.

Another essential element to illustrate the racial character of emergency powers is the focus on Islam and religion within political debates, emphasising the category of the 'Islamic radical other'. For example, reflecting on the application in Algeria, police forces did not profile and arrest Algerians who 'look like non-orientalised', meaning those wearing 'European clothes' (Lambert 2021: 64) (translation by the author). In 2005, political actors argued that the youth population in the *quartiers populaires* had been trained and manipulated by 'radical Islamists' (Lambert 2021: 235). Another expression of the vernacular is the Operative Sentinelle in 2015.[12] Through its military powers it securitised the space and the everyday by profiling French Muslims, closing places of worship, and profiling women wearing the hijab and men with beards and/or white men who had converted to Islam (Mechaï and Zine 2018), all under the cover of protecting 'sensitive' points. Additionally, political debates to ban the hijab in public space erupted every time emergency measures were activated and implemented (e.g., in 2004 in schools, in 2010 public spaces, in 2017 with the ban of the burkini, etc.). Lastly, to further demonstrate the racial and colonial continuum of counter-terrorism approaches, we compare the framing of Islamic terrorism in 2015 and terrorism perpetrated by white terrorists such as Bretons and Corses in the 1960s and 1970s. The French government never activated nor implemented emergency measures to deal with the latter's acts of terrorism.

Thus, the state of emergency as a counter-terrorism tool represents what Quijano called the coloniality of power (2000). Not only does the discourse on terrorism construct an external terrorist other, but it also draws upon a colonial matrix of powers and relations to depict an 'internal racial other' as an expression of the coloniality of being/non-being. Race is a phenomenon and an outcome of colonial domination (Quijano 2000) and was used as a criterion to classify the population in the power structure of society during colonisation, which has evolved today into new racial geo-cultural identities embedded in Western hegemonic powers. Racial assumptions demonstrate the coloniality of CT power and structures in France. It suggests a historical continuity between the colonial period (colonisation) and the present one (Lambert 2021: 42). It also signifies the colonial structures within contemporary French society (Lambert 2021: 231). A concrete example are the emergency powers which are a 'survival' from the French colonial empire (Vergès 2019: 18) as a contemporary CT tool.

Emergency powers in the hands of the executive are structured by racism and are central to it, racialising French Muslim bodies. While colonisation is over, structures and powers did not disappear (Vergès 2019: 27–8). Coloniality is a process and a movement embedded in French counter-terrorism approaches. The so-called *état d'urgence* is revealing the colonial continuum as the use of colonial powers continuously applied as a contemporary persistence in racialising spaces and bodies.

'Good versus bad Muslims' narratives

The discourse constructs both an external other, while depicting the terrorist enemy, and internal differences. The latter are produced through the discourse on 'Islamic terrorism' or the implementation of counter-terrorism measures, as well as the narrative of 'good versus bad Muslims', which is produced by Western hegemonic powers. This subsection draws upon those discursive assumptions argued to be rooted in a racist and Islamophobic Western epistemological narrative that links terrorism and Islam (Majozi 2018: 180). It leads to vilifying Islam and the Muslim community and produces a discourse on who is 'a good Muslim' and who is 'a bad one'. This narrative is a political discursive strategy (Johnson 2002: 224) argued to be politically and culturally loaded. Jackson (2007: 423) demonstrates that political rhetoric is one of the consequences of the ubiquitous public discourse that depicts Islam and Muslims as a source of terrorism, extremism, and threat, despite the other side of the discourse emphasising the need to protect the 'good Muslims' against those who distort Islam (Hollande 2015b).

To analyse the narrative of 'good versus bad Muslims' embedded in post-Charlie Hebdo and post-Paris attacks' discourse, the analysis is built on Breen-Smyth's work (2014) and her re-definition of 'suspect community' logic, adding a decolonial approach to her analysis. A range of studies investigates the effects of counter-terrorism measures on 'suspect communities' and draws upon Hillyard and others' applications of the 'suspect community' logic. While Hillyard (1993) argues that legislation and security practices produced the 'suspect community' sub-group, Breen-Smyth (2014) re-defines it by reflecting on contemporary counter-terrorism security practices, to fit with the reality experienced by this politically and culturally designed 'suspect community', and to avoid the fixed characteristics perception. That is

> ... as a group of people, or a subset of the population constructed as 'suspect' by mechanisms deployed by the state to ensure national or state security... directed at one specific population by an ethnic, religious, racial, national, or other market and the threat to that security is seen as emanating exclusively

or primarily from them. ... This creates in the public mind a suspiciousness of
people apparently in that category and renders them a 'suspect community'.
(Breen-Smyth 2014: 231–2)

The formation of a 'suspect community' by authorities carries significant
repercussions. It renders as suspect people who may be the innocent target of repressive and punitive measures created by emergency powers. The
community exists in the public's suspicious mind as constructed on and (re)
produced by imagined fears embedded in political actors' discourse on security, insecurity, and terrorism (Nickels et al. 2012). Not only it is produced
through political discourse and the public suspicious mind, it is also historically based upon a colonial, imperialist legacy, an orientalist representation of the 'other', reproduced by political actors in their contemporary
counter-terrorism approaches: the Muslim others. Political actors employ a
narrative to distinguish terrorists from 'good Muslims' in order to diminish
the effects of the label 'suspect community' on them, while using counter-
terrorism policies targeting the same people they seek to protect in their discourse. Counter-terrorism approaches impact the Muslim community and
securitised subgroups, while the Muslim community lives under pressure to
be perceived as 'good Muslims' (Breen-Smyth 2014). It therefore requires
a political performance from them, and/or the manifestation of their positions as being detached from this 'subgroup of the population that is singled
out for state attention as being "problematic"' (Pantazis and Pemberton
2009: 649).

The French decision-makers created a distinction by protecting the
French Muslim community to mitigate the use of politically and culturally
loaded labels depicted in the previous section and diminish the effect of the
'suspect community'. In practice, counter-terrorism approaches continue to
duplicate the 'suspect community' logic. Muslims, constantly discriminated,
are the principal victims of counter-terrorism measures of surveillance, profiling, and targeting (Kundnani 2015). Their bodies, spaces, religion, places
of worship, their quartiers are constantly securitised in the everyday life (see
Kaleem in this volume). I focused in this chapter on one specific manifestation of racial othering, based on the context of its production and construction by the political actors which are the Arabs and Muslims embedded in
French political discourse on terrorism. The context matters for the analysis of the political narratives of 'racial othering' which replace a discourse
on racialised bodies. Arguably, these bodies are a threat to national security and justify surveillance and suspicion according to Western hegemonic
counter-terrorism powers. (Selod 2018) for decision-makers to (re)pro-
duce a discourse that racialised their bodies, those same bodies which, as
argued by the Western hegemonic powers through their counter-terrorism

approaches, threaten security and justify their surveillance, and suspicion. This is particularly significant for the practice of the state-of-emergency measures in France between 14 November 2015 and 31 October 2017; nineteen places of worship were closed, 9,700 FSPRT *fiches* S[13] profiled Muslims for radicalisation (out of 25,000 State Security files), 12,000 people registered in FSPRT;[14] 4,469 house searches were conducted. In other words, the measures particularly targeted the French Muslim community through house raids, house arrests, closure of places of worship, profiling, and increased surveillance. Reflecting on Breen-Smyth's work (2014) on 'suspect community' and the definition of 'racial othering' by Patanzis and Pemberton (2009: 649), the race, ethnicity, religion, class, language, bodies, dress, ideology, or any combinations serve to delineate the sub-group and therefore construct and produce an internal 'other', creating internal differences (Khalid 2017; Tickner 2002: 39). Internal differences find illustration with the narratives of the *déchéance de nationalité*, the postcolonial-enemy-within logic, the colonial continuum of emergency powers, and political debate after the Paris attacks. Therefore, contemporary national security policies portray and depict Muslims as an internal other, treated with continuous suspicion, and illustrate how the French elite continue to demonise a racial other (Fekete 2004). Muslims are constantly constructed within the French political discourse following an orientalist approach and, as a race based on markers commonly associated with Islam (Koning 2016), conceptualised as a postcolonial internal and inferior other, continuously viewed as a potential threat (Rigouste 2011; Smith 2016).

Conclusion

In order to enhance the critical scholarship on terrorism, the analysis examines how the prevailing discourse on terrorism reflects on an entrenched colonial and imperialist framework. Through the lens of a French case study, the research not only reveals the presence of orientalist counter-terrorism discourse but also emphasises the enduring colonial influences within modern society and political choices. Of particular importance is the examination of French counter-terrorism approaches after the Charlie Hebdo and Paris attacks. These instances demonstrate a consistent colonial matrix in the implementation of counter-terrorism measures, as described by Quijano (2000) as the coloniality of power and structure. Not only does it depict a terrorist other from an orientalist standpoint, but it also leads to the (re)production of an internal racial other, and to racialising, stigmatising, profiling the Muslim community, and re-enforcing the 'suspect community' logic

(Breen-Smyth 2014; Hillyard 1993) as a 'postcolonial enemy within'. This chapter provides a coherent analysis of how French counter-terrorism policies build upon coloniality and colonial epistemes of race.

The first part of the analysis underlined a political orientalist discursive construction of terrorists after the Charlie Hebdo and Paris attacks, who are dehumanised using various labels from barbarians, to monsters, or to savages; who are depersonalised as the terrorist enemy, and their actions depoliticised. Additionally, the discursive constructions examined highlight the (re)construction of 'racial othering' via the use of the 'Islamic terrorism' narrative, in which decision-makers associate terrorism and religion through politics of representation of Muslims and Arabs, depoliticising their ideology, and reducing it to savagery and irrationality. The otherness meta-narrative was highlighted both by the discourse on 'Islamic terrorism' as well as on the *déchéance de nationalité*. The *déchéance de nationalité* narratives and policies brought back to the political debate a French nationality ladder, differentiating 'French by birth' and 'French with immigrant background', that would have enabled the political actor to remove the French nationality based on race. Combined with the narrative of 'good versus bad Muslims', this narrative ultimately securitises bodies and strengthens the constructed 'suspect community' in the public's mind. Such orientalist political rhetoric leads to the stigmatisation and the racialisation of the French Muslim community as being the target of counter-terrorism measures through profiling and increased surveillance.

The second part of the analysis uncovered the coloniality of power and structures of French domestic counter-terrorism approaches. The state of emergency implemented in the aftermath of the Paris attacks is an illustration of the coloniality of power in France, as a contemporary CT tool, which originated during the Algerian War. Its application was driven by racial political arguments enabling its activation, which securitised and fragmented groups – Algerians, New Caledonians, *banlieusards*, or Islamic terrorists – and spaces.

To conclude, this volume delves into diverse ways in which colonial legacies and colonial knowledge intersect with the historical and present-day aspects of counter-terrorism and illustrates how enduring effects of colonialism influence contemporary approaches to counter-terrorism in the postcolonial era. The French domestic CT approach serves as an illustration of colonialities influencing contemporary response. This chapter demonstrates that the application of emergency powers, the enemy framing, the *déchéance de nationalité*, the Sentinelle forces, and the suspect community logic are structured by racism. Counter-terrorism measures reveal the colonial continuum. Its contemporary persistence racialises and securitises spaces and bodies as a 'colonial survival measure'. While colonisation is over, its structures and powers did not disappear (Vergès 2019: 27–8).

Notes

1 'Loi Sécurité Intérieure et Lutte contre le Terrorisme': Internal Security and the Fight-Against-Terrorism Bill.
2 Translated from French by the author: 'Français de souche' and 'Français musulman'.
3 After the Charlie Hebdo attacks in January 2015, to dissociate from after the Paris attacks in November 2015.
4 'Quartiers populaires' relates to what Rigouste (2011) developes as the 'quadrillage de l'espace' (Rigouste 2011: 64), i.e., militarisation of the space.
5 Translated from French (by the author): 'ennemi de l'intérieur postcolonial'.
6 Stripping citizenship.
7 Eventually, the French Senate refused this bill, as it would render the person convicted or suspected stateless, for being anti-constitutional.
8 Author's translation of 'échelle de francité ou de pureté identitaire'.
9 Vigipirate acronym for surveillance and protection of facilities against the risk of terrorist bombing attacks. Created in 1978, it is the French national security alarm system.
10 See note 5.
11 Translated from French: 'ennemi de l'intérieur postcolonial'.
12 Operation Sentinelle is a French military operation, launched after the Charlie Hebdo attacks, reinforced after the Paris attacks, which belongs to the State of Emergency.
13 Fiche S translated as S card (stands for state security): a mechanism used by the authorities to flag an individual to be considered as a serious threat to national security.
14 'Fichier des Signalements pour la Prévention de la Radicalisation à caractère Terroriste': File treating prevent and radicalisation with a terrorist character.

References

Adamson, F. B. (2020). 'Pushing the boundaries: Can we "decolonize" security studies?', *Journal of Global Security Studies*, 5(1), 129–35.
Amnesty International (2017). France's permanent state of emergency. www.amnesty.org/en/latest/news/2017/09/a-permanent-state-of-emergency-in-france/ (accessed 29 September 2024).
Anderson, B. R. O. (1991). *Imagined Communities: Reflections on the Origin and Spread of Nationalism*. London and New York: Verso.
Attali, C. and Moussi, D. (2020). 'Islamophobia in France, National Report 2020', in Bayrakli, E. and Hafez, F. (eds) European Islamophobia Report 2020.
Boyle, J. M. (2021). 'Introduction', in Boyle, J. M. (ed.) *Non-Western Responses to Terrorism*. Manchester University Press, pp. 1–19.
Breen-Smyth, M. (2014). 'Theorising the "suspect community": Counterterrorism, security practices and the public imagination', *Critical Studies on Terrorism*, 7(2), 223–40.
Campbell, D. (1998). *Writing Security: United States Foreign Policy and the Politics of Identity*. Minneapolis, MN: University of Minnesota Press.

Cazeneuve, B. (2015). Déclaration de M. Bernard Cazeneuve, ministre de l'intérieur, sur l'enquête concernant les auteurs de l'attentat au siège de l'hebdomadaire "Charlie Hebdo" et de la fusillade de Montrouge (Hauts-de-Seine), le déclenchement du niveau d'Alerte Attentat du plan Vigipirate et la nécessité de préserver le consensus républicain dans la défense de la liberté de la presse et des valeurs de la démocratie, Paris le 8 janvier 2015. www.vie-publique.fr/discours/193476-declaration-de-m-bernard-cazeneuve-ministre-de-linterieur-sur-lenqu (accessed 29 September 2024).

Césaire, A. (2000). *Discours sur le colonialisme, suivi de: Discours sur la Négritude*. Paris: Présence Africaine.

Doty, R. L. (1996). *Imperial Encounters: The Politics of Representation in North-South Relations*. Minneapolis, MN and London: University of Minnesota Press.

Bayrakli. E. and Hafez, F. (eds) (2020). European Islamophobia Report, SETA Foundation, http://fra.europa.eu/en/databases/anti-muslim-hatred/node/6106

Fekete, L. (2004). Anti-Muslim Racism and the European Security State. *Race & Class*, 46, 3–29.

Foucault, M. (1993). *Surveiller et punir: Naissance de la prison*. Paris: Gallimard.

Geisser, V. (2015). 'Déchoir de la nationalité des djihadistes "100 % made in France": qui cherche-t-on à punir?', *Migrations Société*, 162(6), 3–14.

Guéguin, M. (2022). 'The normalisation of exceptional counterterrorism powers: the case of France', PhD thesis. University of Leeds.

Haslam, N. (2006). 'Dehumanization: An integrative review', *Personality and Social Psychology Review*, 10(3), 252–64.

Haslam, N. and Loughnan, S. (2014). 'Dehumanization and infrahumanization', *Annual Review of Psychology*, 65, 399–423.

Hillyard, P. (1993). *Suspect Community: People's Experience of the Prevention of Terrorism Acts in Britain*. London: Pluto Press.

Holland, J. (2016). 'The language of counter-terrorism', in Jackson, R. (ed.) *Routledge Handbook of Critical Terrorism Studies*. Abingdon: Routledge, pp. 203–14.

Hollande, F. (2015a). Déclaration de M. François Hollande, Président de la République, devant le Parlement réuni en Congrès à la suite des attaques terroristes perpétrées à Paris et en Seine-Saint-Denis, Versailles le 16 novembre 2015. www.vie-publique.fr/discours/196856-declaration-de-m-francois-hollande-president-de-la-republique-devant (accessed 29 September 2024).

Hollande, F. (2015b). Déclaration de M. François Hollande, Président de la République, sur la culture contre l'obscurantisme et les fanatismes, à Paris le 14 janvier 2015. www.elysee.fr/francois-hollande/2015/01/14/declaration-de-m-francois-hollande-president-de-la-republique-sur-la-culture-contre-lobscurantisme-et-les-fanatismes-a-paris-le-14-janvier-2015 (accessed 29 September 2024).

Jackson, R. (2007). 'Constructing enemies: "Islamic terrorism" in political and academic discourse', *Government and Opposition*, 42(3), 394–426. https://doi.org/10.1111/j.1477–7053.2007.00229.x

Jackson, R. (2005). *Writing the War on Terrorism: Language, Politics and Counter-Terrorism*. Manchester: Manchester University Press.

Joffé, G. (2021). 'Algeria: Algeria's response to violent extremism', in Boyle, J. M. (ed.) *Non-Western Responses to Terrorism*. Manchester: Manchester University Press.

Johnson, R. (2002). 'Defending ways of life: The (anti)terrorist rhetoric of Bush and Blair', *Theory, Culture & Society*, 19(4), 211–31.

Kelman, H. C. (1979). 'An interactional approach to conflict resolution and its application to Israeli-Palestinian relations', *International Interactions*, 6(2), 99–122.

Khalid, M. (2017). *Gender, Orientalism, and the 'War on Terror': Representation, Discourse, and Intervention in Global Politics*. London: Routledge.

Koning, M. de (2016). ' "You need to present a counter-message": The racialisation of Dutch Muslims and anti-Islamophobia initiatives' *Journal of Muslims in Europe*, 5(2), 170–89.

Kundnani, A. (2015). *The Muslims Are Coming!: Islamophobia, Extremism, and the Domestic War on Terror*. London: Verso.

Lambert, L. (2021). *États d'urgence: Une histoire spatiale du continuum colonial français*. Toulouse : Premiers matins de novembre.

Majozi, N. (2018). 'Theorising the Islamic State: A decolonial perspective', *ReOrient*, 3(2), 163–84.

Mbembe, A. (2011). 'Preface', in Fanon, F., *Oeuvres*. Paris: La Découverte.

Mechaï, Z. (2018). *L'État d'urgence (permanent)*. Paris: MeltingBook.

Nickels, H. C., Thomas, L., Hickman, M. J., and Silvestri, S. (2012). 'Constructing "suspect" communities and Britishness: Mapping British press coverage of Irish and Muslim communities, 1974–2007', *European Journal of Communication*, 27(2), 135–51.

Pantazis, C., Pemberton, S. (2009). 'From the "old" to the "new" suspect community: Examining the impacts of recent UK counter-terrorist legislation', *The British Journal of Criminology*, 49(5), 646–66.

Quijano, A. (2007). 'Questioning "race" ', *Socialism and Democracy*, 21(1), 45–53.

Quijano, A. (2000). 'Coloniality of Power and Eurocentrism in Latin America', *International Sociology*, 15(2), 215–32.

Rigouste, M. (2011). *L'ennemi intérieur*. Paris: La Découverte.

Said, E. W. (2003). *Orientalism*. London: Penguin Classics.

Scrimin, S. and Rubaltelli, E. (2021). 'Dehumanization after terrorism: The role of psychophysiological emotion regulation and trait emotional intelligence', *Current Psychology*, 40(6), 2704–14.

Selod, S. (2018). 'Islamophobia and racism in America', *Contemporary Sociology: A Journal of Reviews*, 47(5), 607–9.

SILT (2017). Loi renforçant la sécurité intérieure et la lutte contre le terrorisme. 30 Octobre 2017.

Smith, H. J. (2016). 'Britishness as racist nativism: A case of the unnamed "other" ', *Journal of Education for Teaching*, 42(3), 298–313.

Taubira, C. (2015). Interview de Mme Christiane Taubira, garde des sceaux, ministre de la justice, avec France Info le 8 janvier 2015, sur l'attentat contre Charlie Hebdo et la lutte contre le terrorisme. www.vie-publique.fr/discours/ 193495-interview-de-mme-christiane-taubira-garde-des-sceaux-ministre-de-la-ju (accessed 29 September 2024).

Tickner, J. A. (2002). 'Feminist Perspectives on 9/11', *International Studies Perspectives*, 3(4), 333–50.

Toros, H. (2016). 'Dialogue, praxis and the state: A response to Richard Jackson', *Critical Studies on Terrorism*, 9(1), 126–30.

Toros, H. (2012). *Terrorism, Talking and Transformation: A Critical Approach*. Abington: Routledge.

Tsoukala, A. (2008). 'Defining the terrorist threat in the post-September 11 era', in Bigo, D and Tsoukala, A. (eds) *Terror, Insecurity and Liberty*. London: Routledge.

Tuastad, D. (2003). 'Neo-orientalism and the new barbarism thesis: Aspects of symbolic violence in the Middle East conflict(s)', *Third World Quarterly*, 24(4), 591–9.

Valls, M. (2015a). 'Déclaration de M. Manuel Valls, Premier ministre, sur l'attentat au siège de l'hebdomadaire "Charlie Hebdo", le suivi par le Gouvernement de la situation, l'appel à la responsabilité et à la prudence dans la diffusion d'informations sur l'événement et la sécurité des futures manifestations d'unité nationale'. www.vie-publique.fr/discours/193475-declaration-de-m-manuel-valls-premier-ministre-sur-lattentat-au-sieg (accessed 29 September 2024).

Valls, M. (2015b). 'Interview de M. Manuel Valls, Premier ministre, à BFM TV le 12 janvier 2015, sur la manifestation républicaine du 11 en hommage à "Charlie Hebdo", le plan Vigipirate et le renforcement des moyens de lutte contre le terrorisme'. www.vie-publique.fr/discours/193540-interview-de-m-manuel-valls-premier-ministre-bfm-tv-le-12-janvier-2 (accessed 29 September 2024).

Valls, M. (2015c). 'Interview de M. Manuel Valls, Premier ministre, à France Inter le 17 novembre 2015, sur les principales mesures annoncées par le président François Hollande devant le Parlement à Versailles trois jours après les attentats perpétrés à Paris et en Seine-Saint-Denis'. www.vie-publique.fr/discours/196836-interview-de-m-manuel-valls-premier-ministre-france-inter-le-17-nov

Vergès, F. (2019). *Un féminisme décolonial*. Paris: La Fabrique.

Wilhelmsen, J. (2017). 'How does war become a legitimate undertaking? Re-engaging the post-structuralist foundation of securitization theory', *Cooperation and Conflict*, 52(2), 166–183.

Zulaika, J. and Douglass, W. (1996). *Terror and Taboo: The Follies, Fables, and Faces of Terrorism*. New York: Routledge.

Part II

Global, national, and everyday counter-terrorism practices

5

Comparative counter-terrorism: All for one, but NOT one for all

Graig R. Klein

Counter-terrorism has become a global governance issue. Bilateral and multilateral cooperation and coordination proliferated at an astonishing level as terrorism and terrorists were catapulted into a global threat following the 11 September 2001 attacks in the United Sates, and subsequent spectacular attacks in Madrid 2004, London 2005, and Mumbai 2008, among many other terrorist attacks. Since the 11 September 2001 terrorist attacks, the international community has invested billions of dollars in counter-terrorism (CT) and governments have, often encouraged by the USA and Western Europe, made it a central pillar of international relations (Renard 2021: 2). The shared international threat of terrorism has encouraged many countries to prioritise CT bilateral and multilateral collaboration and coordination. As a result, some Global South countries have become intimate partners in CT efforts, but many others remain subjugated participants in Global North countries' CT efforts and pursuits of global and national security.[1] Yet, systematic cross-national analyses of CT efforts are largely restricted to Western liberal democracies, in particular North America and Europe. While a large corpus of research on CT in the Global South exists, it is primarily case studies that provide phenomenal depth and within case exploration. There remain few multi-country comparisons studies of Global North and Global South CT.

There is excellent research on CT in the Global South that heavily relies on in-depth case studies and critical analyses (Boyle 2019). Western/Eurocentric models continue to dominate the field, especially in the quantitative study of counter-terrorism even though they risk lacking cross-national external validity and generalisability. This means quantitative theory testing and analyses of CT may produce biased, inefficient, and potentially false results. A consequence of this is that CT remains a patchwork of inefficient policies two-decades after being catapulted to the global governance stage (Renard 2021). Imposing lessons learned from the Global North – both from analytical models and tangible experiences – on Global South countries without accounting for differences in governance structures, regional or local norms, culture, and threat perceptions could be a central cause or source of these inefficiencies. The in-depth case studies of Global South CT efforts identify critical context specific goals, limitations, and perceptions of Global North and/or external and international CT policies, practices, impositions, and implications. But the lack of systematic cross-national explorations and analyses bridging these differences within the Global South or across the North-South divide inhibits comprehensive studies of CT. It also limits the lessons researchers can provide to policymakers for strengthening CT cooperation, implementation, and effectiveness.

This is not for a lack of desire or value to academic and policy communities. Rather, the dearth of public information and resulting limitations on data collection, coding, and measurement are challenges (Lehrke and Schomaker 2016; Schmid et al. 2021: 159). Cross-national empirical analyses of CT efforts and coordination typically test theories and models using samples of Western or democratic countries because they are generally more transparent, allowing for some data collection. For example, Crelinsten and Schmid (1993) analyse CT in Western Europe categorising it into Defensive, Reconciliatory, Criminal Justice, and War models. Building on their work, Pedahzur's (2009) study of Israeli CT shows that intelligence efforts can be included in CT models and that there is significant overlap and boundary sharing among these different models. Van Dongen's (2010) categorisation of CT agencies in ten EU countries adds empirical, or measurable, dimensions that help identify countries' practices. Perliger and Milton (2018) introduce a cross-national CT dataset, but their focus is on bi-lateral cooperation against domestic terrorism and not identifying or measuring countries' CT models. D'Amato's (2021) work brings many of these different pieces together using qualitative data to classify and identify the patchwork of multilateral CT by European countries in the Sahel, but the data remains Euro-centric.

This chapter introduces an alternative approach and potential solution: the Comparative Counterterrorism Project (CCTP), a database of CT legislation and law enforcement, security services, military, and judicial CT efforts. CCTP includes ninety-six countries and administrative territories in the Global North and Global South from 2016 to 2019. Now, CT models that are primarily theorised based on Global North, particularly Western liberal democracies, policies and practices, can also be theorised and analysed in the Global South.

The remainder of the chapter discusses CT models and how they have evolved. It then introduces CCTP in detail leading to a description of the data. Using this new data, countries are classified into counter-terrorism models and submitted to statistical analyses exploring similarities and differences in the Global North and Global South. The analyses show that while global CT coordination and cooperation has resulted in some Global South countries becoming intimate partners in global security, there are important differences in Global North and Global South approaches to CT. Some of these differences are attributed to governance structures and systems, particularly in the Global South, and cannot be explained by terrorist threat, thus affirming that CT is a security *and* political problem. For example, an increased frequency of international terrorist attacks in a Global North country is expected to impact the country's CT approach but does not have a statistically significant effect on Global South CT practices. A country's governance structure (e.g., parliamentary democracy, presidential democracy, or autocracy) influences CT approaches much more in the Global South than in the Global North. We are now better able to ask what motivates CT decision-making, policies, and efforts in the Global South and identify global, regional, and/or local patterns of diffusion, decision-making, and coordination.

CT models

At a foundational level, CT can be a binary classification between offensive and defensive. Offensive CT takes the fight to terrorists to diminish their capabilities, whereas defensive CT focuses on deterrence by increasing the physical and resource costs for conducting attacks. While increased defense improves security by reducing the frequency of attacks, it does not necessarily weaken terrorist groups and can redirect attacks to new or softer targets (Enders and Sandler 1993; Lehrke and Schomaker 2016). Others classify it as proactive, or anticipatory and reactive, or soft power and hard power (Schmid et al. 2021). These differences reflect efforts removing terrorists and/or their resources versus focusing on protecting places and reducing opportunity to attack (McIlhatton et al. 2020). And still others define CT as intervention and prevention (Eijkman and Schuurman 2011), or as upstream and downstream policies focused on security and protection at home versus abroad (Renard 2021). But rigid binary classifications obfuscate how important tactics, categories, types, or strategies are combined when implementing counter-terrorism.

Crelinsten and Schmid (1993) are early innovators for categorising CT beyond binary classifications. They developed four models to CT – defensive, reconciliatory, criminal justice, and war – where each has distinct state aims and means, legal aspects, and agents. Countries prescribing to the defensive model see terrorism as a physical and psychological threat. The reconciliatory model sees it as a political problem. The criminal justice model considers terrorism as a criminal act, and, to the war model, terrorism is an act of war (Crelinsten and Schmid 1993). But their classification relies on rigid boundaries for each model.

Following the 11 September attacks in the United States, the 9/11 Report highlights the need to un-silo CT efforts because the 'responsibility for dealing with terrorism is widely distributed, and lines of jurisdiction tend to be blurred and overlapping, with no clear monopoly of the issue' (Crenshaw 2001: 330). The USA was not alone in realising this. The 2003 European Council stated that counter-terrorism necessitates a multi-faceted strategy integrating policing, judicial, military, economic, and intelligence capabilities (Albrecht 2008). These changes forced CT models to catch-up and evolve to reflect multi-faceted dynamics.

Bhoumik (2004) argues that the expanded intelligence service powers and jurisdiction necessitates adding an intelligence model. But adding models continues upholding artificial boundaries. Pedahzur and Ranstorp's (2001) theorise counter-terrorism as a continuum that accounts for overlapping responsibilities, jurisdictions, and coordination (Boyle 2018). For example, Pedahzur and Ranstorp (2001) develop an expanded criminal justice model based on Israel's mix of war and criminal justice efforts and agents, which is reinforced by some countries' reliance on gendarmeries for CT because they have both military and law enforcement training and jurisdiction (Mustafa 2020). Pedahzur (2009) additionally details the messy boundaries of criminal justice, reconciliatory, and war models of Israeli CT providing more evidence for thinking in a continuum.

Others shift the focus to direct actions classifying CT as (1) doing nothing (2) conciliation (3) legal reform (4), restrictions, and (5) violence (Miller 2007). Bellasio et al. (2018) categorise CT as: (1) military (2) policing, and (3) legal intelligence and capacity building. Van Dongen (2010) uses the EU CT strategy categories of prevent, protect, pursue, and respond and UNODC's categories of CT policies to develop empirically measurable parameters, classifying nine EU countries into maximalist, human agent, and confrontational approaches to CT. Maximalist countries treat terrorism as a 'multifaceted phenomenon' and practice all four EU CT strategies. Human agent countries prefer prevent and pursue to protect and respond, and confrontational countries prefer pursue and 'take the fight... to the terrorists' (van Dongen 2010: 234–5).

The rapid and intense growth in bilateral and multilateral CT cooperation and legislative convergence led to new and more specific areas of CT resulting in broadening some theories and modelling beyond Western and/or liberal democracies. Geographic expansion was forced in part because CT cooperation happens within and outside the West. Shared and cooperative approaches to CT led to a convergence in legislation and regulations (Pokalova 2015; Lehrke and Schomaker 2014; Epifanio 2011; Whitaker 2007; Josua 2021). For example, bilateral cooperation between the USA and Middle East countries is a standard bearer of US CT policy (Dunne and Wehrey 2014). The historical reliance on Western countries for cross-national analysis and CT modelling severely restricts understanding why countries sometimes cooperate in CT and sometimes do not (Perliger and Milton 2018). But, improving our understanding of CT cooperation is challenging because cooperation occurs along multiple dimensions, multiple actors, at different levels of government and governance, and sometimes includes public-private partnerships and private actors (D'Amato 2021).

One way to conceptualise cooperation is to think of it as a three-dimensional patchwork of strategic-political, operational, and procedural cooperation (D'Amato 2021). Another way is Perliger and Milton's (2018) identification of 'pair[s] of countries who have been attacked at least once by the same organization' (207) to analyse causes for bilateral CT cooperation. Reflecting the reality that 'CT policy can no longer remain compartmentalized in one or two policy areas' and that any adequate model must account for newer whole of government approaches, Crelinsten (2018) updates the original four models into multi-layered CT philosophies (363).

The recognition that the boundaries of Crelinsten and Schmid's (1993) CT models can be messy is potentially of more concern for non-US and non-European countries because these countries' police-military and domestic-international jurisdictional boundaries are often overlapping, ill-defined, or interwoven (Boyle 2018). And key to improving cross-national CT modelling is focusing on actions because they show behaviours and not just membership in an organisation (Perliger and Milton 2018). But the dearth of CT data has inhibited large-N cross-national studies of strategies and models that apply to both Western and non-Western, liberal democracies and autocracies, and Global North and Global South countries. In general, CT research suffers from a data problem as there are very few public CT databases (Schmid et al. 2021). There are no easy solutions to the CT data problem. The intrinsic secretive nature of CT and the growing expanse of policy-domains and tactics included in it make cross-national in-depth data collection immensely challenging. But there is hope for continued innovations in CT data collection. The Comparative Counterterrorism Project (CCTP), introduced in the next section, offers a new database measuring multiple dimensions of countries' CT efforts across a diverse sample of ninety-six countries and administrative territories from 2016 to 2019.

The Comparative Counterterrorism Project

The Comparative Counterterrorism Project (CCTP) codes countries' CT efforts using information from United States (USA) Department of State Country Reports on Terrorism (USCRT). The reports identify legislative and legal procedures, policies, kinetic and non-kinetic operations,[2] and judicial processes used in identifying, interdicting, combatting, and prosecuting terrorists and terrorist groups. United States Code, Title 22, Chapter 38, Section 2656f mandates the Department of State provide yearly reports on foreign countries where significant international terrorism occurred, that are state sponsors of terrorism (specifically identified as important in the War on Terror by the US Secretary of State), or that the USA has sought CT cooperation from. Information for USCRT comes from in-country officials, US Embassy staff, and local sources. Some of the stipulations for including countries in USCRT are vulnerable to political processes and decision thus introducing an inherent risk of bias in the inclusion criteria and country assessments. As a result, not all countries are included in USCRT. Also, new countries may not be included in a report until after there are significant increases in the frequency or scale of terrorist attacks. Figure 5.1 highlights this limitation of the primary data source. But similar US State Department Country Reports on Human Rights Practices are the primary data source for gold-standard human rights databases including the Cingranelli-Richards Human Rights Database (Cingranelli et al. 2014), Political Terror Scale (Gibney et al. 2021), and Sub National Analysis of Repression Project (Cordell et al. 2020; 2022).

CCTP uses the 'Overview', 'Terrorist incidents', and 'Legislation, law enforcement, and border security' sections to code countries' CT efforts. From 2016 to 2019, ninety-four countries (Israel and Palestine are separately reported, and both included as separate countries in CCTP), Macau, and Hong Kong are included in USCRT covering a diverse set of government types, levels of economic development, terrorism hotspots, and high-risk terrorist attack target states as seen in Figure 5.1. Countries were included in USCRT every year except for Burundi (2016), Cuba (2019), Democratic Republic of Congo (2018–19), Ireland (2016), and Mozambique (2018–19).

For each country–year, CCTP contains information on new or amended CT laws and codes, which government office or body proposed legislative changes, the objective(s) of the legislation, and the state agent(s) it would affect. It also provides the number of new terrorism cases at different stages of criminal justice and judicial processes (i.e., investigations opened, cases in court, cases dismissed). The date and state agent(s) used in kinetic CT operations included in a country report (i.e., police, gendarmerie, special forces)

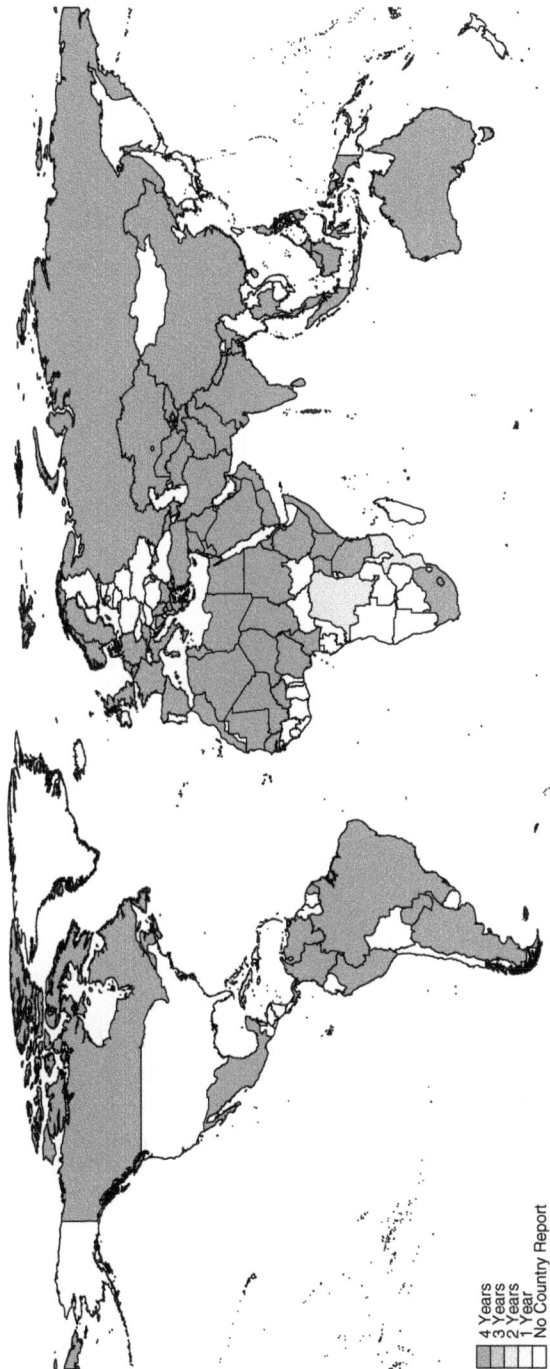

Figure 5.1: CCTP geographic coverage (*source*: author's own work)

Legend:
4 Years
3 Years
2 Years
1 ear
No Country Report

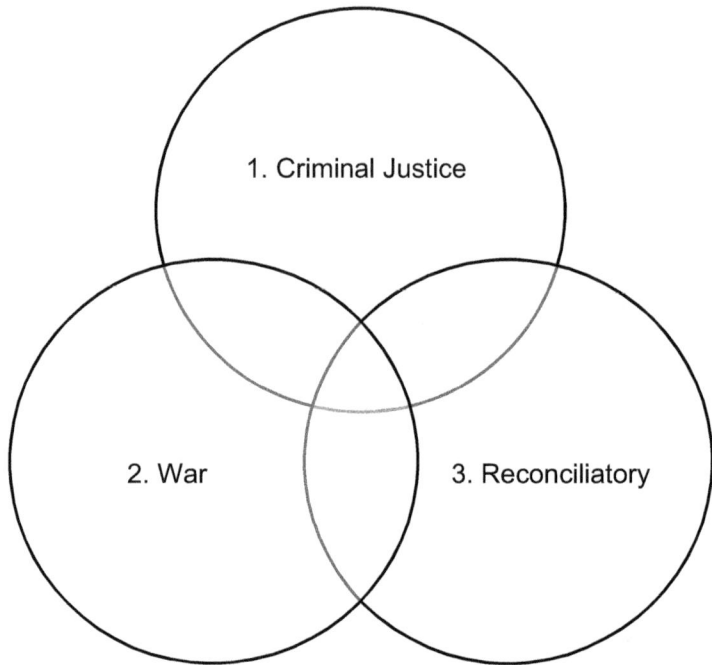

Figure 5.2: CCTP models (*source:* author's own work)

are also coded. If USCRT include information on newly created CT units or agencies, changes to border security, government agencies named as responsible for CT and/or border security (non-kinetic and kinetic operations, as well as general jurisdictional responsibility), names terrorist group or ideologies, specific actions taken against terrorist group(s) or ideology(ies), and/or foreign fighter repatriation(s), deportation(s), and/or citizenship revocation(s), it is coded in CCTP. In addition, qualitative description of CT and border security are included in CCTP.[3]

Using these coded components, multi-dimensional CCTP models are constructed building from Crelinsten and Schmid's (1993) seminal work, but, importantly, overcoming the compartmentalisation of their models. Defensive and intelligence models are omitted because all countries are assumed to take at least minimal defensive measures and employ some level of intelligence collection and analysis. USCRT also lack information on defensive and intelligence efforts. By focusing on criminal justice, war, and reconciliatory models, the classification of countries identifies core philosophies and strategies defining their CT. Figure 5.2 illustrates the effect of considering overlapping boundaries and how it turns three models into seven updated CCTP models of: (1) Criminal Justice, (2) War, (3) Reconciliatory, (4) Criminal Justice–War, (5) Criminal Justice–Reconciliatory, (6) War–Reconciliatory, and (7) Criminal Justice–War–Reconciliatory.

Using Table 5.1, three binary variables are created corresponding to Criminal Justice, War, and Reconciliatory. If any of the CCTP indicators for one of these types of CT are present, then the corresponding binary variable is coded as 1. If none of the CCTP indicators are present, the corresponding binary variable is coded as 0. A country–year can be coded as implementing none, one, two, or all three of the corresponding models. For example, in 99.5 per cent of country–years, the government implemented at least one component of criminal justice (Eritrea 2019 and Albania 2017 were not coded as CJ). The distribution in Table 5.2 shows that in many country–years more than one of Crelinsten and Schmid's (1993) original models are implemented. CCTP helps untangle where this overlap occurs and provides an empirical classification scheme. As seen in Table 5.3, criminal justice efforts are routinely implemented and war and reconciliatory are never exclusive efforts. This verifies Pedahzur and Ranstorp's (2001), Boyle's (2018), and Pedahzur's (2009) emphasis on the importance of considering overlapping boundaries.

CCTP models are classifications that can vary on a yearly basis depending on a country's changes to legislation, kinetic operations, activities within the judicial system, or direct actions by state agents. The country–year unit of observation allows for annual variation so that a country moves from one CCTP model to another if their efforts evolve as seen in Figure 5.3.[4]

There is substantial global diversity in CCTP models and significant variation within countries across the four years. Using 2016 as the initial comparison year, from 2017 to 2019, change in a country's CCTP model from 2016 is observed in 52.8 per cent of country–years. For example, Russia implemented a CJ-W-R model in 2016 and 2017, a CJ-R model in 2018, and a CJ model in 2019. While criminal justice remained a foundation of Russian counter-terrorism, war and reconciliatory efforts vary over time. Brazil's approach to counter-terrorism also varied, but in a different pattern, oscillating between a CJ-W-R model in 2016 and 2018 and a CJ model in 2017 and 2019. India's approach also varies, implementing a CJ-R model in 2016, CJ in 2017 and 2018, and escalating kinetic counter-terrorism in 2019 resulting in a CJ-W-R model. Using this classification scheme, CCTP models can be submitted to statistical analyses to improve our understanding of government's CT efforts.

Table 5.1: Constructing CCTP models

Criminal Justice	CCTP Indicators:
	1. Actions against terrorist group(s)
	  • arrest, border security or deportation, designation as terror organisation, investigations, legal action
	2. Actions against terrorist ideology(ies)
	  • arrest, border security or deportation, investigations, legal action
	3. Law enforcement investigations
	  • investigations opened, investigations closed
	4. Judicial procedures
	  • suspects arrested, prosecution, cases in court, cases waiting trial, charges opened, cases or charges dismissed
	5. Residency/citizenship status
	FTFs deported or repatriated, citizen revocation
	
	CCTP measurement:
	1. all are binary variables [0 = no mention, 1 = mentioned]
	2. all are binary variables [0 = no mention, 1 = mentioned]
	3. count of new cases per country–year
	4. count of new cases per country–year
	5. count of new cases per country–year

War	CCTP indicators:
	1. Actions against terrorist group(s)
	  • CT operations
	2. Actions against terrorist ideology(ies)
	  • CT operations
	3. Kinetic deployments or missions
	
	CCTP measurements:
	1. binary variables [0 = no mention, 1 = mentioned]
	2. binary variables [0 = no mention, 1 = mentioned]
	3. binary variables [0 = no mention, 1 = mentioned]

Reconciliatory	CCTP indicators:
	1. Actions against terrorist group(s)
	  • legislation
	2. Actions against terrorist ideology(ies)
	  • legislation
	3. CT legislative activity
	  • new code or law, amended code or law
	
	CCTP measurements:
	1. binary variables [0 = no mention, 1 = mentioned]
	2. binary variables [0 = no mention, 1 = mentioned]
	3. binary variables [0 = no activity, 1 = activity]

Source: author's own work.

Table 5.2: Distribution of overarching CT by country–year

	Criminal Justice		War		Reconciliatory	
	Freq.	Percent	Freq.	Percent	Freq.	Percent
0	2	0.54	270	72.78	216	58.22
1	369	99.46	101	27.22	155	41.78

Source: author's own work.

Table 5.3: CCTP model distribution per country–year

	Frequency	Percent
Criminal Justice	162	43.90
Criminal Justice–War	52	14.09
Criminal Justice–Reconciliatory	106	28.73
Criminal Justice–War–Reconciliatory	49	13.28
Total	369	100

Source: author's own work.

Statistical analysis

Building from previous studies of counter-terrorism decision-making, counter-terrorism cooperation, and rates or frequency of terrorist attacks, I test three categories of influences on governments' CT choices: (1) security threats, (2) political structures, and (3) socio-economic factors.

Security threats

The first security threat focuses on terrorism by measuring terrorist attack frequency and casualties. The Global Terrorism Database (GTD) (START 2019) provides information on terrorist attacks and the INT_ANY variable is used to define *Domestic Attacks* and *International Attacks* as counts of the number of each type per country–year. *Domestic Casualties* and *International Casualties* are counts of the total number of each type of casualty per country–year. Domestic and international terrorism could present different levels of threat to the government and population. For example, variations in the size, target, and intended audience, all of which underscores perceived security threat, can correlate with an attack being international or

CT Model per Country–Year

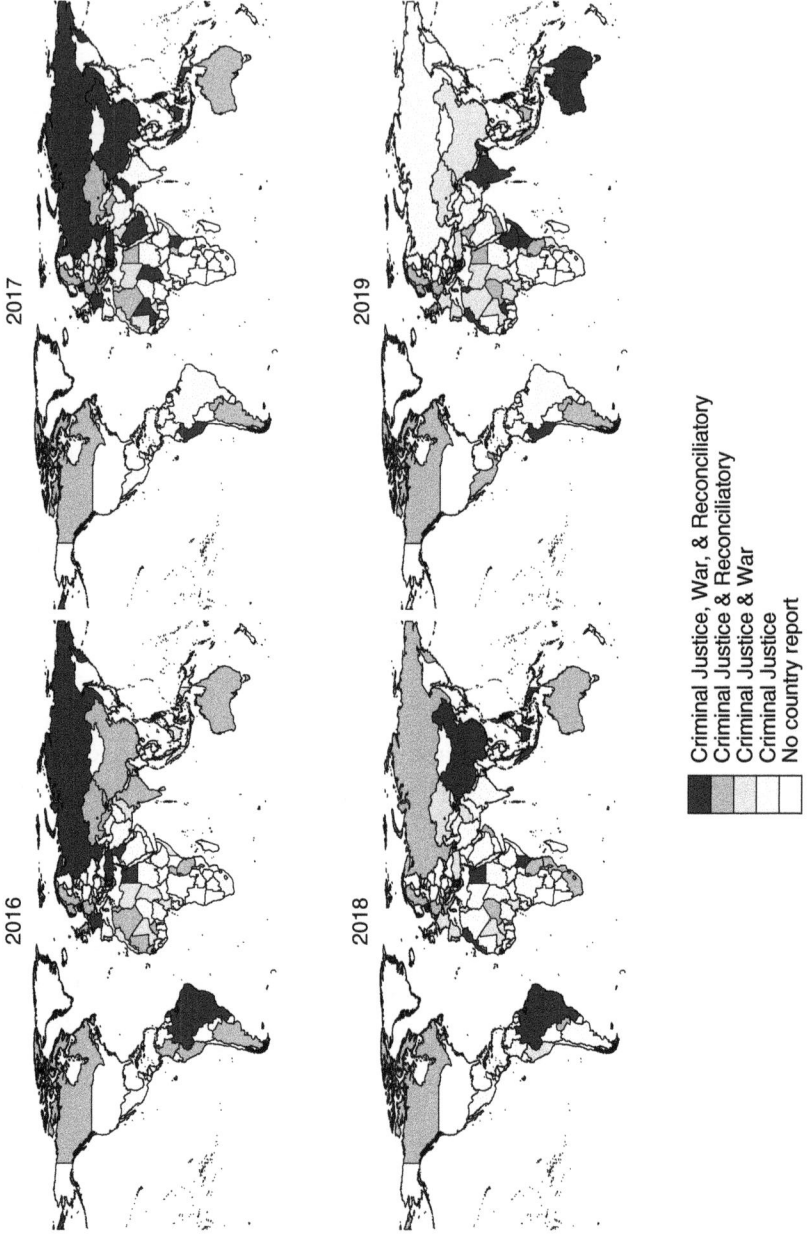

Figure 5.3: Mapping CCTP models per country–year (*source:* author's own work)

domestic (Klein 2016). As a result, international and domestic attacks can motivate different CT efforts.

In the CCTP sample, Domestic Attacks ranges from 0 to 1,295, with 58 per cent of country–years recording 0 attacks. International Attacks ranges from 0 to 1,231, with 45 per cent of country–years recording 0 attacks. Domestic Casualties ranges from 0 to 12,703 and 63 per cent of the sample records 0 casualties. International Casualties ranges from 0 to 15,886 and 29 per cent of the sample records 0 casualties. 8.5 per cent of the country–years recording no domestic casualties, record at least one domestic terrorist attack. And in 12.6 per cent of the country–years with at least one international terrorist attack, there are no casualties recorded To account for these uneven distributions and standardise the measures, I add one and take the natural log.

All measures of terrorist attacks and casualties are implemented as a one-year lag, measuring how terrorism the previous year influences CT in the current year. Including these variables and CT efforts in the same country–year would introduce significant endogeneity into the models as it is impossible at a country–year level of analysis to determine which came first, an increased terrorist threat or CT efforts, or if an increase in terrorist attacks is a response to CT operations.

I also account for armed conflict during the country–year because CT can provide a rationale and tool for governments to combat rebel forces. Using the UCDP/PRIO Armed Conflict Dataset v21.1 (Pettersson et al. 2021; Gleditsch et al. 2002), I include a count measure of all ongoing civil wars in a country–year that have at least twenty-five battle-related deaths. *Armed Conflict* is also implemented as a one-year lag, to reduce endogeneity issues of increased CT triggering conflict in the country–year of observation.

Political structures

Politics and counter-terrorism are inextricably connected. Political leaders decide how to allocate resources and what groups or individuals to target, making CT a political decision. A country's regime type could influence CT decision-making in many ways (Perliger 2012). Democracies take longer to pass new legislation than autocracies because of debate rules and procedures and because autocrats target political opponents with CT legislation (Whitaker 2007). Some regime types are more prone to distorting terrorism threats to legitimise political uses of CT legislation, surveillance and intelligence collection, and law enforcement actions against political rivals and dissidents than others. This happened in MENA following the Arab Spring protests (Josua 2021). To account for this, I include a categorical measure of *Regime Type*: parliamentary democracy, mixed democracy, presidential democracy, civilian autocracy, military autocracy, or royal autocracy (Bjørnskov and Rode 2020).

Human rights practices can also influence CT. The balance of civil liberties and CT is the centre of a large body of scholarship. Countries that do not respect civil liberties and human rights may find it easier to implement punitive and ruthless CT efforts like mass incarcerations and kill-first operations. To account for this, I include a five-category measure of *Human Rights* using the Political Terror Scale, whereby higher scores correspond to worse human rights practices (Gibney et al. 2021). For the analysis I use the measure based on the US Department of State Country Reports on Human Rights Practices.

Socio-economic factors

To account for socio-economic factors that could impact a government's ability to invest in different types of CT, a country's *GDP* per capita and population are included (World Bank 2022a; 2022b). Country size could also impact CT because larger countries have more geographic area in need of security and protection. It could create potential variation in coordination and logistical costs, population centres may be more spread out and distant from one another, or decisions about concentrating security in certain areas and leaving others potentially vulnerable to attack could vary depending on country size. (Mustafa 2020). *Land Area* measures country size in square kilometers (World Bank 2022c). All three measures are operationalised using the natural log.

Summary statistics

To maximise the four years of CCTP data, indicator measures from 2015 to 2019 are used so that the one-year lagged specifications can be included allowing analyses of the full CCTP sample from 2016 to 2019. Summary statistics are included in Table 5.4.[5] This is not an exhaustive list of determinants. It is a starting point to improve our understanding of what influences CT decision-making cross-nationally using a sample of geographically, politically, and economically diverse countries.

Testing CCTP models

A series of binary and multinomial logit regressions are conducted. The binary logit regression specification assumes that governments are selecting a CT type independent of all other options. That is, the government selects one CCTP model or not. For these models, I created four dependent variables corresponding to the CCTP models in Table 5.3. If a country–year practiced a CCTP model, then the corresponding dependent variable

Table 5.4: Summary statistics for determinants of counter-terrorism type

	N	Mean	Std. dev.	Min.	Max.
Domestic attacks$_{(t-1)}$	351	1.42	2.00	0	7.07
International attacks$_{(t-1)}$	351	1.42	1.70	0	7.12
Domestic casualties$_{(t-1)}$	351	1.78	2.60	0	9.41
International casualties$_{(t-1)}$	351	2.01	2.53	0	9.67
Armed conflict	369	0.463	0.804	0	3
Regime type	353	2.28	1.56	0	5
Human rights	357	2.87	1.24	1	5
GDP per capita (ln)	349	8.77	1.47	5.64	11.38
Total population (ln)	362	2.94	1.53	–0.743	7.233
Land area (ln)	363	–1.51	2.32	–10.40	2.80

Source: author's own work.

is coded as 1, otherwise it is coded as 0. Returning to the example of India above, the CJ-R model dependent variable is coded as 1 in 2016 and 0 for 2017–19, the CJ model dependent variable is coded as 1 in 2017 and 2018 and 0 in 2016 and 2019, and the CJ-W-R model dependent variable is coded as 1 in 2019 and 0 for 2016–18.

A government is likely choosing a CCTP model from a menu of options (all CCTP models) though. To account for this, the models are re-estimated using a multinomial logit specification because it assumes each category of the outcome variable (CCTP model) is not independent from the other categories. The multinomial logit requires one of the outcome variable categories to function as a base category because the model estimates the probability of CCTP types relative to it. CJ is set as the base category because it is the most common CCTP model. For the multinomial logit regression, the dependent variable, *CT Model*, is coded 1 for Criminal Justice, 2 for Criminal Justice–War, 3 for Criminal Justice–Reconciliatory, or 4 for Criminal Justice–War–Reconciliatory.

Cross-national results

The logit regression results in Table 5.5 show three interesting patterns. First, the security threat indicators have nearly no statistically significant influence on CCTP model choices. Second, the socio-economic indicators

Table 5.5: CCTP model type, logit regression results

	CJ	CJ–W	CJ–R	CJ–R–W
Domestic attacks$_{(t-1)}$	.410 (.260)	.074 (.256)	–.363 (.272)	–.301 (.251)
International attacks$_{(t-1)}$	.043 (.205)	–.155 (.197)	.052 (.207)	–.067 (.233)
Domestic casualties$_{(t-1)}$	–.340* (.196)	.041 (.198)	.181 (.215)	.195 (.204)
International casualties$_{(t-1)}$	–.076 (.123)	.204 (.133)	–.120 (.139)	.086 (.170)
Armed conflict	–.113 (.224)	–.043 (.337)	.021 (.267)	.221 (.373)
Regime type	.138 (.099)	.077 (.153)	–.243* (.112)	.087 (.129)
Human rights	.476* (.210)	–.121 (.314)	–.576** (.210)	.114 (.266)
Total population (ln)	–.053 (.146)	–.130 (.258)	–.026 (.160)	.376** (.154)
GDP per capita (ln)	.024 (.144)	–.242 (.165)	–.059 (.146)	.182 (.151)
Land area (ln)	–.058 (.084)	.088 (.168)	.057 (.090)	–.102 (.127)
Constant	–1.27 (1.91)	–.589 (2.85)	1.35 (1.94)	–3.95* (1.95)
N	323	323	323	323
Wald X^2 (prob. > X^2)	15.50 (0.1150)	18.75 (0.0435)	38.97 (0.0000)	18.89 (0.0417)

Two-tailed significance test: * p ≤0.05 ** p≤0.01 *** p≤0.001
Robust std. errors clustered by country. Eighty-seven country clusters.
Source: author's own work.

do not have a statistically significant effect. Last, political structures are the most important factors on CCTP model choice. The multinomial logit models produce similar results and are available on the author's webpage.

The only security threat indicator that produces a statistically significant effect is the number of domestic terrorist attack casualties. The more domestic terrorist attack casualties in a country–year, the less likely the government is to implement a CJ model the following year. If domestic casualties change from 0 (the median) to 6 (the mean), and all other variables are held constant at their mean, the likelihood a country implements a CJ model the following year decreases by 27.8 per cent, that is, from 53.3 per cent to 38.5 per cent. This decreased likelihood does not lead to a 1-to-1 trade-off with another model based on the lack of statistical significance domestic casualties has on the other models.

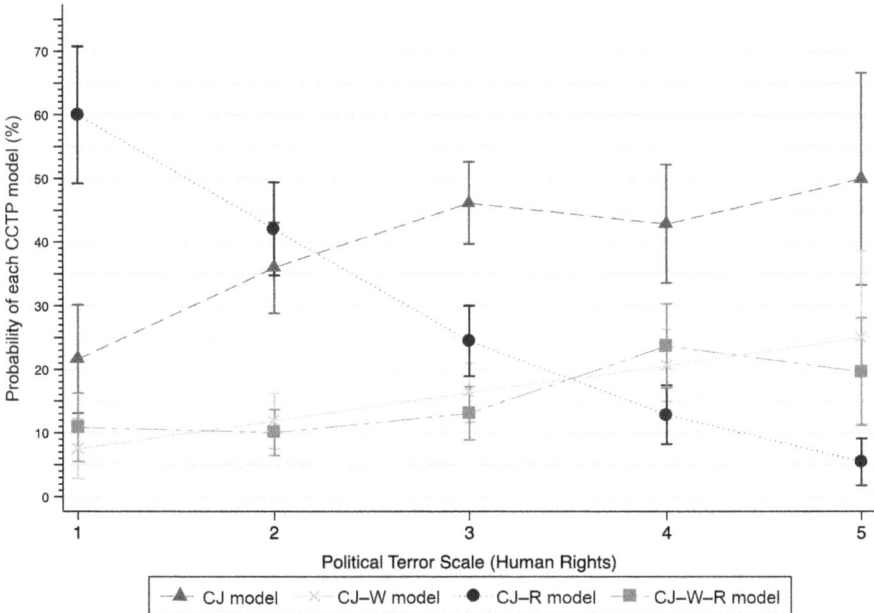

Figure 5.4: Effect of changes in human rights on CCTP model (90 per cent CIs)
(*source:* author's own work)

Both a country's regime type and human rights practices decreases the likelihood of a Criminal Justice–Reconciliatory model. Human rights practices increase the likelihood of a CJ model. Because both political structure measures are categorical variables, interpretation of the effect solely based on the regression results can hide important nuances. That is, the statistical results show that countries with lower human rights practices are more likely to use a CJ model and less likely to use a CJ–R model, but we do not know if this relationship is incremental as countries decrease their respect for human rights or is a consistent effect from most respectful to least respectful.

To dig deeper, using the multinomial logit regression results, Figure 5.4 plots the marginal effect of changes in human rights practices on each CCTP model. On the x-axis, moving from a score of 1 to 5, from left to right, translates to worsening human rights practices. If the confidence intervals overlap, the effect of human rights on the CCTP model are not statistically significant. Including reconciliatory efforts is a preferred CT strategy in countries that fully respect human rights (PTS = 1). As human rights practices worsen, reconciliatory efforts are increasingly excluded and reliance on law enforcement tactics (CJ model) is increasingly likely. The CJ model is the most likely choice for countries with common and consistent violations of human rights (PTS = 3–4). At this tipping point, the predicted probability a country uses a CJ–R model decreases by 59.2 per cent, from a predicted probability of 60 per cent when PTS = 1 to 24.5 per cent when PTS = 3. And the predicted probability a country uses a CJ model increases by 113 per cent from 21.6 per cent to 46.1 per cent. As human rights worsen, the inclusion of war efforts becomes increasingly likely, but not at a statistically significant level.

Regime type also has a statistically significant effect. Figure 5.5 plots the marginal effects of regime type. Democracies are likely to practice CJ or CJ–R models, and within these regime types, only parliamentary democracies are statistically more likely to implement CJ–R instead of CJ. Autocracies are consistently most likely to practice a CJ model at a statistically significant rate. While the CJ model is the most likely CT for autocrats, it is important to highlight that the likelihood of countries using a CJ model does not cross a tipping point at the democratic–autocratic divide. Rather, only parliamentary democracies are statistically less likely than autocracies to use the CJ model. And this difference is substantively small when considering the proximity of the upper confidence interval bound for parliamentary democracies and lower bounds for autocracies. The change in these confidence interval bounds from 35.4 per cent for

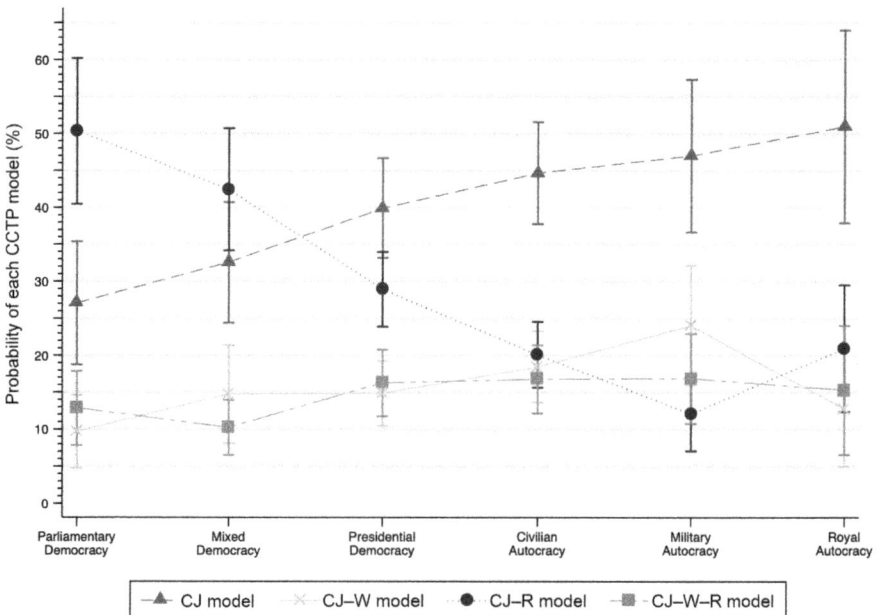

Figure 5.5: Effect of changes in regime type on CCTP model (90 per cent CIs) (*source:* author's own work)

parliamentary democracies to 37.8 per cent for civilian, 36.7 per cent for military, and 37.9 per cent for royal autocracies, is only a 6.8 per cent, 3.7 per cent, and 7.1 per cent increase in probability, respectively. Again, the predicted probabilities for CJ–W and CJ–W-R models remain low across all regime types, and the likelihoods are statistically indistinguishable from each other. For autocracies, the CJ–R model is also indistinguishable from war effort models.

It is not surprising that the predicted probability of the CJ model is statistically significant for autocracies and that reconciliatory efforts are less likely. Autocracies may have less experience and interest in pursuing legislative activity (reconciliatory element) compared to relying on decrees, special orders or operations, and reliance on coercive or repressive state institutions or agents, in particular security services and law enforcement tools and tactics. These important differences in how regime type impacts CT highlight one of the benefits of CCTP: we are able to systematically identify and study how institutional design, political systems, and politics influence CT choices, which was previously inhibited by the traditional and historical studies limited to Western countries and liberal democracies.

To better understand global patterns, the CCTP sample is divided into two sub-sets defined as Global North and Global South. Classifying countries is based on World Bank income economy classifications and geography resulting in unbalanced sub-sets, ninety-seven Global-North country–years and 274 Global-South country–years.[6]

CCTP in Global North and South

As a first cut, a Chi-square test is used to see if there are differences in Global North and Global South CT. A Chi-square test compares the observed frequency of a value with the expected frequency if the variable was randomly distributed. If the test produces a statistically significant Chi-square value, then the observed pattern follows a unique pattern that is statistically significantly different to what a random or average pattern could produce. Testing the distribution of CCTP models, see Table 5.6, shows there are statistically significant differences in Global North and Global South CT (Pearson Chi-square = 29.76, N = 369, Pr = 0.000). In the Global North, CJ and CJ–W models are implemented (i.e., observed) less than is expected, a CJ–R model is implemented more than is expected, and the implementation of a CJ–R–W model nearly meets expected frequency. In the Global South, CJ and CJ–W models are implemented more than is expected, a CJ–R model is implemented less than expected, and a CJ–R–W model, again, nearly meets the expected frequency. This warrants further statistical exploration.

Global counter-terrorism

Table 5.6: CCTP model distribution in Global North and South

	CJ	CJ–W	CJ–R	CJ–W–R	Total
Global North	30	7	48	11	96
Global South	132	45	58	38	273
Total	162	52	106	49	369

Source: author's own work.

The two sub-samples are submitted to the binary and multinomial logit regression specifications applied to the full sample. For the multinomial logit models, the base category for the Global North is CJ–R, as it is the most frequent type, and in the Global South it is CJ. The analyses produce similar results. Again, only the binary logit regression results are reported in Figure 5.6 as a coefficient plot. If the confidence intervals surrounding the point estimates cross the vertical line at 0, then the indicator does not have a statistically significant effect on the likelihood a country–year implements that particular CCTP model. The estimated effect for armed conflict$_{(t-1)}$ is missing in the Global North CJ–W model because armed conflict always equaled 0 in the countries implementing a CJ–W model; there is no variance and thus no relationship to estimate. The larger substantive effect indicated by the scale of the x-axis is an artifact of the comparatively small Global North sample.

The analyses suggest that there are distinct processes leading to different CT efforts in the Global North and Global South. First, security threat indicators show that in the Global North, the number of international terrorist attacks in the previous year has a statistically significant negative effect on the likelihood of CJ–W and CJ–W–R models. This suggests that countries frequently targeted in international terrorist attacks are not expected to systematically increase their offensive responsiveness or engage in militarised counter-terrorism the following year. This could be a consequence of using a one-year lag of the terrorism variables because these countries may react or retaliate immediately to international terrorism, that is, within the same country–year, which is not detected in the models. But, for a CJ–W model, the effect is conditioned by the size of the international terrorist attacks; the more casualties in the previous year, the likelihood a country will implement the CJ–W model increases at a statistically significant level. In the Global South, none of the security indicators exert statistically significant effects on CCTP models.

The socio-economic factors point to important patterns hidden in the global analyses. In the Global North, a CJ–W model is the only one impacted

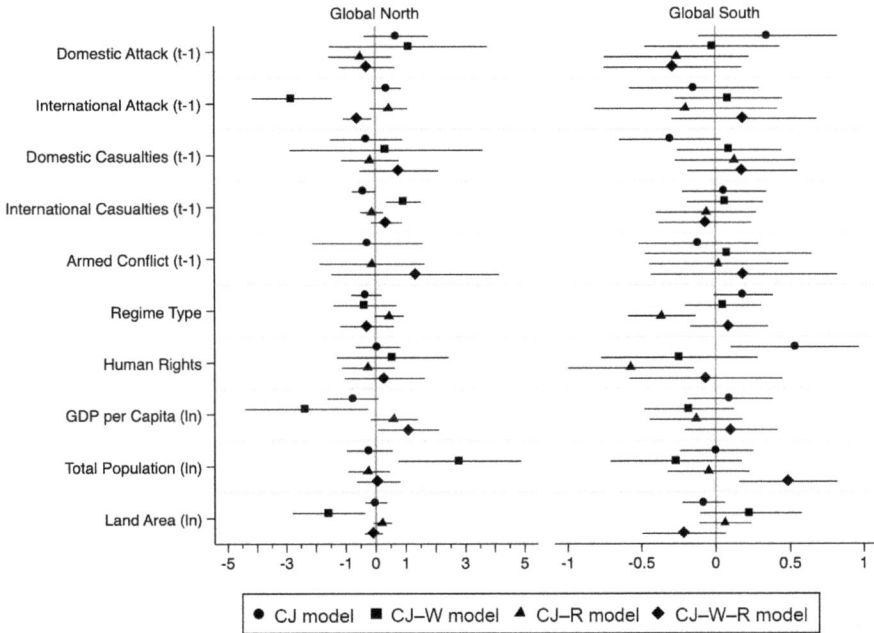

Figure 5.6: CCTP model type by Global North–South, logit regression results
(*source:* author's own work)

by these variables. As country wealth and land size increase, the likelihood
of implementing a CJ–W model decreases. Increasing population increases
the likelihood of this CCTP model. In the Global South, population is
the only statistically significant socio-economic factor. As total population
increases the likelihood of a CJ–W–R model increases. It appears that in
the Global South, governing more people promotes an all-hands-on-deck,
or whole-of-government, approach to counter-terrorism.

As expected from the global analysis, regime type and human rights practices influence a country's CT. But, because the distribution of these variables is quite different in the Global North and Global South, conclusions
from the regression results must be made with caution. In the Global North
estimation sample, most country–years are democracies (61.6 per cent parliamentary, 3.5 per cent presidential, and 22.1 per cent mixed) and 12.8
per cent (11 of 86 country–years) are civilian autocracies (Russia, Bosnia-
Herzegovina, and Singapore [2017–19]). And 89.5 per cent of the sample (9
of 86 country–years) has high respect for human rights. Russia, Israel, and
Bulgaria [2017] are the outliers, and in no country–year do human rights
violations terrorise the entire population (PTS = 5). In the Global South,
country–years are distributed across all regime types with 38 per cent (90 of

237 country–years) practicing some form of democracy. A total of 21.5 per cent of country–years record a high respect for human rights, and 11.4 per cent of country–years record violations terrorising the entire population. To better understand how these variations could impact CT, marginal effects from the multinomial logit models are implemented, akin to the global sample analyses, and presented in Figures 5.7 and 5.8.

Because of the distribution of human rights practices, in Figure 5.7, direct comparisons by the North–South divide are only possible when PTS = 2. At this level of human rights practices, looking across panels, while the predicted probabilities of each CCTP model are similar, there is notable divergence in the Global South where CJ and CJ–R models are statistically significantly more likely than CJ–W and CJ–R–W models. In the Global North, this divergence does not occur as a CJ–W model has overlapping confidence intervals with CJ–W–R and CJ–R models, but there is a statistically significant difference with a CJ model. This may be a result of military capabilities of Global South countries relying on CT cooperation with and intervention by Global North partners to fulfill CT war efforts. This highlights the importance of D'Amato's (2021) research on EU CT strategies

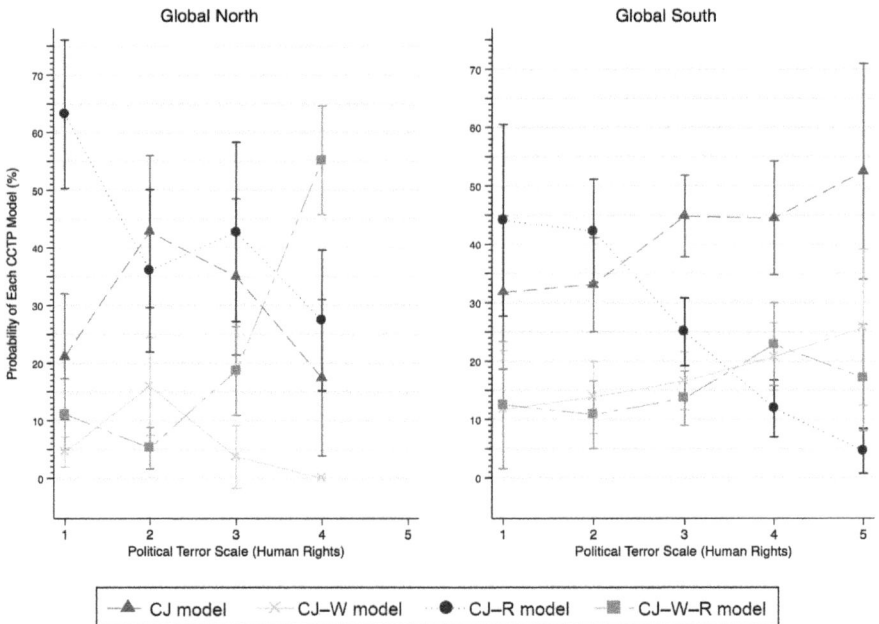

Figure 5.7: Effect of changes in human rights on CCTP model in the Global North and Global South (90 per cent CIs) (*source:* author's own work)

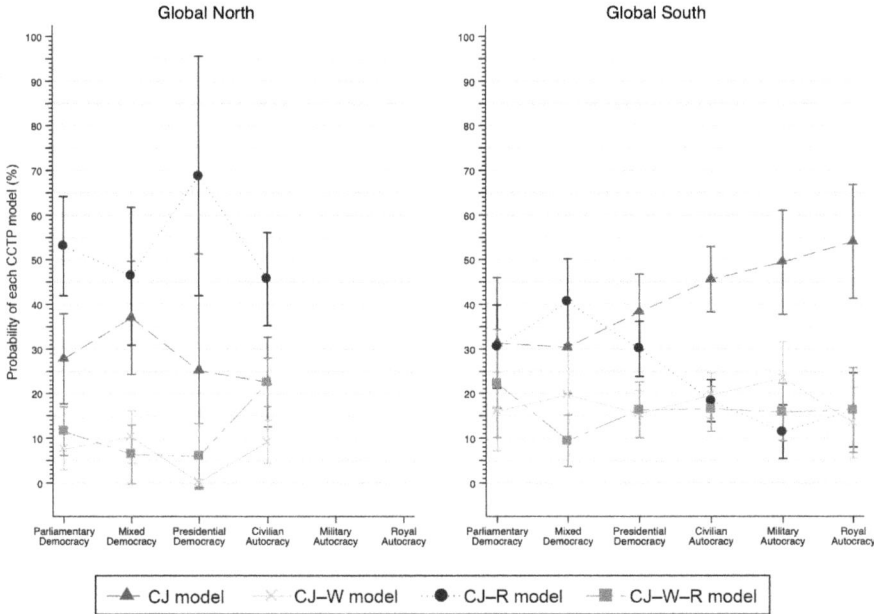

Figure 5.8: Effect of changes in regime type on CCTP model in the Global North and Global South (90 per cent CIs) (*source:* author's own work)

overseas. It also encourages expanding Perliger and Milton's (2018) research to include CT cooperation against international threats.

In the Global North, conclusions can be made when PTS < 3. Countries that perpetrate limited violation of human rights (PTS = 2) are much more likely to employ a CJ model than countries where human rights violations are rare (PTS = 1). Although this change is not statistically significant, nor is the decreased probability of a CJ–R model, the CJ–R model is no longer the most likely strategy. And the likelihood of a CJ–W model is statistically significantly higher, increasing by 248 per cent from 4.6 per cent to 16 per cent.

In the Global South, conclusions can be made when PTS > 1. The association between worsening human rights practices and decreased likelihood of using a CJ–R model observed in the full sample is reinforced. The tipping point is immediately statistically significant as the probability of a CJ–R model decreases by 40.9 per cent from 42.3 per cent to 25 per cent comparing countries with limited violations (PTS = 2) and countries that frequently repress political opponents (PTS = 3). It continues to decrease in statistically significant increments across worsening human rights practices until countries implement widespread human rights violations and target wide swaths of the population rather than repressing political opponents (PTS = 4 and

PTS = 5). The increasing probability of a CJ model and including war/militarised efforts increases as human rights practices worsen, which is likely the result of human rights violators converting their experience and expertise in repressive tools from political repression to CT.

Like the Global North, countries in the Global South with limited human rights violations (PTS = 2) are equally likely to implement a CJ or CJ–R model. As human rights violations increase, Global South countries are most likely to use a CJ model until human rights violations increase to widespread civilian repression (PTS = 5), and the likelihood of CJ–W and CJ–W–R models become statistically indistinguishable from a CJ model.

Turning to regime type, the skewed distribution of the variable between the Global North and Global South again limits direct comparisons in Figure 5.8. Confident conclusions can be drawn when comparing parliamentary democracies, mixed democracies, and civilian autocracies. Presidential democracy is quite rare in the Global North sample, which is responsible for the dramatically larger confidence intervals surrounding the respective predicted probabilities in the left panel.

When comparing across panels, there is significant difference in parliamentary democracies' CT. In the Global North, these countries are most likely, at a statistically significant level, to implement a CJ–R model, followed by a CJ model, which is also statistically significant from the next most likely choice, which is a toss-up between CJ–W and CJ–W–R models. Parliamentary deliberation and institutions appear to encourage the use of reconciliation, law enforcement, and legislation and discourage militarised or war efforts in CT. But in the Global South, a different picture emerges; parliamentary institutions do not translate into a ranked likelihood. Rather, all confidence intervals overlap, and no discernible patterns are identified. This could be partially an artifact of the data because only 6.8 per cent of the Global-South estimation sample is a parliamentary democracy, but nevertheless, this is a significant difference in the role of governance and institutions on CT in the Global North and Global South.

Comparing the CCTP models predicted probabilities in mixed democracies points to a similar difference in the two regions. In the Global North, while the predicted probabilities for CJ and CJ–R are statistically indistinguishable, both are more likely than a country including war or militarised efforts in CT. In the Global South, this regime type is again less influential on CT as seen by the overlapping confidence intervals; only a CJ–W–R model is statistically less likely than CJ–R and CJ models. While a CJ–W model is statistically less likely than the CJ–R model, there is no statistical difference from the CJ model.

Civilian autocracies' CT also differs. In the Global North, these regimes are predicted to use a CJ–R model at a statistically higher rate than the other models, which are all statistically indistinguishable from each other. But in the Global South, these regimes are expected to implement a CJ model at a statistically higher rate than the other models, which are predicted at nearly identical rates. In these regime types the primary CCTP model has a predicted probability of 45–6 per cent in both regions.

In the Global South, autocratic countries are consistently more likely to use a CJ model compared to the other CCTP models. It appears to be a substitution of law enforcement and judicial efforts for legislative and reconciliatory efforts. Perhaps surprisingly, while military autocracies are more likely to use a CJ–W model than other regime types, the higher point prediction is not statistically different than other regimes. Democracies in the Global South appear to follow a mixed-bag approach as many of the confidence intervals overlap, but there seems to be a slight preference to use CJ and CJ–R models. This is much different than in the Global North where these regimes are less likely to include 'W' efforts in their CT strategies.

Conclusion

The analyses highlight important differences in CT in the Global North and Global South. In both regions, terrorist threat does not appear to have consistent or steadfast effects on CT efforts and strategies, at least not at a statistically significant level. While there are some shared patterns of the effect political structures have on CT, there are even more divergent patterns. This variation indicates that local, national, and regional cultural, social, and political institutions are important for CT decision-making and strategy. The analysis verifies what researchers and policymakers already know; CT is not one-size-fits-all, but importantly, identifies how CT practices and policies systematically differ between contexts and across countries. Better recognition and awareness of the sources of variation in and influences on CT is imperative for the decolonisation of CT because it could provide the necessary space, understanding, and cultural awareness and sensitivity that could prove crucial in appropriately confronting terrorism, terrorists, and the scourge on society they unleash. Quite simply, accounting for and respecting cross-national, cultural, and/or regional differences could limit the imposition of Global North CT practices onto the Global South, where they may not work or governments and communities may not be receptive and implore true cross-national and international cooperation that can improve the safety and security of billions of people around the world.

It also points to the need to improve conversations and connections between the wellspring of Global South CT qualitative case studies with data collection efforts, like the CCTP introduced here. Doing so can help identify and measure important dynamics and historical legacies at cross-national and global levels that will lead to new frontiers in CT research. Understanding drivers of Global South CT efforts and strategies is of critical importance as the Global North continues to develop partnerships rather than indentureships with these countries.

Counter-terrorism is not a one-size-fits-all solution. Identifying, recognising, and accounting for variation in governments' calculations, capabilities, and political motivations and how this influences CT efforts and strategies is undeniably important in maximising CT success. The CCTP provides an analytical and quantifiable starting point.

Notes

1 For the purposes of this project, Global North broadly refers to the United States, Canada, Europe, Australia, and New Zealand. Global South is broadly defined as the rest of the world. See the end of cross-national results section and endnote 4 for classification specifications and additional information.
2 Perliger and Milton's (2018) study of bilateral counter-terrorism cooperation provides clear definitions of kinetic and non-kinetic operations that were necessary for classifying different types of cooperation. Kinetic operations are 'military or police operations that were designed to arrest, kill, or otherwise directly intervene against terrorist organizations' (207). Non-kinetic operations are 'joint legislative initiatives, cooperation in eliminating avenues of terrorism finance, funding of one country by another, intelligence sharing, etc.' (207)
3 Coding procedures are on the author's webpage (www.graigklein.com).
4 Albania 2017 and Eritrea 2019 are omitted. USCT reports only provide summaries of terrorism and CT and not information on CT activities.
5 Robustness checks for consistency in model predictions are conducted. A measure of change in attack frequency and casualties from the previous year is created and substituted for the corresponding one-year lag variables. Then terrorism threats are measured by combining GTD's domestic, international, and ambiguous attacks into measures of *Total Attacks* and *Total Casualties*. Results are consistent with the primary analyses and available on the author's webpage.
6 See author's webpage for Global N-S classification.

References

Albrecht, H. 2008. 'Terrorism, risk, and legislation', *Journal of National Defense Studies*, 6, 13–49.
Bellasio, J., Hofman, J., Ward, A., Nederveen, F., Knack, A., Meranto, A. F., and Hoorens, S. (2018). *Counterterrorism Evaluation: Taking Stock and Looking Ahead*. Santa Monica, CA: RAND Corporation.
Bhoumik, A. (2004). 'Democratic responses to terrorism: A comparative study of the United States, Israel and India', *Denver Journal of International Law and Policy*, 33(2), 285–345.

Bjørnskov, C. and Rode, M. (2020). 'Regime types and regime change: A new dataset on democracy, coups, and political institutions', *The Review of International Organizations*, 15(2), 531–51.

Boyle, Michael J. (2018). 'The military approach to counterterrorism', in Silke, A. (ed.). *Routledge Handbook of Terrorism and Counterterrorism*. New York: Routledge, pp. 384–94.

Boyle, M. (ed.). (2019). *Non-Western Responses to Terrorism*. Manchester: Manchester University Press.

Cingranelli, D. L., Richards, D. L., and Clay, K. C. (2014). 'The CIRI human rights dataset', Version 2013.12.05. www.humanrightsdata.com (accessed 18 February 2022).

Cordell, R., Clay, K. C., Fariss, C. J., Wood, R. M., and Wright, T. M. (2020). 'Changing standards or political whim? Evaluating changes in the content of us state department human rights reports following presidential transitions', *Journal of Human Rights*, 19(1), 3–18. DOI: 10.1080/14754835.2019.1671175

Cordell, R., Clay, K. C., Fariss, C. J., Wood, R. M., and Wright, T. M. (2022). 'Disaggregating repression: Identifying physical integrity rights allegations in human rights reports', *International Studies Quarterly*, 66(2), 1–11. DOI: 10.1093/isq/sqac016

Crelinsten, R. D. (2018). 'Conceptualising counterterrorism', in Silke, A. (ed.) *Routledge Handbook of Terrorism and Counterterrorism*. New York: Routledge, pp. 363–74.

Crelinsten, R. D. and Schmid, A. P. (1993). 'Western responses to terrorism: A twenty-five year balance sheet', in Schmid, A. P. and Crelinsten, R. D. (eds) *Western Responses to Terrorism*. New York: Frank Cass, pp. 307–40.

Crenshaw, M. (2001). 'Counterterrorism policy and the political process', *Studies in Conflict & Terrorism*, 24(5), 329–37.

D'Amato, S. (2021). 'Patchwork of counterterrorism: Analyzing European types of cooperation in Sahel', *International Studies Review*, 23(4), 1518–40.

Dunne, M. and Wehrey, F. (2014). *U.S.-Arab Counterterrorism Cooperation in a Region Ripe for Extremism*. Washington, DC: Carnegie Endowment for International Peace.

Eijkman, Q. and Schuurman, B. (2011). 'Preventive counter-terrorism and non-discrimination in the European Union: A Call for Systematic Evaluation. ICCT Research Paper. www.icct.nl/publication/preventive-counter-terrorism-measures-and-non-discrimination-european-union-need (accessed 10 January 2022).

Enders, W. and Sandler, T. (1993). 'The effectiveness of antiterrorism policies: A vector – autoregression-intervention analysis', *American Political Science Review*, 87(4), 829–44.

Epifanio, M. (2011). 'Legislative response to international terrorism', *Journal of Peace Research*, 48(3), 399–411.

Gibney, M., Cornett, L., Wood, R., Hascke, P., Arnon, D., Pisanò, A., Barrett, G., and Park, B. (2021). 'The political terror scale 1976–2020'. www.politicalterrorscale.org (accessed 18 February 2022).

Gleditsch, N. P., Wallensteen, P., Eriksson, M., Sollenberg, M., and Strand, H. (2002). 'Armed conflict 1946–2001: A new dataset', *Journal of Peace Research*, 39(5), 615–37.

Josua, M. (2021). 'What drives diffusion? Anti-terrorism legislation in the Arab Middle East and North Africa', *Journal of Global Security Studies*, 6(3), 1–15.

Klein, G. R. (2016). Ideology isn't everything: Transnational terrorism, recruitment incentives, and attack casualties', *Terrorism & Political Violence*, 28(5), 868–87.

Lehrke, J. P. and Schomaker, R. (2014). 'Mechanisms of convergence in domestic counterterrorism regulations: American influence, domestic needs, and international networks', *Studies in Conflict & Terrorism*, 37(8), 689–712.

Lehrke, J. P. and Schomaker, R. (2016). 'Kill, capture, or defend? The effectiveness of specific and general counterterrorism tactics against the global threats of the post-9/11 era', *Security Studies*, 25(4), 729–62.

McIlhatton, D., Berry, J., Chapman, D., Christensen, P. H., Cuddihy, J., Monaghan, R., and Range, D. (2020). 'Protecting crowded places from terrorism: An analysis of the current considerations and barriers inhibiting the adoption of counterterrorism protective security measures', *Studies in Conflict & Terrorism*, 43(9), 753–74.

Miller, G. (2007). 'Confronting terrorisms: Group motivation and successful state policies. *Terrorism & Political Violence*, 19(3), 331–50.

Mustafa, K. (2020). Who fights terror: Gendarmerie forces and terrorist group termination', *Terrorism & Political Violence*, 34(4), 746–71.

National Consortium for the Study of Terrorism and Responses to Terrorism (START), University of Maryland. (2019). 'The global terrorism database (GTD)'. www.start.umd.edu/gtd (accessed 18 February 2022).

Pedahzur, A. and Ranstorp, M. (2001). 'A tertiary model for countering terrorism in liberal democracies: The case of Israel', *Terrorism & Political Violence*, 13(2), 1–26.

Pedahzur, A. (2009). *The Israeli Secret Service and the Struggle against Terrorism*. New York: Columbia University Press.

Perliger, A. (2012). 'How democracies respond to terrorism: Regime characteristics, symbolic power & counterterrorism', *Security Studies*, 21(3), 490–528.

Perliger, A. and Milton, D. (2018). 'Fighting together? Understanding bilateral cooperation in the realm of counterterrorism', *Dynamics of Asymmetric Conflict*, 11(3), 199–220.

Pettersson, T., Davis, S., Deniz, A., Engström, G., Hawach, N., Högbladh, S., Sollenberg, M., and Öberg, M. (2021). 'Organized violence 1989–2020, with a special emphasis on Syria', *Journal of Peace Research*, 58(4), 809–25.

Pokalova, E. (2015). 'Legislative responses to terrorism: What drives states to adopt new counterterrorism legislation?', *Terrorism & Political Violence*, 27(3), 474–96.

Renard, T. (2021). 'Counter-terrorism as a public policy: Theoretical insights and broader reflections on the state of counter-terrorism research', *Perspectives on Terrorism*, 15(4), 2–10.

Schmid, A. P., Forest, J. J. F., and Lowe, T. (2021). 'Counter-terrorism studies: A glimpse at the current state of research (2020/2021)', *Perspectives on Terrorism*, 15(4), 155–83.

The World Bank (2022a). 'GDP per capita (current US$)'. https://data.worldbank.org/indicator/NY.GDP.PCAP.CD (accessed 18 February 2022).

The World Bank (2022b). 'Population, total'. https://data.worldbank.org/indicator/SP.POP.TOTL (accessed 18 February 2022).

The World Bank (2022c). 'Land area (sq. km)'. https://data.worldbank.org/indicator/AG.LND.TOTL.K2 (accessed 18 February 2022).

U.S. Code. Title 22 – 'Foreign relations and intercourse'. Chapter 38 – Department of State, Sec. 2656f – 'Annual country reports on terrorism'.

van Dongen, T. (2010). 'Mapping counterterrorism: A categorization of policies and the promise of empirical based, systematic comparisons', *Critical Studies in Terrorism*, 3(2), 227–41.

Whitaker, B. E. (2007). 'Exporting the Patriot Act? Democracy and the 'War on Terror' in the third world', *Third World Quarterly*, 28(5), 1017–32.

6

After the bombing of the Norwegian Government Quarter on 22 July 2011: Changes in discourses on urban counter-terrorism 1990–2020

Sissel Haugdal Jore

On 22 July 2011, the bombing of the Norwegian Government Quarter was the first of two terrorist attacks committed by the right-wing extremist Anders Bering Breivik. The bomb was placed inside a van and exploded next to the building where the Norwegian Prime Minister's office was located. Eight people were killed in the explosion: most were government employees, and some were passers-by. More than 200 people were injured. Additionally, the explosion caused enormous material damage (Gjørv, Auglend et al. 2012). Later that day, sixty-nine people, mainly adolescents, were executed on the island of Utøya by the same perpetrator.

In the decade following this attack, Norway has struggled to come to grips with the political implications of the attack and how to rebuild a safe society. The attack was unlike anything previously experienced in Norway. In the aftermath of the terrorist attacks on 22 July 2011, the centre of Oslo was transformed into a city with massive urban security measures, aimed at preventing a similar attack from happening again. The year after, the government decided to rebuild the Government Quarter at the exact same location in the middle of the dense city centre of Oslo with what it referred to as 'a necessary level of security', which entailed building a stand-off zone with massive urban visible and invisible security measures (Ministry of Government Administration, Reform and Church Affairs 2012).

These urban counter-terrorism measures and the Norwegian society's attitudes to this massive implementation of urban security measures have received little academic scrutiny. In the overall climate of the War on Terror, where the focus primarily has been on the threat of Islamic terrorism, concentrating on groups and ideology, the Norwegian news media took the perspective of the government and followed their description of the 22 July 2011 terrorist as a lone and deeply disturbed individual, focusing on the perpetrator as an individual rather than as a member of a terrorist movement, giving him questionable political exposure and not analysing reasons and consequences on a political–societal level (Falkheimer and Olsson 2015; Tellidis and Glomm 2019). Moreover, the coverage differed from the framing of terrorism established after 9/11 in the form of responding to a terrorist attack with war, urban security and surveillance (Falkheimer and Olsson 2015). Instead, the media coverage and research conducted in the time period after 2011 focused almost exclusively on Utøya and on how to prevent radicalisation, whereas the bombing of the Government Quarter and the associated implementation of urban security measures has gained minor attention (Borchgrevink 2013; Hemmingby and Bjørgo 2018).

Since 9/11, the emphasis on hard security measures, such as securing official buildings, airports and public places, has increased drastically, especially in Western countries. In the first decade after 9/11, the focus was primarily directed towards high profile targets, such as government buildings and embassies. However, in the following decade, multiple terrorist attacks, predominately against civilians, using low-tech weapons, such as knives, hand-held firearms, vehicles, or vehicle-borne explosives, moved the focus to securing softer targets and more everyday sites, such as crowded urban spaces, shopping malls and other public spaces where people gather (Hemmingby 2017). However, although 9/11 and the War on Terror increased the focus on protecting high profile targets, just what are considered legitimate urban counter-terrorism measures in a vibrant city centre is not evident. What the citizens and government of a country consider proportional and legitimate counter-terrorism measures will be influenced by many different factors such as threats and crises within a society, geopolitical trends in neighbouring countries, technological development, and cultural-political factors. The Norwegian Government Quarter is an interesting case because the public debate concerning counter-terrorism measures was not launched directly after 9/11 or after the bombing in 2011. Before the 2011 terrorist attack, there had been public discussions regarding the implementation of urban counter-terrorism measures in the Government Quarter. Consequently, the Norwegian Government Quarter can provide insight into how the perceived threat of terrorism and associated counter-terrorism measures have changed over time and into the question of how a terrorist attack can change the public discourse on what are considered legitimate urban counter-terrorism measures. Additionally, the case of the Norwegian Government Quarter can also provide some insight into how a Western country responded to 9/11 and the War on Terror, and whether the US perception of terrorism as a threat was automatically adopted in other Western countries.

This chapter discusses how the 22 July 2011 terrorist attack impacted the legitimacy of urban counter-terrorism measures. It uses the Norwegian

Government Quarter as a case to investigate how the legitimacy of public security measures have changed over the last three decades and whether this attack has led to changes in Norwegian society's attitude towards counter-terrorism measures in the public domain.

The case

The Norwegian Government Quarter consists of eight buildings constructed in the period from 1866 to 1996. Gross floor area is 163,000 m², while the plot area is 29,000 m², of which approximately 12,000 m² constitutes park and recreation areas (Gjørv et al. 2012). Located in the middle of the dense city centre of Oslo, the Government Quarter consists of multiple buildings, hosting ministries, the prime minister's office, local businesses, media houses, the supreme court, political parties, and two churches. It is also a part of the city centre through which ordinary traffic and people pass.

Consequently, the Norwegian Government Quarter is both a traditional hard terrorist target, which hosts the representatives of the Norwegian state, and a soft and civilian target because it is an open district for pedestrians and the location of many private businesses. Subsequently, the implementation of urban security measures at this location will affect not only people working in the government and ministries but also the public and those whose jobs are located within the Norwegian Government Quarter but who do not work for the government. In 2018, it was estimated that the seventy-five-metre standoff security distance from the buildings in the Government Quarter would have consequences for 340 private businesses, with 5,500 employees located within the perimeter of the security zone of the Government Quarter (Jore et al. 2020: 5).

The Government Quarter is, thus, to be understood more as a city district than just a building complex. It was established in 1883 but has expanded and been rebuilt over many time periods. During the time, the Norwegian Government Quarter was under construction, and ever since, architectonic features and its location have been debated (Berg 2016). When the buildings were constructed, pedestrians had access to walk beneath the buildings and cars could park right outside the building where the prime minister's office was located. The debate about securing the buildings started in the period after the terrorist attacks in the United States on 11 September 2001. However, security issues are aspects that are not necessarily open to the public, so public debates concerning the security measures in the Government Quarter have primarily centred around closing streets so that vehicles cannot access the area.

On 22 July 2011, when Anders Behring Breivik left the vehicle-borne explosive device in the Norwegian Government Quarter, no perimeter security obstacles had been put in place to stop the van from driving up in front of the prime minister's building, besides a chain marked with 'no entry' (Gjørv et al. 2012). Breivik parked the van close to the building and left the scene in the direction of another car he had parked nearby which he used to drive to his second attack location on Utøya. CCTV footage showed him armed and disguised in a police-like uniform. Seven minutes passed from when he left the car until the bomb detonated. In the meantime, seventy people passed the wrongly parked car. The bomb killed eight people, and ten others were taken to hospital with life-threatening or serious injuries (The Public Prosecutors 2012). The attack in the Government Quarter led to significant destruction of several government buildings, surrounding streets and buildings in the area (The Public Prosecutors 2012). The reduced presence of government employees, because it was a Friday afternoon in the summer holiday season, together with no building collapse, limited the number of casualties (Meyer et al. 2015). The amount of damage encouraged the Norwegian Government to examine the possibility of redeveloping the Norwegian Government Quarter, to enable most of the ministries to move into it in the future (Ministry of Local Government and Modernisation 2013). In 2012, the government decided that the Norwegian Government Quarter would be rebuilt and protected with the 'necessary security measures' (Ministry of Government Administration, Reform and Church Affairs 2012: 2). The bureaucratic processes of rebuilding the Government Quarter have been extensive. Construction started in 2020, and the first of three building phases is planned to be finalised in 2025. This means that the security measures currently implemented in the Government Quarter are temporary measures that will be replaced with more aesthetic and modern measures in the future rebuilding process.

Theory: Zooming in on urban counter-terrorism

Although terrorism has always been regarded as a possible threat against Norwegian society, what actually constitutes the threat, its magnitude and what are considered legitimate ways to counter the threat, have changed drastically over time (Jore 2012; Larsen 2019). This is not only the case in Norway. Most Western countries have radically changed their perception of the terrorism threat and the legitimacy of counter-terrorism measures over the last decades (Crelinsten 2018; Silke 2018).

Jackson et al. (2011) describe four main categories of counter-terrorism measures: (1) the use of force, (2) intelligence and policing, (3) homeland security, and (4) conciliation and dialogue. The 'use of force' category views terrorism as a special kind of warfare that emphasises military force to destroy, disrupt, deter, or prevent terrorism (Lindahl 2016). The 'use of force category' often presents terrorism as a kind of evil or a national security threat to the survival of the nation state or the values that a nation state is built upon. Since terrorism is understood as an existential threat, states should eradicate it through any means (Jackson et al. 2011; Jore 2012). The assumption behind this category of counter-terrorism measures is that terrorism is not just a criminal or political activity but an extraordinary form of risk which threatens the survival of the nation state. The idea is that terrorism cannot be countered with the use of traditional legal and criminal prevention measures.

On the contrary, the 'intelligence and policing' category views terrorism as a form of criminal activity and a threat that can be countered through the state's security services and the police. If terrorism is perceived as a type of crime, appropriate means will be policing and criminal justice. The assumption is that, by criminalising terrorist activity, possible terrorists will refrain from committing terrorism and the ordinary legal framework will also be appropriate to handle the aftermath of a terrorist attack by punishing terrorist activity. This model also opens the possibility for the rehabilitation of people who have committed acts of terrorism. Included in this category are also intelligence and pre-emptive measures within a legal framework.

The category of 'homeland security' regards terrorism as a manageable security threat that can be mitigated by enhancing society's ability to withstand, delay, or respond to a terrorist threat. This is typically done through enhanced emergency preparedness, strengthening critical infrastructure, and securing high-profile targets and public places. If terrorism is seen as a manageable risk, urban security measures and emergency preparedness measures are considered appropriate (Jore 2012). The assumption behind this category of counter-terrorism measures is that implementing protective security measures will deter possible terrorists from committing a terrorist attack because the chances of carrying out a successful terrorist attack will be reduced (Lindahl 2016).

The category of 'conciliation and dialogue' views terrorism as the result of socio-political grievances and conflicts that can be tackled with nonviolent efforts. If terrorism is seen as a result of oppression and political injustice, then dialogue, political reforms, and conflict resolution will be appropriate means to counter the threat. The assumption behind this category of counter-terrorism measures is that terrorists are rational political activists. Terrorism is caused by socio-economic grievances or political conditions, such as competing religious, ideological or ethnical perspectives; consequently, the solution to preventing terrorism is aimed at removing the structural tensions or inequalities that cause terrorism (Jore 2012).

In addition to these four categories of counter-terrorism, which were developed in 2011, the last decade and the intensive focus on building resilience to radicalisation should be added to the counter-terrorism category overview. Deradicalisation programmes build on the assumption that vulnerable and marginalised individuals can change by therapeutic means and the building of resilience (Jore 2020b; Stephens et al. 2021). The assumption behind this category of counter-terrorism measures is that, by identifying opinions, processes, life events, and situations that have led a possible terrorist into a pathway of violence, society can prevent similar events from happening again. This approach often focuses on the vulnerability of individuals and thus often overlooks structural and political factors (Jore 2020a; Jore 2020b). Such counter-terrorism perspectives are often built on a 'whole of society approach', which has become the dominant Western frame for conducting counter-radicalisation. The whole of society approach entails the involvement of many government departments and agencies of the private and civil sectors and has led to many actors, such as teachers and social workers, who, traditionally, have not had a role in counter-terrorism, having become crucial actors in counter-terrorism (Ragazzi 2017; Sivenbring and Andersson Malmros 2019; Jore 2020a; Andersson Malmros 2021; Sjøen and Mattsson 2022). Table 6.1 shows a summary of the main types of

Table 6.1: The connection between the perception of terrorism as a threat and counter-terrorism measures

Counter-terrorism category	Description of measures	Assumption regarding the nature of the terrorist threat
The use of force	Military power	War, a national security threat
Intelligence and policing	Surveillance, interrogation, arrests	Criminal activity
Homeland security	Reduce vulnerability, emergency management	Manageable risk
Conciliation and dialogue	Focus on root causes, dialogue, negotiation, social justice	Political communication
Deradicalisation programmes	Attitude change, building resilience	Vulnerability, marginalisation

Source: author's own work.

counter-terrorism categories and the connection between the perception of terrorism as a threat and counter-terrorism measures.

According to Renard (2021a; 2021b), most Western countries have changed their counter-terrorism policies away from hard coercive power strategies such as 'the use of force' or 'homeland security' counter-terrorism measures. Nowadays, the predominant perspective for preventing terrorism has moved to more soft non-coercive power strategies, especially 'deradicalisation programmes'. According to this description, it should be expected that states went from 'the use of force' and 'homeland security' approaches to counter-terrorism policies based on 'conciliation and dialogue' and 'deradicalisation programmes'. However, this does not seem to be the case. Western states have not abandoned hard counter-terrorism measures, such as war, military means, and physical security measures. Over the years, numerous European cities have been the subject of a massive implementation of urban counter-terrorism measures, including surveillance cameras, vehicle barriers, bollards, control stations, guards, and electronic face and car sign recognition tools. Despite this, these hard measures have not gained the same scholarly attention in the terrorism research community as soft measures have. Many of these measures have been implemented to protect pedestrians and high-profile targets, for example, government buildings, after terrorist attacks against civilians such as the wave of terrorist attacks by Islamic State in multiple European cities during 2015–18. These measures have drastically changed the landscapes of many cities.

The lack of significant debates concerning these urban security measures can be interpreted as a result of these measures being considered a necessity to protect society from terrorism. However, such measures have not always been regarded as inevitable. The ubiquitous expectation in contemporary Western societies that authorities are responsible for protecting citizens from acts of terrorism is one that most citizens nowadays take for granted. Nevertheless, from a historical perspective, this assumption is new (Crelinsten 2009; Jackson et al. 2011; Crelinsten 2018). Subsequently, there have been massive changes in the perception of terrorism and what constitutes legitimate counter-terrorism measures.

Moreover, what society perceives as effective ways to counter terrorism will depend on how society comprehends terrorism as a threat. Currently, counter-terrorism policies in most countries are much more extensive than in the past, covering a broader variety of actors (Boyle 2021; Crelinsten 2018; Renard 2021b). Although the field of terrorism studies has expanded drastically over the last two decades, the field of counter-terrorism research has not (Lindahl 2016; Renard 2021b). Despite the multiplicity of counter-terrorism measures implemented in Western societies over this period, many terrorism researchers assume that such measures are self-explanatory or consider counter-terrorism as a policy or a practice (Renard 2021a). As a result, counter-terrorism remains significantly under-theorised and under-studied. Furthermore, given the vast number of urban counter-terrorism measures that have been implemented over the last two decades, there is reason to claim that urban counter-terrorism measures have contributed to shaping the public and authorities' perception of terrorism, especially in low-risk Western countries that have little experience of terrorism but, nevertheless, have implemented a variety of urban counter-terrorism measures. This is established, despite the claim from several scholars over many decades that such counter-terrorism measures are intruding on civil liberties, for instance through the implementation of emergency laws and physical security measures, leading to what some have called 'the counter-terrorist state' (Blackbourn and De Londras 2019; Boyle 2021; Renard 2021b).

This chapter tries to fill this research gap by studying the discourse on counter-terrorism in the Norwegian public realm regarding securing the Norwegian Government Quarter. By studying this public discourse, the aim of this chapter is dual: first, to understand how discourses on the threat of terrorism and associated counter-terrorism measures have changed from 1990 to 2020 and, second, to investigate whether the 22 July 2011 terrorist attack changed the perception of the threat and the legitimacy of the associated counter-terrorism measures.

Method: The discourses of urban security counter-terrorism

This chapter generally focuses on the hard measures of urban security and how the discourses regarding terrorism and associated threats and urban security measures have changed since the 1990s. The implementation of urban security measures and the legitimacy of such measures are consequently both a result of occurring terrorist attacks and the perceived threat of terrorism. Additionally, they are related to assumptions regarding the nature of the terrorist threat, as described in Table 6.1.

In a world of multiple threats, the fact that some groups are defined in the security agenda as a terrorist threat against society is a result of the social-political construction of specific groups of activists being framed as an extraordinary type of threat that has a dimension other than that of just being political activists or criminals. Subsequently, what are perceived as a terrorism threat and legitimate associated counter-terrorism measures are contingent on historical, cultural, and political framing (Crelinsten 2021; Jore 2012; van der Veen 2014). This means that our perception of the phenomenon is not just dependent on an actual threat but, to a large degree, dependent on the perception of terrorism as a threat (Braithwaite 2013; Jenkin 2006; Rosenthal et al. 2001). As such, terrorism is not a neutral word used to refer to an independent, objective, ontological phenomenon. The concept and phenomenon of terrorism should rather be understood as a frame that shapes and constructs how individuals and society understand a phenomenon of violence and associated threats (Jackson et al. 2011) and how it should be prevented. This means that what are perceived as effective ways to counter terrorism will depend on how society comprehends terrorism as a threat. In this process, language plays a central role.

In this chapter, argumentative discourse analysis based on Hajer (1995) is applied to investigate how the meaning of terrorism and associated counter-measures have changed over time with regard to the Norwegian Government Quarter. According to Hajer, discourses are defined as 'an ensemble of notions, ideas, concepts and categorizations through which meaning is allocated to social and physical phenomena, and which is produced and reproduced in an identifiable set of practices' (Hajer 1995: 44). This definition of discourse focuses not only on the language and conceptualisation but also on the practices. Applying argumentative discourse analysis to terrorism and counter-terrorism entails that the societal understanding of terrorism at a given time is a product of different discourses in society. By studying how actors in society communicate the threat of terrorism and the necessity of urban counter-terrorism measures in the Government Quarter, it is possible to get a picture of the representation of the risk, giving information about the frames and the discourses within which the terrorism threat is understood. Moreover, discourses to a large degree predetermine how the phenomenon of terrorism as a threat to society is understood and how terrorism should be prevented (Jore 2012).

When many people use the same discourse to conceptualise the world, it frequently solidifies into an institution (Hajer 1995). In the case of terrorism, discourse institutionalisation of terrorism is reflected in the practices of how to deal with terrorism, such as negotiation with – or imprisonment of – terrorists, military operations, or urban security measures. From this perspective, terrorism counter-measures, such as urban security measures, are institutionalisations of terrorism discourses in society. An important aspect of discourse institutionalisations is that, when a discourse has solidified into an institutionalisation, this will facilitate the reproduction of a given discourse. Individuals socialised to see terrorism in a specific discursive framework will reinterpret the phenomenon of terrorism within this framework. Thus, counter-terrorism measures, such as urban security measures, will not only be seen as means for coping with the threat of terrorism but as concrete discourse institutionalisations that support a specific view of the phenomenon of terrorism. Consequently, the urban counter-terrorism measures proposed to secure the Government Quarter should be seen as an institutionalisation of a certain view on terrorism and how it should be dealt with.

Empirics and analysis

The empirical data this chapter is based on are built on several empirical sources. To investigate the changes in the threat of terrorism and the legitimacy of the counter-terrorism measures in the Government Quarter, newspaper articles from the Norwegian Oslo-based newspaper, *Aftenposten*, were investigated. The newspaper articles were collected from the news media search engine Retriever, and sixty-three newspaper articles that mentioned security measures in the Government Quarter were included in the study. These newspaper articles covered the time period between 1990 and 2020. Additionally, twenty-three official documents describing terrorism as a threat or security measures in the Government Quarter were included in the study, such as white papers, commission reports, concept assessments and evaluations. Argumentative discourse analysis, based on Hajer (1995) described in the section above, was applied to investigate how the meaning of terrorism and associated counter-measures have changed over time in regard to the Government Quarter.

The author of this chapter has previously engaged in several projects regarding the security of the Government (Jore et al. 2018; 2020; Meyer et al. 2015) and the Norwegian understanding and conceptualisation of terrorism and counter-terrorism (Jore 2007; 2012; 2016; 2020a; 2023; Jore and Njå 2008; 2009), which this book chapter also is based on.

Results

The Government Quarter – the 10 September approach

At the beginning of the 1990s, the terrorism threat against Norway was neither a topic in the media nor an issue which concerned the authorities or scholars. Terrorism was primarily presented as a political problem in countries other than Norway (Jore 2012; Jore and Njå 2008). If terrorism was discussed as a threat in Norway, it was often related to big events where foreigners who could be a target for political assassination were present. Acts of terrorism were understood as a means of communicating political messages, and terrorism was seen as a form of political communication that primarily was a result of structural factors such as political or socio-economic

injustice (Jore and Njå 2009). To determine whether a political act was terrorism or not, the perpetrator's motivation was important. The assumption
was that the terrorists' goals were to gain sympathy for a political cause
(NOU 1993: 3). Since terrorism was described as a political crime, it was
portrayed not as an extraordinary threat but more as an ordinary criminal
activity that could be handled with dialogue, international cooperation, and
within the ordinary legal framework.

Since terrorism was seen as a form of political activism, possible targets
of terrorism corresponded to the political agendas of terrorism. The terrorism concept in the media and the official documents in the 1990s covered many different groups of perpetrators, such as left-wing and right-wing
extremists, religiously motivated terrorists, and also environmental activists. The terrorists' weapons were mostly related to criminal activities, such
as assassination, civil disobedience, or bombs. Counter-arguments against
why Norway would be considered a legitimate terrorist target existed in the
media, in research, and official documents in the 1990s; it was claimed that
the Norwegian society in the 1990s was geographically remote, homogene-
ous, inclusive, and transparent; all factors that made Norway less of a prob-
able target for terrorism (Jore 2012; NOU 1993). Additionally, the fact that
Norway had a good record in negotiation with extreme groups also made
the nation less of a terrorist target. This conceptualisation of terrorism is,
in line with the 'conciliation and dialogue' perspective on counter-measures,
described by Jackson et al. (2011). This discourse on terrorism was upheld
by the authorities, researchers, and the media, and the assumption of terrorism was that these were rational actors that might as well fight for a
legitimate cause (Jore and Njå 2008).

In the 1990s, terrorism directed against the Government Quarter was
hardly ever mentioned in public documents or the media. In 1990, it was
briefly reported in the media that the windows in the Government Quarter
were protected with an invisible cover to avoid splinters and glass, in case
'terrorists or demonstrators could break the glass and harm those who sit
behind the glass windows' (*Aftenposten* 07.08.1990). To juxtapose terrorism with demonstrators highlights that terrorists were considered to have
political agendas and that they were more to be understood within the range
of ordinary crimes or civil disobedience.

By the end of the 1990s, some scholars and official bodies started to
claim that terrorism could become a threat to Norway. At the time, terrorism was becoming a topic that was more publicly discussed, especially
in relation to the mandates of the Norwegian Armed Forces and the Police
Surveillance Service (Jore 2012; Jore and Njå 2008). These actors claimed
that the Norwegian society was vulnerable and that terrorists could exploit

these vulnerabilities. Accordingly, terrorism would change character in the future to a more dangerous kind that would target civilians and use weapons of mass destruction if the possibility was there (NOU 2000). All these elements were incorporated in the storyline of 'the new threat landscape' which described the new security political era after the Cold War and defined terrorism as one of the threats that could be a reality in the future. However, there was no clear picture of who these possible terrorists actually could be and what their motivation would be for choosing Norwegian targets, and the Government Quarter was not mentioned as a specific target at the time.

The Government Quarter: 11 September 2001–22 July 2011

The terrorist attack in the USA on 11 September 2001 led to an enormous increase in the attention paid to the topic of terrorism in the media, research, and official documents in Norway, as in most other Western countries (Jore 2007; 2012; Jore and Njå 2009). The type of terrorism that had attacked the United States was described as a threat to all democratic societies, including Norway. At the time, the media, research, and authorities had a clearer picture of potential perpetrators against Norwegian society. The terrorism concept was narrowed down to almost exclusively include Islamic terrorism, and it was the motivation, target selection, and potential weapons of these perpetrators that were in focus (Jore 2012). The threat was described as international, but, with the presence of a Muslim population in Norway, some of whose members openly supported violence as a means for political communication, the threat could also come from within Norwegian society. Target selection was no longer necessarily limited to the terrorists' political agendas. Terrorism was described as a threat that would target civilians, aiming to kill as many people as possible. This framing of terrorism resembles the category of 'use of force' described by Jackson et al. (2011) because it focuses on terrorism as a threat to society, democracy, and international peace.

   Although Norway implemented a multiplicity of counter-terrorism measures after 9/11, such as events and celebrity protection, infrastructure and key object protection, legal and regulatory changes, authority strengthening, damage mitigation, and international measures, arguments such as precaution, compliance, solidarity, and moral obligations dominated the justification of the implementation of counter-measures in the public sphere (Jore 2012). These arguments were thus not connected to the threat picture in Norway. This type of argumentation just stated that Norway should comply with what other countries did. This can be attributed to the perception of Norway as a low-risk society with no history of major terrorist activity. But it is probably also related to the fact that the Norwegian perception of terrorism at the time was that terrorism was a form of political communication and political activism, as described in the 'intelligence and policing' and 'conciliation and dialogue' approaches to counter-terrorism.

However, 9/11 shifted Norwegian counter-terrorism policy towards harder measures, such as the 'homeland security' approach. In the years after 9/11, the media focused on high-profile targets, such as the American embassy, but the Government Quarter was also mentioned as a possible target. Two months after 9/11, security personnel in the Government Quarter started the process of evaluating the security measures and emergency plans for the area because they considered the current security regime unsatisfactory and outdated, as it was primarily based on the Cold War's threat landscape and thus not in line with the new threat landscape (Gjørv et al. 2012). Over the years, several threat assessments were conducted, including one scenario that turned out to be almost identical to Breivik's bomb attack. In 2004, the security measures of the Norwegian Government Quarter were considered unsatisfactory and the vulnerabilities deemed unacceptable. The conclusions were that various bomb explosion counter-measures had to be implemented. Among the most important suggested measures were the permanent closing of the street outside the prime minister's office to vehicle traffic with vehicle barriers, measures to reduce glass shrapnel in the event of an explosion, closure of the reception area, and improved façade monitoring, along with several physical, technical, administrative, and operational safety and security measures. Despite this assessment by the security professionals working in the Government Quarter, these measures had yet to be implemented when the terrorist attack took place on 22 July 2011. Except for the closing of the public streets, these discussions were primarily kept within the security community and did not reach the public before 22 July 2011, due to bureaucratic challenges and secrecy (Gjørv et al. 2012).

The closing of the streets outside the prime minister's office followed ordinary procedures for regulation and led to media debates around the necessity of closing the streets because of a potential terrorist threat. The newspaper *Aftenposten*, which had its main office in the Norwegian Government Quarter, wrote in 2007 that:

> Closing the street (Grubbegata) because of a terrorist threat is both hysterical and hypothetical and a mindset we should be spared from. *(Aftenposten* 2007)

This quote illustrates that, although terrorism was considered a potential threat, for many people in Norway, including those that dealt with security in the Norwegian Government Quarter, the idea that terrorism could actually happen in Norway was still distant. Moreover, at the time, counter-terrorism measures were still disputed. The closing of the street surrounding the American and Israeli embassies after 9/11 had triggered massive public criticism, as did the plans around securing the Norwegian Government Quarter. Consequently, the discourse in the years between 11 September 2001 and 22 July 2011 was characterised by discussions on whether terrorism actually posed a threat to Norway. Urban counter-terrorism measures were a controversial and disputed topic, framed within the dichotomous value dilemma of freedom versus security, where freedom was often considered a more important value than security.

The Government Quarter after 22 July 2011

Breivik's twin attack remains the deadliest far-right terrorist attack in the Western world since the Oklahoma City Bombing in 1995. As such, the 22 July 2011 terrorist attack on Utøya triggered massive media coverage. This attack was seen as unprecedented and one which no one had seen coming. Conversely, the attack on the Government Quarter did not gain the same amount of media attention as the shooting spree on Utøya. This was probably because of the character of the target being a well-known conceivable terrorist target and the limited number of casualties in the Government Quarter compared to Utøya where so many adolescents were killed. The attack on Utøya and the Government Quarter triggered massive discussions around whether the attack could have been prevented, and a commission was appointed to investigate this matter. In 2012, this commission (Gjørv et al. 2012) concluded that the attack could have been avoided, among other things through the permanent closing of the streets close to the prime minister's office to traffic, the integration of bollards, etc. According to the commission, if preparedness plans developed in the years after 9/11 2001 had been properly implemented, they would have been enough to thwart the attack. Accordingly, the commission called the tragedy of 22 July 2011 a paradox:

> On the one hand, the terrorist attacks may be the most shocking and incomprehensible acts ever experienced in Norway. Few had envisaged that anything so unreal could become a reality: 77 people were killed. Many more were seriously injured. Thousands suffered terrible human losses, and the material damages are hard to comprehend. All because of one man. On the other hand, we were prepared for several aspects of 22 July. A car bomb scenario at the Government Quarter and several coordinated attacks have been recurring scenarios in threat assessments, as well as for security analyses and emergency exercise scenarios for many years. (Gjørv et al. 2012: 8)

According to the commission, the long-standing efforts to secure the Government Quarter were never limited for budgetary reasons but due to the bureaucratic, leadership, and cultural failures of those working with and in charge of the security measures in the Government Quarter.

The discussions on whether Norway could actually be a terrorist target were no longer an issue in the media. The 22 July 2011 attack had proven that Norway could also be a target for terrorists, and the commission's devastating conclusions of the failure to prevent the attack shifted the media discourse. Urban counter-terrorism was no longer seen as unnecessary and something that should be weighed against civil liberties. As such, 22 July 2011 shifted popular perceptions of security measures from something negative to a necessity. The newspaper *Aftenposten*, which had previously been sceptical about closing the streets surrounding the prime minister's office, now referred to their previous article, in which they had been sceptical regarding urban counter-terrorism, and stated that:

> Today, we just have to acknowledge that we were thoroughly wrong. We underestimated the need to secure some of our most important public buildings. And we joined those who thought the danger of terrorism was so small that it should not be given any weight. Now we have painfully experienced that this was wishful thinking… We still believe in the importance of an open society and an open city. We still believe that we must not be overwhelmed by fear. For, as Prime Minister Jens Stoltenberg has put it, 'a people in fear is not free.' But at the same time, we need to reconsider our view of the need for some security measures around buildings that may be terrorist targets. (*Aftenposten* 25.08.2011)

Consequently, the 'homeland security' approach to countering terrorism gained a stronger foothold in Norway after the terrorist attack in 2011. The lack of sufficient security measures was given as the explanation for why the perpetrator could carry out the attack, and homeland security measures were now described as a necessity by actors that previously had been critical of such hard security measures. However, despite the acknowledgement that terrorism could happen in Norway and that there was a need for some sort of homeland security regime, urban security measures in the Government Quarter were still a disputed topic in the media. During the ten years that have passed since the bomb attack, the Government Quarter reconstruction process has been the target of massive and continuous criticism from many different actors. This criticism has been directed at the demolition of buildings, the architectural features, the costs, the decision to gather all ministries except the Ministry of Defence in one location and at the perimeter security zone around the Government Quarter.

However, one argument has trumped all criticisms: the argument about building security. The argument of security was central to the decisions to rebuild and to relocate and centralise (almost) all ministries and the prime minister's office in the city centre of Oslo. Security was also the key argument for creating an outer perimeter of seventy-five metres (a security zone) around the planned buildings. The intention behind the perimeter was to prevent vehicle-borne threats like the threat scenario that took place on 22 July 2011. However, this decision to rebuild the Government Quarter in a dense city centre and the associated security zone are still disputed because the effects of the urban security measures in the Government Quarter will have consequences that go far beyond the people working in the ministries as the Government Quarter is a central part of the city centre of Oslo. The security zone will consist of multiple layers of security measures, such as surveillance cameras, bollards, control stations, security guards, and probably artificial intelligence such as car sign recognition technology (Jore, Kruke et al. 2020). While the security measures are intended to make those working in the Norwegian Government Quarter safe, these measures also constitute a surveillance regime affecting not only bureaucrats and visitors but everyone using and traversing the cityscape surrounding the complex. However, these arguments were met by the authorities and security personnel as an old-fashioned view of urban security, and urban security measures were described as something that can be integrated into the built environment and serve aesthetic purposes. Instead of implementing counter-terrorism measures that could contribute to a building fear or a hostile environment, urban security measures would be designed as integrated part of a park such as benches, trees, water mirrors, and hilly terrains. The idea was that by redesigning counter-terrorism measure into practical or artistic features these measures would not be perceived by the public as counter-terrorism measures.

This changed attitude towards urban security is also described in the white paper on the 'New Government Quarter'. In this white paper, the new Government Quarter is described as 'green, open and safe' (Ministry of Local Government and Modernisation NOU 2018–2019, 27), and urban security measures are also described here as something that should not be controversial but something that can be a positive element in the urban landscape:

> Physical security measures around the buildings and in the outdoor areas in the Government Building Complex will have an as little as possible unsightly effect on the urban environment. It has been a significant development in this area in recent years in the sense that less neat security measures have been replaced by integrated and aesthetically pleasing solutions. (Ministry of Local Government and Modernisation, NOU 2018–2019, 28)

This approach to counter-terrorism is an attempt to converge hard counter-terrorism measures into more softer measures, which illustrates that there remains scepticism about the homeland security approach in Norway, even for a government complex that has been the scene of a devastating terrorist attack. Consequently, the dichotomous value challenge of freedom versus security that has been strong in the Norwegian public media debate is still present.

The controversy over urban security measures also reappeared in 2020, when the cost estimates for the new Government Quarter rose from NOK 16.3 billion in 2014 to up to NOK 36.5 billion, according to a quality assurance report (Kvalitetssikring av valgt prosjektalternativ (KS2) datert 6. juli 2020).

The Minister of Local Government and Modernisation's response to this was that a key argument for sticking to the plan to rebuild the Norwegian Government Quarter was to reduce the presence of security measures in other places in Oslo:

> In 2012, the police and security authorities considered that a unified ministry community is preferable from a security point of view. It was thus decided that we were to take the Government Quarter back. In my mind, this is also the best solution from an urban development perspective. The alternative is more closed streets and security measures around many different buildings in which the ministries currently sit. This also costs money. (Nikolai Astrup, *Aftenposten* 17.07.2020)

This quote illustrates that even the responsible minister still sees urban security measures as something negative that should be limited to one location.

Discussion

The case of the Norwegian Government Quarter illustrates how the threat perception has changed over time. The traditional Norwegian conceptualisation of terrorism is to regard it as a form of political communication and activism; thus, 'intelligence and policing' and 'conciliation and dialogue' approaches to counter-terrorism were the dominant framing of terrorism as a threat and of how this threat should be prevented. Although 9/11 and the US-led War on Terror altered the focus on terrorism to mass casualty terrorism, motivated by Islamic terrorism, it was still disputed whether terrorism could happen in Norway and whether Norway should sacrifice democratic freedoms and implement hard security measures. As such, there are two different discourses on the nature of terrorism and associated counter-terrorism measures in the Norwegian public and official debate. The first discourse regards terrorism as a political crime and, thus, an ordinary type of risk that can be handled with dialogue, international cooperation, and police methods. This discourse describes terrorists as political activists, with the best way to reduce the risk of terrorism being by dialogue and social justice. The other discourse describes terrorism as an omnipresent societal threat, which legitimates hard homeland security measures (Jore 2012). This second discourse is intertwined with an increased focus on the vulnerabilities of critical infrastructures, dealing with worst-case scenarios encompassing new terrorist weapons and attack strategies focusing on mass casualty terrorism, especially from Islamic terrorism. The shift in discourses cannot exclusively be explained by the terrorist attacks in the USA on 9/11, because both discourses are still present, and the discourse-shift appeared before the terrorist attacks on 9/11 (Jore 2007). Consequently, it is important for the scholars who are comparing counter-terrorism perspectives and discourses between the Global North and South to keep in mind that, even in a Western country such as Norway, there was resistance in the decades following 9/11 to simply import the American official discourse on terrorism and counter-terrorism which favoured hard counter-terrorism approaches based on 'the use of force' and 'homeland security'. Although the 9/11 attacks triggered threats assessment and planning of security measures in the Government Quarter, the planned measures were not carried through and, in the public media debate, there remained scepticism about the type of hard security measures that a 'homeland security' approach entails.

There is no doubt that the terrorist attack on 22 July 2011 was used as an argument for implementing massive security measures in the urban environment and, by this, increasing the power of the state through surveillance and regulating the democratic right of free movement. However, the case of the Government Quarter also illustrates how complicated the relationships between terrorism threat perception and counter-terrorism measures are. It is not a given that a terrorist attack will sway public opinion and the authorities towards legitimating hard homeland security measures. Although the Government Quarter had been massively damaged in a severe terrorist attack, security measures to protect the same scenario from happening again were still a disputed topic in the decade following this attack. This illustrates that the connection between an actual terrorist attack and the will to implement security measures is more complex than many terrorist researchers tend to believe. Citizens' acceptance of counter-terrorism measures is not a straightforward process in which the public passively accepts the media's or the government's presentation of the threat. The public's attitude towards counter-terrorism measures is a complex combination of fear, trust, political factors, and attitude towards civil liberties (Rykkja et al. 2011). The public perception of terrorism is not altered just by a terrorist attack occurring; it is also rooted in historical discourses on what terrorism is and how it should be prevented. Also, within the government and the official bodies, there was resistance to just simply implement hard security measures in the Norwegian Government Quarter. The attempt to redesign hard counter-terrorism measures into more aesthetic art features and everyday features such as benches etc. also indicates that, within the Norwegian authorities, there was a need to soften the hard counter-terrorism measures.

The bombing of the Government Quarter was a severe direct attack on the government and the central government administration. From a symbolic perspective, this was also an attack on the nation and the democratic values on which Norwegian society is founded. The terrorist attack made it visible to everyone that Norway was also exposed to terrorism threats and could be a target of terrorism. Despite this, the media attention after the attack mainly focused on the attack on Utøya and the emergency and rescue situation related to this attack. This is probably related to the fact that the Utøya scenario was seen as a totally unprecedented and unpredictable attack with many more fatalities (especially young people) than the Government Quarter attack. It is worth noticing that many of the measures put in place to prevent radicalisation in Norway after the 2011 attack have not been as controversial as the urban security measures in the Government Quarter. These measures are often seen as a form of safeguarding and preventing marginalisation, and they build on the notions of the Norwegian welfare state (Jore 2020b; Malmros 2019; Sivenbring and Andersson Malmros 2019). As such, this approach to terrorism prevention builds on the traditional Norwegian counter-terrorism approach as seeing counter-terrorism as conciliation and dialogue and the assumption that vulnerable and marginalised individuals can change by therapeutic means and building resilience. Consequently, this study illustrates that, even in Western countries, 9/11 should not be taken as a starting point for understanding counter-terrorism. The Norwegian case illustrates that the way in which terrorism and associated counter-terrorism measures are understood has national and historical roots.

Conclusions

During the period under study, the discourse on terrorism and counter-terrorism has undergone major changes in the framing of what terrorism is and how it should be prevented. Historically, Norwegians have been sceptical about counter-terrorism measures, but 22 July 2011 turned the perception of security measures from something negative to a necessity, by removing the debate on whether Norway would actually be a possible terrorist target. Despite this, the relation between the terrorist attack and the society's willingness to implement far-reaching urban security measures to protect the Norwegian Government Quarter has been the subject of a vociferous public debate, and there is still resistance to accepting hard security measures in the urban environment; attempts have been made to solve it by redesigning the hard measures into more soft and aesthetic measures. The case of securing the Norwegian Government Quarter thus illustrates that the relation between a terrorist attack and the implementation of counter-terrorism measures is much more complicated than often illustrated in contemporary terrorism research. Moreover, Norway also serves as an example of how a social democratic country deals with counter-terrorism within the context of an inclusive society. This study shows that the Norwegian understanding of that terrorism is built on historical discourses and that, despite the devastating terrorist attack on the Government Quarter, Norwegian authorities and the public media debates are not willing to simply accept that terrorism is a threat that should be prevented through hard counter-terrorism measures. Subsequently, there is a need for future CVE research to direct more attention to the counter-terrorism aspects, especially the 'hard', physical urban counter-terrorism. The case of the Norwegian Government Quarter illustrates that there is a need for more research on counter-terrorism strategies and the dilemmas that they are surrounded by and the national and international discourses that lay the foundation for the acceptance and implementation of these measures.

References

Andersson Malmros, R. (2021). 'Translating ideas into actions: Analyzing local strategic work to counter violent extremism', *Democracy and Security*, 17(4), 399–426.

Astrup, N. (2020). '*Vi må bygge et nytt regjeringskvartal*', 17 July, Aftenposten, www.aftenposten.no/meninger/debatt/i/zGvWzb/vi-maa-bygge-et-nytt-regjerings kvartal-nikolai-astrup

Berg, S. K. (2016). 'Heritage value revisited after 22 July 2011 – The Norwegian Government Block as an expression of public values and a national symbol', in *Heritage, Democracy and the Public-Nordic Approaches*. New York: Routledge.

Blackbourn, J. and De Londras, F. (2019). *Accountability and Review in the Counter-terrorist State*. Bristol: Policy Press.

Borchgrevink, A. (2013). *A Norwegian Tragedy: Anders Behring Breivik and the Massacre on Utøya*. Cambridge: Polity Press.

Boyle M. (2021). *Non-Western Responses to Terrorism*. Manchester: Manchester University Press.

Braithwaite, A. (2013). 'The logic of public fear in terrorism and counter-terrorism', *Journal of Police and Criminal Psychology*, 28(28), 95–101.

Crelinsten, R. (2021). *Terrorism, Democracy, and Human Security: A Communication Model*. London: Routledge.

Crelinsten, R. (2018). 'Conceptualising counterterrorism', in Silke, A. (ed.) *Routledge Handbook of Terrorism and Counterterrorism*. London: Routledge, pp. 363–74.

Crelinsten, R. (2009). *Counterterrorism*. Cambridge: Polity Press.Department for Central Government Buildings, Security and Administrative Services https://www.regjeringen.no/en/dep/kmd/subjects/Housing-and-building-policy/thegovernment-buildingcomplex/rebuilding-the-government-building-compl.html?id=712726 (accessed 7 March 2014).

Falkheimer, J. and Olsson, E.-K. (2015). 'Depoliticizing terror: The news framing of the terrorist attacks in Norway, 22 July 2011', *Media, War & Conflict*, 8(1), 70–85.

Gjørv, A. B., Auglend, R. L., Bokhari, L., Enger, E. S., Gerkman, S., Hagen, T., Hansen, G. H. B., Paulsen, M., and Straume, K. (2012). 'Rapport fra 22. juli-kommisjonen', *Norges Offentlige Utredninger* 14.

Hajer, M. A. (1995). *The Politics of Environmental Discourse: Ecological Modernization and the Policy Process*. Oxford: Clarendon Press.

Hemmingby, C. (2017). 'Exploring the continuum of lethality: Militant Islamists' targeting preferences in Europe', *Perspectives on Terrorism*, 11(5), 25–41.

Hemmingby, C. and Bjørgo, T. (2018). 'Terrorist target selection: The case of Anders Behring Breivik', *Perspectives on Terrorism*, 12(6), 164–76.

Jackson, R., Jarvis, L., Gunning, J., and Breen-Smyth, M. (2011). *Terrorism: A Critical Introduction*. London: Bloomsbury Publishing, pp. 1–14.

Jenkin, C. M. (2006). 'Risk perception and terrorism: Applying the psychometric paradigm', *Homeland Security Affairs*, 2(2).

Jore, S. H. (2007). 'The Norwegian research on terrorism 1996–2006: Paradigms and attitudes towards security measures', *Risk, Reliability and Societal Safety*: 2579–86.

Jore, S. H. (2012). 'Counterterrorism as risk management strategies' (PhD thesis no. 178), University of Stavanger.

Jore, S. H. (2016). 'Norwegian media substantiation of counterterrorism measures', *Journal of Risk Research*, 19(1), 101–18.

Jore, S. H. (2020a). 'Countering radicalisation in Norwegian terrorism policy', *Nordic Societal Security*, 179, 179–98.

Jore, S. H. (2020b). 'Is resilience a good concept in terrorism research? A conceptual adequacy analysis of terrorism resilience', *Studies in Conflict & Terrorism*, 46(1), 1–20.

Jore, S. H. (2023). 'On security and safety', *Risk Discourse and Responsibility*, 336, 232.

Jore, S. H. and Njå, O. (2008). 'Protection from half-criminal windows breakers to mass murderers with nuclear weapons: Changes in the Norwegian authorities' discourses on the terrorism threat', *Safety, Reliability and Risk Analysis. Theory, Methods and Applications*, 3077–84.

Jore, S. H. and Njå, O. (2009), 'Terrorism risk as a change stimulus to the Norwegian society', *Reliability, Risk and Safety. Theory and Applications*: 2265–74.

Jore, S. H. and Njå, O. (2012). *The Relation between Terrorism Risk Discourses and Aviation Security*. 11th International Probabilistic Safety Assessment and Management Conference and the Annual European Safety and Reliability Conference 2012, PSAM.

Jore, S. H., Utland, I.-L. F., and Vatnamo, V. H. (2018). 'The contribution of foresight to improve long-term security planning', *Foresight*, 20(1), 68–83.

Jore, S. H., Kruke, B. I., and Olsen, O. E. (2020). 'Vurdering av konsekvenser ved etablering av ytre perimeter rundt nytt regjeringskvartal'. https://uis.brage.unit. no/uis-xmlui/bitstream/handle/11250/2653567/Rapport_86.pdf?sequence=1 (accessed 13 January 2022).

Larsen, A. G. (2019). 'Threatening criminals and marginalized individuals: Frames and news conventions in reporting of radicalization and violent extremism', *Media, War & Conflict*, 12(3), 299–316.

Lindahl, S. (2016). 'Critical evaluation of counterterrorism', in Jackson, R. (ed.) *Routledge Handbook of Critical Terrorism Studies*. London: Routledge, pp. 214–24.

Malmros, R. A. (2019). 'From idea to policy: Scandinavian municipalities translating radicalization', *Journal for Deradicalization*, 18(18), 38–73.

Meyer, S. F., Jore, S. H., and Johansen, K. W. (2015). 'Troublesome trade-offs: Balancing urban activities and values when securing a city-centre governmental quarter', *City, Territory and Architecture*, 2(2), 1–15.

Ministry of Government Adminstration, Reform and Church Affairs (2012). *Mandate for Concept Study of Future Government Building Complex*. Ministry of Government Administration, Reform and Church Affairs, Oslo.

Ministry of Local Government and Modernisation (2013). 'Rebuilding the government building complex'.

Ministry of Local Government and Modernisation (NOU 2018–2019). 'New Government Building Complex'.

NOU (1993). *Strafferettslige regler i terroristbekjempelsen [Legislature in Counter-Terrorism]*. Report from the Security Commission, appointed by the Ministry of Justice and the Police 26 October 1990, submitted 11 February 1993, NoU 1993:3. Ministry of Justice and the Police, Oslo.

NOU (2000). *Et Sårbart Samfunn. Utfordringer for Sikkerhets–Og Beredskapsarbeidet I Samfunnet*. Sårbarhetsutvalget, Oslo. 24.

Ragazzi, F. (2017). 'Countering terrorism and radicalisation: Securitising social policy?', *Critical Social Policy*, 37(2), 163–79.

Renard, T. (2021a). 'Counter-terrorism as a public policy', *Perspectives on Terrorism*, 15(4), 2–10.

Renard, T. (2021b). *The Evolution of Counter-terrorism Since 9/11: Understanding the Paradigm Shift in Liberal Democracies*. London: Routledge.

Rosenthal, U., Boin, A., and Comfort, L. K. (2001). *Managing Crises: Threats, Dilemmas, Opportunities*. London: Charles C Thomas Publisher.

Rykkja, L. H., Lægreid, P., and Fimreite, A. L. (2011). 'Attitudes towards anti-terror measures: The role of trust, political orientation and civil liberties support', *Critical Studies on Terrorism*, 4(2), 219–37.

Silke, A. (ed.). (2018). *Routledge Handbook of Terrorism and Counterterrorism*. Routledge.

Sivenbring, J. and R. Andersson Malmros (2019). 'Mixing logics: Multiagency approaches for countering violent extremism', 1764750_korrekt-versionmixing-logics_digital_korrekt.pdf (gu.se)

Sjøen, M. M. and Mattsson, C. (2022). 'Depoliticising political violence: State-centric and individualised discourses in the Norwegian counterterrorism policy field', *Scandinavian Journal of Educational Research*, 67(6), 1–14.

Stephens, W., Sieckelinck, S., and Boutellier, H. (2021). 'Preventing violent extremism: A review of the literature', *Studies in Conflict & Terrorism*, 44(4), 346–61.

Tellidis, I. and Glomm, A. (2019). 'Street art as everyday counterterrorism? The Norwegian art community's reaction to the 22 July 2011 attacks', *Cooperation and Conflict*, 54(2), 191–210.

The Public Prosecutors (2012). *Indictment*. Oslo Public Prosecutors, Oslo.

van der Veen, A. M. (2014). '3 The power of terrorism frames', *Arguing Counterterrorism: New Perspectives*, 74.

7

'It takes a village': The collective securitisation of social policy related to preventing and countering violent extremism in the European Union

Inés Bolaños-Somoano

'We have moved on from a State-centric, regalian internal security frame…. In a decade, we have achieved [regarding internal security] what in the frames of exterior policy and common security we have not achieved in 50 years! Why is that?' (Interviewee 1)

In the last two decades, the way that counter-terrorism has been conceptualised, framed and implemented has fundamentally changed (Coaffee and Wood 2006). Whereas shortly after 9/11, reactive, retaliating, and repressive measures were dominant (Coolsaet 2010), the focus has since over ten years ago shifted towards anticipatory measures that try to prevent rather than react to terrorism. Such measures come under the umbrella term 'P/ CVE', Prevention of Radicalisation or Prevention and Countering of Violent Extremism, and have come to complement the traditional 'hard approach' to counter-terrorism (CT), based on police work, investigative teams, or intelligence (Stockdale 2013).

P/CVE (Preventing and/or Countering Violent Extremism) or Prevention in short constitutes a pre-emptive 'holistic approach [to counter-terrorism] to ensure a level of stability and cohesion in society so that violent extremism does not occur' (Martini et al. 2020: 3). P/CVE, both in theory and in practice, rests on the practice of state-led, civil society fronted interventions in various spheres, such as education, social/NGO work, and counselling, which were previously not considered part of security policy and rather classified as 'social policy'. But such social policy areas are not being prioritised based on their intrinsic value (i.e., improving school environments to achieve overall better educational results), as other areas of social work are. Public housing might have an impact on decreasing youth crime, but it is promoted by politicians or the state framed as a social concern. Prevention efforts, in contrast, address the same 'root issues' but are justified, for funding and implementation, from a security point of view. These initiatives are meant to minimise and/or anticipate a security threat (terrorism and violent extremism), not to remedy a social malady. This turn to P/CVE has not been limited to Western liberal democracies. The globalisation of counter-terrorism in the last decades, spearheaded by the USA and the United Nations (Martini 2020), has also resulted in the localisation of preventive counter-terrorism by non-Western regimes, often entailing a whole different host of challenges (Boyle 2019: 7).

This chapter provides an empirical account of how a securitisation process of social policy unfolds and is influenced by hegemonic and colonial discourses on Islam and security. It further contributes to literature on collective securitisation by testing existing theories. Finally, it explores much discussed issues of agency in EU institutional processes.

As a main argument, this chapter proposes that the shape of P/CVE policies in Europe today are the result of a process of securitisation of social policy in the European Union.

It further argues that certain EU institutions, chiefly the European Commission, with the tacit support of the Council and the Parliament and in tandem with a few Member States, such as UK (until 2020), the Netherlands, Spain, and France, are the main actors behind this process of securitisation. It concludes by arguing that the wide-spread existence of anti-Muslim discourses in the immediate policy environment has affected this process of securitisation and determined some of its final characteristics, something that brings into question whether P/CVE policies are even applicable to non-Jihadist[1] forms of extremist violence.

The field of decolonial studies offers a valuable critical lens that can enrich our comprehension of counter-terrorism and deradicalisation, especially in today's climate of rising polarisation and hate, particularly towards Muslims and LGTBQ+ individuals. Singh et al. (2016), in their study, posit that external factors, such as policy and societal norms, play a substantial role in fostering moderation, while reminding us of the potential adverse consequences. Thus, while this analysis chapter does not extensively explore the nuanced aspects of the intersection between securitisation and decolonial theory, it does bring forth a historical perspective illuminating the power dynamics influencing our political decision making processes within the domain of counter-terrorism and deradicalisation (Mohamed et al. 2020).

Theoretical framework

This research rests on a theoretical framework built around post-Copenhagen securitisation theory and the study of anti-Muslim biases in Western counter-terrorism. Taking Prevention as a case study, it tries to answer the following research question:

Has there been a securitisation of social policy at the EU level? If so, how did the securitisation process unfold? Who are the main actors, countries and/or institutions behind it?

The idea that security and its provision do not constitute an absolute, objective good in international politics is firmly rooted in the constructivist approaches to studying international security (Gaidaev 2022). The securitisation that securitisation theory describes refers to the successful establishment of a link between an object and a source of threat for the object (Balzacq 2010). This is, securitising is the move towards identifying a phenomenon, event, or person as a source of insecurity, as a threat and/ or a potential danger to the individual. This threat is sometimes directed at the individual, but most frequently it is framed as an existential danger to the state, the national culture or the (political) community. The securitising move, whereby this insecurity status is imposed on a subject or subjects, is divided into two phases: (1) problem framing, that is, creation and dissemination of knowledge explaining that this referent object is to be seen as a threat. Then comes (2) solution formulation meaning that, once the threat has been established and (re)defined, there is a push towards drafting new policy responses to adequately neutralise it (Balzacq 2010).

This chapter follows on the post-Copenhagen conceptualisation of securitisation as rooted 'in a neo- or post-Marxist reading of discourse theory which is marked by a much stronger acknowledgement and consistent incorporation of a distinctly social space of discursive productions' (Stritzel 2014a: 39). Such a discursive approach better captures the agency of the audience response and outlines a framework for the securitising actor–audience response interaction that 'better accounts for securitization theory's linguistic and intersubjective character, addresses this theoretical/empirical conflict, and improves our understanding of how groups select and justify security priorities and costly security policies' (Côté 2016: 542).

Among the numerous variations of post-Copenhagen securitisation theory, this article employs the collective securitisation (CS)[2] theory (Sperling and Webber 2019) as the most adequate to study the European Union. Collective Securitisation theory argues that the power and interests of states are central for the functioning of international organisations, so that said organisations are rarely able to compel powerful states to act against their interests (Sperling and Webber 2019).

CS also shows a high degree of versatility in order to distinguish interest patterns and hidden mechanisms in processes of institutional change, in order to shed light on the fundamental power dynamics and historical contexts that serve as catalysts for the production of radicalisation and extremism (Mohamed et al. 2020) as well P/CVE policies, and preventive counter-terrorism practices. Indeed, the results of the analysis suggest that securitisation theory can offer causal explanations of a particular kind that bridges the analytical gap between pure description and theoretical models. By focusing on 'how is it possible' questions (Robinson 2017: 520), we can show securitisation processes in a historically contextualised way.

Furthermore, this research pairs securitisation theory with a process-tracing methodology. While so far 'process-mechanism explanations have received limited attention from critical, post-structural and constructivist scholars of security', this says little about their adequacy, and rather is 'likely due to the mistaken assumption that process tracing has no place in interpretivist methodologies because of its commitment to causal explanation' (Robinson 2017: 506). Thus, the choice is made to pair process tracing and securitisation theory in order 'to examine the social mechanisms which brought a social phenomenon into being' (Balzacq 2011: 49). This approach strives to be interpretivist in nature, due to the theoretical commitment of post-Copenhagen approaches to understand 'the intersubjective construction of threats' (Robinson 2017: 507).

Finally, the main criticisms directed against securitisation theory, including CS, rest on its inability to properly account for collective agency, that is, for the cacophony of opposing voices across and inside the different institutional bodies (Côté 2016). Being aware of this criticism, a large part of the research design has been geared towards minimising agency issues as outlined in institutionalist literature (Scharpf 1997). First, by moving beyond 'speech acts' to consider other sources of governance and power: agenda setting rules, threat perception formation and sites, for example those of knowledge creation and dissemination. Second, in order to capture the 'collective' institutional voice of the European Union, a wide variety of EU actors are included in the interview sample, not only the European Commission, which is strictly speaking the one tasked with prevention.

Finally, regarding research design, this chapter uses a six-stage model (see Figure 7.1; Lucarelli 2019: 215)[3] and moves away from previous analyses conflating the securitising move and audience response phases (Kaunert and Léonard 2019). Instead, I argue that the key to collective securitisation can only be found in the dialectic relationship existing between actors and phases of the securitising move and the audience response. Moreover, most securitisation processes reveal the existence of a 'hierarchy of audiences' (Coté 2016) in the response phase, some of which have a big impact; we can think of a major member state such as Germany. Other audiences, however, are lower in the hierarchy and not able to impact the final securitisation move to such an extent; such is the case with NGOs or critical scholars arguing

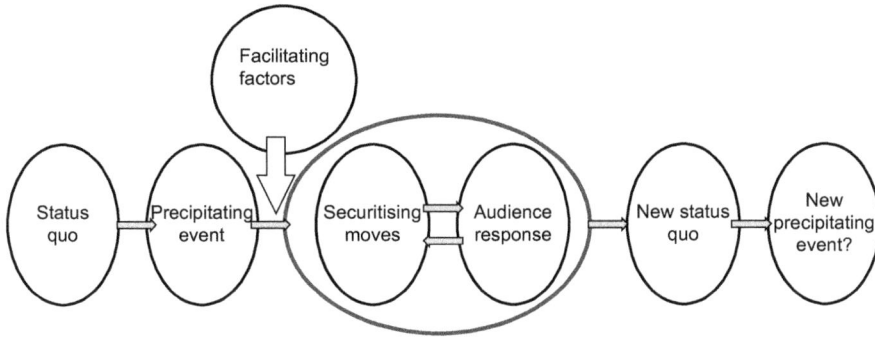

Figure 7.1: Modified collective securitisation model
(*source:* author's own work adapted from Sperling and Webber 2019)

against certain security provisions. This work focuses on the more dominant voices present, namely those of EU institutions and Member States.

Methodologically, a list of pseudo-anonymised interviewees can be found in Table 7.1. Interviews were almost solely conducted using remote methods (Bolaños-Somoano and Thyrard 2022) between late 2019 and the beginning of 2020, manually transcribed and analysed using a grounded theory approach (Locke 2002). Regarding positionality, this research acknowledges that access to the target interviewees was definitely facilitated by my identity as a white, female researcher from a prestigious university, with a good command of English and other Western European languages. In fact, it must be noted that, with the policy actors, my gender identity as a cis woman was a facilitating factor; this positive bias was at times reinforced by a particular performance of femininity that I dub 'good girl persona': 'the "good girl persona" implies actively undermining your own intelligence and assertiveness' (Bolaños-Somoano 2020).

Securitisation and P/CVE in the EU

There were, as of 2022, no studies tracing the securitisation of social policy in the EU. There are, however, some sources addressing the emergence of the EU's Prevention Model (Bossong 2014; 2012), the securitisation of terrorism in the EU broadly, the securitisation of Islam in today's society and political regimes (Bigo et al. 2015; Croft 2012; Eroukhmanoff 2018; Fox and Akbaba 2015; Mavelli 2013; Motilla 2018), and the role of P/CVE programmes as part of the EU's foreign policy (Argomaniz 2012; Gaub and Pauwels 2017). Work on the global development of Prevention notes the wide-spread turn of several large international organisations towards

Table 7.1: List of pseudo-anonymised interviewees

Interviewee	EU institution	Expertise area	Policy role
1.	Commission	Justice and Home Affairs	High-level civil servant
2.	Council	General Secretariat	Policy expert
3.	Commission	DG Home	Policy officer
4.	Commission	Anti-Discrimination	Policy officer
5.	Parliament	Counter-terrorism	Policy officer
6.	Commission	DG Home	High-level civil servant
7.	Parliament	Security Permanent Committee	High-level civil servant
8.	Parliament	EU Internal Security	Policy expert
9.	Parliament	Secretariat	National expert Western Europe
10.	Parliament	External Security	Policy expert
11.	Council	Counter-Terrorism	High-level civil servant
12.	Parliament	TERR Committee	Political advisor
13.	Parliament	Interfaith Dialogue	High-level civil servant
14.	Europol	Counter-Terrorism	Policy officer

Source: author's own work.

favouring P/CVE over police-based counter-terrorism (Tsui 2020). Most of the research on the securitisation of social policy through P/CVE, however, is focused on the United Kingdom and its unique governance arrangement PREVENT (Heath-Kelly 2013; Kaleem 2022; Ragazzi 2017; Winter et al. 2022).

Our present use of CS is informed by the fact that historically rooted Western perceptions about Islamic religious beliefs have permeated discussions on the causes of terrorism, and have had a profound impact on the design and implementation of prevention policy (Cesari 2009; Hussain and Bagguley 2012; Jackson 2007; Kundnani and Hayes 2018; Silke 2018). Such arguments are often tied in with claims of an 'Islamist bias' existent in the underlying logic of global prevention regimes (Kundnani and Hayes 2018). This anti-Muslim bias is well documented across different critical literatures. Chiefly, the decolonial approach suggests that Western states' security policies are intertwined with enduring legacies of colonialism, as well as racist and gendered constructions of the 'other' (Abbas 2021). All these background ideas ultimately feed into counter-terrorism policy and practice, and P/CVE is a prime example of these tendencies.

Indeed, some authors argue that radicalisation has come to be seen as a unique contemporary process linked almost exclusively to Muslims and Muslim/immigrant-related underlying causes (Coolsaet 2016: 27–8), despite the growing threat of right-wing extremism world-wide (Bolaños-Somoano and McNeil-Willson 2022; Somoano 2022).

Within EU counter-terrorism research, there is first a concern with effectiveness and proportionality of action. Accordingly, this paper's findings come to complement EU studies research on security integration, which warns that common EU responses are still undermined by differences in national threat perceptions, and that current EU counter-terrorism suffers from poor implementation and lack of legitimacy, among other problems (Monar 2007: 293). On the other hand, there is also a focus on the role of knowledge creation in EU security governance. First, through 'expert group discussions', which serve to clarify language, set common definitions and channel policy initiatives (Coolsaet 2010: 867). Second, by studying how knowledge creation around prevention, in particular with regards to funding, forces knowledge-creating actors to adapt their outputs to dominant discourses and national preferences (Russo and Selenica 2022).

The present work will hopefully contribute in several ways to the literature. First, by providing an empirical account of how the securitisation process of social policy unfolds and is influenced by hegemonic discourses on Islam and security. Second, by adding to the existing work on collective securitisation theory through empirical analysis and testing of existing theories (Lucarelli 2019). Third, by exploring issues of collective EU agency in an explicit and detailed manner which acknowledges audience responses, composite agencies and the *sui generis* nature of the EU.

Testing the theory: Modified collective securitisation model

Stages 1 and 2: The status quo and the precipitating event

The first stage, the status quo, is characterised by a tendency on the part of the EU and MS to solidarise with the American approach to the War on Terror. In 2001, shortly after the 9/11 attacks, an ad hoc programme of measures was drawn up by the General Secretariat of the Council. In response, the Commission speeded up a 'Proposal for a council framework decision on combating terrorism' (European Council 2001). This document would become the basis for all other proposals to come.

The purpose of this initiative was to confront radicalisation by addressing the key social conditions that may trigger such a process, primarily outside the European Union. Such conditions included poor or autocratic governance, rapid but unmanaged modernisation, and lack of political or economic prospects and of educational opportunities (European 2002). At this point, such conditions were not considered prevalent within the European Union, and the threat was largely perceived as external: 'the terrorism perpetrated by Al-Qa'ida and extremists inspired by Al-Qa'ida' (European Council 2001: para. 3).

In contrast to US-centric assumptions about 9/11, it was the 2004 bombings in Madrid's train station, Atocha, which really got EU Prevention policy moving along[4]. Al-Qa'ida claimed responsibility for the attacks, creating a big echo reminiscent of 9/11. Although historically inaccurate, to many EU citizens the Atocha attacks marked the entry of Jihadist terrorism in Europe. Indeed, the bomb attacks on the public transport systems of Madrid and London, in 2004 and 2005, served as rallying points, 'as catalysers for the creation of a coordinated counter-terrorism policy in Europe' (interviewee 5). Considering the rocky and uneven progress in the previous years, 2004 constituted a 'wake up call'.

The overall impression left by these attacks and the political responses towards them, was that of a 'new kind of terrorism', and that hitherto existing knowledge and legal approaches were no longer fitting. For some MS, terrorism was an ignored or non-problem, whereas most others were familiar with left-wing or separatist violence, therefore feeling unequipped to deal with 'religiously inspired threats'; 'Aside from the initial divergences among MS in their legal approaches to terrorism, or lack thereof, the Jihadist terrorist was new and many MSs were not equipped to deal with it' (interviewee 5).

The local nature of the 2004 and 2005 attacks caused discussions about homegrown terrorism to take centre stage in the political sphere. The identity of the terrorists and their affiliation with Al-Qa'ida constituted an important source of motivation for political action. The fact that many had resided in EU MS for years prior to the attacks led to rising concerns about 'home threats' and 'the threat from within'. Additional worries emerged around regular European Muslims' potential support for terrorism: 'The danger [is] not in a group of seven terrorists, but on the 7,000 people who actively or passively support them; the 700 people that are involved in illicit money-making operations that finance terrorism; etc.... Thus it is necessary to curtail social support...' (interviewee 1).

Counter-radicalisation emerged in 2005. It was officially introduced as one of the four key pillars in the EU's approach to 'combatting terrorism', in the European Union Strategy for Countering Terrorism, which formally instituted prevention as one of the four key pillars in the EU's approach to combatting terrorism (European Council 2005). It was conceived as part of a holistic policy paradigm encompassing all threats against public order, and identifying early prevention as a key step of a larger counter-terrorism strategy (European Commission 2004), thus justifying the intervention in the national social spheres, via coordinated EU action framed as a security measure.

The initial problem framing from 2004 to 2005 would continue to evolve following subsequent attacks, which 'triggered MS interest in increased cooperation and the need for further action within the EU' (interviewee 8). For example, during 2013–14, when the Islamic State self-proclaimed the Caliphate and EU citizens started travelling overseas in greater numbers, the issue of foreign fighters entered Commission discussions. In the UK particularly, the issue of foreign fighters captured significant public and political attention; 'I think in 2013, 2014, when we had the rise of ISIS, this was obviously a totally unprecedented challenge, attracting tens of thousands of Europeans and others to the so-called Caliphate. This had a really unprecedented dimension, so that it was only normal that the focus [of the policies] really shifted' (interviewee 2). And indeed, in the following plan for prevention, foreign fighters were featured explicitly (European Council 2014).

Stage 3: Facilitating factors – new terrorism discourse and inter-institutional cooperation

Aside from the EU-led knowledge production efforts on the field, there were larger discursive tendencies in global security arguing for a distinction between old, political, ideology-driven terrorism and a new, religiously inspired, and apolitical type of terror. The events of 2004 and 2005 only accrued this perception, and the veracity of this discourse was backed up by a perceived increase in terrorist activity on EU soil, which further served to legitimise securitising social policy as a security priority. In a relatively short period of time, most European public audiences and national politicians turned to the EU for a coordinated solution to a global problem, and were willing to accept and even demanded new approaches.

This shift of responsibility was facilitated by another condition: the novelty of prevention as a field. While P/CVE draws from pre-existing national approaches to crime prevention, such were rarely a formalised field but a loose set of practices. Thus, first, it was not previously an area with well-established national institutions and actors who would resist an EU concentration of activity on the field. Rather, the ad hoc creation of this field (primarily funded by EU institutions) facilitated a top–down transmission of knowledge from EU to the MS.

Second, while the EU produces and coordinates most knowledge production and dissemination (including staff training and financing programmes) on prevention aspects, there is no real transfer of competences at the EU level. Initiatives surrounding social policy, like education, mental health, and prison programmes, remain decidedly in national hands, and final implementation of prevention projects is a national choice.

Third and finally, interviewees highlighted the facilitative role played by the EU as a neutral dialoguing party during the Irish Peace Processes. This previous experience probably had a positive effect on MS' considerations of the EU's capacity to act, first as a networking node for opposing policy wants, and second proving the 'efficacy' of EU peace funds to support a grassroots forms of peacebuilding via social policy initiatives (Irvin et al. 2008).

> the regional development policy of the European Union has contributed greatly to this peace. And on what front has Europe played a role? In the social dimension. Not so much in the political or military dimension, not much in the diplomatic dimension, but a lot in the economic-financial-budgetary dimension, the fight against unemployment, increasing university cooperation, etc. (interviewee 1)

In sum, this cumulus of factors facilitated MS cooperation and activity, whilst allowing particularly invested MS and actors to circumvent the thorny issue of communitarisation, the transfer of responsibility for a national policy area to the EU level, that is, of core state powers such as social policy (Genschel and Jachtenfuchs 2016). Especially important here is also the EU's significant funding on prevention, which not only supports its dedicated bodies, but also funds research as well as implementation of P/CVE projects.

While there is no real transfer of competences, there was a de facto transfer of the agenda-setting power from the internal national realm to the EU Commission, where MS in fact compete to put their own conceptualisations first within EU-mediated discussion groups: '[We work] to make sure that the actions taken at the EU level, which are meant to support Member States and stakeholders, are really geared towards their needs, their expectations' (interviewee 2). Furthermore, the resulting EU Prevention paradigm echoes, to a certain extent, fundamental aspects of the EU's discourse of itself as a political order, for example, in its preoccupation with fundamental rights and civil society involvement (Bigo and Tsoukala 2008).

Stage 4: The securitising move – creating P/CVE

In this analysis of P/CVE, the object of securitisation is not terrorism broadly, but social policy and its inclusion in security provisions, legitimised by the threat of extremism. The securitising move is seen on the joint MS and EU's decision to link the 'new terrorism' threat framing with a social policy heavy solution. This solution, called the whole of society approach, rests on the promotion of personal development and emotional resilience, as well as on the alleviation of underlying causes for socio-political disaffection.

In the aftermath of Atocha, efforts coalesced at the EU Commission level to bring together experienced national staff in Brussels. They were familiar with terrorism, coming from the British Home Office, as well as from the Spanish Guardia Civil and National Police, together with Dutch representatives experienced in youth crime prevention. 'The Prevention dimension [of EU CT] is something that emerged naturally in a context of people who were very much aware that, to definitely win against terrorism, you need to work on the social level as well' (interviewee 1). These actors thus declare the centrality of social policy, 'because you cannot foresee all future terrorist organisations or threats, so what do you need to do is make the individual or society more resilient' (interviewee 2); whilst still higlighting a transnational need for 'better and updated knowledge' of Islamist terrorism. As a consequence of this need, an ad hoc research group created in 2006 meant to give the commission 'a starting point' to discuss improved policy responses to terrorism (European Commission 2006).

This is how the European Commission Expert Group on Violent Radicalisation, 'Radicalisation processes leading to acts of terrorism', was established, with a mandate to provide answers on issues of prevention and homegrown radicalisation. This group was multidisciplinary and of elite scholarly composition. A similar group was created in 2017 to deal with new open questions regarding lone actors and foreign fighters (European Commission 2017). EU and national policy makers then drew on this new knowledge to come up with a common policy response, respectful of fundamental rights and integrated in the EU security strategy; 'Scholars [from the Commission Expert Group] taught us that action must be concentrated at the street level, the lowest possible level and the closest to the general population. And the tools for that action are front-line practitioners: police forces, social services, doctors, justice system workers, prison staff, etc.' (interviewee 1).

The resulting policy reflects, first and foremost, Dutch approaches to local action and multi-agency cooperation in youth crime prevention strategies, themselves being heavily influenced by a 2004 AIVD (Dutch Intelligence) report on the long-term threat of Salafism for democracy and social cohesion.[5] The United Kingdom, in turn, was already developing its own PREVENT strategy, which would influence the EU model by highlighting the centrality of civil society and security cooperation strategies. Finally, the Spanish contributions on the field of prevention were police-work oriented as well as political.[6]

While these influences came from different national officials, the resulting efforts were presented as an EU initiative and clearly delineated different duties for EU institutions and MS. Research, knowledge production, training of staff, policy initiatives, and informational efforts would be centralised at the EU Commission and Council levels. MS would be mostly responsible for the adaptation of EU guidelines to local governance and its implementation. The CTC (the European Union's Counter-terrorism Coordinator's Office), on the council's side, would collect political trends and common policy needs, and transmit them to the Commission. The Commission, in turn, would further those needs to institutional research groups and other experts/think-tanks, in order to fill information gaps and propose policy solutions for further discussion with the Council, and eventually, after the Lisbon Treaty, also with the Parliament.

As a result of this cooperation, the EU produced a veritable cascade of policy documents, best practice guidelines, training manuals, and threat indicators, among others. These documents, while different among themselves, do however share some characteristics.

First, most EU policy documents are minimum-consensus documents, which are often vague in terms of project development, implementation timeframes, and assigning explicit duties; they also tend to employ ambiguous language on nationally sensitive topics, such as religiosity. This type of policy output results from harmonising conflicting national interests. Moreover, P/CVE policy outputs are further limited in their scope because of the EU's principle of subsidiarity. Subsidiarity is understood in its double meaning of delegation to national authorities and empowerment of NGOs and civil actors (practitioners) for implementation (see European Commission, December 2017). In practice, this means that the EU devises measures and institutions to complement MS initiatives on P/CVE; but ultimately, it is up to national authorities to implement them, and to practice accountability and democratic oversight. Second, prevention policy outputs have a multi-stakeholder character, requiring, only at the Commission level, the involvement of several DGs: Migration and Home Affairs, Health, Research and Education, as well as informal but constant cooperation with the ECTCO and ad hoc cooperation with other bodies.

There are also important outputs in terms of scholarly research. First, a significant amount of research projects on P/CVE is funded by the Commission, chiefly through the Horizon2020 and Horizon Europe grants, as well ERC grants. These projects mimic EU inter-governmental arrangements by establishing consortiums of actors from different universities, disciplines, and countries to work together on concrete challenges. These research grants often include concrete deliverables in exchange for funding: from databases on polarisation or risk factors, to improving action guidelines, or to didactic materials for other actors to use. The resulting research is seen by EU actors as a great achievement in itself, which they can export as privileged knowledge to other countries and institutions interested in developing similar prevention strategies (European Council 2020). It is important to note that EU funding, either directly from the Commission's budget or via ERC research grants, constitutes one of the key drivers of research and practice of prevention issues in Europe today, with the consequent influence it implies in determining research agendas throughout Europe and abroad (Russo and Selenica 2022).

To conclude, there is a high degree of cooperation across EU institutions on P/CVE efforts. Europol provides strategic predictions and threat perceptions through yearly reports. The EU Council and the ECTC put new issues on the table for political discussion. The EU Commission takes the Council requests, as well as MS requests for action and/or knowledge, and translates them into concrete policy answers to be cycled back to the Council. Finally, the European Parliament fulfils the role of an oversight provider. In 2017, an special committee was established to evaluate the existing EU policy strategy around counter-terrorism (TERR 2018), including prevention efforts. While civil liberties aspects of the CT strategy did cause strong divisions, prevention itself was met with overwhelming support and high degree of consensus. 'Parliament has always stressed the importance of prevention and that is actually very much in line with the Commission's approach to support front-line practitioners to engage with civil society...' (interviewee 2).

These elements point to the EU having a high level of inter-institutional agreement and effective labour division on prevention. This means that, despite each institution having distinct approaches to issues of security and inside dynamics affecting their positions, their positions (of the different EU institutions) are aligned in so far as they all agree on the securitisation of social policy being necessary to fight terrorism, presenting a united front on the part of the securitising move. The practical obstacles posed by the proposed multi-stakeholder transnational governance structure have been an incentive to create specific EU bodies centralising tasks and facilitating cooperation. In general, this is not surprising, as the gradual securitisation of social policy has produced a significant and disordered expansion of bureaucratic actors with competing competencies at the European level, perfectly illustrating the phenomenon known as 'Brusselisation'.

Chiefly, among the new bodies created, is the ECTCO or European Counter-terrorism Coordinator Office, set up in 2005 on Javier Solana's suggestion. The ECTCO was meant to fulfil a coordination role, to maintain an overview of all the instruments at the Union's disposal, to closely monitor the implementation of the EU counter-terrorism strategy, and to ensure an active role for the EU in the fight against terrorism (European Counter Terrorism Coordinator 2011). The ECTCO is a mediator and facilitator, with no direct hierarchical authority and no funding. Under Giles de Kerchove, its first director, it had however considerable political poise and facilitated informal policy exchanges for combined responses.

The second, least researched and most relevant new body is the Radicalisation Awareness Network (RAN). Established in 2011, in the aftermath of the Norway attacks, the RAN initiative was put forward by the EU Commission and is divided since 2021 between RAN Practitioners and RAN Policy Support. The first branch, RAN Practitioners, is managed via a commission procurement contract held by a Dutch company, Radar Avies, whereas the second branch is composed of civil servants working on P/CVE nationally. Its two branches are respectively tasked with training national civil society actors (practitioners), and providing advice to national policy actors on radicalisation and prevention issues. RAN's goal is 'to pool experiences, knowledge and good practices' to a centralised EU level and back to the national level (European Commission 2010: 7).

Stage 5: Audience response

On its part, MS responses to the securitising of prevention by the EU were varied. Some MS were especially active, either because of an institutional tradition of counter-terrorism or due to being directly targeted by a terrorist attack.

As it is the case with EU institutions, MS maintained a relative common front on the ensuing developments of prevention policy. A good example of this is religion, which was initially absent from EU policy documents, but which, as a result of the political pressures following the 2015 Paris attacks, was explicitly included in prevention policy. Following January 2015, French Prime Minister Manuel Valls endorsed this approach, as did his Belgian colleague Charles Michel. The agreement was to characterise Jihadist terrorism as a fanatical ideology wanting to impose its obscurantist vision through extreme violence. National pressures to directly include religion in EU documents were eventually successful. As noted in the previous section, no political or parliamentary conflict took place at the European level to an extent comparable to the ongoing debates on other areas of CT, like data privacy and civil liberties (EAVA 2018).

In general, developments concerned with Jihadist terrorism were met with support across EU institutions and Member States alike. As we see in the previous section, countries like the UK, Spain, the Netherlands, and France were very active and involved in providing nuances and guiding EU policy towards their respective interests. Indeed, for some national entrepreneurs, the EU momentum and the resources devoted to prevention constituted a window of opportunity to gain agenda-setting power in previously unclaimed areas. 'There is a window of opportunity, of around nine months, where politicians can act [on bringing new issues to the table]. What doesn't get done in that period, doesn't tend to get done' (interviewee 1). Originally, these were salient matters for specific countries which spilled over into a general EU concern. This is the case with the inclusion of lone actors, foreign fighters, and vulnerable communities, for example, as very high-profile elements of EU knowledge creation efforts and policy outputs.[7]

Since 2017, the EU Commission has also hosted several High-Level Commission Expert Groups on Radicalisation related to prevention in which nationally sent civil servants and ministry officials exchange priorities and discuss current policy priorities in a more informal setting (European Commission 2017).

The High Level Expert Group on Radicalisation was set up following an initiative of the Directorate General Migration and Home Affairs on 27 July 2017 (European Commission 2017). Having completed its mandate and being subsequently renewed, this group brings together representatives from MS, the EU Commission and relevant EU agencies. Its offers advice on how to improve cooperation and collaboration among national policy stakeholders as well as suggestions to develop targeted measures for preventing radicalisation. It also constitutes a lobbying point for national experts to propose problems and solutions. Several such areas, identified as priorities by Member States, have been selected for further action at EU level, such as prison rehabilitation, online propaganda, education and social inclusion, and the external dimension of radicalisation (High-Level Commission Expert Group on Radicalisation 2018).

MS response to the securitising move is also seen in other, more indirect areas. For example, Europol's European Union Terrorism Situation and Trend reports (TE-SAT) is a vehicle for MS audience response, allowing national interests to enter EU governance and legislation. The yearly TE-SAT reports are compiled relying primarily on national data, but each MS contributes differently to these reports. P/CVE problems are thus primarily defined by certain MS who provide more information, and their framing is going to be more prevalent in how the threat is perceived first at Europol and then at EU institutional level. This approach to problem framing, reliant on MS interests, has led to potentially under- or over-reporting on certain issues depending on varying national interests:

> You have a first problem there, which is that not all Member States feed the same amount of information to Europol: some MSs are very active, others aren't. What you get as a result is that problems are defined by certain MSs which provide more information, and their understanding of terrorism is going to be prevalent in how the threat is perceived at Europol and then at the EU institutional level. Another problem is that things can be over-reported or to the contrary, be under the radar (interviewee 8).

In particular, the Islamist bias present in the EU strategy since its inception has kept certain countries away from the discussions, with at least two observable divides among MS. On the one hand, while almost all Western European MSs have experienced major Jihadist attacks (Spain, France, Italy, Germany, Netherlands, etc.), very few countries in Central and Eastern Europe have had a problem with Jihadism. Consequently, the latter countries tended to stay away from providing data (problem framing) or research/policy solutions regarding Jihadism. On the other hand, these same Western MS are only now starting to collectively address right-wing terrorism as a real threat. The consequence has been that Central and Eastern European Member States (Czech Republic, Slovakia, Romania, etc.) are becoming increasingly involved in terrorism discussions, now that they revolve around an issue they actually have experienced. Germany, however, remains the lead driver of prevention policy and practices addressing right wing extremism and terrorism, pushing for a coordinated and homogenised EU legal framework, among other initiatives.

Thus, another division would be probably between MS that have experienced Jihadist terrorism and those which have not. Most attacks so far have occurred in Western Europe: Spain, France, UK, and Benelux, in contrast to Central and Eastern European countries. This cleavage is likely to be altered by the irruption of a new threat: right-wing terrorism. Until now, Central and Eastern European MS were not very interested in the ongoing EU discussions on counter-terrorism, given the Jihadist angle, but this will change and such MS will go on to take up a bigger role in policy discussions.

Stages 6 and 7: New status quo and new precipitating event

In the final section of this analysis, I will compare the initial status quo with the one resulting from the successful securitising move and introduce the next precipitating event.

First, we must highlight the successful securitisation of social policy, having been incorporated as a cornerstone of EU counter-terrorism. Intervention in social policy as a way to mitigate security risks posed by terrorism and violent extremism have thus become the new status quo. Not only that, in fifteen years, prevention has amassed its own institutional centre of gravity, with new permanent bodies and funding regimes attached. MS have indeed adopted EU guidelines on prevention at the national level. Nevertheless, policy initiatives continue to vary from country to country; in some cases, they are further distorted because of the implementation of the governments' own political biases regarding Islam and security.

A telling example is how slowly prevention developments on right-wing extremism is being accepted, depending on the member state and their political scenes. Right-wing extremist activity in Western Europe and other Western countries has triggered a new participating event, and is indeed the turning point to a new status quo.

'I really think it is based on the attacks. If they are isolated, you don't make much of it, but if you see that there are attacks like in Germany and New Zealand… At a certain point there is a critical mass which then leads Member States and others to say ok, let's re-focus our attention on right wing extremism. There is a before and after Christchurch' (interviewee 2). Thus, the 2019 attacks of Christchurch, New Zealand constituted an early wake-up call for prevention bodies in the EU. But the attacks in Halle and Hanau in Germany, in 2019 and 2020, respectively were the true precipitating event for EU collective action to begin rolling.

Discussion

P/CVE and the securitisation of social policy at the EU level: How and by whom?

Applying the collective securitisation framework to European P/CVE policies, I have been able to trace the process and main actors involved in the securitisation of social policy in the European Union. This is, while a priori prevention policy is part of a security strategy, its implementation is irredeemably linked to action on the social policy spheres: education, youth, citizenship… This Securitization of social policy, heralded by migration scholars, is the product of the risk-oriented policy mentality, which is future-oriented, rather than present-focused, and deploys managerial conception of policing attached to a racialized conception of social order (Ragazzi 2017: 170).

As I have shown, Member States have had direct and indirect ways of influencing the content of EU prevention policy. But while these influences are real, their importance towards the larger institutional development is secondary to the EU's ability to render terrorism prevention a new, actionable field. The EU Commission should be highlighted as the main securitising actor, although this was only possible due to high levels of inter-institutional agreement on the topic, counting with the support of the Council and the Parliament. The securitising move, especially, shows how radicalisation as a policy concept enabled policy makers and epistemic communities to render a simple, understandable, linear narrative around terrorism engagement, making it accessible to EU-proposed problem solving and governance approaches (Heath-Kelly 2013: 396).

In a wide range of areas, knowledge and expertise about a subject is required by policymakers in order to make decisions; thus, the knowledge available influences the way EU policy-makers define the solution to the problem (Haas 1990: 9–12). I therefore argue that the main source of EU influence is the creation of knowledge through expert and practice networks. These actors play a pivotal role in the transfer and diffusion of knowledge by promoting policy innovation; policy diffusion; policy selection, and even policy evolution as learning (Adler and Haas 1992a). The creation of transnational networks of prevention experts, practitioners, and policy-makers with common norms, and the interactions within these networks, were vital to the success of the institutional learning and diffusion processes (Adler and Haas 1992b; Cross 2011; Haas 1990). These networks work both by allowing experts to exchange their ideas during transnational conferences or workshops and by encouraging networking between the epistemic community and the decision-making arena, enabling these new ideas to become official. In the end, successful epistemic communities, aided by institutional resources and constrained by larger international trends, managed to develop a new framing of terrorism and to thus justify the creation of a new area of policy in response: P/CVE.

By privileging ideology over context, policy priorities could be pooled and the challenging task of devising a whole-of-society strategy could bypass sensitive national issues, such as the role of religion in public spheres. The EU was then able to disseminate its model across national settings thanks to its monopoly of knowledge production and dissemination routes, as well as other facilitating factors such as the novelty of the field and MS's various interests in pushing agenda-setting on prevention to the EU level. This situation confirms theoretical expectations about the role and influence of knowledge production and policy diffusion. Indeed, following theoretical expectations from the UK, the radicalisation discourse in Europe should be considered as performative security knowledge (Heath-Kelly 2013: 408). This is an ontology that discursively produces the threats it claims to identify through risk-strategies, rather than acting as a response to already existing risks.

In terms of collective institutional agency, which does the securitising, the lines between EU and MS agency are blurred at times. For example, when a national policy expert proposes policy innovations within a EU Commission policy forum, they are conveying a national interest framed within an EU institutional initiative. There are of course more easily identifiable EU actors, in the shape of the EU Commission and Council bureaucrats, technicians and experts, or MS policy experts. However, a third type of hybrid actor seems to arise from the analysis. This research proposes that this type of actor should be understood as embodying EU collective agency, which cannot be fully understood under either a national or a supranational lens. Rather, it is better seen as the interaction between national interests and EU institutions, conveyed by individual actors or epistemic communities who themselves belong to both denominations, the national and supranational.

To conclude, I will briefly discuss the current prevention governance structure which emerged from the securitising move. MS have retained discretion in implementation regimes, as well as a good degree of influence in agenda setting and research matters. The EU, however, has primacy as a policy coordinator and forum-provider. It also has the upper hand in terms of knowledge creation. As such, these knowledge production circles constitute a primary EU tool to mobilise experts and civil society actors in a flexible framework, and to encourage the circulation of best practices regarding prevention, both inside and outside the EU. For example, through the RAN, the EU can provide an actionable framework without appearing as a norm-provider and circumventing the practicalities of national prevention management. It also allows MSs to participate without the threat of legally binding agreements.

Therefore, knowledge production and expert pooling constitute a costless and safe way to expand the political framing of prevention across national borders, whilst highlighting the important and helpful nature of the EU as a security actor. Also present is the EU focus on the role of knowledge creation through 'expert group discussions', to clarify language, set common definitions, and channel divergent policy initiatives (Bossong 2012: 1; Coolsaet 2010: 867). The disaggregated stages of collective securitisation come close in several points to the EU hard CT literature. Namely, they reveal that EU initiatives on counter-terrorism are more reactive than proactive, and that their acceptance by MS depends on the respect of national sovereignty. EU Prevention measures indeed answer to stimuli by external discourses on terrorism, security shocks and political pressures. Member States remain untouched in their prerogatives and specificities. This brings us to a second point on the resulting governance of P/CVE. Although originally conceived as an ideology-free approach to terrorism, the EU prevention model was developed in response to a security threat often framed in terms of Islam and religiosity rather than political struggle. Examples of this include the fact that many current programmes are targeting Jihadist-vulnerable communities, that is, Muslim communities. A similar trend is true of research projects, which are still primarily concerned with issues of radicalisation among Muslim and migrant communities. We can thus talk of a leftover Islamist bias in EU prevention. It remains to be seen whether the EU's copy-and-paste approach to right-wing violence can be successful.

Conclusions and further research

This contribution has explored the process of collective securitisation of social policy in the European Union. It has observed, at the case study level, the emergence of a new type of counter-terrorism, which focuses on root causes and ideological/religious pull factors, while relying on social work and employing a whole-of-society logic. This approach is ontologically rooted on the concept of radicalisation which is inextricably linked to an Islamist bias.

Within these developments, this research has highlighted how the concatenation of security shocks, conducive discursive conditions and EU/MS policy interests have fraught the evolution of the field. The lack of domestic versions of the policy field, together with EU patronage and dynamic role as policy coordinator, meant a high degree of inter-institutional and transnational cooperation at the EU sphere. In the current situation, MS retain most implementation competences, whilst the EU collaborates by producing and distributing innovative knowledge on the field among MS, EU policy makers, and implementation actors.

Finally, this research concludes by proposing some avenues for future research, which would benefit from addressing the CS shortcomings outlined in the discussion. First, stronger theoretical and empirical tests are needed connecting crisis as opportunity (Boin et al. 2009) and process tracing methodologies (Beach and Pedersen 2016) to securitisation models. Such linkages would compensate for the lacking micro-analysis and would help to integrate this model within larger EU studies and institutional analysis literature. Moreover, securitisation theory requires a mixed-methods approach, which would combine traditional interview data with quantitative data derived from institutional activity and composition.

Second, in this chapter, I have conducted an examination of the development and pragmatic obstacles associated with the formulation and execution of counter-radicalisation strategies within the EU. These challenges hint on the need to strike a delicate equilibrium between efficacy, legitimacy, and societal integration. The discipline of decolonial studies presents valuable viewpoints that have the potential to enhance counter-terrorism and deradicalisation approaches at both the policy and implementation levels within the EU.

Thus, I recommend that additional research on EU P/CVE should effectively incorporate decolonial insights, so as move beyond the critique and promote the advancement of alternative human security paradigms prioritising pluralism, participation, and justice. By integrating these perspectives, the EU has the potential to enhance the efficacy and inclusivity of its P/CVE strategies while limiting discriminatory national approaches and anticipating social and cultural backlash against counter-terrorism as a whole.

This chapter is based on the author's PhD study, exploring preventive counter-terrorism in the EU, completed at the European University Institute in Florence.

Notes

1 The author acknowledges that the use of the label 'Jihadist' or 'Jihadism' is not without issues. However, more neutral labels such as 'religious extremism' paint a picture of neutrality not to be found in the data, as both EU documents and interviewees confirm a preoccupation with ISIS and ISIS-inspired violence in this period, and not with, for example, Christian nationalist violence.

2 Collective securitisation is a further theoretical development of securitisation theory: the influential framework for security and international relations analysis proposed by the Copenhagen School (Buzan et al. 1998). This school, currently in its second generation, has underwent many changes. For lack of space, only the present strand of securitisation theory used is discussed. For an in-depth discussion, see Stritzel (2014b) and Knudsen (2001).

3 For lack of space, this research will conflate the first and last two stages, status quo and precipitating event, and new status quo and new precipitating event, into one section. This should not be taken as a theoretical assumption that these two stages are indistinguishable.

4 The relevance of Atocha and the 2005 London bombings have been explored previously only in regard to domestic effects on internal security reform (Reinares 2009).

5 Said report was probably prompted by the murder of a film director in Amsterdam in 2004 by a presumed Jihadist.

6 A Spanish politician, Javier Solana, would be of great help in the future inclusion of prevention as a legitimate policy field within the EU CT Strategy.

7 This type of knowledge creation also heavily relies on Commission-funded and guided research, usually through the RAN or Horizon20/Horizon Europe research grants, moving away from academia. 'I don't think academics are involved nor sought after that much at this point, in terms of evidence bases for radicalisation models and so on. Or at least not academia outside the EU institutions, so there are experts within institutions and those are consulted but academia at large isn't very involved at this point' (interviewee 8).

References

Abbas, T. (2021). *Countering Violent Extremism: The International Deradicalization Agenda*. London: I.B. Tauris. https://doi.org/10.5040/9781838607258

Adler, E. and Haas, P. M. (1992a). 'Conclusion: Epistemic communities, world order, and the creation of a reflective research program', *International Organization*, 46(1), 367–90. https://doi.org/10.1017/S0020818300001533

Argomaniz, J. (2012). 'A rhetorical spillover? Exploring the link between the European Union Common Security and Defence Policy (CSDP) and the external dimension in EU counterterrorism', *European Foreign Affairs Review*, 17, 35–52.

Balzacq, T. (2011). 'Enquiries into methods: A new framework for securitization analysis', in *Securitization Theory: How Security Problems Emerge and Dissolve*, PRIO New Security Studies. New York: Routledge, pp. 45–68.

Balzacq, T. (2010). *Understanding Securitisation Theory: How Security Problems Emerge and Dissolve*. London: Routledge.

Beach, D. and Pedersen, R. B. (2016). *Causal Case Study Methods: Foundations and Guidelines for Comparing, Matching and Tracing*. Ann Arbor: University of Michigan Press.

Bigo, D., Carrera, S., Guild, E., Guittet, E.-P., Jeandesboz, J., Mitsilegas, V., Ragazzi, F., and Scherrer, A. (2015). 'The EU and its counter-terrorism policies after the Paris attacks', *Liberty and Security in Europe*, 84, 27 November. CEPS Pap. Lib. Secur. Eur, pp. 1–16.

Bigo, D. and Tsoukala, A. (2008). *Terror, Insecurity and Liberty: Illiberal Practices of Liberal Regimes After 9/11*. New York: Routledge.

Boin, A., Hart, P., McConnell, A. (2009). 'Crisis exploitation: Political and policy impacts of framing contests', *Journal of Euopean. Public Policy*, 16(1), 81–106. https://doi.org/10.1080/13501760802453221

Bolaños-Somoano, I. (2020). 'Gender and danger: The 'good girl persona' in institutional fieldwork', *New Ethnographer*, accessed 5 August 2023. https://thenewethnographer.com/the-new-ethnographer/ux7ugsabn07b457slo8rz7ltcsn2e4

Bolaños-Somoano, I. and McNeil-Willson, R. (2022). *Lessons From the Buffalo Shooting: Responses to Violent White Supremacy*. The Hague: ICCT.

Bolaños-Somoano, I. and Thyrard, A. (2022). From a back-up plan to a purposeful research design. Using remote fieldwork in two EU case studies', *Politique Européenne*, 78(4), 32–46.

Bossong, R. (2014). 'EU cooperation on terrorism prevention and violent radicalization: Frustrated ambitions or new forms of EU security governance?', *Cambridge Review of International Affairs*, 27(1), 66–82. https://doi.org/10.1080/09557571.2013.839627

Bossong, R. (2012). 'Assessing the EU's added value in the area of terrorism prevention and violent radicalisation', DIW., Economics of Security Working Paper 19.

Boyle, M. J. (ed.) (2019). *Non-Western Responses to Terrorism: New Directions in Terrorism Studies*. Manchester: Manchester University Press.

Buzan, B., Waever, O., and Wilde, J. de (1998). *Security: A New Framework for Analysis*. Boulder, CO: Lynne Rienner Publishers.

Cesari, J. (2009). 'The securitisation of Islam in Europe', CEPS Challenge Paper No. 15, Changing Landscape of European Liberty and Security. 9 April, Berlin: Centre for European Studies.

Coaffee, J. and Wood, D. M. (2006). 'Security is coming home: Rethinking scale and constructing resilience in the global urban response to terrorist risk', *International Relations*, 20(4), 503–17. https://doi.org/10.1177/0047117806069416

Coolsaet, R. (2016), ' "All radicalisation is local": The genesis and drawbacks of an elusive concept', *Egmont-Royal Institute for International Relations*, 84, 1–49.

Coolsaet, R. (2010). 'EU counterterrorism strategy: Value added or chimera?' *International Affairs*, 86(4), 857–73. https://doi.org/10.1111/j.1468–2346.2010.00916.x

Côté, A. (2016). 'Agents without agency: Assessing the role of the audience in securitization theory', *Security Dialogue*, 47(6), 541–58. https://doi.org/10.1177/0967010616672150

Croft, S. (2012). *Securitizing Islam. Identity and the Search for Security*. Cambridge: Cambridge University Press. https://doi.org/10.1017/CBO9781139104142

Cross, M. (2011). *Security Integration in Europe: How Knowledge-Based Networks are Transforming the European Union*. Ann Arbor: University of Michigan Press.

EAVA (2018). 'The fight against terrorism: Cost of non-Europe report', *European Parliamentary Research Service*, https://epthinktank.eu/2018/05/28/the-fight-against-terrorism-cost-of-non-europe-report/ (accessed 11 February 2020).

Eroukhmanoff, C. (2018). "It's not a Muslim ban!" Indirect speech acts and the securitisation of Islam in the United States post-9/11', *Global Discourse*, 8(1), 5–25. https://doi.org/10.1080/23269995.2018.1439873

European Commission (2004). 'Final communication from the commission to the council and the European parliament: Prevention, preparedness and response to terrorist attacks', https://eur-lex.europa.eu/LexUriServ/LexUriServ.do?uri=COM:2004:0698:FIN:EN:PDF

European Commission (2006). 'Commission decision of 19 April 2006 setting up a group of experts to provide policy advice to the Commission on fighting violent radicalisation, OJ L, https://eur-lex.europa.eu/legal-content/EN/ALL/?uri=CELEX:32006D0299

European Commission (2010). 'The EU internal security strategy in action: Five steps towards a more secure Europe. Communication from the Commission, https://eur-lex.europa.eu/LexUriServ/LexUriServ.do?uri=COM:2010:0673:FIN:EN:PDF

European Commission (2017). 'Commission decision of 27.7.2017 setting-up the High-Level Commission Expert Group on radicalisation'.

European Council (2001). 'Conclusions and plan of action of the extraordinary European Council meeting', SN 140/01.

European Council (2002). 'Council framework decision of 13 June 2002 on combating terrorism (2002/475/JHA)'. https://doi.org/10.1007/978–3-642–18896–1_46

European Council (2014). 'Revised EU Strategy for combating radicalisation and recruitment to terrorism'.

European Council (2020). 'Council conclusions on EU external action on preventing and countering terrorism and violent extremism', 8868/20, https://eur-lex.europa.eu/LexUriServ/LexUriServ.do?uri=COM:2004:0698:FIN:EN:PDF

European Counter Terrorism Coordinator (2011). 'EU Action Plan on combating terrorism', https://data.consilium.europa.eu/doc/document/ST-15358-2009-INIT/en/pdf

Fox, J. and Akbaba, Y. (2015). 'Securitization of Islam and religious discrimination: Religious minorities in Western democracies, 1990–2008', *Comparative European Politics*, 13, 175–97. https://doi.org/10.1057/cep. 2013.8

Gaidaev, O. S. (2022). ' "Danger: Security"! Securitization Theory and the Paris School of International Security Studies', *MGIMO Review of International Relations*, 15(1), 7–37. https://doi.org/10.24833/2071–8160–2022–1-82–7-37

Gaub, F. and Pauwels, A. (2017). '*Counter-terrorism cooperation with the Southern Neighbourhood*', Policy brief. Policy Department, Directorate-General for External Policies.

Genschel, P. and Jachtenfuchs, M. (2016). 'More integration, less federation: The European integration of core state powers', *Journal of European Public Policy*, 23, 42–59. https://doi.org/10.1080/13501763.2015.1055782

Haas, E. B. (1990). *When Knowledge is Power: Three Models of Change in International Organizations*. Berkeley: University of California Press.

Heath-Kelly, C. (2013). 'Counter-terrorism and the counterfactual: Producing the 'radicalisation' discourse and the UK PREVENT strategy', *British Journal of Politics and International Relations*, 15, 394–415. https://doi.org/10.1111/j.1467–856X.2011.00489.x

High-Level Commission Expert Group on Radicalisation (2018). 'High-Level Commission Expert Group on Radicalisation (HLCEG-R): final report', Directorate-General for Migration and Home Affairs, Brussels.

Hussain, Y. and Bagguley, P. (2012). 'Securitized citizens: Islamophobia, racism and the 7/7 London bombings', *Sociological Review*, 60, 715–34. https://doi.org/10.1111/j.1467–954X.2012.02130.x

Irvin, C., Fissuh, E., and Byrne, S. (2008). 'The role of the European Union Peace II Fund and the International Fund for Ireland in building the peace dividend in Northern Ireland', *International Politics*, 47, 229–50.

Jackson, R. (2007). 'Constructing Enemies? Islamic Terrorism in political and academic discourse', *Government and Opposition*, 42(3), 394–426. https://doi.org/10.1111/j.1477–7053.2007.00229.x

Kaleem, A. (2022). 'The hegemony of Prevent: Turning counter-terrorism policing into common sense', *Critical Studies on Terrorism*, 15(2), 267–89. https://doi.org/10.1080/17539153.2021.2013016

Kaunert, C. and Léonard, S. (2019). '*The collective securitisation of terrorism in the European Union*, West European Politics 42(2), 261–77. https://doi.org/10.1080/01402382.2018.1510194

Knudsen, O. F. (2001). 'Post-Copenhagen security studies: Desecuritizing securitization', *Security Dialogue*, 32(3), 355–68. https://doi.org/10.1177/0967010601032003007

Kundnani, A. and Hayes, B. (2018). *The globalisation of countering violent extremism policies. Undermining Human Rights, Instrumentalising Civil Society*. Amsterdam: Transnational Institute.

Locke, K. (2002). 'The grounded theory approach to qualitative research', in Drasgow, F. and Schmitt, N. (eds) *Measuring and Analyzing Behavior in Organizations: Advances in Measurement and Data Analysis*, The Jossey-Bass Business & Management Series. Hoboken, NJ: Jossey-Bass/Wiley, pp. 17–43.

Lucarelli, S. (2019). 'The EU as a securitising agent? Testing the model, advancing the literature', *West European Politics*, 42(2), 413–36. https://doi.org/10.1080/01402382.2018.1510201

Martini, A. (2020). *Legitimising Countering Extremism at an International Level: The Role of the United Nations Security Council, Encountering Extremism*. Manchester: Manchester University Press.

Mavelli, L. (2013). 'Between normalisation and exception: The securitisation of Islam and the construction of the secular subject', *Millennium Journal of International Studies*, 41(2), 159–81. https://doi.org/10.1177/0305829812463655

Mohamed, S., Png, M.-T., and Isaac, W. (2020). 'Decolonial AI: Decolonial theory as sociotechnical foresight in artificial intelligence', *Philosophy & Technology*, 33, 659–84.

Monar, J. (2007). 'Common threat and common response? The European Union's counter-terrorism strategy and its problems', *Government & Opposition*, 42(3), 292–313. https://doi.org/10.1111/j.1477–7053.2007.00225.x

Motilla, A. (2018). 'Security and religious radicalization: Securitization of Islam in Europe', *Stato Chiese e Pluralismo Confessionale*, 1.

Ragazzi, F. (2017). 'Countering terrorism and radicalisation: Securitising social policy?', *Critical Social Policy*, 37(2), 163–79. https://doi.org/10.1177/026101831 6683472

Reinares, F. (2009). 'After the Madrid Bombings: Internal security reforms and prevention of global terrorism in Spain', *Studies in Conflict and Terrorism*, 32(5), 367–88. https://doi.org/10.1080/10576100902836767

Robinson, C. (2017), 'Tracing and explaining securitization: Social mechanisms, process tracing and the securitization of irregular migration', *Security Dialogue*, 48(6), 505–23. https://doi.org/10.1177/0967010617721872

Russo, A. and Selenica, E. (2022). 'Actors and sites for knowledge production on radicalisation in Europe and beyond', *Contemporary European Studies* 30(2), 236–54. https://doi.org/10.1080/14782804.2021.1997729

Scharpf, F. W. (1997). 'Games real actors play: Actor-centered institutionalism in policy research', in *Theoretical Lenses on Public Policy*. Boulder, CO: Westview Press.

Silke, A. (2018). *Routledge Handbook of Terrorism and Counterterrorism*. New York: Routledge. https://doi.org/10.4324/9781315744636

Singh, P., Sreenivasan, S., Szymanski, B.K., and Korniss, G. (2016). 'Competing effects of social balance and influence', *Physical Review E*, 93(4), 1–8.

Somoano, I.B. (2022). 'The right-leaning be memeing: Extremist uses of Internet memes and insights for CVE design', *First Monday*, 27(5). https://doi.org/ 10.5210/fm.v27i5.12601

Sperling, J. and Webber, M. (2019). 'The European Union: Security governance and collective securitisation', *West European Politics*, 42(2), 228–60. https://doi.org/ 10.1080/01402382.2018.1510193

Stockdale, L. P. D. (2013). 'Imagined futures and exceptional presents: A conceptual critique of 'pre-emptive security', *Global Change, Peace & Security*, 25(2), 141–57. https://doi.org/10.1080/14781158.2013.774342

Stritzel, H. (2014a). 'A securitization theory post-Copenhagen School', in Stritzel, H. (ed.) *Security in Translation: Securitization Theory and the Localization of Threat*, New Security Challenges Series. London: Palgrave Macmillan, pp. 38–51. https://doi.org/10.1057/9781137307576_3

Stritzel, H. (2014b). *Security in Translation: Securitization Theory and the Localization of Threat*. London: Palgrave Macmillan.

TERR, S.C. on T. (2018). *TERR: Overview of Activities during the mandate (2017–2018)*. European Parliament, Brussels.

Tsui, C.-K. (2020). 'Interrogating the concept of (violent) extremism: A genealogical study of terrorism and counter-terrorism discourses', in Martin, A., Ford, K., and Jackson, R. (eds) *Encountering Extremism*. Manchester: Manchester University Press, pp. 21–39.

Winter, C., Heath-Kelly, C., Kaleem, A., and Mills, C. (2022). 'A moral education? British values, colour-blindness, and preventing terrorism', *Critical Social Policy*, 42(1), 85–106. https://doi.org/10.1177/0261018321998926

8

The individual and the intimate in counter-terrorism: The case of the British government's Prevent strategy

Amna Kaleem

In their report entitled 'The globalisation of countering violent extremism', Kundnani and Hayes provide a comprehensive account of a new front in the War on Terror that situates policing activities within the domestic spheres (2018). They chart the emergence of Countering Violent Extremism (CVE) programmes and security logics in the post-9/11 era, their co-optation of the 'hearts and minds' rhetoric from counter-insurgency (COIN) tactics (Dunlap 2016; Sabir 2017), and their institutionalised adoption by international organisations. This report is a useful resource in understanding how the international logics of counter-terrorism have migrated into domestic security infrastructures. This chapter will take this work forward by moving beyond the focus on the macro-level organisational structures and situating this enquiry within the intimate politics of everyday. Studying the enactment of the British government's Prevent strategy, I will draw on the findings of fifty-five semi-structured interviews conducted with educators, medics, and social workers to unpack the personal politics of counter-terrorism policies. This approach is useful because by restricting our focus to international organisations or states, we situate the coercion of security policing outside of our immediate surroundings. The violence of counter-terrorism and the injustices perpetrated in the name of security stay confined to far-flung spaces like Guantánamo Bay or the Abu Ghraib prison. Furthermore, as the editors of this volume explain, this analysis restricts our understanding of CVE policies as 'extraordinary, emergency legislation' that are at odds with the values of Western liberal democracies. By shifting our analytical gaze to the individual and the intimate in the everyday, we learn that these policies are not exceptional measures but rather a continuation of colonial epistemic violence. This helps us see that the War on Terror is being waged within our communities, with our bodies serving as the terrain where international and domestic security logics converge. As Finden, Yousaf, and Guéguin in this volume discuss, this approach also helps us situate the violence of the security state within the framework of coloniality that reveals a through line between imperialist subjugations and modern-day liberal politics

(Abu-Bakare 2022; Cruz 2021; Khan 2021; Ndlovu-Gatsheni 2015). When we look at how threat and (in)security are articulated in banal social interactions, we learn that colonial ideas of the threatening 'other' are being reproduced in everyday discourses. As such, by foregrounding the role of the individual in CVE policies, this chapter addresses the conceptual enquiries of this volume and makes the racialised violence of modern coloniality visible.

CVE has not only opened up new fronts in the global War on Terror, it has also significantly expanded the scope of this one-sided warfare. These programmes aim to tackle the threat of terrorism before it manifests by targetting it pre-emptively (Heath-Kelly 2013). With the understanding that 'extremist ideas' lead to acts of political violence, CVE policies aim to neutralise these cognitive threats before they can turn into actions. However, this form of policing is not just pre-emptive, it is also expansive as extremist thoughts and ideas can emerge anywhere in the society. Therefore, the infrastructure to manage this threat pre-emptively has to be just as widespread. As such, CVE takes surveillance and policing outside the traditional infrastructures of state security and shifts security responsibilities to civilians (Kaleem 2022a). These individuals do not belong to any law enforcement agencies nor have formal training in surveillance work; they are 'ordinary' citizens who get tasked with conducting counter-terrorism work. When these people get mobilised to take on security responsibilities, everyday interactions become surveillance-gathering opportunities and mundane social spaces turn into avenues of counter-terrorism governance. This diffusion of security logics and practices into the civic life has created securitised identities, spaces, and interactions, all of which contribute to extending the War on Terror into our domestic spheres. By looking at how CVE policies are enacted, this chapter will situate the analysis of counter-terrorism at the grassroots level, where the individual and the intimate get mobilised to manage security concerns.

This approach is also important because moving our level of analysis to the grassroots helps us appreciate the intimacy inherent in the enactment of CVE policies. These rely on mobilising people and tasking them to disturb the banal peace and mutual trust of their social interactions to conduct counter-terrorism policing. While these initiatives may originate in policy papers and legislative instruments drawn up within the higher echelons of power, CVE policies get enacted within and through situations that are not so much defined by hierarchical power but by principles of trust and confidentiality. Therefore, to understand the intimate politics of CVE, we foreground the lowest rungs of the power hierarchy and focus on the individuals, practices, and spaces where counter-terrorism policies are being enacted and experienced.

Case study and methods

The British government's Prevent Strategy places a statutory obligation on civilians working in welfare state sectors such as health, education, and social work, to monitor people for signs of extremism and to keep them from 'being drawn into terrorism' (Home Office 2015; 2011). As a result, teachers, doctors, and social workers come under a legal duty to conduct surveillance on their students, patients, and service users and make a Prevent referral about them if they are deemed to be vulnerable to radicalisation. Prevent was first publicly released in 2006 in response to the 7/7 bombings in London.[1] The policy signalled a shift in British government's approach to security to target what was seen as a 'homegrown threat'. As such, Prevent can be seen as one of the first CVE interventions that opened up domestic outposts of the global War on Terror (Abbas 2019; Abbas et al. 2021; Briggs 2010; Choudhury 2007; Spalek and Imtoual 2007; West 2017). Despite being embedded in the flagship counter-terrorism strategy, Prevent is presented as a 'pre-criminal' intervention that takes place before a crime has been committed (Heath-Kelly 2017). This framing is deployed to encourage ordinary citizens to engage with the policy as it relies on them for its operationalisation. By detaching Prevent from traditional modes of surveillance, the state not only maintains but also repurposes the intimacy of social interactions for counter-terrorism purposes. This makes it a useful starting point to understand how CVE policies enter the domestic sphere and assign new identities and security responsibilities to civilians. In my research, I identify these individuals as 'ordinary citizens' because even though they are frontline professionals working for different state-run institutions. They are not part of the security infrastructure, therefore, when they get tasked with counter-terrorism work, their 'ordinariness' becomes important.

Within Prevent Duty enactment, we can find two sets of citizens interacting with the state who can be roughly divided into 'suspects' and 'agents'. Those who work for the different welfare state sectors get cast as agents of the state while the people they have to monitor become potential suspects by default. This is an arbitrary divide imposed by the state and these labels are very unstable as any individual can find themselves on either side of this metaphorical security border. However, this does help us see how different pockets of the civil society are targeted. On one side we have the frontline staff who have to take on security responsibilities, on the other are those citizens who by interacting with the former become subjected to this surveillance. We can look at either of these groups and learn valuable lessons about how mundane activities like going to school or consulting a medical professional have turned into (in)security making opportunities. My research focuses on the first group of individuals: the frontline staff who have a legal obligation to enact the Prevent Duty as part of their professional work. It is useful to focus on this group of individuals because even though the scope of Prevent Duty is being expanded, at the current stage, these civilians have a clearly defined role in this CVE policy (Smith 2023).

This chapter draws on the findings of fifty-five interviews conducted between 2019 and 2020 with primary and secondary schoolteachers, university lecturers, social workers, medical professionals, and Prevent co-ordinators working in the north of England.[2] I recruited participants through snowball sampling and focused on getting a representative sample from different frontline sectors of health, education, and social work to understand the influence of professional and social dynamics on staff engagement with Prevent Duty, I discuss how these play out in the final section. While I prepared a thematic questionnaire, the interviews were conducted in a semi-structured format to follow the participants' train of thought and learn how they articulate concepts of threat and security (Soss 2015: 165). A majority of the participants had received some form of Prevent training and those who had not received a training were aware of the policy. The interview data was analysed using thematic coding to identify how participants interacted with the policy, how they identified their role in CVE, and if the diffusion of surveillance and policing had an impact on their professional and personal lives. Through iterative coding cycles, I was able to see how citizens articulated compliance with Prevent, how they spoke about loyalty and responsibility, and whether anyone associated Prevent with spying and surveillance. These insights thus, explain how ordinary citizens understand their counter-terrorism obligations and what motivates them to undertake this surveillance work.

This focus on the role of the individuals is crucial to understand the expansion of the Prevent Duty across different parts of the society. My research findings show that while citizens are introduced to this policy as a professional obligation, they do not just engage with Prevent as a professional duty, they connect it to a wider civic responsibility of protecting other people. This takes their role as Prevent operatives beyond the confines of their professional sectors and into their personal lives. When viewed as a moral or a civic duty, citizens do not stop 'doing' Prevent work when they are off-the-clock; the practice of monitoring seamlessly flows from their professional to their personal spheres. As such, by focusing on why ordinary citizens engage with a CVE policy like the Prevent Duty and how they enact it, we can chart the course counter-terrorism policies take at the grassroots level of the society and how they expand the scope of this policing.

A feminist epistemological approach to studying counter-terrorism

My research is rooted in feminist epistemology that guides us to 'make visible' those domains of activity that are considered too ordinary or trivial to matter in politics (Enloe 2014). By opening up new sites, activities, and identities and seeing the power politics at play therein, feminist scholarship has been instrumental in recalibrating our understanding of what should be seen as political. As such, Enloe's assertion that the 'personal is political' has served as the guiding principle of my work. By shifting our focus to the private and the trivial, Enloe opens up a new terrain that should be explored in our efforts to understand how the world works (2014). In the study of counter-terrorism, this 'feminist curiosity' directs us to the lived experience of ordinary citizens and how they conceptualise security threats and their mitigation (Aradau and Huysmans 2014; Enloe 2004). Before I proceed, I would like to clarify that while I am using a feminist approach to study the enactment of CVE policies, this is not a gendered analysis of Prevent Duty. As Åhäll explains, feminist knowledge creation goes 'beyond studies of gender' to understand the dynamics of our everyday politics. This chapter presents a more general study of how counter-terrorism policies operate at the grassroots level with the focus placed on the lived experiences of ordinary citizens. (2019: 154; 2016: 159).

A feminist epistemological approach, thus, turns our attention to the political through the personal and the intimate, but not in a way that maintains the latter as a sphere with sealed borders hosting activity that is strictly contained inside. When approached from a feminist perspective, the personal is anything and everything that is suffused with a power dynamic. This makes visible bodies, emotions, stories, interactions, and affects as political processes that inform power relations between citizens and the state (Åhäll 2016: 158). By privileging the personal, feminist epistemology gives us a new language to talk about those thought processes of individuals that inform their engagement with Prevent. As discussed earlier, even though people come into contact with the Prevent Duty in their professional capacities, their actions are steeped in a personal politics of care. Applying a feminist lens on this, we can see this as a 'personalisation' of professional obligations. Prevent appeals to citizens' sense of duty, to the need to protect the vulnerable, and to shoulder their civic responsibilities. As such, we cannot separate the personal and the intimate from Prevent because it relies on these personal instincts to mobilise citizens. Similarly, while the civic relationships targeted by Prevent take place in a professional setting, that is, between a teacher and their student, a doctor and their patient, they are informed by principles of trust and confidentiality. It is the personal connection that citizens forge within these professional spaces that has been securitised by Prevent Duty. Therefore, it is important to situate the study of Prevent within the personal, the mundane, and the everyday, because without the personal, there can be no Prevent enactment.

By privileging the individual and the intimate, this approach also lets us look beyond elite actors to ordinary people as not just the recipients of politics but also as actors that shape politics. This accords agency to those who are normally seen as passive subjects, as bodies that are 'acted upon' (Enloe 2014: 35). As such, when we approach these actors as creators of politics and possessors of power, we not only situate them within security politics, we also identify their contribution in making or disrupting security. Counter-terrorism then becomes a practice that is not solely defined by the states and elite actors, but also by ordinary people who can either engage with it positively or disrupt it as they undertake mundane civic activities.

Foregrounding the personal and fixing our analytical gaze on civilians also allows us to enter spaces and understand interactions that are not new per se but that are usually overlooked in the analyses on where security politics unfolds. As such, privileging the ordinary, the individual, opens up 'everyday' as a space where we can look to find the emergence of new meanings of security and counter-terrorism (Huysmans 2009; Nyman 2021; Stanley and Jackson 2016). It is useful to recognise 'everyday' as a site of (in)security making because this is where counter-terrorism policing unfolds. People are reminded to 'see it, say it, sorted' at train and underground stations in the UK (British Transport Police 2016), they are told 'Actions Counter Terrorism' when they go to the cinema (Leicestershire Police 2018), their vigilance is even requested when honouring the passing of a monarch (Metropolitan Police Events [@MetPoliceEvents], 2022). Not only is counter-terrorism and (in)security diffused within the everyday, it works by securitising the mundane activities of ordinary citizens, who then become both its subjects and agents. While these put different demands on individuals and some are more mundane than others, the diversity of these calls for citizens' participation in policing shows the widespread nature of counter-terrorism policing. Focusing on the intimate in the everyday also helps us understand 'how' citizens engage with CVE policies. As this chapter will discuss, the everyday reality of Prevent enactment yields a variety of interactions that come about through a negotiation of different concerns. Some people feel uneasy about Prevent's disproportionate focus on Muslims, while others see it as a form of spying. The following sections will discuss how people manage these doubts to engage with the policy. Therefore, this approach allows us to capture the narratives that convince individuals to become part of the security state. This exploration is important because all of these constitute the political reality of not just the Prevent Duty, but our civic existence in an increasingly securitised society.

Finally, focusing on the everyday also serves the normative aim of uncovering the violence of security politics when it is camouflaged within the mundanity of civic life. By diffusing Prevent Duty obligations within professional and civic obligations, the state hides the coercion of counter-terrorism policing within the sanitised frames of 'safeguarding' and 'pre-crime space' (Goldberg et al. 2017; Heath-Kelly 2017). If we continue to see the everyday as a site where politics does not happen, we give the state the cover to hide these (in)security-making interventions (Huysmans 2009). As such, by adopting a feminist epistemology, we can uncover how and why citizens get co-opted into security politics, how they respond to this responsibilisation, and what the scope of civic subjection, complicity, and agency is within these domestic counter-terrorism regimes.

Counter-terrorism at the grassroots level: Prevent Duty enactment and citizens' perspectives

By allocating security responsibilities to citizens employed in health, education, and social work sectors, the British state has not only extended the reach of its coercive sphere, it has also expanded the network of civic exchanges that take place between the security state and citizens. Within the context of Prevent, these interactions influence the conduct of all citizens, whether they are the ones being given the responsibility to carry out security obligations or the citizens who are at the receiving end of these counter-terrorism measures. This chapter focuses on the experiences of the former to identify the dominant narratives that facilitate the co-optation of citizens into the state's security infrastructure as they find themselves turning into both the agents and subjects of counter-terrorism policing. To understand the personal politics of counter-terrorism, this discussion will be divided into the themes of threat identification and threat mitigation. The first theme will help us understand how individuals tasked with enacting the Prevent Duty are introduced to the idea of threat and encouraged to use social interactions to monitor people. This discussion shows how people end up relying on vague ideas of who looks like a threat and act upon their own 'gut instincts'. Under the theme of threat mitigation, I focus on how people deal with their own concerns about the Prevent Duty and negotiate these doubts to engage with the policy.

Threat identification

CVE policies like the Prevent Duty operate on the basis of stopping radicalisation which is defined by the Prevent strategy as a process through which individuals 'come to support terrorism and forms of extremism leading to terrorism' (Home Office 2011: 108). The idea of radicalisation securitises the personal in two different but connected ways. It provides a roadmap for identifying threats (where none exist yet) and shifting responsibilities to the citizens. In addition to this, the very concept of radicalisation becomes an 'actionable' device. As Strausz and Heath-Kelly explain, Prevent makes radicalisation 'knowable, controllable, potentially treatable' (2019). Within the day-to-day enactment of Prevent, radicalisation is presented as a symptom to be spotted and managed. This approach takes radicalisation outside the confines of academic and policymaking discourses and makes it a risk that can not only be identified but should also be tackled by everyone. Almost all the frontline professionals who have a legal obligation to enact the stipulations of the Prevent strategy receive some form of training that varies from a day-long workshop to a 30-minute e-learning module. While the content may vary, the core message revolves around countering radicalisation of vulnerable individuals with rudimentary details of what constitutes radicalisation (Home Office 2015b; Strausz and Heath-Kelly 2019; Younis and Jadhav 2019). This makes the act of counter-extremism policing more personal and intimate as not only are relationships of trust and confidence being used to conduct this monitoring. People are also being left to make their own judgements about who can be radicalised. In my interviews with frontline staff, I noticed that while people were clear that their job was to stop radicalisation, they could not always tell me what radicalisation is and, depending on their personal outlooks, their identifying criteria for radicalisation also varied:

> I think they might have given definitions of radicalisation and extremism perhaps or used these words, but certainly there was no mention of what will make you think that they are being radicalised or that somebody is trying to poach them and what should be the trigger questions you ask or what are the red flags that you should look for, basically left a lot to the imagination. Basically, to listen to your gut. (HE13, A&E Doctor)

This encouragement to rely on one's gut feeling has also been reported in other studies of Prevent strategy (Dresser 2019; Strausz and Heath-Kelly 2019). This signals a further shifting of responsibilities to individuals. Not only do they have to monitor vulnerability to radicalisation, they also have to identify what can or cannot be evidence of radicalisation. Furthermore, this power to assign the risk embeds private interactions between citizens with security logics that are formed through racialised discourses. They make judgements based on their own notions of what a terrorist looks like drawn from pop culture depictions and mainstream discourses (Hanif 2021; Pears 2022). It is within these interactions, where an individual makes a judgement about another, we find the influence of not just the global practices of counter-terrorism but also the historical and colonial logics of who is seen as a threat. As Abu-Bakare and Khan have explained in their work, the ideas of 'terrorism' and 'counter-terrorism' predate the events of 9/11 and as such the figure of the threatening 'other' is also a legacy of imperialist politics (2022; 2021). It is the 'deep, sticky coloniality' at work that results in a Muslim person of colour being seen more as a threat than their white counterparts (Khan 2021: 499). I observed this in an interview with a social worker, who spoke about the risk of radicalisation and extremism informed by wider narratives on race and security:

> I think when people think of Prevent, they have got a very clear picture in their head of what somebody who that might be… so, in XXX, majority of people we worked with were white British, and I don't think when people think of Prevent, they have a picture in their head of someone who is white, British. (LA11, social worker)

The idea of threat gets formed through the fault lines of religion, race, and class because people form these opinions based on the collective common sense around who is seen as a productive member of the society and who is considered a deviant other in need of disciplining. We can see this in politicians talking about the perils of 'Islamist extremism' and Muslim school children being referred to Prevent for innocuous activities (Jenrick 2022; Taylor 2022; Townsend and Stein 2021). Even though the recent iterations of Prevent Duty trainings state that being Muslim or religious is not necessarily an indicator of radicalisation, Prevent is enacted with the inherent belief that the actual threat comes from Muslims. This was stated by a Prevent co-ordinator I interviewed who said that Prevent funding goes to areas with 'BME population because the number one threat is Islamist threat' (PC-ED01). Similar insights came up time and again in conversations where casual observations betrayed a reliance on mainstream ideas of what a risky body looks like (Bhattacharyya 2008). I noticed this in an interview with a secondary schoolteacher who seemed to regard the religious conservatism of their Muslim students as something the school should monitor:

> There is a general pressure on the girls from each other in the Muslim section of our school to dress modestly and to wear a hijab and to conform within that group and so I think the school has under-assessed that [i.e., the risk of radicalisation of these girls] than over[-assessed this risk]. (secondary schoolteacher, ED01)

Interestingly, this schoolteacher otherwise had a nuanced view of what should be seen as radicalisation and during our conversation they did say that wearing a hijab does not mean a student is becoming radicalised. However, despite this understanding, they flagged the conservative views of their students as a concern to be managed by the school. A social worker also echoed this viewpoint when they discussed the case of a young man who they thought was at risk:

> A young man I worked with, he started attending the mosque, he was a white British man, started attending the mosque, he grew a beard, he became… very much all he ever spoke about was how good these people were and he was going to go and do their work. (social worker, LA08)

These quotes show that by leaving people to form opinions about threat and vulnerability based on their gut instincts, Prevent allows them to act on their biases. These biases then get operationalised in social interactions where teachers, doctors, and social workers start looking at their students, patients, and service users through a securitised lens of threat identification. When assessed within the remit of Prevent Duty enactment, these concerns come to be seen as threats to national security.

Interestingly, in some instances, my research participants who belonged to minority communities also spoke a similar language of security. A Muslim doctor (HE04) explained Prevent as a 'moral duty' that we should engage with to keep everyone safe. While discussing security threats, they referenced a failed 2007 terror attack at Glasgow Airport that was planned by two Muslim men (Brocklehurst 2017). Similarly, another Muslim doctor (HE17) discussed that even though the Prevent training they took featured the case study of far-right extremism, they considered the dominant threat to be coming from Muslims and therefore the Prevent training should focus on depicting them as a threat. These insights show the effectiveness of the mainstream security discourses that even Muslim people adopt and reproduce the colonial logics of Prevent Duty and situate the threat within the image of a Muslim person.

This attitude was also observed in the insights of a Muslim social worker who dismissed criticism of Prevent's inherent racism as a branding problem (LA09). This social worker had decades of experience working with ethnic minority families in different parts of England and was quite familiar with the grievances related to the issues of racism and discrimination. However, with reference to Prevent, they appeared to dismiss these grievances as misconceptions that need to be corrected by a different branding. Their engagement with Prevent was rooted in the idea that Prevent was started with 'very good aims' of protecting young people who saw themselves 'fighting a crusade' when 'they have been born and brought up in this country'. They not only situated the problem of radicalisation within Muslim communities, they also saw Prevent as waging a battle of ideas against these deviant viewpoints. This shows that security logics travel temporally (the continuation of the colonial logics) and spatially (from the international to the domestic), and become sedimented as 'common sense' ideas that we adopt without giving them much thought (Kaleem 2022b). These ideas get reproduced and reinforced through the CVE structures in social interactions. As the next section will demonstrate, within Prevent Duty enactment, people start thinking of surveillance work as a form of safeguarding and engage with this policy as not just their professional, but also civic and moral duty. The idea of identifying and mitigating threats then becomes a responsibility for securitised citizenry.

While Prevent has predominantly focused on the British 'Muslim community' as a site of intervention, over the past few years there has been an acknowledgement of the threat posed by far-right extremism. This is also pointed as a counter-argument when arguments about Prevent's racism are made. The supporters of the policy claim that Prevent is not racist because recently there have been more far-right referrals (Grierson 2018). However, this framing hides the fact that Prevent operates on mainstream prejudices; while in the case of Muslims, it's the colonial logics of the 'dangerous other'. In the case of far-right extremism, the threat is situated within the demographic of white, working class communities, with the assumption that they are more vulnerable to radicalisation. In my interviews, when teachers and social workers spoke about the threat of far-right extremism they discussed it with reference to their work in 'working-class areas' (ED01, ED02, LA05). A schoolteacher who taught in an area serving this demographic complained about the Prevent training course they took for its focus on a stereotypical idea of threat:

> The Prevent course that I did on my laptop, the option of going with the [scenario featuring] white one [far-right extremist], was a lad who went to the football and met some blokes there and there were all bald with tattoos and having British flags, singing and that itself is a real generalisation of football fans, as being Northern, racist… It's almost like them saying that if you're a white kid who goes and watches football, you're at risk of being radicalised. (primary schoolteacher, ED09)

The focus of Prevent Duty on far-right extremism is presented as a proof that the policy is colour-blind (Winter et al. 2021; Younis and Jadhav 2020). However, this stereotypical portrayal shows that within the racialised logics of Prevent, the threat of far-right extremism is situated within the overt displays of racism deemed to be restricted to a certain demographic, while the threat of religious extremism is seen to be present throughout the supposedly monolithic 'Muslim community'. As such, even within this supposed colour-blind approach, there are exceptions in place to restrict the scope of policing along racialised and colonial logics. This exceptionalism has been further underscored by the recent review of the Prevent strategy conducted by William Shawcross who blamed the policy for focusing too broadly on 'extreme right-wing' by targeting 'mildly controversial or provocative forms of mainstream, right-wing leaning commentary that have no meaningful connection to terrorism or radicalisation' (Shawcross 2023: 7). This viewpoint was reiterated by then Home Secretary Suella Braverman who critiqued the Prevent Duty for equating 'fascists with perfectly respectable centre-right figures' and espousing 'cultural timidity' and 'institutional hesitancy' in tackling 'Islamism' (Braverman 2023). These interventions show us that the threat of far-right extremism can only be conceived within narrow parameters of class-based prejudice while allowing 'mainstream right-wing opinions' to evade any scrutiny. Furthermore, this also underscores the coloniality of the Prevent project as the recent focus on the far right is seen as a failure to capture the real threat coming from the Muslim other.

This theme has explored the colonial roots of threat identification within Prevent Duty enactment, helping us connect these grassroots interactions to international logics of security and counter-terrorism. The next theme will extend this discussion by focusing on how these ideas of threat identification create conditions of permissibility for an intrusive counter-terrorism policy within our everyday social interactions. Here, I will shift the focus to how individuals make sense of the Prevent Duty to show how once the idea of a threat is embedded in the collective common sense, people negotiate their discomfort with the idea of monitoring and spying on their fellow citizens. As such, the following theme of threat mitigation will show us how the coloniality of Prevent Duty manifests at the grassroots level.

Threat mitigation

To draw out the multifaceted nature of the lived reality of counter-terrorism, this chapter will focus on the instances where people oscillate between complying with Prevent Duty or resisting it. These actions see citizens weigh different options that lead them to often act against their initial judgements or park their doubts. This discussion allows us to unpack a space of deliberation where citizens negotiate clashing narratives of Prevent's statutory duty, their civic and professional obligations, their sense of responsibility, and their feelings and circumstances. By taking stock of how people deliberate over Prevent, we get to understand how and why they engage with their counter-terrorism obligations and what narratives influence this engagement.

Interview data show that when it comes to articulating the Prevent Duty and implementing it in daily professional routines, there are blurred boundaries between what is deemed acceptable by people and what they would end up doing. In my research, some participants demonstrated a critical engagement with the policy and were wary of some or most aspects of Prevent and the impact it can have on certain communities. However, despite their reservations with the policy, they agreed to comply with it, albeit with some hesitation. This shows that the narratives of security and protection from the threat of 'terrorism' are strong enough to neutralise opposition to invasive security policies. By looking at how people make sense of Prevent Duty and convince themselves to engage with it despite their doubts, we can understand the process through which people learn to act against their instincts or negotiate with them to deal with less than ideal conditions. This shows that through this process of deliberation citizens take stock of their Prevent Duty responsibilities as conveyed to them through dominant narratives of threat and security. They may feel uneasy about complying with Prevent Duty and may feel that their actions could harm the vulnerable person in their care, but this could be overridden by a concern for the safety of other people around them or a sense of responsibility to the state.

As I have discussed in my previous work (Kaleem 2022b), re-framing Prevent as a safeguarding duty has been instrumental in not only convincing people to engage with it but to also connect it with a broader sense of civic responsibility. Once people start seeing surveillance work as a means to protect those who are vulnerable and fulfilling a civic duty, the policy stops becoming a coercive intervention in civic life and becomes a necessary component of the duty of care (Busher et al. 2019: 441). This came through very clearly in interview insights of participants who had a favourable view of the policy. However, we can find similar narratives emerging in those cases where there was a more critical form of engagement with the policy. This shows that the narrative of Prevent Duty being a safeguarding intervention gets accepted even by those who have certain reservations about it. As this discussion will demonstrate, when presented within the discourse of threat and security, Prevent allows people to act in counter-intuitive ways. This is evident in the process of internal negotiation that takes place before any formal engagement with Prevent, whereby an individual makes sense of the policy, their positionality, and their professional and civic duties. Tracking this process provides useful insights into the intimate politics of counter-terrorism that cannot be accessed through a top–down analysis of security policies.

The deliberation over whether to engage with Prevent Duty or not is often characterised by conflicting thought processes as was evident in the discussion with a primary schoolteacher (ED09). As a white, British man, he spoke about the policy's tendency to make him look differently at minorities. He acknowledged that Muslim communities feel threatened by Prevent and that white working-class youth could be more at risk of prejudicial Prevent referrals for 'racist views' without any effort to understand their grievances. They also expressed concerns about the expanding remit and securitisation of civic activity, asking if any kind of radical politics could be targeted by Prevent. Throughout the interview they demonstrated a thoughtful assessment of the Prevent Duty and its impact on different communities. However, while they expressed concerns and acknowledged different critiques of Prevent, they justified their engagement with the policy by prioritising their responsibilities over personal misgivings:

> I know there's quite a lot of opposition to Prevent… I'm not completely comfortable with it, although I also see some reasons for it too. So, yes, it's not like I'm just fully behind [it]… I just feel there is a duty in terms of just as an adult in the position of care, it is my duty to help children or vulnerable people, based on my professionalism, rather than because I have to do it for Prevent or for the police or something or the government. (primary schoolteacher, ED09)

By taking account of the negative impacts of the Prevent Duty but then side-stepping them to fulfil his duty to 'children and vulnerable people', this teacher is attempting to disconnect Prevent from the wider security agenda, rooting it in the intimate politics of safeguarding. Here we see a reverse of what we discussed in the previous theme. While people articulate threats through the international and colonial logics of the dangerous other, the mitigation of this threat is seen through the prism of intimate politics devoid of any coercive influences. This does not mean that coloniality is not at play here, it is very much influencing these decisions because even though people see the potential harms this policy can do, they believe risks can be mitigated by focusing on the duty of care aspect of their role. They may not identify their focus on protecting children as an act in service of the government, but this thought process is rooted in a wider ethos of being a responsible citizen. It is interesting because on the surface, they seem to be shunning the government-assigned label of an active citizen, instead thinking their motivations are rooted in something more organic. This schoolteacher has doubts about the negative impacts of this policy but since this is presented as a way of protecting children, they are opting to see Prevent as being disjointed from its coercive elements. In addition to a sense of obligation towards their pupils, this engagement with Prevent is also informed by an urge to do the 'right thing' (ED09). Here we can see how the British state has successfully co-opted the principles of safeguarding and duty of care to a point that even when individuals are conscious of the policy's harms, they end up complying with it as it is seen as a way of protecting people against the threat of radicalisation. As such, it is useful to look at how individuals make sense of the Prevent Duty to understand which narratives cut through and convince people to become part of the wider security infrastructure.

We can also observe this negotiation over the concern that Prevent is a surveillance tool. While the policy is overwhelmingly framed as safeguarding, several participants made unprompted linkages between Prevent and surveillance. A teacher seemed to oscillate between their discomfort with the idea of 'spying' on pupils and the recognition that the government needs help. Their intervention shows a confusion between their professional duty to their pupils and their duty as a citizen, with them negotiating over where their ultimate responsibility lies:

> The reason I'm there is to teach them languages, it's not to do all this other stuff, but I have to recognise that I can't do that job without caring about children… Just as a person, I have a responsibility to notice if something is not right and to act on that… The initial fear with the Prevent Duty was am I being used as a kind of spy? I don't… am I involved in counter-terrorism? I don't think I should be! But equally, I understand that we are hundreds of eyes on the ground in places that the government can't get to. (secondary schoolteacher, ED16)

Here we can see the duty of care principles colliding with fears of being co-opted into a surveillance programme. This secondary schoolteacher is also torn between wanting to protect their pupils and resisting being part of a coercive regime. Similarly, they are also conscious of their role as a citizen in helping the state. They accept their duty to safeguard children, but they also do not want to do 'counter-terrorism'. We can see the push and pull of different factors in this brief quote. They talk about their fears convincingly, but they ultimately decide to prioritise their duty to the children, which in this case means complying with Prevent. They mention civic duty that shows that they are also cognisant of their role in the society as a citizen who serves as the eyes and ears of the state. The phrase 'hundreds of eyes on the ground' betrays a surveillance logic but despite their concerns about the coercion of such practices, they are, perhaps inadvertently, advocating this approach to fulfil their professional and civic duties. This is particularly interesting because during our interview, they talked about not being 'immensely loyal to the government' and often disagreeing with the 'way the government teaches' (ED16). They also mentioned they would ignore teaching government-mandated lessons if they didn't agree with it. However, despite their general scepticism of the state, they also see their place in the security infrastructure due to their proximity to the grassroots and their responsibility towards their pupils. As such, despite their critique of the government, they also hold views consistent with those of a security-state-activated citizen. By mapping these processes of deliberation, we can see how people often advocate actions that may not necessarily match their wider belief systems.

A similar dichotomous approach was revealed by a social worker (LA01) who also explained their role in the Prevent Duty as an agent of the state due to their proximity to people. While they were not very enthusiastic about the inclusion of Prevent Duty in their professional role, they understood why that is the case:

> I can see why we would be the ones that would be able to identify concerns... with Prevent, I feel like we can probably be the eyes, it's very big brother... like just watching, snooping and things like that, it's probably what they want us to do... I think if somebody was obviously glaringly like oh God! we are very worried about this child, this young person whose got a keen interest in... I don't know... but then what is extremism as well, could be a lot of things. (social worker, LA01)

They use the term 'big brother' that attaches a negative connotation to the act of monitoring others, and they express uncertainty about what can be identified as extremism, but they still situate themselves within the security state as a professional and a citizen. Interestingly, this linkage between Prevent and surveillance was made by participants from different sectors. This shows that despite the policy's generally successful attempts to present this work as safeguarding, the narrative about spying also cuts through. This tension was evident in some discussions where the perception of Prevent as a surveillance policy was brought up unprompted by the participants. However, they seemed to make a calculation between the 'worry of spying' or 'being spied on' and the overall safety of people, opting for the latter, albeit with some unease:

> I don't want to live in a state where you feel your neighbour is watching you all the time and I don't really believe in the idea of making it people's duty to spy on each other... but equally I think there is a duty, if you know harm is going to occur you should try to prevent it. (secondary schoolteacher, ED01)

This quote reveals that compliance with Prevent comes with certain reservations, but it also shows that the common-sense around civil liberties alters when it gets dominated by concerns around security (Kaleem 2022b). This hesitation reveals how securitisation of normal safeguarding practices dilutes the coercion of security policies in favour of ensuring one's active participation in the society and assisting the state. From teachers to social workers, we can see a similar message being articulated about the unease with spying which then takes a backseat to the overriding concern for keeping the public safe from the threat of radicalised individuals who can commit acts of political violence. This also shows that when security logics enter the mainstream discourse, they create little pockets of exceptional activity that permit otherwise questionable practices. What is most interesting is that these exceptions sit alongside seemingly progressive ideas that people hold. As such, one can have both very progressive views on individual liberty and freedom, and simultaneously advocate or tolerate a security state and facilitate the creation of a mass surveillance infrastructure. Within the enactment of Prevent Duty, this tension is reconciled by people thinking of their engagement with the policy through the narratives of safeguarding and duty of care. When surveillance works comes to be seen as a way of protecting others, the sharp edges of its coercion get blunted and it becomes more acceptable.

Conclusion

This chapter has focused on uncovering the connections between the supposedly binary concepts of international/personal and modern/colonial within the study of counter-terrorism. By focusing on the individual and the intimate in the enactment of Prevent Duty, we open up the everyday and the personal as sites where the coercion of security state takes place. Furthermore, by looking at how and why citizens engage with their counter-terrorism obligations under the Prevent Duty, we get insights on who is seen as a threat to security and how this threat is mitigated. We find how dominant discourses on security get reproduced in everyday interactions with people making judgements about threat and risk along racial and class lines. Making this coercion visible thus, helps us make connections between these normalised acts of surveillance and the colonial logics of disciplining the deviant other.

By exploring how these threats are mitigated, we unpack the internal negotiations people undertake to justify their engagement with a security policy. It is important to make these explorations because the weaponisation of the intimacy of social interactions is not accidental, it is by design. The diffusion of counter-terrorism work within civil society has been carried out to make use of the bonds of intimacy and trust that uphold the fabric of civic life. CVE relies on securitising the mutual trust and confidence students have in their teachers, patients have in their doctors, and service users have in the social workers they let into their private spaces. We have to explore the enactment of these policies at the grassroots level and within the everyday mundanity to understand how these policies have become part of our civic life. The spaces in which a teacher communicates with their pupils or a doctor treats their patients are now security terrains and their interactions are surveillance opportunities. This helps us understand that our personal spaces serve as the domestic outposts of the global War on Terror and we become the conduits for reproducing the coloniality of the security state.

Notes

1 7/7 bombings refer to the terrorist attack in London on 7 July 2005 where four suicide bombers denotated explosives across Central London killing fifty-two people.
2 Style note: I have chosen to identify my research participants through identity numbers rather than assigning pseudonyms because this could result in imposing racial identities on my participants. People have different names that may not always correspond to their ethnic or religious identity; therefore, I prefer to use participant identity numbers.

References

Abbas, T. (2019). 'Implementing 'Prevent' in countering violent extremism in the UK: A left-realist critique', *Critical Social Policy*, 39(3), 396–412.

Abbas, T., Awan, I., and Marsden, J. (2021). 'Pushed to the edge: The consequences of the "Prevent Duty" in de-radicalising pre-crime thought among British Muslim university students', *Race Ethnicity and Education*, 26(6), 719–34.

Abu-Bakare, A. (2022). 'Exploring mechanisms of whiteness: How counterterrorism practitioners disrupt anti-racist expertise', *International Affairs*, 98(1), 225–43.

Åhäll, L. (2019). 'Feeling everyday IR: Embodied, affective, militarising movement as choreography of war', *Cooperation and Conflict*, 54(2), 149–66.

Åhäll, L. (2016). 'The dance of militarisation: A feminist security studies take on "the political"', *Critical Studies on Security*, 4(2), 154–68.

Aradau, C. and Huysmans, J. (2014). 'Critical methods in international relations: The politics of techniques, devices and acts', *European Journal of International Relations*, 20(3), 596–619.

Bhattacharyya, G. (2008). *Dangerous Brown Men*. London: Zed Books Ltd.

Braverman, S. (2023). 'Counter-terrorism strategy (CONTEST) 2023 launch'. www.gov.uk/government/speeches/counter-terrorism-strategy-contest-2023-launch (accessed 25 July 2023).

Briggs, R. (2010). 'Community engagement for counterterrorism: Lessons from the United Kingdom', *International Affairs*, 86(4), 971–81.

British Transport Police (2016). 'See It Say It Sorted – new national campaign', 30 July, www.btp.police.uk/latest_news/see_it_say_it_sorted_new_natio.aspx (accessed 17 May 2019).

Brocklehurst, S. (2017). 'The day terror came to Glasgow Airport', *BBC News*, www.bbc.co.uk/news/uk-scotland-40416026 (accessed 26 July 2023).

Busher, J., Choudhury, T., and Thomas, P. (2019). 'The enactment of the counter-terrorism "Prevent duty" in British schools and colleges: beyond reluctant accommodation or straightforward policy acceptance', *Critical Studies on Terrorism*, 12(3), 440–62.

Choudhury, T. (2007). *The Role of Muslim Identity Politics in Radicalisation*. London: Preventing Extremism Unit.

Cruz, J. D. (2021). 'Colonial power and decolonial peace', *Peacebuilding*, 9(3), 274–88.

Dresser, P. (2019). ' "Trust your instincts – act!" PREVENT police officers' perspectives of counter-radicalisation reporting thresholds', *Critical Studies on Terrorism*, 12(4), 605–28.

Dunlap, A. (2016). Counter-insurgency: Let's remember where prevention comes from and its implications', *Critical Studies on Terrorism*, 9(2), 380–5.

Enloe, C. (2004). *The Curious Feminist: Searching for Women in a New Age of Empire*. Berkeley, CA: University of California Press.

Enloe, C. (2014). *Bananas, Beaches and Bases: Making Feminist Sense of International Politics*. Berkeley and Los Angeles, CA: University of California Press.

Goldberg, D., Jadhav, S., and Younis, T. (2017). 'Prevent: What is pre-criminal space?', *BJPsych Bull*, 41(4), 208–11.

Grierson, J. (2018). 'White people make up largest proportion of British terror arrests', *The Guardian*, 13 September, www.theguardian.com/uk-news/2018/sep/13/white-people-make-up-largest-proportion-of-terror-arrests-figures-show (accessed 25 July 2023).

Hanif, F. (2021). *British Media's Coverage of Muslims and Islam (2018–2020)*. London: Centre for Media Monitoring.

Heath-Kelly, C. (2017). 'The geography of pre-criminal space: Epidemiological imaginations of radicalisation risk in the UK Prevent Strategy, 2007–2017', *Critical Studies on Terrorism*, 10(2), 297–319.

Heath-Kelly, C. (2013). 'Counter-terrorism and the counterfactual: Producing the 'radicalisation' discourse and the UK PREVENT strategy', *The British Journal of Politics and International Relations*, 15(3), 394–415.

Home Office (2015a). 'Counter-Terrorism and Security Act 2015', www.legislation. gov.uk/ukpga/2015/6/contents/enacted (accessed 25 July 2023).

Home Office (2015b). 'Home office Prevent training and wrap for schools', *Educate Against Hate*, https://educateagainsthate.com/teachers/prevent-training/ (accessed 20 May 2019).

Home Office (2011). 'Prevent strategy', https://assets.publishing.service.gov.uk/gov ernment/uploads/system/uploads/attachment_data/file/97976/prevent-strategy-review.pdf (accessed 25 July 2023).

Huysmans, J. (2009). 'Insecurity and the Everyday', in Noxolo, P., Huysmans, J. (eds) *Community, Citizenship and the "War on Terror": Security and Insecurity*. Basingstoke: Palgrave Macmillan, pp. 196–207.

Jenrick, R. (2022). 'We can't keep turning a blind eye to Islamist extremism', *The Telegraph*, 12 April, www.telegraph.co.uk/politics/2022/04/12/cant-keep-turn ing-blind-eye-islamist-extremism/ (accessed 26 July 2023).

Kaleem, A. (2022a). 'Citizen-led intelligence gathering under UK's Prevent Duty', in Ben Jaffel, H., Larsson, S. (eds) *Problematising Intelligence Studies Towards: A New Research Agenda*. London: Routledge, pp. 73–95.

Kaleem, A. (2022b). 'The hegemony of prevent: Turning counter-terrorism policing into common sense', *Critical Studies on Terrorism*, 15(2), 267–89.

Khan, R. M. (2021). 'Race, coloniality and the post 9/11 counter-discourse: Critical terrorism studies and the reproduction of the Islam-terrorism discourse', *Critical Studies on Terrorism*, 14(4), 498–501.

Kundnani, A. and Hayes, B. (2018). *The Globalisation of Countering Violent Extremism policies: Undermining Human Rights, Instrumentalising Civil Society*. Amsterdam: Transnational Institute.

Leicestershire Police (2018). 'Action counters terrorism', www.leics.police.uk/pol ice-forces/leicestershire-police/areas/leicestershire-force-content/c/campaigns/ 2019/action-counters-terrorism/ (accessed 23 September 2022).

Metropolitan Police Events [@MetPoliceEvents] (2022). 'If you're out and about in London this weekend to honour Her Majesty The Queen, please stay vigilant. If you spot something suspicious, please report it to our officers or a steward', X, https://t.co/nbYy45hOKd (accessed 25 July 2023).

Ndlovu-Gatsheni, S. J. (2015). 'Decoloniality as the future of Africa', *History Compass,* 13(10), 485–96.

Nyman, J. (2021). 'The everyday life of security: Capturing space, practice, and affect', *International Political Sociology*, 15(3), 313–37.

Pears, L. (2022). 'Protecting whiteness: Counter-terrorism, and British identity in the BBC's Bodyguard', *Millennium*, 1–22.

Sabir, R. (2017). 'Blurred lines and false dichotomies: Integrating counterinsurgency into the UK's domestic "war on terror"', *Critical Social Policy*, 37(2), 202–24.

Shawcross, W. (2023). 'Independent review of Prevent', www.gov.uk/government/ publications/independent-review-of-prevents-report-and-government-response/ independent-review-of-prevent-accessible (accessed 25 July 2023).

Smith, B. (2023). 'Counter-terror Prevent duty could be expanded to DWP, Border Force and asylum staff', *Civil Service World*, www.civilserviceworld.com/prof essions/article/prevent-review-duty-expanded-dwp-border-force-asylum-staff (accessed 27 July 2023).

Soss, J. (2015). 'Talking our way to meaningful explanations: A practice-centered view of interviewing for interpretive research', in Schwartz-Shea, P. and Yanow, D. (eds) *Interpretation and Method: Empirical Research Methods and the Interpretive Turn*. New York: Routledge, pp. 161–82.

Spalek, B. and Imtoual, A. (2007). 'Muslim communities and counter-terror responses: "Hard" approaches to community engagement in the UK and Australia', *Journal of Muslim Minority Affairs*, 27(2), 185–202.

Stanley, L. and Jackson, R. (2016). 'Introduction: Everyday narratives in world politics', *Politics*, 36(3), 223–35.

Strausz, E. and Heath-Kelly, C. (2019). 'Seeing radicalisation? The pedagogy of the Prevent strategy', in Edkins, J. (ed.) *Routledge Handbook of Critical IR*. Abingdon, Oxon: Routledge, pp. 161–75.

Taylor, D. (2022). 'Anger over referral of vulnerable boy, 11, to counter-radicalisation scheme', *The Guardian*, 26 January, www.theguardian.com/uk-news/2022/jan/ 26/anger-over-referral-of-vulnerable-boy-11-to-counter-radicalisation-scheme (accessed 4 July 2022).

Townsend, M. and Stein, J. (2021). 'Muslim boy, 4, was referred to Prevent over game of Fortnite', *The Observer*, 31 January, www.theguardian.com/uk-news/ 2021/jan/31/muslim-boy-4-was-referred-to-prevent-over-game-of-fortnite (accessed 4 July 2022).

West, J. (2017). 'Civic resilience: Securing ' "resilient communities" ' to prevent terrorism', in Chandler, D. and Coaffee, J. (eds) *Routledge Handbook of International Resilience*. Abingdon: Routledge, pp. 318–30.

Winter, C., Heath-Kelly, C., Kaleem, A., and Mills, C. (2021). 'A moral education? British values, colour-blindness, and preventing terrorism', *Critical Social Policy*, 42(1), 85–106.

Younis, T. and Jadhav, S. (2020). 'Islamophobia in the National Health Service: An ethnography of institutional racism in PREVENT's counter-radicalisation policy', *Sociology of Health & Illness*, 42(3), 610–26.

Younis, T. and Jadhav, S. (2019). 'Keeping our mouths shut: The fear and racialized self-censorship of British healthcare professionals in PREVENT training', *Cultural and Medicine Psychiatry*, 43(3), 404–24.

Part III

Counter-terrorism, radicalisation,
and right-wing extremism

9

The securitisation of Muslims and the growth of far-right extremism in Canada

Naved Bakali and Barbara Perry

In the context of the War on Terror, policies and discourses about the Canadian national security landscape have shifted towards targeting and policing Muslims, such that they have become a 'suspect community'. This has resulted in the securitising of Muslims in Canada. Though some may argue that the securitisation of Canadian Muslims is the outgrowth of anti-Muslim racism and bias that has come about from the 9/11 attacks and the subsequent War on Terror, this chapter traces the roots of these manifestations as part of broader historical practices associated with the racialised logics of coloniality (Jamil 2022). This chapter examines the securitisation of Canadian Muslims in the War on Terror through surveillance and racial profiling, which has resulted in the arrests of dozens of Muslims involved in half-baked terrorist plots precipitated and catalysed by agent provocateurs; anti-terrorism legislations, which have normalised states of exception for Muslims with regards to their civil rights; as well as restrictions of movement of Muslim bodies through a no-fly list, which in some instances has falsely identified children and infants. Ultimately, the disproportionate targeting of Muslims in the War on Terror not only violates the rights and freedoms of Canadian Muslims, but it also draws attention away from other serious threats to Canadian society (Bakali 2018). These threats include the rapid growth of white supremacist and far-right extremist groups, which have targeted racialised and minority communities, including Muslims. The most prominent examples of this include the mass shooting of Muslims at a Quebec City mosque in 2017 and the murder of a Muslim family in London, Ontario, in 2021.

The chapter begins with a discussion of the historical context of Canada as a white settler society. This exploration of Canada will assert that the notion of exaltation (Thobani 2007) is central to the racialised logics that have been employed to cast out racialised 'others' from the nationalist space. Through this mindset of exaltation, it becomes clearer how and why Muslims have become the objects of securitisation in the War on Terror. The next section of the chapter discusses how Muslims have been framed as a security threat in the War on Terror. Thereafter, the chapter will examine how Canadian Muslims, specifically, have experienced securitisation. The chapter will then turn to examine how other threats have flown under the radar with regards to security policies and discourses in Canada through a discussion of the rapid growth of far-right extremist activism.

Historicising the racialised logics of Canada as a white settler society

The land mass referred to as Canada was colonised by the British and French empires in the 1500s and was constructed as a settler society. Settler societies in this chapter refers to nations that were intended to be permanent European settlements through imperialist encounters (Bakali and Hafez 2022). The formation of Canada as a settler society was predicated on the killing and dispossession of Indigenous communities – an injustice which continues to this day. Throughout Canada's early history, strident efforts were made to keep it as a white settler society. This was reflected in early immigration policies established in the 1800 and 1900s, which prevented non-white migrants from settling on the land. For example, the Immigration Act of 1910 prevented people of African descent from immigrating to Canada on the basis of 'climatic unsuitability', which presumed that unfamiliarity with the cold climactic conditions would prevent successful settlement in the nation (Williams 1997). Asian migrants were also prevented from settling in Canada. This occurred through the Chinese Head Tax (1885–1923), a fee charged for each Chinese person entering the country. This tax varied from $50 to $500, effectively discouraging and preventing Chinese migrants from settling in Canada (Chan 2016). Another example of callous immigration policies can be seen in the Continuous Journey Clause. This law prevented Asian immigrants from settling in Canada if they did not travel directly from their home nation on a continuous journey to arrive to Canada. In 1914 this law was put to the test when a group of 367 Indian migrants boarded on the Komagata Maru ship and attempted to enter Canada through a continuous journey from Japan to Vancouver Harbour. The overwhelming majority of these passengers were denied settlement in Canada and were forced to return to India (Hawkins 1989). The racialised logics undergirding these white supremacist immigration laws and policies were also present in the educational projects of erasure and assimilation of Indigenous communities.

Through residential schooling, the Canadian government forcibly removed Indigenous children from their families and required them to attend schools administered by the church with the purpose of erasing their heritage and assimilating them to European-Canadian religion, culture, and ways of living (Hanson 2009).[1] Indigenous children were severly punished if they spoke their native languages or acknowledged their Indigenous culture and heritage. Beyond this, the children attending these schools were subjected to many other forms of psychological, physical, and sexual torture (Hanson 2009). The horrid conditions Indigenous children were subjected to in these schools resulted in the deaths of untold numbers of children. In 2021, over 1,300 unmarked graves in proximity to residential schools across Canada were discovered, which were believed to be the remains of children who attended and died in these schools (Gilmore 2021). The racialised violence experienced by Indigenous communities through these spaces have been traumatic and have had enduring effects. In Robina Thomas' (2014) study of Canadian residential schooling policies, she notes that not only did these schools contribute to the cultural genocide of Indigenous communities, but also inflicted sexual, physical, mental, and spiritual abuse on Indigenous children, which have affected generations. As the above discussion illustrates, there has been a historic legacy of preserving Canada as a white settler society through immigration policies, as well as cultural genocide. In more contemporary times, the preservation of Canada as a white settler society has been perpetuated through promoting national mythologies and imaginaries. This has been described by some as 'exaltation' (Thobani 2007).

Exaltation is the process of attributing certain imagined qualities which characterise the nationality of a people. Those who do not embody these qualities are considered strangers to the national community. As Thobani (2007: 6) mentions, 'national subjects who fail to live up to the exalted qualities are treated as aberrations… The failings of outsiders, however, are seen as reflective of the inadequacies of their community, of their culture, and, indeed, of their entire "race"'. In other words, there are certain imagined qualities inherent within English/French white Canadians. Those qualities exalt them above others and define who gets to be a 'real' Canadian. Those who do not fit within the mould of the Canadian national subject are believed to be outsiders who do not truly belong within the nation. Such a difference warrants a change in behaviour towards, and treatment of certain classes of citizens. The notion of exaltation is meant to preserve a national imaginary, which excludes undesirable 'others'. In the case of Muslims, this casting out is operationalised through constructing them as threatening objects of securitisation in the War on Terror.

The securitisation of Muslims in the War on Terror

Through the War on Terror, a meta-narrative of Islam and Muslims has emerged, transcending Global North and South barriers (Bakali and Hafez 2022). This meta-narrative has been influenced and structured by works and ideas associated with securitisation theory. Securitisation theory argues that national security is not limited to military security interventions. It extends beyond this to encompass state policies, apparatuses, and actions to address domestic challenges, which may also pose an existential threat. Securitisation policies are a function and reflection of prevailing politics and relations of power within a society. Critiques of securitisation theory maintain that this approach to national security is undergirded by an ideological project, which frame the subjects of securitisation as non-normative or being in a state of exception. In other words, securitisation theory reinforces the notion of 'otherness' with regards to objects of securitisation (Bakali 2019). In developing this critique, Howell and Richter-Montpetit (2019) assert that securitisation theory is underpinned by the concepts of civilisationism, methodological whiteness, and anti-black racism. As such, racist political thought is integral to it and the objects of securitisation exist in racialised threat imaginaries (Ibrahim 2005).

Extending Howell and Richter-Montpetit's analysis further, we can see how anti-Muslim bias and thought has significantly influenced the securitisation of Muslims in the policy making of nation states around the globe and framed them as an existential concern in the War on Terror. It is important to note here that the notion of securitisation assumes that when an issue is identified as a security threat, it is not always grounded in evidence or objectivity. Rather, a threat manifests through what Wæver (2003: 10) refers to as a 'speech act'. This is the simple utterance of an issue as being a security concern. By framing something or someone as a security threat, it becomes one (Wæver 2003). Through this process a 'new social order' is created (Balzacq 2005: 171), which justifies extreme emergency measures to eliminate potential threats. Theoretically, anyone can securitise an issue or people. However, according to Taureck (2006) the ability to securitise or being an actor of securitisation is dependent upon power. Those with sufficient power and authority are able to create the perception of a threat politically and socially. According to Wæver (1995: 55), this power and authority remains in the hands of state representatives, who can assert a 'special right to use whatever means necessary' to contain supposed security concerns and threats. Historically, Canada has deemed various groups as threatening to the white Canadian imaginary, as manifested in the immigration policies and schooling practices discussed above. The following section explores how Muslims have been the objects of securitisation and classified as a threatening 'Other' to the Canadian national imaginary in the context of the War on Terror.

The policing of Canadian Muslims in the War on Terror

There have been several terrorism related cases in Canada in the aftermath of the War on Terror (Leman-Langois 2018). However, most of these cases were not prosecuted and punished as acts or attempted acts of terrorism, unless the perpetrators were Muslims (Bakali 2016). One of the most notable attempted terrorism plots since the War on Terror, which likely garnered the most widespread media attention was the case of the 'Toronto 18' in 2006. The Toronto 18 was a group of eighteen young Muslim men, varying in ages from their early teens to their twenties, residing in the Canadian city of Toronto. These eighteen young men were all arrested on suspicion that they were a part of a terrorist cell that was plotting multiple terrorist attacks on prominent Canadian buildings including the Toronto Stock Exchange. Eventually, seven of the eighteen men had their charges stayed, while the remaining suspects pled or were found guilty of terrorism related offences (CBC News 2008). The sentences of these young men varied from two and a half years to life imprisonment. It is worth noting here that three of the eleven men sentenced in this case accepted plea bargain deals and were able to get off on time served. When examining the details of this terrorism plot, several problematic points emerge. Much of the evidence against the accused in this case was procured through interactions from two informants employed by the Royal Canadian Mounted Police (RCMP), Mubin Sheikh and Shaher Elsohemy. These informants provided a firearm, three tons of ammonium nitrate for making explosives, as well as arranged for the warehouse space to store the ammonium nitrate. Furthermore, Sheikh and Elsohemy were each paid $300,000 and $4 million, respectively, for their services (CBC News 2010). Without the 'assistance' of these informants, the key pieces of evidence upon which the case was built would not exist. The case of the Toronto 18, as with many other terrorism cases against Muslims in the War on Terror, reveals how law enforcement resorted to a lucrative incentive structure for multiple agent provocateurs who actively encouraged defendants to engage in criminal activity to build a case against them (Center for Human Rights and Global Justice 2011).

In another incident, a British Columbia couple, John Nuttall and Amanda Korody, were also lured into a terror plot by an RCMP agent provocateur. The attempted attack involved planting bombs at the British Colombia Legislature in a 'Canada Day Bomb Plot'. The mentally unstable methadone addicts were found guilty on three terrorism related charges in 2013, even though Nuttall repeatedly expressed concerns about the legitimacy of the plot and desperately sought spiritual advice from a religious scholar or family members about engaging in such actions. Every time Nuttall expressed such concerns the undercover RCMP officer prevented him from seeking such guidance. Furthermore, the RCMP officer convinced the couple that he was a member of a powerful international terrorist organisation that would likely kill them if they did not go through with the plot. Eventually, in 2016, a British Colombia judge stayed the charges against Nuttall and Korody, stating that law enforcement agents used trickery and subterfuge to manipulate the couple, effectively creating a terrorist threat instead of foiling one (Trumpener 2016). In addition to half-baked terrorist plots, orchestrated and incited by undercover law enforcement agents, the Canadian Government has also passed legislation which has disproportionately targeted Muslims, reinforcing archetypal portrayals of Muslims as terrorists.

The Anti-Terrorism Act (2001 and 2015) and the Immigration and Refugee Protection Act are both examples of the targeted laws, which have securitised Canadian Muslims. Measures within the Anti-Terrorism Act (2001) include:

> the strengthening of state powers of surveillance and detention; the imposition of greater restrictions on immigration and refugee policies; the increased scrutiny of immigrants and refugees (both at the borders and within the country) and a strengthening of the powers of deportation; a commitment to fighting the war against terrorism under the leadership of the Bush administration, most specifically to participate in the war on Afghanistan; and the intensification of intelligence, security, and military alliances with the United States. (Thobani 2007: 348)

Through this legislation, Canadian Muslims have been racially profiled and intimidated by Canadian Security Intelligence Services (CSIS). Most notably, provisions within this law allowed for the illegal detention, extraordinary rendition, and torture of Maher Arar, a Canadian citizen of Syrian descent in 2002 (Mazigh 2009). The Immigration and Refugee Protection Act authorises the Minister of Citizenship and Immigration in conjunction with the Solicitor General to issue a security certificate. A security certificate permits:

> the detention and expulsion of non-citizens who are considered to be a threat to national security. Detainees have no opportunity to be heard before a certificate is issued, and a designated judge of the federal court reviews most of the government's case against the detainee in a secret hearing at which neither the detainee nor his counsel is present. The detainee receives only a summary of the evidence against him. Detention is mandatory for non-permanent residents… and there is no possibility of release unless a person leaves Canada, or the certificate is struck down, or if 120 days have elapsed and deportation has still not taken place. (Razack 2008: 26)

Security certificates, like the provisions in the Anti-Terrorism Act, suspend rights and due process for non-citizens residing within Canada. Critics contend that they are an example of pre-emptive punishment in which people are being punished before they have committed any crime or wrongdoing. As Razack (2008) discusses, these provisions have stripped away basic fundamental rights of Muslim men. Such a situation, where the suspension of the law (i.e., stripping away fundamental basic human rights) becomes the law, can be described as one where there is a proliferation of 'camps' (Arendt 1944). These are spaces that legally authorise the 'suspension of law and the creation of communities of people without "the right to have rights"… camps are places where the rules of the world cease to apply' (Razack 2008: 7). The danger of camps and the logic that underlies these spaces is that they normalise the violence enacted by the state as actions associated with the law and therefore legitimise and sanitise them.

Additionally, detainees deported to their countries of origin as a result of a security certificate face the possibility of torture there. Muslims detained on the grounds of security certificates since the onset of the War on Terror include Hassan Almrei, Mohammed Mahjoub, Mohammed Jaballah, Mohamed Harkat, and Adil Charkaoui. All men have at some point languished in prison for a number of years and have spent varying amounts of time in solitary confinement (Razack 2008). All five men have spent time under house arrest with extremely strict conditions, some of whom felt the house arrest conditions were so humiliating and difficult that they preferred to return to prison. The policing of Muslims in Canada has also included restrictions on movement through a no-fly list.

The freedom of movement that Canadian citizens are privy to, is a right that most take for granted. In the War on Terror, some Muslims have had this freedom restricted through the presence of the Specified Persons List, also commonly referred to as the 'no-fly list'. The no-fly list was created in 2007 and expanded through Bill C-51 in 2015. The aim of this measure was to prevent people who may pose a security threat or people suspected of wanting to participate in terrorist activities from flying to other places (Jamil 2022). It is unknown precisely who, and how many people are on this list, as this information is limited to government officials involved in creating this list. However, based on media reporting on the issue, it is evident that Muslims have been disproportionately targeted by this legislation. One of the more frustrating aspects of this mechanism is that false positives routinely occur. A false positive is when someone with the same or similar name to individuals who appear on the list are flagged and prevented from travelling. Even young children have been erroneously identified through this system. In 2016, the parents of a six-year-old Ontario boy named Syed Adam Ahmed, spoke to Canadian media voicing their concerns of how their young child routinely had to undergo additional security checks because his name would be flagged whenever they travelled by air (CBC News 2016a). After the story of Syed Adam Ahmed aired, other Muslim families came forward with similar incidents of their children being falsely identified through the no-fly list. The ages of these children varied from six months to seventeen years old (CBC News 2016b). One would naturally assume that a child less than one year of age would pose no threat or warrant any concern of engaging in terrorist activities. However, as Muslims have been securitised in the War on Terror, a constant state of exception exists, regardless of how illogical this may be.

The securitisation of Canadian Muslims has brought about cases of entrapment, the passing of targeted legislation in which due process and civil rights have been routinely violated, as well as restrictions in the freedom of movement. Additionally, Canadian Muslims have experienced severe stigmatisation and associations with violence, oppression, and terrorism, framing them as undesirable 'Others' within the white Canadian imaginary (Bakali and Soubani 2021). In the process of securitising Muslims, other more serious and apparent threats to the nation have gone largely undetected. In particular, there has been a failure to cast the securitised gaze to far-right extremism, to which we now turn.

(Non-)securitisation of right-wing extremism

Narratives around the 'threat environment' (Monaghan and Walby 2012) have somehow evaded serious consideration of right-wing extremism (RWE). Rather, in a study published in 2015, Perry and Scrivens identified over 120 incidents of violence associated with right-wing extremists in Canada between 1980 and 2014, ranging from criminal harassment, to arson, to murder. To put that in context, during the same period of time, there were seven incidents associated with Islamist inspired extremism. More recent studies completed after this one have identified over 300 active far-right groups (Davey et al. 2020; Perry, Hofmann, and Scrivens 2023). An even more dramatic illustration of the risk posed by this movement are the mass murders that we have witnessed in Canada between 2014 and 2021. In 2014, Justin Bourque shot and killed three RCMP officers (Perry and Scrivens 2020). His behaviour was shaped by an anti-authority and anti-police stance derived from his right-wing views (Bakali 2019). In January of 2017, Alexandre Bissonnette killed six Muslim men at prayer. A frequently posted photo shows Bissonnette sporting a 'Make America Great Again' hat, a reflection of his admiration for Donald Trump and other right-leaning populists such as France's Marine Le Pen (Perry 2019). This would not be the last time far-right extremist would fatally target Muslims, as another mass murder occurred in London, Ontario, in 2021 when four members of the Afzaal family were struck and killed by a twenty-year-old man who had been consuming white supremacist narratives online since his mid-teens (Carruthers 2021). Similarly, Alek Minassian's van attack in Toronto in 2018 took ten lives. Minassian is an adherent of the misogynistic arm of the movement, Incel, or Involuntary Celibate (CTVNews 2022). For Incels, women's increasing freedom and empowerment represent unacceptable threats to masculinity and the right that it implies to control women's bodies. For all of this, RWE is still very low on the list of priorities for law enforcement and intelligence communities.

The RWE movement is spread widely across the country. When Perry and Scrivens published the 2015 report, they conservatively estimated that there were over one hundred active groups across the country, with particular concentrations in Quebec, Ontario, Alberta, and BC (Perry and Scrivens 2015). Since approximately 2016 – a time period corresponding to Trump's ascendency – we have seen dramatic growth in the numbers, visibility, and online/offline activism associated with the extreme right. An updated study of right-wing extremism conducted by the second author, Ryan Scrivens, and David Hofmann documented closer to 300 groups currently active. This includes new groups (e.g., Proud Boys; La Meute), and new chapters of already existing groups (e.g., Blood and Honour; PEGIDA). With increased numbers has come increased visibility, not least of which is manifest in the far-right rallies and demonstrations that have peppered the country since 2016. Hardly a weekend goes by that there is not a handful of such events to be found nationwide. And unlike patterns we observed in our 2015 report, today's groups are finding ways to put aside their differences in the interests of 'uniting the right', as so clearly expressed at Charlottesville, USA in 2021, where a 'Unite the Right' rally was held, culminating in violent confrontations between white supremacists and protesters. In an attempt to collectively empower the movement as a whole, groups that might previously have engaged in conflict across ideological lines are now creating coalitions, especially at the aforementioned rallies, or during street patrols.

The presence of the latter at such events raises another important caveat. Many of the groups are characterised by a much more aggressive stance, and distressingly, an obsession with heavy weaponry. The Proud Boys smugly proclaim – along with their 'western chauvinism' – that 'We love our guns.'[2] Online images of groups like La Meute[3] show a similar attachment to arms, including automatic weapons. The III%ers,[4] however, take this to the extreme. Allegedly drawing on the training provided by former – and likely current – members of the armed services, the III%ers are actively engaged in paramilitary training in preparation for what they see as the inevitable 'Muslim invasion'. The combination of arms, training and xenophobia is a potentially deadly one (Perry, Hofmann, and Scrivens 2023).

Failure to monitor

In their comprehensive study of right-wing extremism in Canada, Perry and Scrivens (2018) highlighted what was then a widespread tendency among law enforcement to minimise the threat of right-wing extremism. Indeed, police officers themselves acknowledged this relative lack of attention to RWE. This seemed to be especially problematic in rural areas, where police officers indicated that 'no one knows' the risk because no one is monitoring activity. But this was also the case in urban areas, even in those where RWE activity was widely known. An officer in one Ontario city that had long been the site of significant far-right organising and activity expressed concern that 'we're not doing enough' to confront the known activists. Another in the same community admitted that 'until something happens, we're not looking at them'. This was readily apparent when a march composed of twenty to twenty-five neo-Nazis carrying White Pride flags and intoning racist chants led adherents through the downtown. However, there was no attempt to engage or monitor the activists. On the contrary, officers in the hate crime and diversity portfolios had no prior knowledge of the event, indicating that they were not paying close attention to the local movement (Perry and Scrivens 2018).

In addition to the neglect paid to any known right-wing presence, some police personnel deny – at least publicly – that there is any risk associated with the right. Instead, they downplay the potential for organised violence, referring to them variously as 'three man wrecking crews' or 'losers without a cause'. This was the case even in communities where officers acknowledged the presence of right-wing group membership into the hundreds (Perry and Scrivens 2018).

This tendency to disregard the threat posed by RWE was made readily apparent during the 2022 convoys and the occupation of Ottawa. Law enforcement have been roundly criticised for their apparent lackadaisical approach to the demonstrations that plagued so many communities in January and February of that year. The most besieged city, Ottawa, suffered through three weeks of crowds and trucks strangling the downtown area. Businesses closed, residents stayed indoors or left the city, shelters and soup kitchens restricted entry. These were reasonable responses to the ongoing harassment and violence directed toward homeless, COVID-19-masked, racialised, and queer communities. The convoy's occupation of Ottawa was anything but the 'peaceful' and 'joyous' gathering that its proponents and organisers claimed. It was a right-wing inspired and informed strategy of intimidation of both government and citizens (Smith and Amarasingam 2022).

Yet in spite of community calls for a forceful police effort to close down the occupation, the truckers and their supporters were allowed to remain in place from 22 January until 23 February 2022. Moreover, there were strong indications of police sympathy for the convoys. Law-enforcement-specific social media accounts with such monikers as Mounties for Freedom and Police for Freedom were riddled with support for the convoys, and critiques of COVID-19-related mandates. An open letter on the Facebook page of Mounties for Freedom – which also made claims of the 'peaceful' and 'loving' nature of the convoy – was signed by the likes of Derek Sloan and Randy Hillier, prominent Conservative politicians, both of whom have been severely criticised for their racist, and/or homophobic narratives, as well as the dissemination of COVID-19 disinformation. An RCMP officer in BC, and the current BC Chapter leader for Police for Freedom posted a video in which she also demonstrates sympathy with the movement, referring to the 'tyrannical state' – another common trope of the contemporary far right, which misrepresents recent state mandates.[5] An OPP officer was recorded by a trucker bound for Ottawa, telling the driver 'I get what you are doing. I support you 100%.'[6] It is no surprise that, when posted on TikTok, it drew both favourable and critical attention. Another OPP officer came under severe criticism when an observer tweeted a video of him offering his cruiser as a 'photo booth' for convoy participants.[7] Finally, even after the convoy had been designated a criminal event, police officers continued to donate funds to their GiveSendGo account before it was closed down (Oved 2022).

The lack of response to right-wing extremism is attributable in part to the locus of responsibility for extremism within police services. Some services place extremism within the largely under-resourced and under-staffed hate crime and/or diversity portfolios. Others assign it to the gang unit, where RWE groups are not equated – definitionally or operationally – with non-white gangs. Yet others embed the onus within the broader mandate of extremism units. As the first half of this paper highlights, that is fraught with difficulty as law enforcement remain obsessed with Islamist extremism – as well as left wing extremism – and so pay little attention to other forms of 'homegrown' extremism. The failure to take seriously RWE is likewise embedded in the contemporary exercise of securitisation discussed above. In particular, it calls to mind the reference to Wæver (1995: 55), who noted that agents of the state can assert a 'special right to use whatever means necessary' to contain supposed security concerns and threats. Yet until Trudeau's federal government invoked the Emergencies Act on 14 February 2022, those 'means' were not, in fact, brought into play. In keeping with the longer trajectory of denying the RWE threat, there appeared considerable resistance to intervene in a predominantly white movement, in spite of the stated intent of organisers to overthrow the sitting government.

We should not be surprised by the relative lack of action against RWE activism. Law enforcement bodies – in varied guises – were developed to support the colonialist project of the state. The social and legal order defended by police was also that of a colonial state, seeking to exclude or at least regulate native peoples who were seen to stand in the way of 'progress'. Specifically, law enforcement became the key means by which to 'police' racialised spaces, and by which to facilitate the assimilative process. The race and place of Indigenous people on Turtle Island was defined and regulated by an array of intertwined formal and informal mechanisms of social control: missionaries, boarding schools, the military, even public health facilities. Underlying the power and success of each of these, however, were formal policing agencies. Harring's (1994: 13) comments on the American context also apply to Canadian history:

> Bureau of Indian Education (BIA) schools could not function without compulsory attendance laws and BIA police to arrest or threaten parents for not sending children to school. BIA farmers could not teach the Indians to farm without laws and police to prevent Indians from killing their stock for food. Christian churches could not convert without laws to bar traditional ceremonial activities. Land could not be allotted without laws to punish Indians who resisted.

Thus, police functioned explicitly to force the imposition of Western values and behaviours, and the suppression of traditional ways of living. This is not simply an historical artifact, but a practice that continues today, as Derek Gregory (2004: 7) observes: 'the capacities that inhere within the colonial past are routinely reaffirmed and reactivated in the colonial present', affecting not just Indigenous people but racialised communities as well. Sherene Razack (2020: 17) concurs, asserting that,

> Settler colonialism is an ongoing project that preserves intact its colonial, spatial and legal structures. Dispossession continues apace with extraction as the engine that drives the racial project of accumulation. We can expect, then, that both the ghost of slavery and the ghost of settler colonialism animate institutions such as prisons and policing.

Consequently, police and the power they exert are intended to support rather than disrupt the sort of narratives and appeals to racial superiority that are embedded in RWE movements.

Failure to address a right-wing presence sends a dangerous message of tolerance. It empowers and emboldens groups and individuals who begin to think that they are under the radar and thus untouchable. Whether this is the reality or the perception is immaterial. If members and potential members believe that they can act with impunity, they will be drawn to online and offline activism. They are correct in assuming that their engagement with RWE narratives and actions will go unnoticed and unbothered – unbothered because of the ideological alliances between the far-right and sympathetic law enforcement bodies. The alignment enables the contemporary racist, homophobic, Islamophobic, and ironically even anti-authority movement to thrive. As Castle (2021: 231) observes, 'when police consistently ignore white power mobilisation, and collude with members of these groups during a documented global increase in far-right extremism, they expose the institution's foundation in a white supremacist ideology that has animated police power' since both Canada and the US emerged as settler colonial states.

Failure to name

Just as RWE activity goes unmonitored, so too does it go unnamed in Canada. In 2020, Perry and Scrivens cited the absence of attention to right-wing terrorist attacks on Canada's Integrated Terrorism Assessment Centre (ITAC) website. While international in scope, the published list included only one such attack – Anders Breivik's murders in Norway in 2011. Until 2021 – in the aftermath of the deadly Charlottesville Unite the Right rally – no RWE groups were on the country's list of terrorist entities. Within two years, seven such groups would make their way onto the list. Aside from this, the focus of the Canadian security community tends to be on global, and especially Islamist extremism. Successive Public Reports on the Terrorist Threat to Canada published by Public Safety Canada (2013; 2014; 2016; 2017; 2018) reinforce this imbalance. Indeed, from 2013 to 2016, there was no reference whatsoever to RWE. Ironically, the 2013 and 2014 reports acknowledged that no attacks by Muslim extremists occurred in Canada in 2012 or 2013, nor had any Canadians been killed on domestic soil by Al-Qaida or other Islamist inspired extremists. Yet as noted above, RWE attacks on individuals and property were fairly widespread during this time. Nonetheless, the 2013 Public Report on the Terrorist Threat to Canada (Public Safety Canada 2013) warned that 'homegrown violent extremists still pose a threat of terrorist attack in North America'. In an oblique reference that might be referring to far-right motives – or far-left, or single issue, or any other form of ideologically motivated extremism – the 2013 report also claims that the 'homegrown violent extremism can be based on other causes' – aside from the Al-Qa'ida influences – 'but is more limited in scope and scale than the activities of terrorist entities listed under the Criminal Code', effectively dismissing the risk. The two subsequent reports (Public

Safety Canada 2014; 2016) would also be silent on RWE. It was not until 2017 (Public Safety Canada 2017) that explicit mention was made to the RWE threat, but only to dismiss it. Three paragraphs in the twenty-one-page document referred to RWE while nonetheless downplaying the threat:

> The extreme right-wing is not an ideologically coherent group and historically, extreme right-wing violence in Canada has been sporadic and opportunistic… As there has been a rise in hate-related incidents reported to police in Canada, there is always the potential for extreme right-wing motivated violence to occur in the future. (Public Safety Canada 2017: 7)

The last such report in 2018 (Public Safety Canada 2018) offers a confused and confusing treatment of RWE, across just four or five paragraphs in total in the thirty-seven-page document. Inexplicably, the Public Report on the Terrorist Threat to Canada report for 2018 (Public Safety Canada 2018: 3) claimed that the 'principal terrorist threat to Canada continues to stem from individuals or groups who are inspired by violent ideologies and terrorist groups, such as Daesh or al-Qaida (AQ)'. As an aside, it did note that Canada 'also remains concerned about threats posed by those who harbour right-wing extremist views' (Public Safety Canada 2018: 3). The same year that an Incel-inspired man killed ten people in the downtown Toronto van attack, the report stated that no terrorist attacks had been committed by terrorist groups or their followers. Yet late in the report, the van attack was mentioned. A tally of terrorist incidents from 2014 to 2018 also made no reference to RWE attacks (Public Safety Canada 2018). During that period of time, attacks grounded in some variant of RWE ideology were responsible for at least nineteen deaths (Moncton, Quebec City, Toronto). But again, each of these incidents was later mentioned with little comment. In short, there was undue caution, indeed, unwillingness to designate such incidents as terror-related. Together, these unbalanced reports suggest a resistance to attributing terrorist intent to white perpetrators. Their violence is not recognised as ideologically motivated, and it is certainly not understood as embedded in white (supremacist) culture. Indeed, the sanitised public and political narratives around the risks associated with far-right persist even in cases where the threat is realised – as in the instances of RWE mass murders noted here.

There is no reason why the violence associated with the murders noted above should not be characterised as terrorist incidents. The definition adopted in Canada in Section 83.01 of the Canadian Criminal Code refers to an act committed 'in whole or in part for a political, religious, or ideological purpose, objective or cause with the intention of intimidating the public… with regard to its security, including its economic security, or compelling a person, a government or a domestic or international organisation to do or to refrain from doing any act'. The Canadian Criminal Code also identifies terrorist activities as those that endanger a person's life, risks posed to the health and safety of the public, death and bodily harm with the use of violence, significant property damage, and interference or disruption of essential systems, facilities, or services, to name but a few. In short, three boxes must be ticked for an act to be considered terrorist in Canada: physical threat or violence; ideological, political or religious motivation; and intention to intimidate. There is little question by now that the incidents noted here tick each of those boxes.

As an example of the unequal consideration given to Islamist inspired and RWE inspired violence, consider three incidents that occurred within months of each other. Perry and Scrivens (2020) assessed the representations of these three cases. In early June 2014, twenty-four-year-old Justin Bourque crept through the city of Moncton, New Brunswick, armed with a high-powered rifle and shotgun. The anti-authoritarian survivalist was hunting RCMP police officers and killed three and injured two others (CBC News 2014). On 20 October 2014, Martin Couture-Rouleau ran down two Canadian Armed Forces members at the Integrated Personnel Support Centre (IPSC) in Saint-Jean-sur-Richelieu, Quebec. One died while the other was seriously injured. Just days later, on 22 October 2014, Michael Zehaf-Bibeau drove to the National War Memorial and fatally shot a Canadian soldier on ceremonial sentry duty. While there were striking similarities across all three incidents, it is also readily apparent that they were treated very differently in the press as well as by politicians and security services. Indeed, there was a rush to identify both Couture-Rouleau's and Zehaf-Bibeau's attacks as terrorist incidents. Curiously, though, this was not the case for Bourque.

There is not much to distinguish the three acts from one another or from the definition of terrorism offered above. Bourque was just as clearly motivated by his ideological stance as were Couture-Rouleau and Zehaf-Bibeau. Nonetheless, while these three separate events shared similar characteristics that constitute 'acts of terrorism' in the legal and academic sense, both the media and political representations of these events were skewed in terms of whom they implied ought to be defined as a terrorist (Perry and Scrivens 2020). The reactions highlighted the complex question of why two lone wolf attacks, inspired loosely by radical Islam, were framed as acts of terrorism while the other, motivated by far-right ideologies, was simply identified as murder or 'cop-killing'. The disparate consideration of Bourque's attack on the one hand, and those of Couture-Rouleau and Zehaf-Bibeau on the other, confirm Mythen and Walklate's (2006: 14) contention that representations of 'the terrorist threat have been ambiguous, patchy and ill conceived'. Specifically, such constructions in the Canadian context have been narrowly defined and highly dependent on the standard trope of Islamist extremism to the exclusion of more common domestic forms of violence associated with right wing extremism. Writing on the UK experience, Kundnani (2012) draws much the same conclusion, highlighting the tendency to distinguish between Islamist inspired violence as embedded in Muslim culture and identity, whereas RWE violence is atomistic and shaped by personal troubles. In short, the former is grounded in cultural pathologies, the latter in individual pathologies.

Ongoing work updating the 2018 study by Perry and Scrivens (2018) continues to find this bifurcation between public order (RWE) and national security (Islamist inspired). In line with the implied narratives found in the public terrorism reports noted above, many law enforcement officers that we spoke to asserted a similar claim, arguing that the crimes of the extreme right were of less concern to them – as extremism experts – than those of Islamist actors. Frequent references were made to 'free speech' when speaking of RWE actors, as if that somehow justified their actions. No such leeway – even around freedom of religion, for example – was allowed for Muslims. RWE terrorism's 'capacity to escape the label and thus, the regulation precisely signifies white privilege. Right-populism has been legitimised as part of a putative struggle for "national unity" and "Canadian values" and its targets are instead cast as problems to be eradicated' (Kwak 2020: 1184).

Failure to prosecute

Kwak (2020) is correct to suggest that the failure to name terrorism perpetrated by RWE actors also results in the failure to confront it through prosecutions. Michael Nesbitt (2021) provides a comprehensive assessment of the contexts in which Canada's terrorism provisions are invoked, and the findings reinforce the trend whereby Islamist and far right violence attract widely disparate legal treatment. Between 2001 and 2019, fifty-six individuals were charged with terrorism related offences – none of these were associated with RWE. As Nesbitt (2021: 39) decries, this is in spite of the fact, as highlighted previously in this paper, that 'over the same time period in Canada, far-right extremism killed or injured more people and was responsible for more domestic criminal incidents than AQ-inspired extremism'. Admittedly, since that time there has been some incremental shift, in that two recent incidents of RWE violence were met with terrorism charges. In the first, in May 2020, an Incel-inspired youth was charged in the machete attack on two women at a Toronto massage parlour (CBCNews 2023); in the second, a young man faces terrorism charges after killing four members of a

London Muslim family by driving his truck over them in 2021 (Carruthers 2021). The response to these later cases may well be, in part, due to public and media criticism of previous incidents of murder that did not attract terrorism charges, as in the case of the Quebec City mosque murders or the Moncton police murders. It is particularly glaring that the even more lethal Toronto van attack did not lead to terror-related charges.

The findings in Canada parallel those observed in the USA where there is de jure distinction between 'foreign' – that is, Islamist inspired – and 'domestic terrorism' – aka right-wing inspired. The tendency to levy more serious legal repercussions on international terrorists – 'them' – than on domestic terrorists – 'us' – is explicitly embedded in the law in the USA. In so doing, the law embodies the cultural predilection to ascribe a greater degree of threat to foreign, often racialised communities. It thus encapsulates associations linking Muslims, foreigners, non-whites, and terrorists in the popular imagination. The 'international terrorism' side of the divide conjures images of violent, dark-skinned Muslims, who threaten us here and abroad. The 'domestic terrorism' category conveys an entirely different social meaning: if one can envision a white Christian American as a terrorist at all, he remains nonetheless 'one of us' (Sinnar 2019: 1397).

It may well be that similar dynamics are playing out, de facto, in Canada in the absence of parallel legislation. While we do not have the same legal divide between international and domestic terrorism, there is a similar discursive divide here whereby Islamist-inspired terrorism is understood to be 'foreign' and more threatening, relative to the 'homegrown' terrorism associated with RWE. This is borne out by the narratives found in the Public Reports on the Terrorist Threat to Canada noted above, wherein the primary focus of concern continues to be the global Islamist threat. Considerable attention is also paid to 'foreign fighters' who leave Canada to travel to fight in support of ISIS and Daesh, or to train under their tutelage. In the 2018 report (Public Safety Canada 2018: 11–12), it is suggested that extremist travellers returning to Canada 'could' or 'might' pose any number of 'security threats', including terrorist attacks, inciting others to engage in attacks, or facilitating attacks elsewhere. No such alarm was raised when Canadian and American members of groups like The Base and Atomwaffen Division travelled to Ukraine to train with the far-right nationalist Azov battalion (Khaikin 2020). When it was later revealed that the Canadian military was 'briefed' by the same battalion in Ukraine in 2018 – prior to the Russian invasion – even that highly problematic fact received fleeting attention. In fact, the Azov exploited the photo op that this had presented, and reproduced the pictures in their online propaganda, lending some measure of legitimacy to their extreme right-wing narratives (Pugliese 2021). Looking beyond the Canadian borders, another infamous far right 'foreign fighter' might include Brenton Tarrant, who killed fifty-one Muslims in the Christchurch terrorist attacks. He had travelled widely across Europe, engaging with RWE activists online and offline (Roach 2021).

The tendency to characterise Islamist inspired extremism, but not right-wing extremism as global and transnational is a related blind spot in Canadian responses to risk. It is not only Islamist inspired extremists who have international ties that apparently heighten their threat level. The far-right movement is inherently global in scope, reflecting as it does adherence to white European nationalism. Indeed, what stands out about so many contemporary white supremacist groups is their allusion to a collective 'we' that transcends national boundaries (Back 2002; Caiani and Kröll, 2014). Adherents of the far-right pledge allegiance to particular nation states: Sweden, Germany, or Canada, for example. Each refers to their imagined nation as the great white homeland. However, otherwise diverse nationalists pledge a more profound allegiance to the mythic *white* nation, wherein nationality comes to be defined not by state, geography, or citizenship, but by race. More than pan-Canadian, or pan-European, the appeal is to join the fraternity of pan-Aryanism, wherein online extremists assert a common lineage, traceable to white Aryan cultures of Western Europe (Perry and Scrivens 2016). In short, the contemporary RWE movement is also a global rather than simply domestic threat.

It is important to note, finally, that in contrast to the application of terror related charges in cases of Islamist inspired crimes, right-wing extremists are more likely to draw hate crime charges – although even that is rare. A study by Department of Justice Canada found that between 2007 and 2020, only fourty-eight published cases considered hate as an aggravating factor at sentencing (Provost-Yombo and McDonald 2020). Keep in mind that, during that same period, police-reported hate crimes numbered well over 10,000 (Wang and Moreau 2022). Furthermore, between 2009/2010 and 2019/2020 Canadian courts heard just eighty-one cases under hate propaganda provisions, resulting in a finding of guilt in 43 per cent of the cases, of which just 34 per cent resulted in custodial sentences. In Nesbitt's (2021) analysis, this translates into a pattern wherein, between December 2001 and December 2019, all seventeen hate propaganda cases and applications of sentencing enhancement cases involved individuals motivated by far-right ideologies (Nesbitt 2021: 41).

In addition to the disparities in charging, Nesbitt (2021) also noted sharp divides in sentencing options and outcomes. Hate propaganda provisions allow for up to two years in prison, whereas the most common terrorism related offences could draw from ten years incarceration up to life. In practice, this has resulted in disparate sentencing outcomes:

since 2001 the average length of incarceration for those convicted of hate speech under s 319(1) and s 319(2) is 6.8 months, while the average length of non-custodial punishment for a conviction under the same sections is 10 months; by contrast, between 2001 and 2019, the average custodial sentence for a terrorism offender was 13 years and all offenders received custodial sentences. (Nesbitt 2021: 52)

Clearly, in practice, Canadian prosecutors and courts treat Islamist-inspired extremists far more harshly than their RWE counterparts. The divide between terrorism and hate crime designations also has symbolic implications. They have very different connotations in terms of the implied threat, harm, and culpability. The terrorist threat posed by extreme right groups is typically obscured 'when attacks on non-government targets, such as abortion clinics or members of unpopular or stigmatised religions, ethnic, racialised, sexual minorities, immigrants or gypsies are defined as "hate crimes", thus suggesting that such attacks are no more than expressions of personal prejudice' (Jaggar 2005: 204). However, the intent of 'hate crime' and of much of the violence associated with the extreme right is not only or even primarily intimidation of an individual, but of their community. In short, terrorism shares the same continuum as hate crime, while clearly occupying the extreme end of the scale.

Sinnar (2019: 1364–6) highlights a number of key implications that derive from the unequal balance between prosecutions of Islamist and right-wing extremist activity. First and foremost, it both assumes and reinforces the notion that Muslims are the primary perpetrators of terrorism in the USA and in Canada. These skewed perceptions and reactions can then be exploited by politicians and the public alike to justify and in fact heighten the punitive response to a narrowly defined range of terrorist actions and individuals. Ultimately, as with any such government imperative, the application of the terrorist label to one brand of terrorism but not the other reinforces the climate of hate that perpetuates private acts of hatred and violence.

Conclusion

Within the national imaginary, Canada is envisioned as a multicultural society that celebrates the various cultures and backgrounds of its citizenry as parts of an enriching mosaic (Haque 2012). This framing of the nation gives rise to the false notion that Canada is a post-racial society. This implies that notable racial progress has been made and that we have now entered a phase in our societal development in which racism is a concern of the past (Barnes, Chemerinsky, and Jones 2010). Consequently, some critics argue that the notion of multiculturalism masks the racist past of the nation while simultaneously cloaking the existing inequities, alienation, and prejudices that continue to impact racialised members of society (Thobani 2007). Historically, Canada has engaged in genocide and has wrought generational trauma to Indigenous communities through residential schools; has instituted racist immigration laws, preventing Asian and African migrants from settling, to keep Canada a white nation; and more contemporarily, has instituted legislation in the aftermath of the War on Terror, which has targeted and securitised the Muslim subject. The racialised logics, which undergird these actions are rooted in the settler colonial past of Canada, which has been sanitised through a national mythology of Canada as a multicultural state. This inability to recognise the institutionalisation of racism, particularly in relation to security practices and policies, have allowed for the growth and proliferation of far-right extremist groups within Canada, which are overwhelmingly white supremacists and pose a far greater security threat to the state then the 'otherised' Muslim subject.

The reach of RWE groups has expanded across the nation and the threat that they pose is often overlooked by law enforcement. Furthermore, in the post-COVID era, evidence suggests that many members of law enforcement are sympathetic to and in some cases members of these groups themselves. The failure to acknowledge RWE and the threat it poses has serious implications. As Nesbitt (2021: 51) observes, '[c]alling one group terrorists and another merely hateful matters... not just socially and culturally. Law has a normative, social, and communicative function'. By minimising far-right crimes, the sentencing of such crimes becomes more lenient. When the legal system does not treat these crimes with the appropriate level of seriousness, the potential for far-right crimes and groups to grow only increases (Nesbitt 2021).

There is an essential need for a more balanced approach in mitigating security threats in the Canadian context that are divorced from the racialised logics of settler colonialism, which exclusively perceive the notion of terrorism through Muslim 'Otherness' (Bakali 2019). This process is unattainable without first recognising the institutionalisation of racist practices and policies within the national security apparatus as well as broader Canadian society. A thorough critical self-examination, acknowledgement, and commitment to unlearning and decolonising is a prerequisite for any type of reform to occur.

Notes

1 Mandatory attendance for Indigenous children at these schools was from 1894 until 1947, however these schools persisted until the last decades of the t century.
2 'The Proud Boys' actions belie their disavowals of bigotry: Rank-and-file Proud Boys and leaders regularly spout white nationalist memes and maintain

affiliations with known extremists. They are known for anti-Muslim and misogynistic rhetoric. Proud Boys have appeared alongside other hate groups at extremist gatherings such as the "Unite the Right" rally in Charlottesville, Virginia. Former Proud Boys member Jason Kessler helped organise that event, which brought together a broad coalition of extremists including Neo-Nazis, antisemites and militias' (Southern Poverty Law Centre, nd). It is notable that Proud Boys was founded by Canadian Gavin McInnes.

3 La Meute (French for 'the pack') is a Quebec far-right group that was founded by two former military personnel. They are generally considered to be Islamophobic, anti-immigrant, and ultranationalist (*Le Soleil* 2018; Patriquin 2017; Montpetit 2017).

4 III%ers are part of the broader militia or patriot movement, who proclaim themselves the true defenders of 'the nation', asserting that the current government is incapable of doing so and is in fact contributing to the demise of their homeland. The state is held to be by turns tyrannical and weak, having succumbed to the undue demands of minorities, immigrants and globalists. Patriots are thought to be especially likely to draw their membership from military (armed services) and paramilitary institutions (law enforcement), to train in paramilitary maneuvers, and to be heavily armed (e.g., III%ers). The III%ers, specifically, are informed by rabid Islamophobia, and actively train to defend Canada from what they see as the inevitable invasion by Muslims (Lamoreux 2017). Bloggers and commenters on social media make frequent references to the 'threat' of Islam, to the risk of terrorist attacks, and to the 'take-over' of Canada by Islam.

5 https://police4freedom.ca/members/maria-chirdaris/

6 https://www.tiktok.com/@bamybear/video/7063926421722254597?is_copy_url=1&is_from_webapp=v1&lang=en

7 https://twitter.com/CBCOttawa/status/1492342150671052804

References

Arendt, H. (1944). 'Race-thinking before racism', *The Review of Politics*, 6(1), 36–73.

Back, L. (2002). 'Aryans reading Adorno: Cyber-culture and twenty-first century racism', *Ethnic and Racial Studies*, 25(4), 628–51.

Bakali, N. (2019). 'Challenging terrorism as a form of 'Otherness': Exploring the parallels between far-right and Muslim religious extremism', *Islamophobia Studies Journal*, 5(1), 99–115.

Bakali, N. (2018). 'The redefining of far-right extremist activism along Islamophobic lines', *Islamic Perspective*, 19(1), 1–18.

Bakali, N. (2016). *Islamophobia: Understanding Anti-Muslim Racism through the Lived Experiences of Muslim Youth*. Rotterdam: Sense Publishers.

Bakali, N. and Hafez, F. (2022). *The Rise of Global Islamophobia in the War on Terror: Coloniality, Race, and Islam*. Manchester: Manchester University Press.

Bakali, N. and Soubani, N. (2021). 'Hijab, Gendered Islamophobia, and the Lived Exoeriences of Muslim Women', *Yaqeen Institute for Islamic Research*, 17 August, https://yaqeeninstitute.ca/read/paper/hijab-gendered-islamophobia-and-the-lived-experiences-of-muslim-women (accessed 2 December 2023).

Balzacq, T. (2005). 'The three faces of securitisation: Political agency, audience and context', *European Journal of International Relations*, 11(2), 171–201.

Barnes, M., Chemerinsky, E., and Jones, T. (2010). 'A post-race equal protection?', *Georgetown Law Journal*, 98, 967–1004.

Caiani, M. and Kröll, P. (2014). 'The transnationalization of the extreme right and the use of the Internet', *International Journal of Comparative and Applied Criminal Justice*, 39(4), 331–51.

Carruthers, D. (2021). 'Thousands mourn London Muslim family killed in alleged hate attack', London Free Press, https://lfpress.com/news/local-news/thousands-mourn-london-muslim-family-killed-in-alleged-hate-attac (accessed 14 January 2023).

Castle, T. (2021). 'Cops and the Klan: Police disavowal of risk and minimization of threat from the far right', *Critical Criminology*, 29(2), 215–35.

CBCNews (2023). 'Incel-inspired Toronto massage parlour murder was act of terror, judge rules', 6 June, www.cbc.ca/news/canada/toronto/incel-toronto-massage-killing-terrorism-1.6867177

CBCNews (2016a). Markham boy, 6, on no-fly list, parents say, 3 January, www.cbc.ca/news/canada/toronto/markham-security-travel-watchlist-1.3387890 (accessed 23 August 2022).

CBCNews (2014). 'Justine Bourque: Latest revelations about man Charged in Moncton Shooting', *CBC News: Canada*, 5 June, www.cbc.ca/news/canada/new-brunswick/justin-bourque-latest-revelations-about-man-charged-in-moncton-shooting-1.2665900

CBCNews (2008). 'Key events in the case', *CBC News: Canada*, 4 June, www.cbc.ca/news/canada/toronto-18-key-events-in-the-case-1.715266

CBCNews (2010). 'Not in for the money: Toronto 18 informant', *CBC News: Canada*. 16 January. www.cbc.ca/news/canada/toronto/not-in-it-for-money-toronto-18-informant-1.946925

Center for Human Rights and Global Justice (2011). *Targeted and Entrapped: Manufacturing the 'Homegrown Threat' in the United States*. New York: Center for Human Rights and Global Justice.

Chan, A. (2016). 'Chinese head tax', *The Canadian Encyclopedia,* www.thecanadianencyclopedia.ca/en/article/chinese-head-tax-in-canada (accessed 18 July 2021).

CTVNews (2022). 'Alek Minassian sentenced to life in prison with no parole for 25 years in Toronto van attack', 13 June, https://toronto.ctvnews.ca/alek-minassian-sentenced-to-life-in-prison-with-no-parole-for-25-years-in-toronto-van-attack-1.5944169

Davey, J., Guerin, C., and Hart, M. (2020). *An Online Environmental Scan of Right-wing Extremism in Canada*. London: ISD.

Gregory, D. (2004). *The Colonial Present*. Malden: Blackwell.

Hanson, E. (2009). 'Residential schools', *Indigenous Foundations*, https://indigenousfoundations.arts.ubc.ca/the_residential_school_system/ (accessed 15 December 2021).

Haque, E. (2012). *Multiculturalism within a Bilingual Framework: Language, Race, and Belonging in Canada*. Toronto: University of Toronto Press.

Harring, S. (1994). *Crow Dog's Case: American Indian Sovereignty, Tribal Law, and United States Law in the Nineteenth Century*. Cambridge: Cambridge University Press.

Hawkins, F. (1989). *Critical Years in Immigration: Canada and Australia Compared*. Kingston: McGill-Queen's University Press.

Howell, A. and Richter-Montpetit, M. (2019). 'Is securitisation theory racist? Civilizationalism, methodological whiteness, and antiblack thought in the Copenhagen School', *Security Dialogue*, 51(1), 3–22.

Ibrahim, M. (2005). 'The securitisation of migration: A racial discourse', *International Migration*, 43(5), 163–87.

Jaggar, A. (2005). 'What is terrorism, why is it wrong, and could it ever be morally permissible?', *Journal of Social Psychology*, 36(2), 202–17.

Jamil, U. (2022). 'The racialised logics of Islamophobia in Canada', in Bakali, N. and Hafez, F. (eds) *The Rise of Global Islamophobia in the War on Terror: Coloniality, Race, and Islam*. Manchester: Manchester University Press, pp. 1–21.

Khaikin, L. (2020). 'The right wing checkpoint for Canada's intervention in Ukraine', *Canadian Dimension*, 21 May, https://canadiandimension.com/articles/view/the-right-wing-checkpoint-for-canadas-intervention-in-ukraine

Kundnani, A. (2012). *Blind Spot? Security Narratives and Far-Right Violence in Europe*. The Hague: International Centre for Counter-Terrorism.

Kwak, L. J. (2020). 'Problematizing Canadian exceptionalism: A study of right-populism, white nationalism and conservative political parties', *Oñati Socio-Legal Series*, 10(6), 1166–92.

Lamoureux, M. (2017). 'The Birth of Canada's Armed, Anti-Islamic, 'Patriot' Group.' *Vice*, www.vice.com/en_uk/article/new9wd/the-birth-of-canadas-armed-anti-islamic-patriot-group

Leman-Langlois, S. (2018). 'Canada', in Silke, A. (ed.) *Routledge Handbook of Terrorism and Counterterrorism*. London: Routledge.

Lewis, H. (2021). 'Mapping the missing: Former residential school sites in Canada and the search for unmarked graves', *Global News: Local*, 15 September, https://globalnews.ca/news/8074453/indigenous-residential-schools-canada-graves-map/ (accessed 15 December 2021).

Mazigh, M. (2009). *Hope and Despair: My Struggle to Free My Husband, Maher Arar*. New York: Emblem Editions.

Monaghan, J. and Walby, K. (2012). 'Making up 'terror identities': Security intelligence, Canada's integrated threat assessment centre and social movement suppression', *Policing and Society*, 22(2), 133–51, DOI: 10.1080/10439463.2011.605131.

Mythen, G. and Walklate, S. (2006). 'Criminology and terrorism: Which thesis? Risk society or governmentality?', *British Journal of Criminology*, 46, 379–398.

Nesbitt, M. (2021). 'Violent crime, hate speech or terrorism? How Canada views and prosecutes far-right extremism (2001–2019)', *Common Law World Review*, 50(1), 38–56.

Oved, M., LaFleche, G., McKeen, A., and Wang, S. (2022). 'Ontario police officers are named in leaked list of donors to the "Freedom Convoy"', *The Star*, 22 February, www.thestar.com/news/investigations/2022/02/22/ontario-police-officers-are-named-in-leaked-list-of-donors-to-the-freedom-convoy.html

Perry, B. (2019). 'Breaking the peace: The Quebec City Terrorist Attack', in Zempi, I. and Awan, I. (eds) *The Routledge International Handbook of Islamophobia*. London: Routledge, pp. 275–85.

Perry, B. and Scrivens, R. (2020). 'Who's a terrorist? What's terrorism? Comparative media representations of lone-actor violence in Canada', in Littlewood, J. Dawson, L. L., and Thompson, S. (eds) *Terrorism and Counter-Terrorism in Canada*. Toronto: University of Toronto Press.

Perry, B. and Scrivens, R. (2018). *Right-Wing Extremism in Canada*. London: Palgrave.

Perry, B. and Scrivens, R. (2016). 'White Pride worldwide: Constructing global identities online', in Schweppe, J. and Walters, M. (eds) *The Globalisation of Hate: Internationalising Hate Crime?* London: Oxford University Press.

Perry, B. and Scrivens, R. (2015). *Right Wing Extremism in Canada: An Environmental Scan*. Ottawa: Public Safety Canada.

Perry, B., Hofmann, D., and Scrivens, R. (2023). 'Right-wing extremism in Canada environmental scan 2.0', Public Safety Canada.

Provost-Yombo, K., Louden, C., and McDonald, S. (2020). *Hate as an Aggravating Factor at Sentencing: A Review of the Case Law from 2007–2020*. Ottawa: Department of Justice Canada.

Public Safety Canada (2013). 'Public report on the terrorist threat to Canada', www.securitepublique.gc.ca/cnt/rsrcs/pblctns/trrrst-thrt-cnd/trrrst-thrt-cnd-eng.pdf

Public Safety Canada (2014). 'Public report on the terrorist threat to Canada', www.publicsafety.gc.ca/cnt/rsrcs/pblctns/2014-pblc-rpr-trrrst-thrt/index-en.aspx

Public Safety Canada (2016). 'Public report on the terrorist threat to Canada'.

Public Safety Canada (2017). 'Public report on the terrorist threat to Canada', www.publicsafety.gc.ca/cnt/rsrcs/pblctns/pblc-rprt-trrrst-thrt-cnd-2017/index-en.aspx

Public Safety Canada (2018). 'Public report on the terrorist threat to Canada', www.publicsafety.gc.ca/cnt/rsrcs/pblctns/pblc-rprt-trrrsm-thrt-cnd-2018/index-en.aspx

Pugliese, D. (2021). 'Canadian officials who met with Ukrainian unit linked to neo-Nazis feared exposure by news media: documents', *Ottawa Citizen*, 28 November https://ottawacitizen.com/news/national/defence-watch/canadian-officials-who-met-with-ukrainian-unit-linked-to-neo-nazis-feared-exposure-by-news-media-documents

Razack, S. (2020). 'Settler colonialism, policing and racial terror: The police shooting of Loreal Tsingine', *Feminist Legal Studies*, 28(1), 1–20.

Razack, S. (2008). *Casting Out: The Eviction of Muslims from Western Law & Politics*. Toronto: University of Toronto Press.

Roach, K. (2021). 'Counterterrorism and the challenges of terrorism from the far right', *Common Law World Review*, 50(1), 3–20.

Sinnar, S. (2019). 'Separate and unequal: The law of "domestic" and "international" terrorism', *Michigan Law Review*, 117(7), 1333–404.

Smith, P. and Amarasingam, A. (2022). *Right-Wing Populism, Conspiracy Theories, and the Canadian Trucker Convoy*, Right-Wing Extremism: Experts Symposium, Oshawa, Ontario.

Southern Poverty Law Centre (no date). Proud Boys. www.splcenter.org/fighting-hate/extremist-files/group/proud-boys

Taureck, R. (2006). 'Securitisation theory and securitisation studies', *Journal of International Relations and Development*, 9(1), 53–61.

Thobani, S. (2007). *Exalted Subjects: Studies in the Making of Race and Nation in Canada*. Toronto: University of Toronto Press.

Thomas, R. (2014). 'Violence and terror in a colonized country: Canada's Indian residential school system', in Perera, S. and Razack, S. (eds) *At the Limits of Justice: Women of Colour on Terror*. Toronto: University of Toronto Press, pp. 23–37.

Tumpener, B. (2016). 'Crown seeks "Terrorism Peace Bond" for couple convicted then freed in B.C. Legislature bomb plot', *CBC Website*. 29 July, www.cbc.ca/

news/canada/british-columbia/crown-seeks-peace-bond-for-john-nuttall-and-amanda-korody-under-fear-of-terrorism-criminal-code-section-1.3701536

Wæver, O. (2003). 'Securitisation: taking stock of a research programme in security studies', draft, http://zope.polforsk1.dk/securitytheory/oletext/ (accessed 18 January 2006).

Wæver, O. (1995). 'Securitization and desecuritization', in Lipschutz, R. D. (ed.) *On Security*. Columbia University Press.

Wang, J. and Moreau, G. (2022). *Police-Reported Hate Crime in Canada, 2020*. Ottawa: Statistics Canada.

Williams, D. (1997). *The Road to Now: A History of Blacks in Montreal*. Montreal: Vehicule Press.

10

The spectre of the predatory Muslim man: Tracing far-right gendered imaginaries and counter-terrorism policies in the cases of love jihad and the Great Replacement

Eviane Leidig

The War on Terror was an inflection point in the convergence of anti-Muslim political activism and counter-terrorism policies around the world. The rise of the contemporary far-right, constituted as part of the broader 'Islamophobia industry' (Cockbain and Tufail 2020), can be situated in relation to the increasing surveillance and stigmatisation of Muslim communities. Critical terrorism scholars have noted that terrorism generates a securitised response because its instrumentalisation maintains gendered and racialised power hierarchies within society, often discrediting violence embedded in patriarchal white supremacist political systems (Gentry 2020). Yet, more recently, others have identified a shifting focus towards far-right extremism and terrorism among counter-terrorism and prevention efforts (Martini and da Silva 2022). Decades of counter-terrorism policies designed to address Islam as a categorised threat are often ill suited for, and not translatable to, the far-right. This chapter takes a critical stance of what Jarvis (2022) identifies as the problem-solving approach towards far-right terrorism and extremism, which has been increasingly viewed as a policy concern that is securitised to fit within pre-existing frameworks of (Western) counter-terrorism models. While far-right terrorism and extremism has indeed been 'typically approached as a fully-formed threat to be identified, assessed, and addressed' (25) within terrorism studies, and researchers should remain critical of these underlying assumptions and logics, this argument contains a major oversight.

Far-right terrorism and extremism has indeed become securitised, but the far-right per se has not. One blind spot concerns the 'mainstreaming' of far-right narratives in ways that are rendered invisible because such narratives are built upon widely accepted norms and values, even within democratic societies (Mondon and Winter 2020). Consequently, this hints at Jarvis' (2022: 25–6) recommendation to pursue ontological analysis, and map the production of discourses and dispositifs as it pertains to wider political discourses. By understanding this holistic relationship, we can begin to fully situate the apparatus of activity constituting far-right activism, politics, and violence by state and non-state actors. A related criticism is the notion of far-right terrorism and extremism as an exemplary problem that exists outside of the remit and operations of the state. Yet, when considering the interconnected relationship between far-right state and non-state actors, far-right terrorism and extremism are no longer exceptional. On the contrary, we can trace how far-right ideological agendas become embedded into mainstream counter-terrorism frameworks. The dynamic between state enacted counter-terrorism policies and far-right non-state actors has not been rigorously explored at a global or transnational scale beyond the attention paid to implications of state terrorism within critical terrorism studies (Silke 2018: 72).

In addition, scholarship critically examining the role of gender in counter-terrorism and P/CVE programmes has drawn attention to the reproduction of gender norms and logics concerning women and men (Rothermel 2020; Skejlsbæk, Hansen, and Lorentzen 2020; White 2020). Discourses on gender feature women primarily as victims, including sexual and gender-based violence, and rarely as perpetrators of extremism, thus reinforcing a binary of 'predominately female victimhood and predominately male violent extremism' (Rothermel 2020: 729). Yet, feminist approaches to studying terrorism and violent extremism unpack women's agency and different forms of engagement, as well as the impact of gender-based structural and cultural violence to reassess what constitutes terrorism, and critiques counter-terrorism and P/CVE responses as state paternalism (Brown 2021).

While previous research within critical terrorism studies drawing upon a feminist approach has effectively highlighted how these logics operate within state counter-terrorism and prevention models, less attention has been paid to how non-state far-right actors drive these narratives in their activism. Such assumptions are weaponised by far-right actors, both men and women, in order to construct 'our' women as constantly under threat from violent, Muslim male others. By engaging in metapolitics, that is, shaping the discourses and mobilisation strategies towards political change, these actors aim to shift public opinion with the ideological goal of cultural hegemony (Maly 2018). The underlying assumption is that spreading far-right ideas through a metapolitical approach will initiate a change in public consciousness and ultimately in the political establishment. Hence, this chapter explores how far-right metapolitical actors influence counter-terrorism policies through gendered narratives of Muslim male sexuality.

This chapter employs a comparative analysis of two case studies: 'love jihad' in India and the Great Replacement in Europe. Love jihad refers to the conspiracy theory of Muslim men who intentionally seduce and marry

Hindu women with the purpose of converting them to Islam (Frydenlund and Leidig 2022), while the Great Replacement, originating from the French *Nouvelle Droite* (New Right) of the 1960s, proclaims that 'white European populations are being deliberately replaced at an ethnic and cultural level through migration and the growth of minority communities' (Davey and Ebner 2019: 7). Despite variation in these two conspiracy theories, both narratives are sexual and gender dynamics that are foundational to far-right anxieties of demographic change. In both contexts, grassroots activism has played a key role in shaping perceptions of Muslim demographic threat. Research shows that the securitisation of Muslim communities is linked to such 'templates' of anti-Muslim hostility and stereotypes, which are globally circulated in anti-terrorism policies and de-radicalisation programmes (Kundnani and Hayes 2018). This chapter seeks to explore how such templates are constructed on the basis of far-right metapolitical discourse of gendered representations and its influence on counter-terrorism policies, which is more explicit in the case of India (given a far-right government currently in power), and implicit within Europe with regards to legislation and government measures (cf. this volume).

Far-right demographic anxieties

This chapter builds upon theories of gender and nationalism, in particular 'femonationalism' (Farris 2017), or the emancipatory rhetoric of women's rights which mobilises on 'the profound danger that Muslim males constitute for western European societies, due, above all, to their oppressive treatment of women' (2). Although this discourse derives from some feminist agendas, Farris argues that right-wing nationalist and neoliberal actors simultaneously articulate it to advance their ideological claims. The European far-right has weaponised on these anti-Islam themes in order to simultaneously proclaim gender equality while portraying Muslim male sexuality as an existential threat to 'native' European women who are constantly in fear of sexual oppression. The politics of reproduction and population policies are well documented in the context of far-right conceptions of the Great Replacement theory (Goetz 2021), but the connection to femonationalism has not been made explicit (except by Tebaldi 2021).

Similarly, this chapter extends the discussion of femonationalism and the Great Replacement as conceptualised in the European context, to compare with depictions of Muslim male sexuality vis-à-vis *Bharat Mata* (Mother India) prominent within Hindutva (i.e., Hindu nationalism). Here, gender and the nation are equated with the persistent threat of Muslim masculinity to Hindu femininity, with the former 'imagined as foreign, violent,

fanatical, intolerant, untrustworthy and anti-national', but most importantly, as hypersexual and deliberately overpopulating to achieve demographic dominance (Anand 2007: 259). Hindu women, on the other hand,
are the daughters of *Bharat Mata*, presented as innocent, naïve, pure, and
the cultural reproductive vessels of the nation. In recent years, this gendered dichotomy has transformed into a conspiracy promoted by Hindutva
activists known as 'love jihad'. Accordingly, Muslim men are constructed as
inflicting terror, aiming to spread their political ideology (i.e., Islamisation)
through intimate, romantic encounters with 'vulnerable' Hindu girls. The
love jihad neologism, once confined to fringe Hindutva circles, has become
increasingly widespread in usage, in part due to digital media proliferation
of the term (Frøystad 2021). Thus, love jihad and the Great Replacement,
despite some contextual differences, share concerns of the perceived threat
of sexual domination and subjugation from the Muslim minority, encapsu-
lated by the spectre of the predatory Muslim man.

Interestingly, both Hindu nationalist and European far-right actors share
the myth of the hypersexualised, barbaric Muslim man as a legacy of colonial epistemologies. Whilst constructions of the predatory Muslim male
originate from British colonialism in India (Menon 2010: 37–8) to create
categories of divide-and-rule between Hindus and Muslims, within Europe,
Orientalist schools of thought constructed the figure of the Muslim man
through essentialist framings of aggression, violence, and uncivilised. This
'othering' would eventually feed into modern Islamophobia escalated by
the War on Terror, as well as underpin far-right nationalist imaginaries of
Muslim invasion and population replacement (see Bangstad 2019).

Driving the narratives of love jihad and the Great Replacement are the
BJP-led Hindutva movement in India and the pan-European youth organisation the Identitarian Movement, respectively. Hindutva is a far-right ideology
and movement that aims to achieve a Hindu *rashtra*, or state, in modern-
day India in which Hindus are defined through primordial ethnic identity
(Leidig 2020). According to Hindutva, Muslims are viewed as the enemy;
as 'foreign' and an 'invasion' despite centuries of Islam present on the subcontinent. The Hindutva movement consists of a wide spectrum of organisations called the *Sangh Parivar* (Family of Organisations), including the
current ruling political party, the *Bharatiya Janata Party* (BJP) led by Prime
Minister Narendra Modi. Under Modi's government, the BJP has effectively
advanced a Hindutva agenda through legislation that frames Muslims as
second-class citizens and an existential threat to national security (Leidig
and Mudde 2023). Over the last decade, Hindutva grassroots activists such
as the *Akhil Bharatiya Vidyarthi Parishad* (ABVP), a student-run organisation with several branches on university campuses, have actively mobilised on the 'love jihad' narrative. This type of metapolitical action should

be viewed in congruence with the fact that 'this idiom remained largely unknown beyond Hindu nationalist activists until the BJP began to prepare for the general election that would take place in May 2014' (Frøystad 2021: 6). Importantly, the love jihad conspiracy began to be increasingly recognised and used in popular parlance during the first Modi administration (2014–2019), supplemented with anecdotes in media coverage. More recently, the male-only militant group *Bajrang Dal* has aimed to spread awareness of love jihad through vigilante activity of campaigns and patrols, seeking to enforce the policing of Hindu-Muslim relations. This shift to overt vigilantism, marked as confrontational and violent, in the public sphere reflects a new political climate that favours the Hindutva agenda. As a result of ABVP and Bajrang Dal activities, the passage of BJP governed state-level laws aims to stymie love jihad under the guise of anti-religious conversion through marriage, discussed below.

On the other hand, the Identitarian Movement (also known as Generation Identity), is a youth-led, pan-European social movement that aims to 'restore' Western civilisation by engaging in metapolitical activism and tactics. It derives from the *Nouvelle Droite* (New Right), institutionalised through the *Groupement de Recherche et d'Études pour la Civilisation Européenne* (Research and Study Group for European Civilization), or GRECE. As a reactionary backlash to 1960s counterculture, GRECE was founded in 1968 as an intellectual body to challenge the ideological hegemony of the elite political left (Šima 2021). Such efforts would be strategically driven through metapolitical action, in order to slowly shift public consciousness towards long-term, political transformation. Ideas developed by GRECE, such as a pan-European identity and the concept of ethnopluralism (preserving separate ethno-cultural regions), have influenced the modern Identitarian Movement. While GRECE was already opposed to multiculturalism, the Identitarians adapted it to contemporary debates on immigration, most notably spearheading the Great Replacement narrative. The Great Replacement, a theory developed by French author Renaud Camus in 2010, posits that white native Europeans are being demographically and culturally replaced by non-European migrants, specifically from North African and sub-Saharan Muslim populations. With an increase in the number of Islamist terrorist attacks in Europe in the 2010s, and the 'refugee crisis' of 2015, European public opinion became conducive to the Great Replacement theory. The Identitarian Movement seized upon the opportunity to advance the Great Replacement discourse in its campaigning efforts to 'save' Western civilisation from Islam; through 'controlled provocation', the Identitarians engaged in media stunts aimed for virality on social media such as simulating a terrorist attack in a flash mob in central Vienna (Ebner 2020: 44).

These social media savvy activists pursue metapolitical strategies to achieve long-term social change; they seek to alter public consciousness through digital activism in order to obtain cultural hegemony. Consequently, much of their activity has been analysed within the literature on social movements through the lens of collective action repertoires, political opportunity structures, and resource mobilisation (see, e.g., Nissen 2020). While this body of literature is highly informative for understanding the success (and failures) of the Identitarians as an organisation, its focus on the internal dynamics tells us little about the external influence of the organisation on mainstream politics (for exception on the Identitarians' influence on mainstream media see Castelli Gattinara and Bouron (2020), especially on the formation of state policies. Meanwhile, the type of digital activism engaged in by Hindutva actors has thus far been documented in terms of top-down mobilisation (Chadha and Guha 2016; Jaffrelot and Verniers 2020) and its effects on fostering offline violence, usually targeting minority communities (Banaji et al. 2019; Banaji 2018; Nizaruddin 2021). However, with the exception of Udupa (2018), social media practices and affordances have not been explored in-depth, nor through the prism of metapolitics. In positioning far-right metapolitical tactics in the online milieu, what Maly (2019) describes as 'algorithmic activism', these social media activists exploit platforms to circulate viral, sensationalist content that will generate views and shares to shape public opinion and achieve their ultimate goal of legislative and political change. This chapter takes a step further by connecting discourses of far-right algorithmic activism with the logics of state policies designed as counter-terrorism measures.

Methodology

To empirically situate narratives of far-right metapolitical digital activism, this chapter utilises a qualitative content analysis of YouTube videos, Telegram channels, and Twitter posts as its methodological approach to explore how activists produce and circulate tropes related to love jihad and the Great Replacement online. It focuses on activists that are connected to the BJP-led Hindutva movement in India and the pan-European youth organisation the Identitarian Movement in France, Germany, and Austria, who promote these conspiracy theories in order to advance far-right agendas. The official Twitter accounts of Akhil Bharatiya Vidyarthi Parishad (ABVP) and Bajrang Dal were manually searched, coded, and analysed for mention of love jihad, religious conversion, and interfaith relations. Given the limited amount of results produced by ABVP and Bajrang Dal explicitly mentioning love jihad (seven and sixteen tweets respectively) using Twitter's search function, this data collection was supplemented with content originating from well-known Hindutva activists such as journalists Nupur Sharma and Swati Goel Sharma mentioned in the examples below.

Similarly, the official Telegram channels and YouTube accounts of Identitarian Movement branches were scraped, coded, and analysed. A custom Python scraper for Telegram was used to scrape the first post to the most recent post of each channel (end date January 2022), before each channel was manually coded and analysed for references to the Great Replacement, great migration, and 'Reconquista' (a popular call to action referring to the historical event). However, given the vast quantity of data related to these themes, a more specific approach was taken that focused on the explicit connection between gender and sexuality, especially portrayals of Muslim men, as it relates to the Great Replacement.

Data collection comprised of the *Génération Identitaire* (GI) main Telegram channel of 1,848 posts including text, image, and video, from October 2017 to the last post in March 2021, with 118 posts coded; the GI Lyon Telegram channel of 738 posts, from May 2018 to March 2021, with 60 posts coded; the GI Paris Telegram channel of 243 posts, from May 2018 to February 2021, with 18 posts coded; and former official spokesperson Thaïs d'Escufon's Telegram channel of 251 posts, from January 2021 to January 2022, with 15 posts coded. Additionally, the GI YouTube channel posted 126 videos from August 2012 to February 2021, and subsequently eleven videos from January 2013 to January 2021 were coded and analysed. Thaïs d'Escufon posted four videos on her YouTube channel from June 2021 to January 2022, with three videos that were coded and analysed.

The data collection of the German-speaking Identitarians included the Austrian *Identitäre Bewegung* (IB) *Österreich* Telegram channel of 108 posts including text, image, and video, from June 2018 to August 2021, with 6 posts coded; the German *Identitäre Bewegung Deutschland* main Telegram channel of 1,312 posts from June 2018 to January 2022, with 41 posts coded; the IB Sachsen Telegram channel of 326 posts from June 2018 to January 2022, with 19 posts coded; and official spokesperson Martin Sellner's Telegram channel of 3,310 posts from July 2017 to January 2022, with 71 posts coded. Additionally, IB and Sellner's YouTube channels have since been terminated by the platform (Sellner's since 2020) and are no longer accessible, but 10 IB videos were coded for analysis.

Overall, the selection of these social media platforms and groups/ branches, reflects their levels of active content generation and high follower count. It should be noted that the Identitarian Movement was banned by the French Government in 2021 on the grounds of promoting 'an ideology inciting hatred, violence and discrimination on the basis of one's origin, race or religion', as well as having received monetary donation from the

2019 Christchurch terrorist (Darmain 2021). Consequently, the organisation halted its activities, including social media content, but individuals previously affiliated with it, such as Thaïs d'Escufon, continue to produce content independently.

Circulating myths of love jihad and the Great Replacement

By comparing the social media practices of far-right metapolitical activists, this chapter illustrates how local ideological narratives of Muslim male sexuality transcend into global Islamophobic tropes through media hyperconnectivity. In particular, a few themes arise for comparative analysis. The first theme concerns the portrayal of Muslim men as hypersexualised, abusive, and violent through love jihad and the Great Replacement narratives.

Within the Indian context, the student organisation ABVP actively mobilised on the issue of love jihad at the beginning of Modi's first administration, tweeting back in 2014:

#ABVP: Who Coined 'Love Jihad'? Not Us

#ABVP #lovejihad" (ABVP Karnataka, Twitter, 23 September 2014)

The tweet includes a link to a news story claiming that the perpetrators self-describe their action as an act of 'love jihad', thus giving legitimacy to Hindutva activists' conspiracy theory of 'Islamisation' of India. As indicated above, however, more recently the male-only militant group, Bajrang Dal, has been at the forefront of public campaigning on this issue.

In one tweet (Figure 10.1) explaining the purpose of love jihad as 'a religious obligation' of Islam, an accompanying photo features a woman in a burka with her eyes peering through cage bars and a bloody *bindi* (a forehead mark often worn by married Hindu women) dripping down her nose. The implication is that Hindu women who convert to Islam as a result of love jihad, such as this photo representation, become violently imprisoned and oppressed with their Hindu identity taken away. A red *bindi* traditionally symbolises honor, love, and prosperity in Hinduism, but as a consequence of inter-faith marriage to a Muslim man, the image warns that Hindu women will become dishonoured and enslaved by Islam.

Frequently shared online are the plethora of anecdotes concerning instances of alleged love jihad between Hindu women and Muslim men:

Case of Love Jihad in Kerala. A man named Sajjad trapped Hindu girl Nimisha in a love trap. After marriage, she was converted to religion. She was given the name Fatima. #LoveTrap (Bajrang Dal, Twitter, 20 September 2020, translated from Hindi)

Figure 10.1: What is love jihad? 27 December 2021
(*source:* @BajrangdalOrg/Twitter)

19-year-old Priya, who became a victim of love jihad in Panipat, married Abdul seven months ago. After having illicit relations with women and Priya protesting, he started beating her. Later it was found that there are five children of Abdul too. #CrushIslamicSexGang (Bajrang Dal, Twitter, 16 October 2020, translated from Hindi)

Assam: Rafiul Hussain poses as Hindu to marry girl, forces conversion to Islam, then abandons her. (Bajrang Dal, Twitter, 22 December 2021)

In carrying out the heinous murder of 19-year-old Ekta Deshwal, the accused Shakib's father, brother, friend, along with sisters-in-law Reshma and Ismat, supported it. #LoveJihadIsReal (Bajrang Dal, Twitter, 18 July 2020, translated from Hindi)

> Baghpat police arrest Akram, his wife Rukshar, for forcing woman to convert to Islam after sexually exploiting, impregnating her (Nupur Sharma, Twitter, 20 November 2020)

These stories of supposed love jihad incidents centre exclusively on the portrayal of young, innocent Hindu 'girls' who have become victims of manipulation and abuse at the hands of sex-driven Muslim men – similar to the sexual grooming narratives of Muslim perpetrators in the UK (see Cockbain and Tufail 2020). As the daughters of *Bharat Mata*, these Hindu women symbolise the violation of the nation by supposed 'anti-national' forces, in which Hindu nationalism becomes synonymous with Indian nationalism, discussed further below.

The Identitarians likewise warn of the sexual threat of Muslim men, but framed through the image of the 'rapefugee' as an instigator of the Great Replacement. While the 'rapefugee' – a derogatory term described by Thorleifsson (2019: 524) as 'fantasies about the threatening "hypermasculinity" of male, dark-skinned foreign men that threaten white women' – is presented through the discourse of immigration in the European context, that is, 'invasion', it is imagined in anecdotes of young, white European women as victims. The citizenship status of the 'rapefugee' is encoded through representations of sexual violence enacted on 'our territory', as the example below illustrates:

> This morning the activists of Génération Identitaire Normandie went to Place de la Pucelle in Rouen to retrace the scene of the crime of Julien and Elise.
>
> In December 2015, a repeat migrant raped then killed Élise and strangled Julien. Barely released from prison after a conviction for rape, the state did not deport him, but released him.
>
> What was he still doing in France? These deaths could have been avoided if the law had been respected.
>
> A savage double murder in Rouen, hundreds of rapes in Cologne, attacks all over our territory, this situation is unacceptable.
>
> The migratory invasion must stop. For Élise, for Julien: let's expel the illegal immigrants! [1] (GI France, Telegram, 3 April 2019)

Stories of rape are not only directly linked to the immigration status of perpetrators, but also mobilise fear by invoking a protective response in 'native' men:

> His name was Tommie Lindh. A few days ago, this 19-year-old Swede was walking down the street when he overheard a chilling scene: a 14-year-old girl was being raped by an African. He feels the ground give way under his feet but doesn't think, he rushes. A fight breaks out. *Tommie only thinks of protecting the one who could be his sister*. Despite the age difference, Tommie does not

back down and tries to push the rapist away. Faced with the courage of this young Swede, the migrant sees red. He pulls out a knife. Tommie refuses to step aside. He was then stabbed several times. The young man collapses on the ground. A few hours later, he died in hospital.

Assaults, rapes, murders… Europeans never stop paying for the ravages of the migratory invasion.

Let's pay tribute to Tommie, not the victim, but the hero. He acted as each of us should in the same situation. May his example inspire us and his courage flow through our veins.[2] (GI France, Telegram, 19 May 2020; emphasis mine)

The anecdote portrays Tommie Lindh as a martyr, whose moral convictions to intervene in the situation was driven by 'protecting the one who could be his sister' from the 'rapefugee'. The Identitarians consistently promote the notion that white European men must be mobilised to protect 'our' women (sisters, girlfriends, wives, mothers, etc.) from migrant rapists, which they link to the threat of population replacement wrought by 'migratory invasion' (see Figure 10.2).

This display of masculinity, as being the protector, taps into the desire of white European men to feel valued and respected among the far-right (see Miller-Idriss 2017), contrary to feeling ashamed of exercising their 'natural', 'biological' masculinity in mainstream society. 'This notion of

Figure 10.2: 'Population replacement', 6 May 2019
(*source:* @IdentitaereDeutschland/Telegram)

Figure 10.3: 'Save Europe', 17 May 2019
(*source*: @IdentitaereDeutschland/Telegram)

masculinity is often contrasted to what is believed to be espoused by Muslim men who are then made into normative deviants, being "anti-West", "anti-modern", "anti-liberal", "anti-women" and "dangerous beings"' (Kinnvall 2015: 525). As 'righteous defenders' (Thorleifsson 2019), then, far-right men view it as their duty to protect white European women and children. Figure 10.3, with description text that translates to 'Save Europe', features a white woman holding her baby wearing a t-shirt logo that displays 'fighting for the rebirth of Europe'.

Like Hindu women, white European women embody purity and person-ify the nationalist imaginary. This reproductive logic entails that they must be 'saved' from the sexual threat and excesses of Muslim immigrant men crossing into Europe's borders. All young women face this potential danger, according to the Identitarians in the example of Figure 10.4.

A young 'southerner' with 'dark, curly hair', presumably a Tunisian or Afghan, lured a young girl on October 25th into a staff toilet in a Hamburg shopping centre. Then he raped her relentlessly.

However, thanks to replacement migration and settlement policies, two out of three young people in Hamburg fit the 'southern' description of the perpetrator.

Hamburg, a historically left city that is ruled by communists, is turning into the capital of imported sex offenders. *Anyone who has a daughter* should get

POLIZEI JAGT DIESEN TRIEBTÄTER!

Vergewaltigung auf Hamburgs feinster Shopping-Meile

Er missbrauchte ein Mädchen (15) abends i

WER KENNT DEN MIGRANT?

Jetzt ermittelt das Hamburger LKA42 (Sexualdelikte): Gesucht wird nach einem Verdächtigen, der dunkle, gelockte Haare hat und bei der Tat Jeans und Nike-Turnschuhe trug. Er hat ein südländisches Erscheinungsbild, könnte Tunesier bzw. Afghane sein.

HAMBURG: HAUPTSTADT FREMDER TRIEBTÄTER?

MSlive

Figure 10.4: Hamburg again: 'Südländer' raped 15-year-old on the toilet, 13 November 2021 (*source:* @IdentitaereDeutschland/Telegram)

her out of this sexual prey zone as soon as possible.[3] (IB Deutschland/Sellner, Telegram, 13 November 2021; emphasis mine)

The Identitarians frame the urgency of saving daughters, particularly teenagers, who are most vulnerable and 'innocent' in their sexuality, from being 'lured' by Muslim men, much like the 'victims' of love jihad discourse in India. Relatedly, urban areas are envisioned by the far-right as sites of social decay, or dystopian enclaves (see Thorleifsson 2019), characterised by violence, criminality, and moral bankruptcy. Likewise, narratives of love jihad have gained resonance within the urban public sphere in India as 'a liberatory space where these young women, who are unmindful of their own social and bodily boundaries, became especially vulnerable to seduction, conversion, violence and trafficking' (Tyagi and Sen 2020: 9). The discourse of love jihad is a means for Hindu nationalists to police the choice and mobility of young Hindu women 'in accordance with a gendered Hindu civil order', permissible through ' "good male violence" (e.g., anti-Love Jihad proponents and activists) in the name of women's security' (Tyagi and Sen 2020: 1; 18). Thus, both the love jihad and Great Replacement conspiracy theories are anchored in the spatial imagination of urban life, where the safety and security of 'our' women are under threat from predatory Muslim men.

Another common tactic employed by both the Identitarian and Hindutva activists in their digital activism is their 'uncovering' of the 'truth' as to the scale of these phenomena. They position their activism as 'revealing' what has been hidden from the public. For the Identitarians, connecting stories of rape and sexual assault to statistics on migration and crime is a means of constructing evidence for their worldview. In one example, the government is viewed as complicit in turning a blind eye to sexual assaults faced by 'native' European women, built within the grander narrative of the Great Replacement.

[The state of] NRW [North Rhine-Westphalia] corrects numbers upwards: every 2nd day a gang rape

The quiet, politically correct existence in the consumer paradise BRD [Bundesrepublik Deutschland, Federal Republic of Germany] is bought dearly. The prize is the bodies and souls of young German women. A gang rape occurs every other day in NRW alone.

The Home Office was forced to release the true numbers after they omitted 70 group molestations through a 'faulty database query'.

The perpetrators, mostly migrant youth gangs, lure their often underage victims to remote places where they rape them for hours. Nobody helps them, nobody hears their screams.

Not only she but the whole nation is being raped by this! Anyone who knows about these acts and does not do everything possible to throw the perpetrators out of the country and to call the political accomplices to account is partly to blame. Anyone who comfortably lives on in an apolitical life accepts the price: the desecrated bodies of German girls.[4] (IB Deutschland, Telegram, 9 September 2021; emphasis mine)

In addition to symbolically equating the incident of rape of one woman to the rape of the nation, the Identitarians blame the political establishment for failing to tell the truth to the public, implying that it only did so after facing demands – a common rhetorical tactic among far-right activists, but especially with cases of sexual grooming (Leidig 2019: 87).

Whereas in India, 'evidence' is relayed through the reporting of love jihad cases to indicate its widespread nature.

> Menace of alleged Love Jihad spreading across India like wildfire: 20 cases reported from UP and other states in the last 2 months (Nupur Sharma, Twitter, 18 September 2020)

With love jihad 'spreading across India like wildfire', the aim of the narrative is to rouse moral panic. This bears resemblance to what Gentry (2020) argues as constructing terrorism as a moral challenge that draws binaries between good and bad in order to maintain power hierarchies. Here, the 'bad' perpetrators of love jihad (i.e., Muslim men) need to be contextualised in opposition to 'good' Hindu women who fall victim as a result of manipulation. Since Hindu women represent the daughters of *Bharat Mata* (Mother India), they personify the nation as under attack.

A noteworthy shift, however, has been the securitisation of love jihad by the state in response to the rise of alleged cases.

> Minor gang-raped, forced conversion to Islam, threats, caste abuse: Details of 11 cases in which UP [Uttar Pradesh] SIT [Special Investigation Team], formed to probe Love Jihad, found criminality (Nupur Sharma, Twitter, 26 November 2020)

The mandate of a police team tasked with intervention in cases of supposed love jihad represents a major repositioning of love jihad as a conspiracy theory promoted by metapolitical activists towards its institutionalisation as a security concern within the state apparatus through law enforcement mechanisms. This relationship is further explored in the following section.

From metapolitics to counter-terrorism policies

In India, state-led legislation prohibiting interfaith (i.e., Hindu-Muslim) marriage and religious conversion has directly responded to Hindutva activists campaigning against love jihad (Nielsen and Nilsen 2021). Tweets from Bajrang Dal exemplify calls for such legislative action:

> After 17 days of hard struggle, the efforts of Bajrang Dal got success in Jind, Haryana.
> The jihadi who ran away with a minor girl from a poor Hindu family was arrested by the police in Saharanpur.
> @mlkhattar Sir, fulfill your promises or else the public will decide your future. #LoveJihadLaw (Bajrang Dal, Twitter, 2 January 2021, translated from Hindi)
> Law against love jihad should be framed in every state says #VHP General Secretary Shri @MParandeVHP (Bajrang Dal, Twitter, 8 January 2021)

Unlike the Identitarian Movement in Europe, Hindutva activism consists of a much larger online ecosystem in which conspiratorial narratives of love jihad spread across a vast network of anonymous and non-affiliated accounts. These scales of interaction – from anonymous users to established organisations, political parties, and state legislative bodies – reflects how the Hindutva apparatus operates according to a more deeply connected network of power dynamics.

The effect has been institutionalised processes of securitisation and governance according to Hindu nationalist statecraft in which Malji and Raza (2021: 7–8) note a recent shift from viewing Islamist terrorism solely as an external threat that is addressed through border securitisation policies towards a combined focus of an internal threat, exemplified through love jihad. 'Since 2014 [the first Modi administration], the BJP and Hindutva groups have scaled up efforts to warn about love jihad… During the 2019 elections, BJP officials and their allies campaigned on the urgent threat within and at the borders by potential infiltrators and radicalized Muslims…', mobilising voters on the fear of demographic shift (Malji and Raza 2021: 3). Muslim migration from surrounding countries such as Bangladesh is deliberately linked to the fear of love jihad within Hindu communities, bolstered by sensationalist stories on social media of alleged cases. Hindutva and BJP politicians have mobilised on this anxiety, resulting in support for stricter immigration policies and securitised borders.

In the second Modi administration (2019–2024), 'eight states across India have implemented some form of anti-conversion law or proposal that prevents any form of religious conversion based on coercion', with interreligious marriages being the target of anti-conversion laws despite not being illegal, thus suggesting Hindu women as being coerced by Muslim men (Malji and Raza 2021: 4). This state-level legislation is the outcome of successful campaigning by Hindutva politicians and activists who claim that love jihad is a threat to Hindus, with a 2021 survey finding that '54% strongly believe there is a widespread "love jihad" conspiracy to convert Hindu women to Islam and 60% supports laws against it'.

Yet the gendered logics of love jihad have thus far not been examined through the lens of counter-terrorism. This is despite the fact that Hindutva discourse equating Muslims with terrorism escalated in India as a result of the global War on Terror (Anand 2007; Frøystad 2021), providing the catalyst for securitising India's Muslim population, including the policing of conjugal order. The tweet below displays that the Muslim man as an internal sexualised 'other' has become subsequently linked to the threat of terrorism:

> Explosive finding by Uttar Pradesh's anti-terrorism squad (ATS): Poor girls from weak communities targeted and trapped [by] Muslim boys for conversion to Islam. Racket run from Delhi's [Muslim majority neighbourhood] Jamia Nagar (Swati Goel Sharma, Twitter, 21 June 2021)

Policing romantic relations between Hindu women and Muslim men was once privy to Hindu male vigilante 'anti-Romeo squads', a campaign promise of the BJP that was later initiated by the Uttar Pradesh State Government through law enforcement (Chacko 2020). However, these acts of moral policing have shifted from vigilantism to the state-led police force Anti-Terrorism Squad (ATS), whose main objective is to prevent and counter terrorist attacks. Love jihad has thus not only become a securitised issue, but the expansion of state resources has led to its classification of needing a counter-terrorism response. The shift in focus of policing resources aligns with the 'ad hoc' characteristics of India's counter-terrorism approach, which relies on laws that are 'short-sighted, reactive and draconian' (Singh 2019: 169; 172).

Within Europe, the passage of anti-immigrant and anti-refugee legislation spearheaded by populist radical right parties can be directly linked to far-right grassroots mobilisation on these issues (Castelli Gattinara 2018), in part articulated through the Great Replacement theory (Leconte 2019). In 2018, the Identitarians organised a 'Defend Europe' mission to block refugee boats in the Mediterranean Sea from entering European borders. A couple years later, French Minister of the Interior Gérald Darmanin announced the creation of a Franco-Italian police brigade to patrol smuggling gangs bringing in migrants. As the Identitarian movement in France illustrates, the goals of their activism must be enforced within the political establishment in order to be effective, albeit through constant vigilance:

> GI congratulate themselves when Gérald Darmanin uses one of their proposals. However we remain vigilant regarding the effective establishment of these patrols. On the other hand, we remind the Minister of Interior that without a real fight against migratory invasion, this type of measure is useless.[5] (GI Lyon, Telegram, 3 August 2020)

The Identitarians especially focus on measures related to remigration and mobilising against the 'ethnic vote', which is directly linked to fear of demographic change, rhetorically labelled as a 'demographic bomb' of white European women who have become 'victims' of Islam (Martin Sellner, Telegram, 5 October 2021). 'Through the framing of gender issues as cultural concerns, for example family violence, forced marriage, genital mutilation, and honor killings, [far-right] parties and movements have been able to securitize immigration and institute gendered boundaries' (Kinnvall 2015: 524), as represented in Identitarian propaganda. Interestingly, the Identitarians also call for appropriate action to be taken in the form of monitoring 'sham marriages', that is, marriages for the purpose of naturalisation leading to citizenship:

Examples of remigration measures… monitoring sham marriages for naturalization.[6] (GI France, YouTube, 10 December 2020)

This presents a corresponding narrative to the fear of religious conversion through marriage in the Indian context, although the Identitarians differ with respect to immigration whereas in India, Muslims are not predominately framed through immigration status but as a dangerous fifth column.

However, the connection between far-right metapolitical activism and its influence on counter-terrorism policies in Europe is not as explicit as India with regards to direct effects on legislation and government measures. National and regional responses in Europe focus on the intersection of (Muslim) immigration and (Islamist) terrorism (Abbas 2019), but analyses have not linked these racialised regimes with the direct influence of far-right metapolitical activist narratives of Muslim male sexuality on legislation. By scrutinising the relationship between 'mainstream' counter-terrorism frameworks and 'far-right' immigration and reproductive politics, this chapter contributes to a nuanced understanding of power dynamics and the production of knowledge by far-right actors at the state level. Identitarian propaganda intertwines Muslim immigration and 'native' population replacement as a parallel development with increased Islamist terrorism:

> Dresden, Paris, Nice, Vienna… the list of Islamist attacks is constantly expanding and makes it clear that Islamist terror is a Europe-wide phenomenon. These tragic developments can be traced back to mass migration flows from predominantly culturally different regions. Demographic developments and the resulting formation of parallel societies offer the Islamists safe havens and increase the risk of terrorism.[7] (IB Deutschland, Telegram, 14 November 2020)

As Kinnvall notes, re/debordering practices among European far-right actors, that is, migration and the rise of parallel societies, has been linked to fears of losing control in accordance with 'the development of EU policies on security, migration, and discrimination' (2015: 518). These fears, Kinnvall argues, 'have become powerful ingredients for the institutionalization and performance of policies and debates', often invoking the threat of Islam and Muslim immigration (519–522). The narrative promoted by the Identitarians reflects a broader association held between (Muslim) immigration, border security, and (Islamist) terrorism, manifested in the 'Counter-terrorism agenda for the EU: Anticipate, prevent, protect, respond' (European Commission 2020), which heavily focuses upon securitising Europe's borders in response to the potential threat of terrorism – implying that such threats originate from outside the EU rather than directing counter-terrorism efforts towards addressing the internal far-right threat.

Yet the group proscription of the Identitarians in France in 2021 reflects one of the 'range of governmental actions and initiatives aimed at reducing the far-right threat' (Jarvis 2022: 15), albeit at a national rather than EU level. This action, however, has had little effect on the mainstreaming of far-right discourse in the political arena (see Michael 2018: 107), with the Identitarian agenda having influenced the French presidential elections in 2022, and the discourse of the Great Replacement being articulated by candidates during campaigning. Éric Zemmour, a far-right pundit, spread anti-immigrant and anti-Islam views channeled through his political party Reconquête (Reconquest). Zemmour openly supports the Great Replacement narrative and has called for measures such as stopping immigration of Muslim Africans and banning 'non-French' names that prevent immigrants from assimilating into French culture (*New York Times* 2021). Zemmour was fully embraced by Identitarian activists for espousing their views of the Great Replacement.

In one recorded conversation between French activist Thaïs d'Escufon and Austrian leader Martin Sellner about the French elections and Zemmour, Sellner explicitly mentions that 'I think the most important and interesting thing for us is that Eric Zemmour is unapologetically speaking about invasion, the Great Replacement' (13:23). Sellner shares a clip of a televised interview with Zemmour relating these talking points:

> Today we don't have immigration anymore. In reality, we have invasion and colonisation. Invasion because people are coming without anyone asking and we don't want them to come but they are forcing our borders. And a colonisation because they are imposing their traditions and customs and their religion to a foreign country, to which one way or another they impose in increasingly vast portions of territory.[8]

In describing immigration as an 'invasion' and 'colonisation', Zemmour reproduces the Identitarians' Great Replacement rhetoric. Yet, such far-right rhetoric has also become 'mainstreamed' as evidenced by the conservative presidential candidate, Valérie Pécresse, who explicitly mentioned the Great Replacement at a high-profile campaign rally (*Politico* 2022). Following the 2015 Charlie Hebdo terrorist attacks, Pécresse vocally supported the creation of a French equivalent to the USA Patriot Act as a counter-terrorism measure (*New York Times* 2016). Thus, the acceptance and eventual adoption of far-right metapolitical discourse and goals within a counter-terrorism framework remains possible given the persistent mainstreaming of far-right ideas within the broader political system (see Mondon and Winter 2020), which is still viewed as disconnected from far-right terrorism and political violence as a fringe phenomenon.

Conclusion

Overall, this chapter reflects on the scales of interaction that occur between grassroots far-right metapolitical activism and state-led counter-terrorism frameworks, integrating the operative function of gendered representations. Through a comparative study of the love jihad and Great Replacement conspiracy theories of demographic change, it foregrounds the spectre of the predatory Muslim man as a symbolic sexual threat to 'native' majoritarian populations. Thus, despite their different respective goals, far-right activists in both postcolonial contexts engage in a similar trope of Muslim male sexuality. This chapter critically examines how this narrative becomes superseded into counter-terrorism policies, in which sexuality and reproductive politics become securitised as a perceived threat through both implicit and explicit ways. In the case of India, the fear of love jihad has been instituted into law enforcement mechanisms such as anti-terrorism squads – traditionally tasked with monitoring terrorist threats to national security – which now police Hindu-Muslim romantic relations to prevent acts of Islamisation. Meanwhile, in Europe, the mainstreaming of far-right discourse reinforces the association held between (Muslim) immigration, border security, and (Islamist) terrorism as an external threat, with the implicit projection that demographic change will be the consequence if not acted upon. In both contexts, far-right grassroots actors such as Hindutva and Identitarian activists have mobilised on these conspiracy theories to influence public opinion, and ultimately, influence government legislation that responds to these threats through a counter-terrorism framework.

The author would like to thank Hanna Rigault Arkhis, Naledi Tilmann, and Joshua Farrell-Molloy for their research assistance on this chapter.

Notes

1 English translations have been provided in the text with original quotes in endnotes.

Ce matin les militants de Génération Identitaire Normandie sont allés place de la Pucelle à Rouen pour retracer la scène du crime de Julien et Elise.

En décembre 2015, un migrant multirécidiviste a violé puis tué Élise et a étranglé Julien. À peine sorti de prison après une condamnation pour viol, l'Etat ne l'a pas expulsé, mais l'a relâché.

Que faisait-il encore en France? Ces morts auraient pu être évitées si la loi avait été respectée.

Un double meurtre sauvage à Rouen, des centaines de viols à Cologne, des agressions un peu partout sur notre territoire, cette situation est inacceptable.

L'invasion migratoire doit cesser. Pour Élise, pour Julien: expulsons les clandestins!

2 Il s'appelait Tommie Lindh. Il y a quelques jours, ce Suédois de 19 ans se balade dans la rue quand il surprend une scène glaçante: une adolescente de 14 ans est en train de se faire violer par un Africain. Il sent le sol se dérober sous ses pieds mais ne réfléchit pas, il fonce. Une bagarre éclate. Tommie ne pense qu'à protéger celle qui pourrait être sa sœur. Malgré la différence d'âge, Tommie ne recule pas et tente de repousser le violeur. Face au courage de ce jeune Suédois, le migrant voit rouge. Il sort un couteau. Tommie refuse de s'écarter. Il est alors poignardé à plusieurs reprises. Le jeune homme s'effondre sur le sol. Quelques heures plus tard, il décèdera à l'hôpital.

Agressions, viols, assassinats...les Européens n'en finissent plus de payer les ravages de l'invasion migratoire.

Rendons hommage à Tommie, non pas à la victime, mais au héros. Il a agi comme chacun de nous devrait le faire dans la même situation. Puisse son exemple nous inspirer et son courage couler dans nos veines.

3 Schon Wieder Hamburg: "Südländer" vergewaltigt 15 Jährige am Klo

Ein junger "Südländer" mit "dunklen, gelockten Haaren", mutmaßlich ein Tunesier oder Afghane lockte ein junges Mädchen am 25.10. in eine Mitarbeitertoilette in einem Hamburger Einkaufszentruum. Dor vergewaltigte er sie schonungslos.

Dank der Ersetzungsmigration und Siedlungspolitik passen allerdings in Hamburg zwei von drei Jugendliche auf die "südländische" Täterbeschreibung.

Hamburg, eine erzlinke Stadt, die quasi von Kommunisten regiert wird, verwandelt sich in die Hauptstadt importierter Triebtäter. Wer eine Tochter hat sollte sie schleunigst aus dieser sexuellen Beutezone rausholen.

4 NRW korrigiert Zahlen nach oben: jeden 2. Tag eine Gruppenvergewaltigung

Das ruhige, politisch Korrekte Dasein im Konsumparadies BRD ist teuer erkauft. Der Preis sind die Körper und Seelen junger Deutscher Frauen. Jeden 2. Tag findet allein in NRW eine Gruppenvergewaltigung statt.

Das Innenministerium musste die wahren Zahlen veröffentlichen, nachdem sie 70 Gruppenschändungen durch eine "fehlerhafte Datenbankabfrage" unterschlagen hatten.

Die Täter, meist migrantische Jugendbanden, locken ihre, oft minderjährigen Opfer an abgelegene Orte, wo sie sie stundenlang vergewaltigen. Keiner hilft ihnen, niemand hört ihre Schreie.

Nicht nur sie sondern die ganze Nation wird dadurch vergewaltigt! Jeder der von diesen Taten weiß und nicht alles tut um die Täter aus dem Land zu schmeißen und die politischen Mittäter zur Rechenschaft zu ziehen ist mitschuld. Jeder der ein apolitisches Leben gemütlich weiterlebt nimmt den Preis in Kauf: geschändete Körper Deutscher Mädchen.

5 Génération Identitaire se félicite de voir Gérald Darmanin reprendre nos propositions. Nous restons néanmoins vigilants quant à la mise en place effective de ces patrouilles. D'autre part, nous rappelons au ministre de l'Intérieur que sans lutte réelle contre l'invasion migratoire, ce type de mesures ne constituent que des coups d'épée dans l'eau.

6 "mesures de émigration... on surveille beaucoup plus les mariages blancs"

7 Dresden, Paris, Nizza, Wien...die Liste islamistischer Anschläge erweitert sich stetig und verdeutlicht, dass es sich beim islamistischen Terror um ein europaweites Phänomen handelt. Zurückzuführen sind diese tragischen Entwicklungen auf massenhafte Migrationsströme aus überwiegend kulturfremden Regionen. Die demographischen Entwicklungen und den daraus resultierenden Bildungen von Parallelgesellschaften bieten den Islamisten hierbei Rückzugsräume und erhöhen die Terrorgefahr.

8 Nous n'avons plus d'immigration, en vérité nous avons une invasion et une colonisation. Une invasion parce que c'est des gens qui viennent alors qu'on ne leur a pas demandé de venir et qu'on ne veut pas qu'ils viennent mais ils forcent nos frontières. Et une colonisation parce qu'ils imposent leurs moeurs et leurs coutumes et leur religion à un pays qui est étranger, à qui de gré ou de force imposent dans des parties de territoire de plus en plus vastes.

References

Abbas, T. (2019). *Islamophobia and Radicalisation: A Vicious Vycle*. Oxford: Oxford University Press.

Anand, D. (2007). 'Anxious sexualities: Masculinity, nationalism and violence', *The British Journal of Politics and International Relations*, 9(2), 257–69.

Apuzzo, M. and Erlanger, S. (2016). 'Patriot Act idea rises in France, and is ridiculed', *New York Times*, 16 January 2016, www.nytimes.com/2015/01/17/world/europe/patriot-act-idea-rises-in-france-and-is-ridiculed.html (accessed 1 December 2022).

Banaji, S. (2018). 'Vigilante publics: Orientalism, modernity and Hindutva fascism in India', *Javnost-The Public*, 25(4), 333–50.

Banaji, S., Bhat, R., Agarwal, A., Passanha, N., and Pravin, M. S. (2019). 'WhatsApp vigilantes: An exploration of citizen reception and circulation of WhatsApp misinformation linked to mob violence in India', LSE.

Bangstad, S. (2019). 'Bat Ye'or and Eurabia', in Sedgwick, M. (ed.) *Key Thinkers of the Radical Right*. Oxford: Oxford University Press, pp. 170–84.

Brown, K. E. (2021). 'Feminist responses to violent extremism', in Väyrynen, T., Parashar, S., Féron, E., and Confortini, C. C. (eds) *Routledge Handbook of Feminist Peace Research*. Abingdon, Oxon: Routledge, pp. 136–47.

Castelli Gattinara, P. (2018). 'Europeans, shut the borders! Anti-refugee mobilisation in Italy and France', in della Porta, D. (ed.) *Solidarity Mobilizations in the 'Refugee Crisis'*. Cham: Palgrave Macmillan, pp. 271–97.

Castelli Gattinara, P. and Bouron, S. (2020). 'Extreme-right communication in Italy and France: Political culture and media practices in CasaPound Italia and Les Identitaires', *Information, Communication & Society*, 23(12), 1805–19.

Caulcutt, C. (2022). 'France's Pécresse comes under fire for reference to far-right conspiracy theory', *Politico*, 14 February, www.politico.eu/article/france-pecresse-slammed-for-great-replacement-reference/ (accessed 1 December 2022).

Chacko, P. (2020). 'Gender and authoritarian populism: Empowerment, protection, and the politics of resentful aspiration in India', *Critical Asian Studies*, 52(2), 204–225.

Chadha, K. and Guha, P. (2016). 'The Bharatiya Janata Party's online campaign and citizen involvement in India's 2014 election', *International Journal of Communication*, 10, 4389–406.

Cockbain, E. and Tufail, W. (2020). 'Failing victims, fuelling hate: Challenging the harms of the 'Muslim grooming gangs' narrative', *Race & Class*, 61(3), 3–32.

Darmanin, J. (2021). 'France bans far-right group Generation Identity', *Politico*, 3 March 2021, www.politico.eu/article/france-bans-far-right-group-generation-identity/

Davey, J. and Ebner, J. (2019). *'The Great Replacement': The Violent Consequences of Mainstreamed Extremism*. London: Institute for Strategic Dialogue.

Ebner, J. (2020). *Going Dark: The Secret Social Lives of Extremists*. London: Bloomsbury.

European Commission (2020). *A Counter-Terrorism Agenda for the EU: Anticipate, Prevent, Protect, Respond*. Brussels, https://eur-lex.europa.eu/legal-content/EN/TXT/PDF/?uri=CELEX:52020DC0795&from=EN (accessed 1 December 2022).

Farris, S. R. (2017). *In the Name of Women's Rights*. Durham, NC: Duke University Press.

Frydenlund, I. and Leidig, E. (2022). 'Introduction: "love jihad": Sexuality, reproduction and the construction of the predatory Muslim male', *Religions*, 13(3).

Frøystad, K. (2021). 'Sound biting conspiracy: From India with "love jihad"', *Religions*, 12(12), 1064.

Gentry, C. (2020). *Disordered Violence: How Gender, Race and Heteronormativity Structure Terrorism*. Edinburgh: Edinburgh University Press.

Goetz, J. (2021). 'The Great Replacement': Reproduction and population policies of the far right, taking the Identitarians as an example', *DiGeSt-Journal of Diversity and Gender Studies*, 8(1), 60–74.

Jaffrelot, C. and Verniers, G. (2020). 'The BJP's 2019 election campaign: Not business as usual', *Contemporary South Asia*, 28(2), 155–77.

Jarvis, L. (2022). 'Critical terrorism studies and the far-right: Beyond problems and solutions?', *Critical Studies on Terrorism*, 15(1), 13–37.

Kinnvall, C. (2015). 'Borders and fear: Insecurity, gender and the far right in Europe', *Journal of Contemporary European Studies*, 23(4), 514–29.

Kundnani, A. and Hayes, B. (2018). 'The globalisation of countering violent extremism policies', Amsterdam: Transnational Institute. www.preventwatch.org/wp-content/uploads/2021/08/014092_26ca35cecec34464a5419fb6e72bf7e9.pdf. (accessed 1 December 2022).

Leconte, C. (2019). 'The socio-political career of the expression "the Great Replacement" among right-wing party networks in Germany: The case of the Alternative for Germany (AfD) party', *Politix*, 2, 111–34.

Leidig, E. (2020). 'Hindutva as a variant of right-wing extremism', *Patterns of Prejudice*, 54(3), 215–37.

Leidig, E. (2019). 'Immigrant, nationalist and proud: A Twitter analysis of Indian diaspora supporters for Brexit and Trump', *Media and Communication*, 7(1), 77–89.

Leidig, E. and Mudde, C. (2023). 'Bharatiya Janata Party (BJP): The overlooked populist radical right party', *Journal of Language and Politics*, 22(3), 360–77.

Malji, A. and Raza, S. T. (2021). 'The securitization of Love Jihad', *Religions*, 12(12), 1074.

Maly, I. (2019). 'New right metapolitics and the algorithmic activism of Schild & Vrienden', *Social Media+ Society*, 5(2), 1–15.

Maly, I. (2018). 'The global New Right and the Flemish identitarian movement Schild & Vrienden: A case study', *Tilburg Papers in Culture Studies*, 220.

Martini, A. and da Silva, R. (2022). 'Editors' introduction: Critical terrorism studies and the far-right: New and (re) new (ed) challenges ahead?', *Critical Studies on Terrorism*, 15(1), 1–12.

Menon, K. D. (2010). *Everyday Nationalism*. Philadelphia: University of Pennsylvania Press.

Michael, G. (2018). 'Right-wing terrorism: The strategic dimensions', in Silke, A. (ed) *The Routledge Handbook of Terrorism and Counterterrorism*. London: Routledge, pp. 98–108.

Miller-Idriss, C. (2017). 'Soldier, sailor, rebel, rule-breaker: Masculinity and the body in the German far right', *Gender and Education*, 29(2), 199–215.

Mondon, A. and Winter, A. (2020). *Reactionary Democracy: How Racism and the Populist Far Right Became Mainstream*. London: Verso.

Nielsen, K. B and Nilsen, A. G. (2021). 'Love jihad and the governance of gender and intimacy in Hindu nationalist statecraft', *Religions*, 12(12), 1068.

Nissen, A. (2020). 'The Trans-European Mobilization of "Generation Identity"', in Norocel, C., Hellström, A., and Bak Jørgensen, M. (eds) *Nostalgia and Hope: Intersections between Politics of Culture, Welfare, and Migration in Europe* Cham: Springer, pp. 85–100.

Nizaruddin, F. (2021). 'Role of public WhatsApp groups within the Hindutva ecosystem of hate and narratives of "CoronaJihad"', *International Journal of Communication*, 15(18).

Onishi, N. (2021). 'From TV to the French Presidency? A right-wing star is inspired by Trump', *New York Times*, 17 September 2021, www.nytimes.com/2021/09/17/world/europe/zemmour-france-presidency-trump.html (accessed 1 December 2022).

Rothermel, A.-K. (2020). 'Gender in the United Nations' agenda on preventing and countering violent extremism', *International Feminist Journal of Politics*, 22(5), 720–41.

Šima, K. (2021). 'From identity politics to the identitarian movement', in: Barkhoff, J. and Leerssen, J. (eds) *National Stereotyping, Identity Politics, European Crises*. Leiden: Brill.

Silke, A. (2018). 'State terrorism', in *The Routledge Handbook of Terrorism and Counterterrorism*. London: Routledge, pp. 66–73.

Singh, R. (2019). 'Counterterrorism in India: An ad hoc response to an enduring and variable threat', in Boyle, M. J. (ed) *Non-Western Responses to Terrorism*. Manchester: Manchester University Press, pp. 153–83.

Skjelsbæk, I., Hansen, J. M., and Lorentzen, J. (2020). 'Hopes and misguided expectations: How policy documents frame gender in efforts at preventing terrorism and violent extremism', *Politics, Religion & Ideology*, 21(4), 469–86.

Tebaldi, C. (2021). 'The terrorist and the girl next door: Love jihad in French femonationalist nonfiction', *Religions*, 12(12), 1090.

Thorleifsson, C. (2019). 'The Swedish dystopia: Violent imaginaries of the radical right', *Patterns of prejudice*, 53(5), 515–33.

Tyagi, A. and Sen, A. (2020). 'Love-Jihad (Muslim sexual seduction) and ched-chad (sexual harassment): Hindu nationalist discourses and the Ideal/deviant urban citizen in India', *Gender, Place & Culture*, 27(1), 104–25.

Udupa, S. (2018). 'Enterprise Hindutva and social media in urban India', *Contemporary South Asia*, 26(4), 453–67.

White, J. (2020). 'Gender in countering violent extremism program design, implementation and evaluation: Beyond instrumentalism', *Studies in Conflict & Terrorism*, 46(7), 1–24.

11

Conspiracy theories and right-wing extremism: The case of Q-Anon

Dean J. Smith, Ewan Bottomley, and Kenneth Mavor

During the COVID-19 pandemic, the relationship between conspiracy theories and anti-government extremism came into sharp focus. This was no clearer than in the case of the Q-Anon phenomenon that has swept through the North American political landscape (Zihiri et al. 2022). This conspiracy theory proposed that the then president, Donald Trump, was waging an apocalyptic battle against a cabal of satanic paedophiles who secretly controlled the United States. The exact relationship between conspiratorial ideation and political extremism is still not entirely clear. However, some shared areas have been identified by previous research, such as an overlap in highly structured thinking styles that are aimed at making sense of societal events (van Prooijen et al. 2015). This chapter aims to build upon the work of previous scholars by reviewing work on the psychology of conspiracy theories and exploring the relationship between endorsement of Q-Anon beliefs and a disposition towards seeing the world as a dangerous and competitive place. The endorsement of these worldviews has been argued to underpin authoritarian beliefs in the form of right-wing authoritarianism and social dominance (Duckitt 2001). This chapter also calls for this research to more explicitly incorporate emerging theories of conspiracy beliefs, both within, and beyond the Western context.

Capitol Hill Riot

The events of 6 January 2021 were a watershed moment in the political history of the United States. Just before 2:00 pm, attackers began attempts to breach the doors of the Capitol Building in Washington DC. At 2:11 pm they succeeded, quickly followed by rioters streaming into the National Security Hall (Zurcher 2021). Following this, countless images and videos of individuals carrying pro-Trump signs, Confederate flags, and apparel referencing 'Q', were posted on social media. Sources from the law enforcement and intelligence communities later demonstrated that the attack had been particularly instigated by two organised extremist groups, the Proud Boys, and the Oath Keepers (Homeland Security Staff Report 2021).

Security sources later reported that militia groups had attempted to storm the Capitol Building to disrupt the ratification of the electoral victory of Joe Biden (Homeland Security Staff Report 2021). A common conspiracy theory advocated by members of the pro-Trump far right has been that the 2020 US presidential election was stolen, the legitimate winner being Donald Trump. Statements made by rioters indicated that they believed they were performing their patriotic duty as Americans to stop the government being controlled by a group of Satan worshiping paedophiles (Bleakley 2023).

Following the expulsion of the rioters from the Capitol building, a sequence of events that left one law enforcement agent and four rioters dead (Healy 2021), public attention was directed to the Q-Anon conspiracy. Multiple rioters carried signs and clothing emblazoned with 'Q' symbols and slogans; the motivating factors behind the attack were conspiratorial in their origins (Spocchia 2021). To understand this in more depth, we will elaborate the specific characteristics and claims of the Q-Anon conspiracy and put this in the context of emerging literature on the psychology of conspiracy ideation.

The role of Q-Anon

The Q-Anon conspiracy theory emerged in its current form in 2017. Q-Anon differs from most conspiracy theories in that its adherents have directed their conspiratorial beliefs into real world political action (Garry et al. 2021: 2).

There have been a multitude of claims made by Q-Anon and its adherents. One of the central claims of the conspiracy is that there is a secret cabal of individuals present within US society (some versions also include an international dimension to the network). This network contains members of the democratic party, major media figures, individuals from Hollywood, and certain elements of the science and technology community, such as the former Microsoft CEO Bill Gates. Q-Anon claims that these individuals are secretly in control of the United States; that they traffic in children, whom they sexually abuse, murder, and cannibalise; often in a ritualised satanic fashion (Bleakley 2023; Zadrozny and Collins 2018).

Q-Anon adherents base their information on online statements posted on various anonymous message boards such as 4chan and 8chan, by an individual (or individuals) referring to themselves as 'Q'. The 'Q' moniker is a reference to a Q-level security clearance, the highest level of security clearance associated with the US Department of Energy (McIntosh 2022;

Rothschild 2021). In these 'Q-Drops', information that comprises the foundation of the Q-Anon mythos has been laid out. The term 'Drops' refers to the dropping of information on public forums by the individual(s) claiming the identity of 'Q'. According to this narrative, the only individual who can stop the cabal of satanic paedophiles is Donald J. Trump; claimed to be secretly waging a covert war against these individuals in the name of the American people (Zadrozny and Collins 2018). A large part of the Q-Anon mythos has merged with Donald Trump's cult of personality and is endorsed by his most fanatical supporters. At the heart of Q-Anon is Donald Trump (Papasavva et al. 2020).

Before the current version of the Q-Anon conspiracy, a prototype version surfaced in 2016. During the presidential race, John Podesta, the then campaign manager of presidential candidate Hilary Clinton, was subject to a form of hacking in which his emails were leaked. Several of these emails referred to a pizza restaurant in Washington DC, later identified as Comet Ping Pong (Fisher et al. 2016; Rothschild 2021). The emails involved Podesta suggesting to a colleague that they go for a cheese pizza. In the parlance of some internet communities, cheese pizza has become a euphemism for child pornography (i.e., CP) (Rodríguez-Ferrándiz 2022). Various right-wing influencers and online social media groups interpreted these references as indicating that a deep-state run, child sex trafficking ring was based out of the basement of the restaurant. Despite the extreme nature of the claims, and the total lack of evidence, on 16 December 2016, a twenty-nine-year-old North Carolina man, Edgar Madison Welch, travelled to Washington DC and entered the restaurant wielding an AR-15 assault rifle (Kennedy 2017). The event ended in Welch firing several shots inside the building, however no one was injured. Welch later explained to police that he believed the basement of the building was harbouring a child sex trafficking ring run by Hilary Clinton. The building in question had no basement and no children were on the premises (Kennedy 2017). The event and the underlying conspiracy became known as 'Pizzagate'. The underlying elements of this theory, of 'elites' trafficking in or harvesting the blood of children represents a recent resurgence in antisemitic conspiratorial thinking that is present in many right-wing extremist movements in the United States (Michael 2018).

Another central tenet of the Q-Anon conspiracy is that the 2020 US presidential election was rigged in favour of Donald Trump's opponents. As noted by analysts, claims of election tampering were being circulated months in advance of polling day (Goodman and Carmichael 2020). The perceived illegitimacy of the election result has been quoted by Q-Anon supporters as one of the primary motivational factors behind the 6 January incident, with a vast increase in social media activity surrounding the event (Bleakley 2023; McIntosh 2022). However, it should be noted that as Q-Anon has become an international phenomenon, and that different national manifestations have different characteristics (Zihiri et al. 2022). The social and cultural context in which extremist movements manifest is of paramount importance and an understanding that focuses exclusively on Western manifestations will fall short of a clear understanding (Boyle 2019). The question then emerges: In a Western context, what drives people to endorse such conspiratorial views that most of the population would find difficult to believe?

Psychology of conspiracy theories

Conspiracy theories have been broadly defined as 'a secret plot involving two or more powerful actors to bring about, an often malevolent, goal' (Pigden 1995: 6). Historically much of the research on the psychology of conspiracy theories focused on the individual characteristics of those who endorsed them. However, more recent research has focused on the social psychological dynamics of conspiracy theories, as they often result in groups formed by believers sharing a social identity (Douglas et al. 2016). In the psychology of conspiracy theories there are two broad themes: the motivational factors that lead to individuals or groups endorsing conspiratorial thinking; and the environmental or situational factors that facilitate conspiratorial thinking. This chapter will focus on the former.

Motivational factors

Douglas et al. (2017) have suggested that, based on recognised patterns in conspiratorial ideation, three underlying psychological factors may contribute to endorsement of conspiracy theories. These are the *epistemic, existential*, and *social* motives. The epistemic motives suggest that conspiracy theories are used to reduce feelings of uncertainty (Douglas et al. 2017; van Prooijen and Jostman 2013). Evidence also supports the idea that, when events are large-scale, low-level mundane or ordinary explanations are regarded as unsatisfactory (Leman and Cinnirella 2013). Douglas et al. (2016) have also found a correlation between endorsement of conspiracy theories and hypersensitivity to agency detection, defined as 'the tendency to attribute agency and intentionality where it does not (or is unlikely to) exist' (Douglas 2019: 10).

Current research has demonstrated that individuals of differing political ideologies will interpret the same information differently (Jerit and Barabas 2012). Lodge et al. (2013) have suggested that one mechanism that could explain this is motivated reasoning. When confronted with facts that contradict their predispositions, individuals may interpret the added information in a way that is compatible with their pre-existing beliefs. Within the US context, motivated reasoning has frequently been seen in conjunction with partisan politics (Duran et al. 2017; Edelson et al. 2017; Enders et al. 2018). This literature suggests that the specific conspiracy theories that an individual will endorse strongly relate to their pre-existing beliefs. For example, during the 2022 Russian invasion of Ukraine, multiple online conspiracies associated with Q-Anon spread throughout right-wing aligned social media platforms (Alba and Thompson 2022). These included claims that Russia's actions were to prevent a 'New World Order', or to destroy 'biolabs' being used to create the next global pandemic (Jackson 2022). The epistemic uncertainty resulting from these geopolitical events caused a form of motivated reasoning that interpreted these events within the context of the pre-existing Q-Anon belief system.

Existential motivations are the result of individuals turning to conspiracy theories to satisfy their existential needs (Douglas 2017).

> people who lack agency and control may reclaim some sense of control by believing conspiracy theories because they offer the opportunity to reject official narratives and allow people to feel they possess a better account. (Douglas 2019: 8)

Some studies have also shown that conspiratorial beliefs are associated with feelings of powerlessness (Abalakina-Paap et al. 1999; Pratt 2003) and existential anxiety (Newheiser, Farias, and Tausch 2011). Van Prooijen and Douglas (2018) have suggested that two major processes underly this existential uncertainty: pattern perception and agency detection. People will see causal relationships where none exist and believe that there is a perceived, intentional, and often malevolent agency behind certain events. Evidence suggest that these processes activate more acutely when experiencing emotional distress and feelings of danger (van Prooijen and Douglas 2018).

Finally, there are the social motives. These are the tendency for individuals to desire a positive image of both themselves, and the group(s) they belong to. Endorsing conspiracy theories can be associated with a need to be seen as unique, or even superior to other individuals (Imhoff et al. 2017; Lantian et al. 2017). At the level of social groups, conspiracy theories reflect the basic underlying structure of intergroup conflict (van Prooijen and Douglas 2018). Conspiracy theories may also be used to explain certain aspects of intergroup relations, particularly if there is a perceived injustice. Usinski and Parent (2014) found that the belief that outgroup members were conspiring against the ingroup was more likely to emerge if the ingroup considered itself undervalued, underprivileged, or under threat. For instance, Mashuri et al. (2014) found a correlation between the belief that Western nations have unfairly victimised Muslims, and a conspiracy theory that stated that terrorist activities conducted by Muslim extremists were either instigated, or perpetrated, by Western intelligence agencies.

Van Prooijen and colleagues (van Prooijen and Douglas 2018; van Prooijen et al. 2015) have suggested that there is a strong social identity component to conspiratorial thinking, with two common motivational processes being the desire to uphold a strong ingroup identity and protection against a hostile outgroup. This relates to Douglas and colleagues' (2017) model, with social motivations to promote the ingroup being a central motivation in the endorsement of conspiratorial thinking. To explore these social motives further, we identify several useful ideas from social identity theory that help inform our analysis of conspiracy theories.

Social identity and threat perception

A potential link between the psychology of conspiracy theories and acts of intergroup violence may be derived from social identity theory and associated models of intergroup conflict.

In their paper 'Making a virtue of evil: a five-step social identity model of the development of collective hate', Reicher et al. (2008) explore how individuals could conclude that acts of extreme political violence against their outgroup are morally virtuous. The five-step model proposed by Reicher et al. (2008) is as follows.

Step 1: Identification – creating a cohesive ingroup.
  This first step draws from the social identity tradition, in particular self-categorisation theory (Tajfel and Turner 1979; Turner et al. 1986). Here individuals form a shared collective identify around a common core, be that identity, politics, ideological, racial, religious etc. From this, members gain clear psychological benefits from collective identity.

Step 2: Exclusion – placing targets outside the ingroup.
  Once the boundaries of what constitutes 'us' have been drawn, then individuals who fall outside this category are considered 'other'. Ingroup identity can be further reinforced by reference to the existence of a salient outgroup.

Step 3: Threat – the outgroup seen as endangering the enactment of ingroup identity.
  A response involves withdrawing benefits and acting with hostility towards outgroup members. In its most advanced form, this could involve constructing the outgroup as an existential threat to the continued survival of the ingroup.

Step 4: Virtue – representing the ingroup as uniquely good.
  In this case, virtue is uniquely ascribed to members of the ingroup. Ingroup identity is associated with morality and positive displays of

virtue. Consequently, outgroup identity is therefore often associated with depravity and immorality.

Step 5: Celebration – eulogising inhumanity as the defense of virtue.

At this point, violence against outgroup members can be seen as virtuous, as Reicher et al. (2008: 25) state:

> Once all the pieces are in place, it becomes easy to see how genocide can be made something to celebrate. Where 'they' are defined as not being of 'us' and as being against 'us,' and where, in addition, we create a Manichean view of the world in which we represent good and they represent evil, then their defeat – if necessary, their destruction – becomes a matter of preserving virtue.

In terms of this five-step model, steps 3 and 4 have major implications for our understanding of conspiracy narratives. Moral denigration of the outgroup and exaltation of the ingroup are common features (van Prooijen et al. 2015) of such narratives. However, what is particularly interesting is that this social identity model also emphasises the role of outgroup threat previously mentioned by van Prooijen and Douglas (2017).

Perspectives on threat: Dangerous and competitive worldviews

The perception of threat to the ingroup can influence the endorsement of conspiratorial beliefs, and this can take a range of forms. For our empirical study we focused on two specific motivational factors which relate to threat to the group or the individual: whether they view the world as competitive (vs. uncompetitive), or dangerous (vs. safe). These factors have been highlighted by Duckitt (2001) as key motivational factors which are associated with right-wing authoritarianism and endorsement of social hierarchy and could potentially relate to extreme conspiratorial beliefs.

Those that endorse a competitive worldview see the world as 'dog-eat-dog', where those that are the strongest prosper, whilst those that are weak will be unsuccessful. Those that endorse such a viewpoint tend to believe that it is a survival of the fittest, where life outcomes are naturally a competition between people. This opinion has been associated with belief in a social dominance hierarchy, where society can be viewed as a hierarchy with different tiers of dominance (for a meta-analysis, see Perry, Sibley, and Duckitt 2013). Those that endorse a competitive worldview also tend to report higher levels of right-wing authoritarianism (Perry et al. 2013).

Similarly, those that endorse a dangerous worldview tend to view the world as unsafe, lawless, and with much to fear. This viewpoint that the world is a dangerous place is associated with right-wing authoritarian beliefs (Perry et al. 2013). In this case, those endorsing dangerous worldviews may be more likely to endorse conspiratorial thinking as they perceive the world to be threatening, believing that they live in a time of unrest and danger. As such, the dangerous worldview believer may have existential motivations for engaging with conspiratorial thinking.

A Study of Q-Anon views on the political right

To explore several of the factors which we have identified above and their implications for extremity of real-world beliefs in the Q phenomenon, we conducted a study of participants from the USA who were broadly on the political right. We constructed a measure of Q beliefs based on published and social media sources, and also made use of measures of two kinds of motivational threats: belief in a dangerous world, and belief that the world is a competitive jungle (Duckitt 2001). In this preliminary study we simply wanted to see if these broad factors do indeed predict increased extremity of belief in various Q tenets.

Methods

Participants

This study used a survey constructed in Qualtrics. The survey was distributed using the online survey platform Prolific. The inclusion criteria were limited to individuals who did not vote for the Democratic candidate in 2016. This opened the participant pool up to Republicans and the small number of individuals who voted for independent candidates. This specific criterion was chosen to cast as wide a net as possible within the US right-wing spectrum. A notable part of this research desired to look at the relationship that the Q-Anon conspiracy theory had with the US political right, not merely at 'card carrying' Q-Anon supporters. As a result, this seemed like the best sampling method to gain the respondents we hoped for. From this criteria, 232 respondents were recorded. We used pairwise deletion to deal with missing data, meaning that we used the data of the participants who responded to a complete scale (i.e., all the questions in a particular variable) where this data was available.

Materials

The first set of questions were designed to measure endorsement of the Q-Anon conspiracy theory. These were a set of twelve questions derived from scholarly and journalistic sources (Garry et al. 2021; Rothschild 2021) as well as analysis of social media posts (see Table 11.1). The questions in this section were designed to assess the participants' endorsement of each of the individual claims of the Q-Anon conspiracy, and to explore potential variation in endorsement of different specific claims.

Dangerous and competitive worldviews

After evaluating the current state of the research on conspiracy theories, the specific claims of Q-Anon, and the social identity model of group violence, the relevance of the Social World View scale became apparent. The Social World View scale (SWV scale), developed by Duckitt et al. (2001), is used

Table 11.1: The twelve questions developed by the researchers to gauge endorsement of the Q-Anon conspiracy theory

Question	Q-Anon Scale
1.	Donald Trump is the legitimate winner of the 2020 presidential election.
2.	Hollywood, the Democratic Party, and the mainstream media are conspiring with foreign powers against the American people.
3.	The Q-Anon statements about an approaching 'storm' against Donald Trump's opponents is certain to happen.[1]
4.	There is an established paedophile ring within the democratic party.
5.	Donald Trump is waging a covert war against paedophiles hidden in the establishment.
6.	Anti-fascist organisations and Black Lives Matter activists were behind the attack on the Capitol Building on 6 January.
7.	Prominent members of the Democratic Party are guilty of treason against the United States.
8.	Members of the Republican Party who have opposed Donald Trump are guilty of treason.
9.	American media is biased in favour of the political left.
10.	Donald Trump should be allowed to hold the office of president, beyond the two terms allowed by the constitution.
11.	America can only be truly safe with Donald Trump as leader.
12.	To preserve the presidency of Donald Trump, violence against his opponents is justified.

Source: authors' own work.

to indicate the extent to which the participant considers their social environment to be hostile. The first categories explore perceptions of danger. Individuals who score highly consider their social environment to be incredibly hostile, where danger and death lurk around every corner. The second explores the extent to which the participant considers their social environment to be competitive. Individuals who score highly on this scale view their social environment as a competitive jungle, in which only a minority of individuals can achieve success, and even safety, often at the detriment of others. Individuals who rank low on this scale tend to view their environment as much less challenging, holding a worldview that emphasises cooperation over competition.

While these worldview scales were designed to evaluate attitudes towards competition as held by individuals, these beliefs are likely to be based heavily on how groups as well as individuals are seen in society. As Douglas et al. (2017) have stated, the social motives underlying conspiratorial thinking involve holding one's group in high esteem. It may be reasonable to believe that the higher an individual is in the competitive worldview scale, the more likely they are to endorse conspiracy theories that suggest their outgroup is attempting to illegitimately oust them from positions of power and security. The Q-Anon mythos describes an apocalyptic war between good and evil with the fate of the entire world at stake and involves elaborate conspiracies and convoluted logic to maintain that Donald Trump is still the rightful president. The mythos kicked into violent overdrive when the power of the American right was threatened by the 2020 electoral outcome.

This study therefore explored the relationship between the social worldview scales of Duckitt et al. (2001) and the endorsement of the Q-Anon conspiracy theory (see Table 11.2). The primary hypothesis of this study is that there is a positive association between the endorsement of a dangerous and competitive worldview and the Q-Anon conspiracy.

Control questions

Several control questions were included to obfuscate the goal of the survey. It was anticipated that if the participants were immediately aware of the goals of the survey it might result in a defensive reaction, with participants either answering inaccurately or producing 'pro-social' answers to questions that did not reflect their actual beliefs. To avoid this, talking points that are usually associated with the US political left, such as critical race theory, were also included to avoid any potential negative reaction from the participants.

Table 11.2: Dangerous worldview and competitive jungle questions

Competitive jungle	Dangerous worldview
It is a dog-eat-dog world where you have to be ruthless at times.	My knowledge and experience tell me that the social world we live in is basically a safe, stable, and secure place in which most people are fundamentally good.
There is really no such thing as 'right' and 'wrong'. It all boils down to what you can get away with.	It seems that every year there are fewer and fewer truly respectable people, and more and more persons with no morals at all who threaten everyone else.
One of the most useful skills a person should develop is how to look someone straight in the eye and lie convincingly.	Although it may appear that things are constantly getting more dangerous and chaotic, it really is not so. Every era has its problems, and a person's chances of living a safe, untroubled life are better today than ever before.
My knowledge and experience tell me that the social world we live in is basically a competitive 'jungle' in which the fittest survive and succeed, in which power, wealth, and winning are everything, and might is right.	Any day now chaos and anarchy could erupt around us. All the signs are pointing to it.
Basically, people are objects to be quietly and coolly manipulated for one's own benefit.	There are many dangerous people in our society who will attack someone out of pure meanness, for no reason at all.
Life is not governed by the 'survival of the fittest'. We should let compassion and moral laws be our guide.	The 'end' is not near. People who think that earthquakes, wars, and famines mean God might be about to destroy the world are being foolish.
It is better to be loved than to be feared.	My knowledge and experience tell me that the social world we live in is basically a dangerous and unpredictable place, in which good, decent, and moral people's values and way of life are threatened and disrupted by bad people.
Do unto to others as you would have them do unto you, and never do anything unfair to someone else.	Despite what one hears about 'crime in the street', there probably isn't any more now than there ever has been.

Table 11.2   (Cont.)

Competitive jungle	Dangerous worldview
Honesty is the best policy in all cases.	If a person takes a few sensible precautions, nothing bad is likely to happen to him or her; we do not live in a dangerous world.
One should give others the benefit of the doubt. Most people are trustworthy if you have faith in them.	Every day as society become more lawless and bestial, a person's chances of being robbed, assaulted, and even murdered go up and up.

Source: authors' work derived from Duckitt et al. (2001).

Procedure

Participants were provided with a general information sheet explaining the general political focus of the survey, as the brief of the experiment stated it was looking at political polarisation. The participants responded to the questions on a seven-point Likert scale with one being strongly disagree and seven being strongly agree. The questions were randomised to prevent any ordering effects, and attention check items were included in the survey. On completion, the participants were debriefed, explaining the purpose of the research.

Results

Descriptive stats

The mean values for each of the twelve Q-Anon questions are reported in Table 11.3. The questions were reported on a seven-point Likert scale with a scale mid-point of four. From the scale means we can see that most participants did not endorse the statements apart from Question 9 (see Figure 11.1).

This item shows general support from the right-leaning sample, although the distribution suggests even on the right there is a sub-sample that disagrees with this statement. The general support for this item shows that it is not distinctive even though it is part of the 'Q' ideology. At the other end of the scale, we can see items that most people, even in our 'non-Democrat' sample would disagree with (with the strong modal response being too strongly disagree). Only those at the extreme of the sample would fully

Table 11.3: Means and standard deviations (SD) for the 12 Q-Anon endorsement questions (the questions were rated on a seven-point Likert scale)

Question	Mean Score	Standard Deviation
1.	2.84	2.059
2.	3.19	1.808
3.	3.05	1.432
4.	3.74	1.777
5.	3.08	1.593
6.	2.69	1.685
7.	3.63	1.798
8.	1.98	1.347
9.	4.61	1.817
10.	1.89	1.488
11.	2.23	1.699
12.	1.8	1.250
overall mean	2.89	

Source: authors' own work.

endorse these items with strong agreement. The distribution of responses for the question with the lowest mean (Question 12), can be seen in Figure 11.2. Only about 5 per cent of our sample would endorse violence to preserve the presidency of Donald Trump. Less than 0.5 per cent of the sample would strongly endorse this. However, that still potentially represents a large group of potential supporters for an event such as the 6 January Capitol Building riot.

Scale construction and correlation analysis

The 'Dangerous worldview' and 'Competitive jungle' scales are well-established; items were reversed as necessary, and combined to create the final scales. The Q-Anon items were generated specifically for this study. We conducted a factor analysis on these items, which confirmed that they fell into a strong single factor. The items were then combined (by taking a mean) to create a composite Q-Anon beliefs scale. Although the scale consists of several items that are strongly skewed, there are also many items with moderate means and low skew even on these 'Q' oriented beliefs. Although

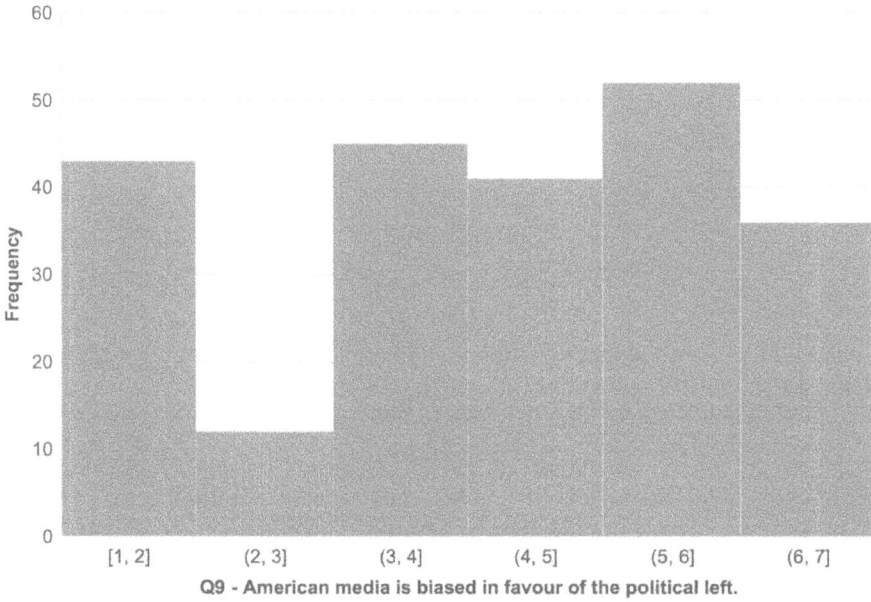

Figure 11.1: Distribution of answers on a seven-point Likert scale for Question 9, 'American media is biased in favour of the political left' (*source:* authors' own work)

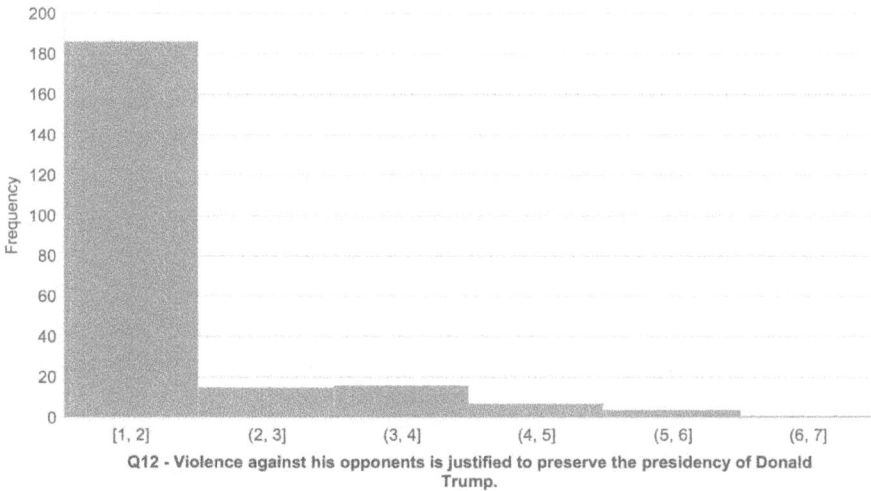

Figure 11.2: Distribution of answers on a seven-point Likert scale for Question 12 'Violence against his opponents is justified to preserve the presidency of Donald Trump' (*source:* authors' own work)

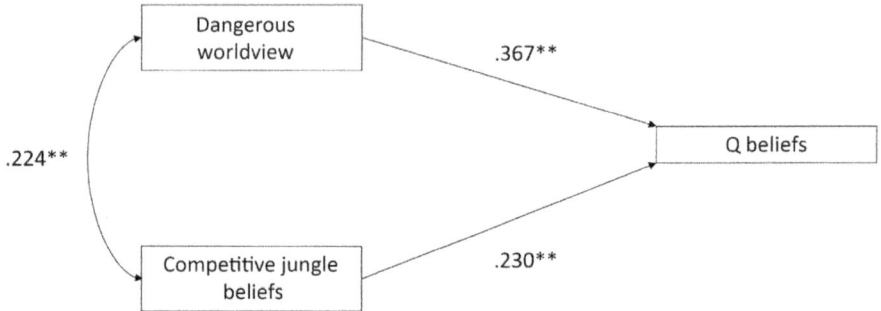

Figure 11.3: A model showing the correlation between competitive jungle beliefs and dangerous worldview (curved arrow), as well as the standardised coefficients between the predictor variables and Q Beliefs (*source:* authors' own work)

hard-core 'Q' conspiracy believers will only represent a small portion of our sample, many of our non-Democrat sample seem willing to at least partially endorse these 'Q' beliefs. For that reason, we believe we can infer something about the tendency to endorse some components of this ideology based on their endorsement of perceived social threat (dangerous world and competitive jungle beliefs).

A correlational analysis between both the dangerous worldview and the competitive jungle with the Q-Anon factor revealed moderate positive correlations (Dangerous worldview r (225) = .422, p <.001 and Competitive jungle r (225) = .319, p<.001 respectively). A linear regression was used to explore the relationship between Q-Anon endorsement, dangerous worldview, and competitive jungle. The results revealed that both dangerous worldview (R^2 = .178, F (1,225) = 48.881, p < .001) and competitive jungle (R^2=.228, F (2,224) = 33.125, p < .001) significantly positively predicted Q-Anon beliefs (see Figure 11.3).

Discussion

Our purpose in this chapter is to use the Q-Anon conspiracy case to draw several sets of insights. As a general case study, the Q-Anon belief set allows us to illustrate emerging theories of conspiracy beliefs that go beyond simple individual motivational factors to incorporate group-based motivations. We introduce recent social psychological work on the social identity factors that exacerbate conspiratorial thinking. These include various kinds of threats, including epistemic, existential, and social threat motives. When the threats are sufficiently extreme, these may meet the five criteria for collective hate (Reicher et al. 2008).

The primary hypothesis this study investigated was the relationship between endorsement of the Q-Anon conspiracy theory, and the two social worldviews. Our results found that both aspects of the Social World View scale were positively and independently associated with Q-Anon endorsement. This demonstrates how beliefs about the world are associated with conspiratorial thinking and extreme political views.

One question showed an overall level of support for belief in media bias, although showing evidence of bimodality in the responses. Several other items with means close to the centre of the scale (and exhibiting some bimodality) include beliefs that the outgroup Democrats are paedophiles and traitors. Whilst these responses are central tenets of the Q-Anon conspiracy theory, they are not unique to Q-Anon alone. The social identity model of collective hate would suggest that in times of increased conflict, groups may attribute various expressions of immorality to the outgroup.

Our factor analysis showed that a coherent set of belief items capturing the core tenets of the Q-Anon conspiracy could be developed. Although the true extremist believers in 'Q' (those who strongly endorse many the beliefs) represent a small minority, a much larger proportion of people who identify as being on the political right endorse at least some of these items. This Q-Anon scale may prove useful in future studies to help identify those at the more extreme end of the spectrum for further exploration.

We also established the association between more strongly endorsing various 'Q' beliefs and two established forms of threatening worldview. The correlation analysis demonstrated that seeing the world as dangerous and as a competitive jungle is significantly associated with Q-Anon beliefs. Furthermore, regression analysis showed that these are distinctive effects, each being significant even after controlling for each other. Although we did not include right-wing authoritarianism (RWA; Altemeyer 1992) and social dominance orientation (SDO; Pratto et al. 1994), these have been consistently associated with dangerous world views and competitive jungle views respectively. Therefore, we would also expect that RWA and SDO would also both be associated with endorsement of Q-Anon beliefs and future research could explore these broader associations.

Our results support previous work done by Douglas and van Prooijen (2017) who suggest that a major motivational factor underlying conspiratorial ideation is the role of 'existential threat' coming from the perception of great social uncertainty originating from the actions of a malevolent outgroup. The results found that an endorsement of Q-Anon supporting statements correlated with an endorsement of a dangerous worldview. This relates to the existential motivational factors stated by Douglas et al. (2017) when they stated that conspiracy theories can often be motivated by a desire to lessen the fear of existential danger. This is also supported by work by an

Prooijen et al. (2017) who notes that a common theme amongst conspiracy theories is a general feeling of danger and threat from a malevolent external force. It has been argued (Rothschild 2021) that the Q-Anon conspiracy is a mixture of various pre-existing conspiracy theories located within the context of North American popular culture. It is therefore no surprise that this conspiracy theory will follow the patterns of its predecessors.

Though not a controllable variable, given the nature of this research, it is worth noting that this research took place in summer 2021 during the COVID-19 and was done in response to the 6 January Capitol attack. However, it should be noted that researchers have suggested that COVID-19 sparked an increase in conspiracy theory endorsement in the United States (Douglas 2021). This is notable due to the previously stated relevance of socially disruptive events, such as terror attacks, natural disasters economic collapses, and civil wars (van Prooijen 2017). This was not through design. Previous research has emphasised the upturn in conspiratorial endorsement during time of great social upheaval and uncertainty (Douglas et al. 2017).

The social identity aspect of this research is also notable. The Q-Anon statements developed via content analysis include characteristics supportive of the social identity model of collective hate developed by Reicher et al. (2008). Two major themes apparent in the Q-Anon doctrine is the perception of existential threat coming from an outgroup (usually identified as a democrat aligned 'deep state'), and the perception of extreme immorality on the part of this outgroup. These themes alone provide a level of support for the five-step model set out by Reicher et al. (2008). Step 3 in this model involved the perception of the outgroup as representing a particular threat to the continued survival of the ingroup. This perception is supported both by the results of this study and by previous research conducted on the content of the Q-Anon belief system (Rothschild 2021). What is also notable is the presence of strong moralistic elements withing the Q-Anon beliefs system, one that paints their opponents as 'Satan worshiping child molesters', and their supporters as 'God fearing patriots'. This recurrent theme provides support for the Reicher et al. (2008) model. Future research could also explore this moral element in conspiratorial thinking in more detail.

Implications

The current study highlights the importance of motivational factors in the study of extremist beliefs. If dangerous or competitive worldviews are associated with extremist beliefs, this could highlight key new variables to consider when trying to understand motivations for extremist behaviour. As such, we highlight the key and vital link between social psychology and counter-terrorism. An understanding of the possible motivations of extremism can help with the creation of practical preventative measures to help prevent terrorist activity.

The current study also brings right-wing extremism into focus. The results of the current study demonstrate that right-wing extremism is associated with the idea that the world is dangerous. This focus on right-wing extremism is something that can be overlooked in counter-terrorism approaches and could benefit from further investigation through the lens of a counter-terrorism perspective. It should be noted, however, that whether conspiratorial thinking is more prevalent on the political right, especially the far right, is a matter of some debate. The association has been supported by research conducted by Galliford et al. (2017), and further studies (Bruder et al. 2013; Grzesiak-Feldman et al. 2009) have found a link between conspiratorial thinking and right-wing authoritarianism, as developed by Altemeyer (1996). However, other research found no relationship between conspiracy theories and right-wing politics (Oliver et al. 2014; Uscinski et al. 2014) or right-wing authoritarianism (Berinsky 2012). Douglas et al. (2019) suggest that this disparity may be related to issues with methodology and the socio-cultural factors present when much of the data was gathered. Regardless, given the clear links between worldviews and right-wing extremist beliefs, we believe this topic requires the attention of future research.

Beyond Western cultures

Examining whether ingroup threat can encourage conspiratorial thinking across multiple contexts could be very useful in terms of broadening the scope of counter-terrorism research. Whilst there is a small pool of research that examines the motivational factors that are related to conspiratorial thinking, these have overwhelmingly studied participants in the US. Therefore, whether the link between threat, worldviews, and conspiratorial thinking is specific to the US is unclear. It is possible that this link is obtainable in other countries and cultures, or that the motivational psychological predictors that have been the subject of investigation are only relevant in the Western context. As such, in line with other chapters in this volume, we call for greater examination of non-Western samples in both psychology and counter-terrorism work.

Conclusion

In conclusion, we argue that the Q-Anon conspiracy belief set is a useful case-study to explore recent work on the psychology of conspiracy theories. We also found a positive relationship between endorsement of the Q-Anon conspiracy theory and view of a dangerous and competitive (strongly hierarchically organised) world. This supports previous research on conspiracy theories more generally that emphasises the role of existential uncertainty as a motivating factor. These results also provide support for the social identity model of collective hate, by showing that perception of outgroup threat and immorality potentially acts as a motivating factor towards acts of political violence. Finally, we support the call for research to be broadened to explore the kinds of questions we illustrate here in conspiracy theories specific to other cultural contexts.

References

Abalakina-Paap, M., Stephan, W., Craig, T., and Gregory, W. (1999). 'Beliefs in conspiracies', *Political Psychology*, 20(3), 637–47. https://doi.org/10.1111/0162–895x.00160

Alba, D. and Thompson, S. (2022). ' "I'll Stand on the Side of Russia": Pro-Putin sentiment spreads online', *The New York Times*, 25 February, www.nytimes.com/2022/02/25/technology/russia-supporters.html (accessed 11 March 2022).

Altemeyer, B. and Hunsberger, B. (1992). 'Authoritarianism, religious fundamentalism, quest, and prejudice', *International Journal for the Psychology of Religion*, 2(2), 113–33. https://doi.org/10.1207/s15327582ijpr0202_5

Altemeyer, B. (1996), *The Authoritarian Specter*. Cambridge, MA: Harvard University Press.

Berinsky, A. (2012). 'Rumors and health care reform: Experiments in political misinformation', *British Journal of Political Science*, 47(2), 241–62. https://doi.org/10.1017/s0007123415000186

Bleakley, P. (2023). 'Panic, pizza and mainstreaming the alt-right: A social media analysis of Pizzagate and the rise of the QAnon conspiracy', *Current Sociology*, 71(3), 509–25. https://doi.org/10.1177/00113921211034896

Boyle, M. J. (2019). 'Introduction', in Boyle, M. J. (ed.) *Non-Western Responses to Terrorism, New Directions in Terrorism Studies*. Manchester: Manchester University Press, pp. 1–20. https://doi.org/10.7228/manchester/9781526105813.003.0001

Bruder, M., Haffke, P., Neave, N., Nouripanah, N., and Imhoff, R. (2013). 'Measuring individual differences in generic beliefs in conspiracy theories across cultures: Conspiracy mentality questionnaire, *Frontiers in Psychology*, 4, 1–15. https://doi.org/10.3389/fpsyg.2013.00225

Douglas, K., Sutton, R., Callan, M., Dawtry, R., and Harvey, A. (2016). 'Someone is pulling the strings: Hypersensitive agency detection and belief in conspiracy theories', *Thinking & Reasoning*, 22(1), 57–77. https://doi.org/10.1080/13546783.2015.1051586

Douglas, K. M., Sutton, R. M., and Cichocka, A. (2017). 'The psychology of conspiracy theories', *Current Directions in Psychological Science*, 26(6), 538–42. https://doi.org/10.1177/0963721417718261

Douglas, K. M., Uscinski, J. E., Sutton, R. M., Cichocka, A., Nefes, T., Ang, C. S., and Deravi, F. (2019). 'Understanding conspiracy theories', *Political Psychology*, 40, 3–35.

Douglas, K. M. (2021). 'COVID-19 conspiracy theories', *Group Processes & Intergroup Relations*, 24(2), 270–5. https://doi.org/10.1177/1368430220982068

Duckitt, J. (2001). 'A dual-process cognitive-motivational theory of ideology and prejudice', *Advances in Experimental Social Psychology*, 33, 41–113. https://doi.org/10.1016/S0065-2601(01)80004-6

Duckitt, J. and Sibley, C. G. (2007). 'Right wing authoritarianism, social dominance orientation and the dimensions of generalized prejudice', *European Journal of Personality: Published for the European Association of Personality Psychology*, 21(2), 113–30.

Duran, N., Nicholson, S., and Dale, R. (2017). 'The hidden appeal and aversion to political conspiracies as revealed in the response dynamics of partisans', *Journal Of Experimental Social Psychology*, 73, 268–78. https://doi.org/10.1016/j.jesp. 2017.07.008

Edelson, J., Alduncin, A., Krewson, C., Sieja, J., and Uscinski, J. (2017). 'The effect of conspiratorial thinking and motivated reasoning on belief in election fraud', *Political Research Quarterly*, 70(4), 933–46. https://doi.org/10.1177/1065912917721061

Enders, A. and Smallpage, S. (2018). 'On the measurement of conspiracy beliefs', *Research & Politics*, 5(1). DOI: 205316801876359.

Fisher, M., Woodrow Cox, J., and Herman, P. (2016). 'Pizzagate: from rumor, to hashtag, to gunfire in D.C.', *Post*, 6 December 2016, www.washingtonpost.com/local/pizzagate-from-rumor-to-hashtag-to-gunfire-in-dc/2016/12/06/4c7def50-bbd4-11e6-94ac-3d324840106c_story.html?utm_term=.ef9c2b1edc2f (accessed 28 June 2021).

Galliford, N. and Furnham, A. (2017). 'Individual difference factors and beliefs in medical and political conspiracy theories', *Scandinavian Journal of Psychology*, 58(5), 422–28. https://doi.org/10.1111/sjop. 12382

Garry, A., Walther, S., Rukaya, R., and Mohammed, A. (2021). 'QAnon conspiracy theory: Examining its evolution and mechanisms of radicalization', *Journal for Deradicalization*, 26, 152–216.

Goodman, J. and Carmichael, F. (2020). 'US election 2020: "rigged" votes, body doubles and other false claims', *BBC News*, 17 October 2020, https://www.bbc.co.uk/news/54562611 (accessed 28 June 2021).

Grzesiak-Feldman, M. and Irzycka, M. (2009). 'Right-wing authoritarianism and conspiracy thinking in a Polish sample', *Psychological Reports*, 105(2), 389–93. https://doi.org/10.2466/pr0.105.2.389–393

Healy, J. (2021). 'These are the 5 people who died in the Capitol Riot', *New York Times*, 11 January, www.nytimes.com/2021/01/11/us/who-died-in-capitol-building-attack.html (accessed 28 June 2021).

Homeland Security Staff Report. (2021). www.rules.senate.gov/imo/media/doc/Jan%206%20HSGAC%20Rules%20Report.pdf (accessed 11 March 2022).

Imhoff, R. and Lamberty, P. (2017). 'Too special to be duped: need for uniqueness motivates conspiracy beliefs', *European Journal of Social Psychology*, 47(6), 724–34. https://doi.org/10.1002/ejsp. 2265

Jackson, J. (2022). 'QAnon embraces Russia conspiracy theories on Ukraine labs, *Newsweek*, 10 March 2022, www.newsweek.com/qanon-embraces-russia-conspiracy-theories-ukraine-labs-1686816 (accessed 11 March 2022).

Jerit, J. and Barabas, J. (2012). 'Partisan perceptual bias and the information environment', *The Journal of Politics*, 74(3), 672–84. https://doi.org/10.1017/s0022381612000187

Kennedy, M. (2017). '"Pizzagate" gunman sentenced to 4 years in prison', *NPR*, 22 June, www.npr.org/sections/thetwo-way/2017/06/22/533941689/pizzagate-gunman-sentenced-to-4-years-in-prison?t=1624918541906 (accessed 28 June 2021).

Lantian, A., Muller, D., Nurra, C., and Douglas, K. (2017). '"I know things they don't know!"', *Social Psychology*, 48(3), 160–73. https://doi.org/10.1027/1864–9335/a000306

Leman, P. and Cinnirella, M. (2013). 'Beliefs in conspiracy theories and the need for cognitive closure', *Frontiers in Psychology*, 4, 1–10. https://doi.org/10.3389/fpsyg.2013.00378

Lodge, M. and Taber, C. S. (2013). The *Rationalizing Voter*. New York: Cambridge University Press.

Mashuri, A. and Zaduqisti, E. (2014). 'The role of social identification, intergroup threat, and out-group derogation in explaining belief in conspiracy theory about terrorism in Indonesia', *International Journal of Research Studies in Psychology*, 3(1), 35–50. https://doi.org/10.5861/ijrsp.2013.446

McIntosh, J. (2022). 'The sinister signs of QAnon: Interpretive agency and paranoid truths in alt-right oracles', *Anthropology Today*, 38(1), 8–12. https://doi.org/10.1111/1467–8322.12697

Michael, G. (2018). 'RIGHT WING TERRORISM: The strategic dimensions', in Silke, A. (ed.) *Routledge Handbook of Terrorism and Counterterrorism*. London: Routledge, pp. 98–108.

Newheiser, A., Farias, M., and Tausch, N. (2011). 'The functional nature of conspiracy beliefs: Examining the underpinnings of belief in the Da Vinci Code conspiracy', *Personality and Individual Differences*, 51(8), 1007–11. https://doi.org/10.1016/j.paid.2011.08.011

Oliver, J. and Wood, T. (2014). 'Conspiracy theories and the paranoid style(s) of mass opinion', *American Journal of Political Science*, 58(4), 952–66. https://doi.org/10.1111/ajps.12084

Papasavva, A., Blackburn, J., Stringhini, G., Zannettou, S., and De Cristofaro, E. (2020). '" Is it a Qincidence?": A first step towards understanding and characterizing the QAnon movement', Proceedings of the Web Conference 2021 preprint arXiv:2009.04885.

Pigden, C. (1995). 'Popper revisited, or what is wrong with conspiracy theories?', *Philosophy of the Social Sciences*, 25(1), 3–34. https://doi.org/10.1177/004839319502500101

Perry, R., Sibley, C., and Duckitt, J. (2013). 'Dangerous and competitive worldviews: A meta-analysis of their associations with social dominance orientation and right-wing authoritarianism', *Journal of Research in Personality*, 47(1), 116–27. https://doi.org/10.1016/j.jrp. 2012.10.004

Pratt, R. (2003). 'Theorizing conspiracy', *Theory and Society*, 32(2), 255–71. https://www.jstor.org/stable/3108580

Pratto, F., Sidanius, J., Stallworth, L. M., and Malle, B. F. (1994). 'Social dominance orientation: A personality variable predicting social and political attitudes', *Journal of Personality and Social Psychology*, 67(4), 741.

Reicher, S., Haslam, S., and Rath, R. (2008). 'Making a virtue of evil: A five-step social identity model of the development of collective hate', *Social and Personality Psychology Compass*, 2(3), 1313–44. https://doi.org/10.1111/j.1751–9004.2008.00113.x

Rodríguez-Ferrándiz, R. (2022) 'The Plandemic and its apostles: Conspiracy theories in pandemic mode', in Filimowicz, M. (ed.) *Digital Totalitarianism.* London: Routledge, pp. 62–83. https://doi.org/10.4324/9781003173304

Rothschild, M. (2021). *The Storm Is upon Us: How QAnon Became a Movement, Cult, and Conspiracy Theory of Everything.* London: Blackstone Publishing.

Spocchia, G. (2021). 'What role did Qanon play in the Capitol riot?', *The Independent*, 9 January 2021, www.independent.co.uk/news/world/americas/us-election-2020/qanon-capitol-congress-riot-trump-b1784460.html (accessed 28 June 2021).

Tajfel, H. and Turner, J. C. (1979). 'An integrative theory of inter-group conflict', in Austin, W. G. and Worchel, S. (eds) *The Social Psychology of Inter-group Relations.* Monterey, CA: Brooks/Cole, pp. 33–47.

Turner, J. and Oakes, P. (1986). 'The significance of the social identity concept for social psychology with reference to individualism, interactionism, and social influence', *British Journal Of Social Psychology*, 25(3), 237–52. https://doi.org/10.1111/j.2044–8309.1986.tb00732.x

Uscinski, J. E. and Parent, J. M. (2014). *American Conspiracy Theories.* New York: Oxford University Press.

van Prooijen, J. and Jostmann, N. (2013). 'Belief in conspiracy theories: The influence of uncertainty and perceived morality', *European Journal of Social Psychology*, 43(1), 109–15. https://doi.org/10.1002/ejsp. 1922

van Prooijen, J. W., Krouwel, A. P., Boiten, M., and Eendebak, L. (2015). 'Fear among the extremes: How political ideology predicts negative emotions and out-group derogation', *Personality and Social Psychology Bulletin*, 41(4), 485–97. https://doi.org/10.1177/0146167215569706

van Prooijen, J. (2017). 'Why education predicts decreased belief in conspiracy theories', *Applied Cognitive Psychology*, 31(1), 50–8. https://doi.org/10.1002/acp. 3301

van Prooijen, J. W. and Douglas, K. M. (2018). 'Belief in conspiracy theories: basic principles of an emerging research domain', *European Journal of Social Psychology*, 48(7), 897–908. https://doi.org/10.1002/ejsp. 2530

Zadrozny, B. and Collins, B. (2018), 'How three conspiracy theorists took 'Q' and sparked Qanon', *nbcnews*, 15 August 2018, www.nbcnews.com/tech/tech-news/how-three-conspiracy-theorists-took-q-sparked-qanon-n900531 (accessed 28 June 2021).

Zihiri, S., Lima, G., Han, J., Cha, M., and Lee, W. (2022). 'QAnon shifts into the mainstream, remains a far-right ally', *Heliyon*, 8(2), 1–7. https://doi.org/10.1016/j.heliyon.2022.e08764

Zurcher, A. (2021). 'Trump impeachment trial: What verdict means for Trump, Biden and America', *BBC News*, 13 February, www.bbc.co.uk/news/world-us-canada-56057849

Index

9 781526 178619